The Art of Prolog

Leon Sterling
Ehud Shapiro
with a foreword by David H. D. Warren

The Art of Prolog

Advanced Programming Techniques
Second Edition

The MIT Press
Cambridge, Massachusetts
London, England

This book was composed and typeset by Paul C. Anagnostopoulos and Joe Snowden using ZzTEX. The typeface is Lucida Bright and Lucida New Math created by Charles Bigelow and Kris Holmes specifically for scientific and electronic publishing. The Lucida letterforms have the large x-heights and open interiors that aid legibility in modern printing technology, but also echo some of the rhythms and calligraphic details of lively Renaissance handwriting. Developed in the 1980s and 1990s, the extensive Lucida typeface family includes a wide variety of mathematical and technical symbols designed to harmonize with the text faces.

Library of Congress Cataloging-in-Publication Data
Sterling, Leon
      The art of Prolog : advanced programming techniques / Leon
Sterling, Ehud Shapiro ; with a foreword by David H. D. Warren.
          p.   cm. — (MIT Press series in logic programming)
      Includes bibliographical references and index.
      ISBN 978-0-262-19338-2 (hardcover : alk. paper), 978-0-262-69163-5 (paperback)
      1. Prolog (Computer program language) I. Shapiro, Ehud Y.
II. Title. III. Series.
QA76.73.P76S74   1994
005.13'3—dc20   93-49494
                                                                    CIP

To Ruth, Miriam, Michal, Danya, and Sara

Contents

Figures

Programs

Series Foreword

The logic programming approach to computing investigates the use of logic as a programming language and explores computational models based on controlled deduction.

The field of logic programming has seen a tremendous growth in the last several years, both in depth and in scope. This growth is reflected in the number of articles, journals, theses, books, workshops, and conferences devoted to the subject. The MIT Press series in logic programming was created to accommodate this development and to nurture it. It is dedicated to the publication of high-quality textbooks, monographs, collections, and proceedings in logic programming.

Ehud Shapiro
The Weizmann Institute of Science
Rehovot, Israel

Foreword

Programming in Prolog opens the mind to a new way of looking at computing. There is a change of perspective which every Prolog programmer experiences when first getting to know the language.

I shall never forget my first Prolog program. The time was early 1974. I had learned about the abstract idea of logic programming from Bob Kowalski at Edinburgh, although the name "logic programming" had not yet been coined. The main idea was that deduction could be viewed as a form of computation, and that a declarative statement of the form

P if Q and R and S.

could also be interpreted procedurally as

To solve P, solve Q and R and S.

Now I had been invited to Marseilles. Here, Alain Colmerauer and his colleagues had devised the language Prolog based on the logic programming concept. Somehow, this realization of the concept seemed to me, at first sight, too simpleminded. However, Gerard Battani and Henri Meloni had implemented a Prolog interpreter in Fortran (their first major exercise in programming, incidentally). Why not give Prolog a try?

I sat at a clattering teletype connected down an ordinary telephone line to an IBM machine far away in Grenoble. I typed in some rules defining how plans could be constructed as sequences of actions. There was one important rule, modeled on the SRI planner Strips, which described how a plan could be elaborated by adding an action at the end. Another rule, necessary for completeness, described how to elaborate a plan by inserting an action in the middle of the plan. As an example for the planner to work on, I typed in facts about some simple actions in a "blocks world" and an initial state of this world. I entered a description of a goal state to be achieved. Prolog spat back at me:

?

meaning it couldn't find a solution. Could it be that a solution was not deducible from the axioms I had supplied? Ah, yes, I had forgotten to enter some crucial facts. I tried again. Prolog was quiet for a long time and then responded:

DEBORDEMENT DE PILE

Stack overflow! I had run into a loop. Now a loop was conceivable since the space of potential plans to be considered was infinite. However, I had taken advantage of Prolog's procedural semantics to organize the axioms so that shorter plans ought to be generated first. Could something else be wrong? After a lot of head scratching, I finally realized that I had mistyped the names of some variables. I corrected the mistakes, and tried again.

Lo and behold, Prolog responded almost instantly with a correct plan to achieve the goal state. Magic! Declaratively correct axioms had assured a correct result. Deduction was being harnessed before my very eyes to produce effective computation. Declarative programming was truly programming on a higher plane! I had dimly seen the advantages in theory. Now Prolog had made them vividly real in practice. Never had I experienced such ease in getting a complex program coded and running.

Of course, I had taken care to formulate the axioms and organize them in such a way that Prolog could use them effectively. I had a general idea of how the axioms would be used. Nevertheless it was a surprise to see how the axioms got used in practice on particular examples. It was a delightful experience over the next few days to explore how Prolog actually created these plans, to correct one or two more bugs in my facts and rules, and to further refine the program.

Since that time, Prolog systems have improved significantly in terms of debugging environments, speed, and general robustness. The techniques of using Prolog have been more fully explored and are now better understood. And logic programming has blossomed, not least because of its adoption by the Japanese as the central focus of the Fifth Generation project.

After more than a decade of growth of interest in Prolog, it is a great pleasure to see the appearance of this book. Hitherto, knowledge of how to use Prolog for serious programming has largely been communicated by word of mouth. This textbook sets down and explains for the first time in an accessible form the deeper principles and techniques of Prolog programming.

The book is excellent for not only conveying what Prolog is but also explaining how it should be used. The key to understanding how to use Prolog is to properly understand the relationship between Prolog and logic programming. This book takes great care to elucidate the relationship.

Above all, the book conveys the excitement of using Prolog—the thrill of declarative programming. As the authors put it, "Declarative programming clears the mind." Declarative programming enables one to concentrate on the essentials of a problem without getting bogged down in too much operational detail. Programming should be an intellectually rewarding activity. Prolog helps to make it so. Prolog is indeed, as the authors contend, a tool for thinking.

David H. D. Warren
Manchester, England, September 1986

Preface

Seven years have passed since the first edition of *The Art of Prolog* was published. In that time, the perception of Prolog has changed markedly. While not as widely used as the language C, Prolog is no longer regarded as an exotic language. An abundance of books on Prolog have appeared. Prolog is now accepted by many as interesting and useful for certain applications. Articles on Prolog regularly appear in popular magazines. Prolog and logic programming are part of most computer science and engineering programs, although perhaps in a minor role in an artificial intelligence or programming languages class. The first conference on Practical Applications of Prolog was held in London in April 1992. A standard for the language is likely to be in place in 1994. A future for Prolog among the programming languages of the world seems assured.

In preparing for a second edition, we had to address the question of how much to change. I decided to listen to a request not to make the new edition into a new book. This second edition is much like the first, although a number of changes are to be expected in a second edition. The typography of the book has been improved: Program code is now in a distinctive font rather than in italics. Figures such as proof trees and search trees are drawn more consistently. We have taken the opportunity to be more precise with language usage and to remove minor inconsistencies with hyphenation of words and similar details. All known typographical errors have been fixed. The background sections at the end of most chapters have been updated to take into account recent, important research results. The list of references has been expanded considerably. Extra, more advanced exercises, which have been used successfully in my Prolog classes, have been added.

Let us take an overview of the specific changes to each part in turn. Part IV, Applications, is unchanged apart from minor corrections and tidying. Part I, Logic Programs, is essentially unchanged. New programs have been added to Chapter 3 on tree manipulation, including heapifying a binary tree. Extra exercises are also present.

Part II, The Prolog Langauge, is primarily affected by the imminence of a Prolog standard. We have removed all references to Wisdom Prolog in the text in preparation for Standard Prolog. It has proved impossible to guarantee that this book is consistent with the standard. Reaching a standard has been a long, difficult process for the members of the committee. Certain predicates come into favor and then disappear, making it difficult for the authors of a text to know what to write. Furthermore, some of the proposed I/O predicates are not available in current Prologs, so it is impossible to run all the code! Most of the difficulties in reaching a Prolog standard agreeable to all interested parties have been with builtin or system predicates. This book raises some of the issues involved in adding builtins to Prolog but largely avoids the concerns by using pure Prolog as much as possible. We tend not to give detailed explanations of the controversial nonlogical behaviors of some of the system predicates, and we certainly do not use odd features in our code.

Part III, Advanced Programming Techniques, is the most altered in this second edition, which perhaps should be expected. A new chapter has been added on program transformation, and many of the other chapters have been reordered. The chapters on Interpreters and Logic Grammars have extensive additions.

Many people provided us feedback on the first edition, almost all of it very positive. I thank you all. Three people deserve special thanks for taking the trouble to provide long lists of suggestions for improvements and to point out embarrassingly long lists of typos in the first edition: Norbert Fuchs, Harald Søndergaard, and Stanley Selkow. The following deserve mention for pointing out mistakes and typos in the various printings of the first edition or making constructive comments about the book that led to improvements in later printings of the first edition and for this second edition. The list is long, my memory sometimes short, so please forgive me if I forget to mention anyone. Thanks to Hani Assiryani, Tim Boemker, Jim Brand, Bill Braun, Pu Chen, Yves Deville, George Ernst, Claudia Günther, Ann Halloran, Sundar Iyengar, Gary Kacmarcik, Mansoor Khan, Sundeep Kumar, Arun Lakhotia, Jean-

Louis Lassez, Charlie Linville, Per Ljung, David Maier, Fred Mailey, Martin Marshall, Andre Mesarovic, Dan Oldham, Scott Pierce, Lynn Pierce, David Pedder, S. S. Ramakrishnan, Chet Ramey, Marty Silverstein, Bill Sloan, Ron Taylor, Rodney Topor, R. J. Wengert, Ted Wright, and Nan Yang. For the former students of CMPS411, I hope the extra marks were sufficient reward.

Thanks to Sarah Fliegelmann and Venkatesh Srinivasan for help with entering changes to the second edition and TeXing numerous drafts. Thanks to Phil Gannon and Zoë Sterling for helpful discussions about the figures, and to Joe Gelles for drawing the new figures. For proofreading the second edition, thanks to Kathy Kovacic, David Schwartz, Ashish Jain, and Venkatesh Srinivasan. Finally, a warm thanks to my editor, Terry Ehling, who has always been very helpful and very responsive to queries.

Needless to say, the support of my family and friends is the most important and most appreciated.

Leon Sterling
Cleveland, January 1993

Preface to First Edition

The origins of this book lie in graduate student courses aimed at teaching advanced Prolog programming. A wealth of techniques has emerged in the fifteen years since the inception of Prolog as a programming language. Our intention in this book has been to make accessible the programming techniques that kindled our own excitement, imagination, and involvement in this area.

The book fills a general need. Prolog, and more generally logic programming, has received wide publicity in recent years. Currently available books and accounts, however, typically describe only the basics. All but the simplest examples of the use of Prolog have remained essentially inaccessible to people outside the Prolog community.

We emphasize throughout the book the distinction between logic programming and Prolog programming. Logic programs can be understood and studied, using two abstract, machine-independent concepts: truth and logical deduction. One can ask whether an axiom in a program is true, under some interpretation of the program symbols; or whether a logical statement is a consequence of the program. These questions can be answered independently of any concrete execution mechanism.

On the contrary, Prolog is a programming language, borrowing its basic constructs from logic. Prolog programs have precise operational meaning: they are instructions for execution on a computer—a Prolog machine. Prolog programs in good style can almost always be read as logical statements, thus inheriting some of the abstract properties of logic programs. Most important, the result of a computation of such a Prolog program is a logical consequence of the axioms in it. Effective Prolog programming requires an understanding of the theory of logic programming.

The book consists of four parts: logic programming, the Prolog language, advanced techniques, and applications. The first part is a self-contained introduction to logic programming. It consists of five chapters. The first chapter introduces the basic constructs of logic programs. Our account differs from other introductions to logic programming by explaining the basics in terms of logical deduction. Other accounts explain the basics from the background of resolution from which logic programming originated. We have found the former to be a more effective means of teaching the material, which students find intuitive and easy to understand.

The second and third chapters of Part I introduce the two basic styles of logic programming: database programming and recursive programming. The fourth chapter discusses the computation model of logic programming, introducing unification, while the fifth chapter presents some theoretical results without proofs. In developing this part to enable the clear explanation of advanced techniques, we have introduced new concepts and reorganized others, in particular, in the discussion of types and termination. Other issues such as complexity and correctness are concepts whose consequences have not yet been fully developed in the logic programming research community.

The second part is an introduction to Prolog. It consists of Chapters 6 through 13. Chapter 6 discusses the computation model of Prolog in contrast to logic programming, and gives a comparison between Prolog and conventional programming languages such as Pascal. Chapter 7 discusses the differences between composing Prolog programs and logic programs. Examples are given of basic programming techniques.

The next five chapters introduce system-provided predicates that are essential to make Prolog a practical programming language. We classify Prolog system predicates into four categories: those concerned with efficient arithmetic, structure inspection, meta-logical predicates that discuss the state of the computation, and extra-logical predicates that achieve side effects outside the computation model of logic programming. One chapter is devoted to the most notorious of Prolog extra-logical predicates, the cut. Basic techniques using these system predicates are explained. The final chapter of the section gives assorted pragmatic programming tips.

The main part of the book is Part III. We describe advanced Prolog programming techniques that have evolved in the Prolog programming community, illustrating each with small yet powerful example programs. The examples typify the applications for which the technique is useful. The six chapters cover nondeterministic programming, incomplete data structures, parsing with DCGs, second-order programming, search techniques, and the use of meta-interpreters.

The final part consists of four chapters that show how the material in the rest of the book can be combined to build application programs. A common request of Prolog newcomers is to see larger applications. They understand how to write elegant short programs but have difficulty in building a major program. The applications covered are game-playing programs, a prototype expert system for evaluating requests for credit, a symbolic equation solver, and a compiler.

During the development of the book, it has been necessary to reorganize the foundations and basic examples existing in the folklore of the logic programming community. Our structure constitutes a novel framework for the teaching of Prolog.

Material from this book has been used successfully for several courses on logic programming and Prolog: in Israel, the United States, and Scotland. The material more than suffices for a one-semester course to first-year graduate students or advanced undergraduates. There is considerable scope for instructors to particularize a course to suit a special area of interest.

A recommended division of the book for a 13-week course to senior undergraduates or first-year graduates is as follows: 4 weeks on logic programming, encouraging students to develop a declarative style of writing programs, 4 weeks on basic Prolog programming, 3 weeks on advanced techniques, and 2 weeks on applications. The advanced techniques should include some discussion of nondeterminism, incomplete data structures, basic second-order predicates, and basic meta-interpreters. Other sections can be covered instead of applications. Application areas that can be stressed are search techniques in artificial intelligence, building expert systems, writing compilers and parsers, symbol manipulation, and natural language processing.

There is considerable flexibility in the order of presentation. The material from Part I should be covered first. The material in Parts III and IV can be interspersed with the material in Part II to show the student how larger Prolog programs using more advanced techniques are composed in the same style as smaller examples.

Our assessment of students has usually been 50 percent by homework assignments throughout the course, and 50 percent by project. Our experience has been that students are capable of a significant programming task for their project. Examples of projects are prototype expert systems, assemblers, game-playing programs, partial evaluators, and implementations of graph theory algorithms.

For the student who is studying the material on her own, we strongly advise reading through the more abstract material in Part I. A good Prolog programming style develops from thinking declaratively about the logic of a situation. The theory in Chapter 5, however, can be skipped until a later reading.

The exercises in the book range from very easy and well defined to difficult and open-ended. Most of them are suitable for homework exercises. Some of the more open-ended exercises were submitted as course projects.

The code in this book is essentially in Edinburgh Prolog. The course has been given where students used several different variants of Edinburgh Prolog, and no problems were encountered. All the examples run on Wisdom Prolog, which is discussed in the appendixes.

We acknowledge and thank the people who contributed directly to the book. We also thank, collectively and anonymously, all those who indirectly contributed by influencing our programming styles in Prolog. Improvements were suggested by Lawrence Byrd, Oded Maler, Jack Minker, Richard O'Keefe, Fernando Pereira, and several anonymous referees.

We appreciate the contribution of the students who sat through courses as material from the book was being debugged. The first author acknowledges students at the University of Edinburgh, the Weizmann Institute of Science, Tel Aviv University, and Case Western Reserve University. The second author taught courses at the Weizmann Institute and Hebrew University of Jerusalem, and in industry.

We are grateful to many people for assisting in the technical aspects of producing a book. We especially thank Sarah Fliegelmann, who produced the various drafts and camera-ready copy, above and beyond the call of duty. This book might not have appeared without her tremendous efforts. Arvind Bansal prepared the index and helped with the references. Yehuda Barbut drew most of the figures. Max Goldberg and Shmuel Safra prepared the appendix. The publishers, MIT Press, were helpful and supportive.

Finally, we acknowledge the support of family and friends, without which nothing would get done.

Leon Sterling
1986

Introduction

The inception of logic is tied with that of scientific thinking. Logic provides a precise language for the explicit expression of one's goals, knowledge, and assumptions. Logic provides the foundation for deducing consequences from premises; for studying the truth or falsity of statements given the truth or falsity of other statements; for establishing the consistency of one's claims; and for verifying the validity of one's arguments.

Computers are relatively new in our intellectual history. Similar to logic, they are the object of scientific study and a powerful tool for the advancement of scientific endeavor. Like logic, computers require a precise and explicit statement of one's goals and assumptions. Unlike logic, which has developed with the power of human thinking as the only external consideration, the development of computers has been governed from the start by severe technological and engineering constraints. Although computers were intended for use by humans, the difficulties in constructing them were so dominant that the language for expressing problems to the computer and instructing it how to solve them was designed from the perspective of the engineering of the computer alone.

Almost all modern computers are based on the early concepts of von Neumann and his colleagues, which emerged during the 1940s. The von Neumann machine is characterized by a large uniform store of memory cells and a processing unit with some local cells, called registers. The processing unit can load data from memory to registers, perform arithmetic or logical operations on registers, and store values of registers back into memory. A program for a von Neumann machine consists of a sequence of instructions to perform such operations, and an additional set of control instructions, which can affect the next instruction to be executed, possibly depending on the content of some register.

As the problems of building computers were gradually understood and solved, the problems of using them mounted. The bottleneck ceased to be the inability of the computer to perform the human's instructions but rather the inability of the human to instruct, or program, the computer. A search for programming languages convenient for humans to use began. Starting from the language understood directly by the computer, the machine language, better notations and formalisms were developed. The main outcome of these efforts was languages that were easier for humans to express themselves in but that still mapped rather directly to the underlying machine language. Although increasingly abstract, the languages in the mainstream of development, starting from assembly language through Fortran, Algol, Pascal, and Ada, all carried the mark of the underlying machine—the von Neumann architecture.

To the uninitiated intelligent person who is not familiar with the engineering constraints that led to its design, the von Neumann machine seems an arbitrary, even bizarre, device. Thinking in terms of its constrained set of operations is a nontrivial problem, which sometimes stretches the adaptiveness of the human mind to its limits.

These characteristic aspects of programming von Neumann computers led to a separation of work: there were those who thought how to solve the problem, and designed the methods for its solution, and there were the coders, who performed the mundane and tedious task of translating the instructions of the designers to instructions a computer can use.

Both logic and programming require the explicit expression of one's knowledge and methods in an acceptable formalism. The task of making one's knowledge explicit is tedious. However, formalizing one's knowledge in logic is often an intellectually rewarding activity and usually reflects back on or adds insight to the problem under consideration. In contrast, formalizing one's problem and method of solution using the von Neumann instruction set rarely has these beneficial effects.

We believe that programming can be, and should be, an intellectually rewarding activity; that a good programming language is a powerful conceptual tool—a tool for organizing, expressing, experimenting with, and even communicating one's thoughts; that treating programming as "coding," the last, mundane, intellectually trivial, time-consuming, and tedious phase of solving a problem using a computer system, is perhaps at the very root of what has been known as the "software crisis."

Rather, we think that programming can be, and should be, part of the problem-solving process itself; that thoughts should be organized as programs, so that consequences of a complex set of assumptions can be investigated by "running" the assumptions; that a conceptual solution to a problem should be developed hand-in-hand with a working program that demonstrates it and exposes its different aspects. Suggestions in this direction have been made under the title "rapid prototyping."

To achieve this goal in its fullest—to become true mates of the human thinking process—computers have still a long way to go. However, we find it both appropriate and gratifying from a historical perspective that logic, a companion to the human thinking process since the early days of human intellectual history, has been discovered as a suitable stepping-stone in this long journey.

Although logic has been used as a tool for designing computers and for reasoning about computers and computer programs since almost their beginning, the use of logic directly as a programming language, termed *logic programming*, is quite recent.

Logic programming, as well as its sister approach, functional programming, departs radically from the mainstream of computer languages. Rather then being derived, by a series of abstractions and reorganizations, from the von Neumann machine model and instruction set, it is derived from an abstract model, which has no direct relation to 'or dependence on to one machine model or another. It is based on the belief that instead of the human learning to think in terms of the operations of a computer that which some scientists and engineers at some point in history happened to find easy and cost-effective to build, the computer should perform instructions that are easy for humans to provide. In its ultimate and purest form, logic programming suggests that even explicit instructions for operation not be given but rather that the knowledge about the problem and assumptions sufficient to solve it be stated explicitly, as logical axioms. Such a set of axioms constitutes an alternative to the conventional program. The program can be executed by providing it with a problem, formalized as a logical statement to be proved, called a goal statement. The execution is an attempt to solve the problem, that is, to prove the goal statement, given the assumptions in the logic program.

A distinguishing aspect of the logic used in logic programming is that a goal statement typically is existentially quantified: it states that there exist some individuals with some property. An example of a goal statement is, "there exists a list X such that sorting the list $[3, 1, 2]$ gives X." The mechanism used to prove the goal statement is constructive. If successful, it provides the identity of the unknown individuals mentioned in the goal statement, which constitutes the output of the computation. In the preceding example, assuming that the logic program contains appropriate axioms defining the *sort* relation, the output of the computation would be $X = [1, 2, 3]$.

These ideas can be summarized in the following two metaphorical equations:

program = set of axioms.

computation = constructive proof of a goal statement from the program.

The ideas behind these equations can be traced back as far as intuitionistic mathematics and proof theory of the early twentieth century. They are related to Hilbert's program, to base the entire body of mathematical knowledge on logical foundations and to provide mechanical proofs for its theories, starting from the axioms of logic and set theory alone. It is interesting to note that the failure of this program, from which ensued the incompleteness and undecidability results of Gödel and Turing, marks the beginning of the modern age of computers.

The first use of this approach in practical computing is a sequel to Robinson's unification algorithm and resolution principle, published in 1965. Several hesitant attempts were made to use this principle as a basis of a computation mechanism, but they did not gain any momentum. The beginning of logic programming can be attributed to Kowalski and Colmerauer. Kowalski formulated the procedural interpretation of Horn clause logic. He showed that an axiom

A if B_1 and B_2 and . . . and B_n

can be read and executed as a procedure of a recursive programming language, where A is the procedure head and the B_i are its body. In addition to the declarative reading of the clause, A is true if the B_i are true, it can be read as follows: To solve (execute) A, solve (execute) B_1 and B_2 and . . . and B_n. In this reading, the proof procedure of Horn clause logic is the interpreter of the language, and the unification algorithm, which is at the heart of the resolution proof procedure, performs the basic data manipulation operations of variable assignment, parameter passing, data selection, and data construction.

At the same time, in the early 1970s, Colmerauer and his group at the University of Marseilles-Aix developed a specialized theorem prover, written in Fortran, which they used to implement natural language processing systems. The theorem prover, called Prolog (for Programmation en Logique), embodied Kowalski's procedural interpretation. Later, van Emden and Kowalski developed a formal semantics for the language of logic programs, showing that its operational, model-theoretic, and fix-point semantics are the same.

In spite of all the theoretical work and the exciting ideas, the logic programming approach seemed unrealistic. At the time of its inception, researchers in the United States began to recognize the failure of the "next-generation AI languages," such as Micro-Planner and Conniver, which developed as a substitute for Lisp. The main claim against these languages was that they were hopelessly inefficient, and very difficult to control. Given their bitter experience with logic-based high-level languages, it is no great surprise that U.S. artificial intelligence scientists, when hearing about Prolog, thought that the Europeans were over-excited over what they, the Americans, had already suggested, tried, and discovered not to work.

In that atmosphere the Prolog-10 compiler was almost an imaginary being. Developed in the mid to late 1970s by David H. D. Warren and his colleagues, this efficient implementation of Prolog dispelled all the myths about the impracticality of logic programming. That compiler, still one of the finest implementations of Prolog around, delivered on pure list-processing programs a performance comparable to the best Lisp systems available at the time. Furthermore, the compiler itself was written almost entirely in Prolog, suggesting that classic programming tasks, not just sophisticated AI applications, could benefit from the power of logic programming.

The impact of this implementation cannot be overemphasized. Without it, the accumulated experience that has led to this book would not have existed.

In spite of the promise of the ideas, and the practicality of their implementation, most of the Western computer science and AI research community was ignorant, openly hostile, or, at best, indifferent to logic programming. By 1980 the number of researchers actively engaged in logic programming were only a few dozen in the United States and about one hundred around the world.

No doubt, logic programming would have remained a fringe activity in computer science for quite a while longer hadit not been for the announcement of the Japanese Fifth Generation Project, which took place in October 1981. Although the research program the Japanese presented was rather baggy, faithful to their tradition of achieving consensus at almost any cost, the important role of logic programming in the next generation of computer systems was made clear.

Since that time the Prolog language has undergone a rapid transition from adolescence to maturity. There are numerous commercially available Prolog implementations on most computers. A large number of Prolog programming books are directed to different audiences and emphasize different aspects of the language. And the language itself has more or less stabilized, having a de facto standard, the Edinburgh Prolog family.

The maturity of the language means that it is no longer a concept for scientists yet to shape and define but rather a given object, with vices and virtues. It is time to recognize that, on the one hand, Prolog falls short of the high goals of logic programming but, on the other hand, is a powerful, productive, and practical programming formalism. Given the standard life cycle of computer programming languages, the next few years will reveal whether these properties show their merit only in the classroom or prove useful also in the field, where people pay money to solve problems they care about.

What are the current active subjects of research in logic programming and Prolog? Answers to this question can be found in the regular scientific journals and conferences of the field; the *Logic Programming Journal*, the *Journal of New Generation Computing*, the *International Conference on Logic Programming*, and the *IEEE Symposium on Logic*

Programming as well as in the general computer science journals and conferences.

Clearly, one of the dominant areas of interest is the relation between logic programming, Prolog, and parallelism. The promise of parallel computers, combined with the parallelism that seems to be available in the logic programming model, have led to numerous attempts, still ongoing, to execute Prolog in parallel and to devise novel concurrent programming languages based on the logic programming computation model. This, however, is a subject for another book.

Leonardo Da Vinci. *Old Man thinking*. Pen and ink (slightly enlarged). About 1510. Windsor Castle, Royal Library.

I Logic Programs

A logic program is a set of axioms, or rules, defining relations between objects. A computation of a logic program is a deduction of consequences of the program. A program defines a set of consequences, which is its meaning. The art of logic programming is constructing concise and elegant programs that have the desired meaning.

1 Logic Programs

1   Basic Constructs

The basic constructs of logic programming, terms and statements, are inherited from logic. There are three basic statements: facts, rules, and queries. There is a single data structure: the logical term.

1.1   Facts

The simplest kind of statement is called a *fact*. Facts are a means of stating that a relation holds between objects. An example is

```
father(abraham,isaac).
```

This fact says that Abraham is the father of Isaac, or that the relation father holds between the individuals named abraham and isaac. Another name for a relation is a *predicate*. Names of individuals are known as *atoms*. Similarly, plus(2,3,5) expresses the relation that 2 plus 3 is 5. The familiar plus relation can be realized via a set of facts that defines the addition table. An initial segment of the table is

```
plus(0,0,0).    plus(0,1,1).    plus(0,2,2).    plus(0,3,3).
plus(1,0,1).    plus(1,1,2).    plus(1,2,3).    plus(1,3,4).
```

A sufficiently large segment of this table, which happens to be also a legal logic program, will be assumed as the definition of the plus relation throughout this chapter.

The syntactic conventions used throughout the book are introduced as needed. The first is the case convention. It is significant that the names

```
father(terach,abraham).        male(terach).
father(terach,nachor).         male(abraham).
father(terach,haran).          male(nachor).
father(abraham,isaac).         male(haran).
father(haran,lot).             male(isaac).
father(haran,milcah).          male(lot).
father(haran,yiscah).
                               female(sarah).
mother(sarah,isaac).           female(milcah).
                               female(yiscah).
```

Program 1.1 A biblical family database

of both predicates and atoms in facts begin with a lowercase letter rather than an uppercase letter.

A finite set of facts constitutes a *program*. This is the simplest form of logic program. A set of facts is also a description of a situation. This insight is the basis of database programming, to be discussed in the next chapter. An example database of family relationships from the Bible is given as Program 1.1. The predicates father, mother, male, and female express the obvious relationships.

1.2 Queries

The second form of statement in a logic program is a *query*. Queries are a means of retrieving information from a logic program. A query asks whether a certain relation holds between objects. For example, the query father(abraham,isaac)? asks whether the father relationship holds between abraham and isaac. Given the facts of Program 1.1, the answer to this query is *yes*.

Syntactically, queries and facts look the same, but they can be distinguished by the context. When there is a possibility of confusion, a terminating period will indicate a fact, while a terminating question mark will indicate a query. We call the entity without the period or question mark a *goal*. A fact *P*. states that the goal *P* is true. A query *P?* asks whether the goal *P* is true. A *simple query* consists of a single goal.

Answering a query with respect to a program is determining whether the query is a logical consequence of the program. We define logical consequence incrementally through this chapter. Logical consequences are obtained by applying deduction rules. The simplest rule of deduction is *identity*: from *P* deduce *P*. A query is a logical consequence of an identical fact.

Operationally, answering simple queries using a program containing facts like Program 1.1 is straightforward. Search for a fact in the program that implies the query. If a fact identical to the query is found, the answer is *yes*.

The answer *no* is given if a fact identical to the query is not found, because the fact is not a logical consequence of the program. This answer does not reflect on the truth of the query; it merely says that we failed to prove the query from the program. Both the queries `female(abraham)?` and `plus(1,1,2)?` will be answered *no* with respect to Program 1.1.

1.3   The Logical Variable, Substitutions, and Instances

A logical variable stands for an unspecified individual and is used accordingly. Consider its use in queries. Suppose we want to know of whom `abraham` is the father. One way is to ask a series of queries, `father(abraham,lot)?`,   `father(abraham,milcah)?`,..., `father (abraham,isaac)?`,... until an answer *yes* is given. A variable allows a better way of expressing the query as `father(abraham,X)?`, to which the answer is `X=isaac`. Used in this way, *variables are a means of summarizing many queries*. A query containing a variable asks whether there is a value for the variable that makes the query a logical consequence of the program, as explained later.

Variables in logic programs behave differently from variables in conventional programming languages. They stand for an unspecified but single entity rather than for a store location in memory.

Having introduced variables, we can define a *term*, the single data structure in logic programs. The definition is inductive. Constants and variables are terms. Also compound terms, or structures, are terms. A *compound term* comprises a functor (called the principal functor of the term) and a sequence of one or more arguments, which are terms. A *functor* is characterized by its *name*, which is an atom, and its *arity*, or number of arguments. Syntactically, compound terms have the form $f(t_1, t_2, \ldots, t_n)$, where the functor has name f and is of arity n, and the t_i are the arguments. Examples of compound terms include s(0), hot(milk), name(john,doe), list(a,list(b,nil)), foo(X), and tree(tree(nil,3,nil),5,R).

Queries, goals, and more generally terms where variables do not occur are called *ground*. Where variables do occur, they are called *nonground*. For example, foo(a,b) is ground, whereas bar(X) is nonground.

Definition

A *substitution* is a finite set (possibly empty) of pairs of the form $X_i = t_i$, where X_i is a variable and t_i is a term, and $X_i \neq X_j$ for every $i \neq j$, and X_i does not occur in t_j, for any i and j.   ■

An example of a substitution consisting of a single pair is {X=isaac}. Substitutions can be applied to terms. The result of applying a substitution θ to a term A, denoted by $A\theta$, is the term obtained by replacing every occurrence of X by t in A, for every pair $X = t$ in θ.

The result of applying {X=isaac} to the term father(abraham,X) is the term father(abraham,isaac).

Definition

A is an *instance* of B if there is a substitution θ such that $A = B\theta$.   ■

The goal father(abraham,isaac) is an instance of father(abraham, X) by this definition. Similarly, mother(sarah,isaac) is an instance of mother(X,Y) under the substitution {X=sarah,Y=isaac}.

1.4   Existential Queries

Logically speaking, variables in queries are existentially quantified, which means, intuitively, that the query father(abraham,X)? reads: "Does there exist an X such that abraham is the father of X?" More generally, a query $p(T_1, T_2, \ldots, T_n)$?, which contains the variables $X_1, X_2, \ldots, X_k$ reads: "Are there $X_1, X_2, \ldots, X_k$ such that $p(T_1, T_2, \ldots, T_n)$?" For convenience, existential quantification is usually omitted.

The next deduction rule we introduce is *generalization*. An existential query P is a logical consequence of an instance of it, $P\theta$, for any substitution θ. The fact father(abraham,isaac) implies that there exists an X such that father(abraham,X) is true, namely, X=isaac.

Operationally, to answer a nonground query using a program of facts, search for a fact that is an instance of the query. If found, the answer, or *solution*, is that instance. A solution is represented in this chapter by the substitution that, if applied to the query, results in the solution. The answer is *no* if there is no suitable fact in the program.

In general, an existential query may have several solutions. Program 1.1 shows that Haran is the father of three children. Thus the query `father(haran,X)?` has the solutions {X=lot}, {X=milcah}, {X=yiscah}. Another query with multiple solutions is `plus(X,Y,4)?` for finding numbers that add up to 4. Solutions are, for example, {X=0, Y=4} and {X=1, Y=3}. Note that the different variables X and Y correspond to (possibly) different objects.

An interesting variant of the last query is `plus(X,X,4)?`, which insists that the two numbers that add up to 4 be the same. It has a unique answer {X=2}.

1.5 Universal Facts

Variables are also useful in facts. Suppose that all the biblical characters like pomegranates. Instead of including in the program an appropriate fact for every individual,

```
likes(abraham,pomegranates).
likes(sarah,pomegranates).
    .
    .
    .
```

a fact `likes(X,pomegranates)` can say it all. Used in this way, *variables are a means of summarizing many facts.* The fact `times(0,X,0)` summarizes all the facts stating that 0 times some number is 0.

Variables in facts are implicitly universally quantified, which means, intuitively, that the fact `likes(X,pomegranates)` states that for all X, X likes pomegranates. In general, a fact $p(T_1,...,T_n)$ reads that for all $X_1,...,X_k$, where the X_i are variables occurring in the fact, $p(T_1,...,T_n)$ is true. Logically, from a universally quantified fact one can deduce any instance of it. For example, from `likes(X,pomegranates)`, deduce `likes(abraham,pomegranates)`.

This is the third deduction rule, called *instantiation*. From a universally quantified statement P, deduce an instance of it, $P\theta$, for any substitution θ.

As for queries, two unspecified objects, denoted by variables, can be constrained to be the same by using the same variable name. The fact plus(0,X,X) expresses that 0 is a left identity for addition. It reads that for all values of X, 0 plus X is X. A similar use occurs when translating the English statement "Everybody likes himself" to likes(X,X).

Answering a ground query with a universally quantified fact is straightforward. Search for a fact for which the query is an instance. For example, the answer to plus(0,2,2)? is *yes*, based on the fact plus(0,X,X). Answering a nonground query using a nonground fact involves a new definition: a common instance of two terms.

Definition

C is a *common instance* of A and B if it is an instance of A and an instance of B, in other words, if there are substitutions θ_1 and θ_2 such that $C=A\theta_1$ is syntactically identical to $B\theta_2$.　　　■

For example, the goals plus(0,3,Y) and plus(0,X,X) have a common instance plus(0,3,3). When the substitution {Y=3} is applied to plus(0,3,Y) and the substitution {X=3} is applied to plus(0,X,X), both yield plus(0,3,3).

In general, to answer a query using a fact, search for a common instance of the query and fact. The answer is the common instance, if one exists. Otherwise the answer is *no*.

Answering an existential query with a universal fact using a common instance involves two logical deductions. The instance is deduced from the fact by the rule of instantiation, and the query is deduced from the instance by the rule of generalization.

1.6 Conjunctive Queries and Shared Variables

An important extension to the queries discussed so far is *conjunctive queries*. Conjunctive queries are a conjunction of goals posed as a query, for example, father(terach,X),father(X,Y)? or in general, $Q_1,...,Q_n$?. Simple queries are a special case of conjunctive queries when there is a single goal. Logically, it asks whether a conjunction is deducible from the program. We use "," throughout to denote logical *and*. Do not confuse the comma that separates the arguments in a goal with commas used to separate goals, denoting conjunction.

In the simplest conjunctive queries all the goals are ground, for example, father(abraham,isaac),male(lot)?. The answer to this query using Program 1.1 is clearly *yes* because both goals in the query are facts in the program. In general, the query $Q_1,\ldots,Q_n$?, where each Q_i is a ground goal, is answered yes with respect to a program P if each Q_i is implied by P. Hence ground conjunctive queries are not very interesting.

Conjunctive queries are interesting when there are one or more *shared variables*, variables that occur in two different goals of the query. An example is the query father(haran,X),male(X)?. The scope of a variable in a conjunctive query, as in a simple query, is the whole conjunction. Thus the query $p(X),q(X)$? reads: "Is there an X such that *both* $p(X)$ and $q(X)$?"

Shared variables are used as a means of constraining a simple query by restricting the range of a variable. We have already seen an example with the query plus(X,X,4)?, where the solution of numbers adding up to 4 was restricted to the numbers being the same. Consider the query father(haran,X),male(X)?. Here solutions to the query father(haran,X)? are restricted to children that are male. Program 1.1 shows there is only one solution, {X=lot}. Alternatively, this query can be viewed as restricting solutions to the query male(X)? to individuals who have Haran for a father.

A slightly different use of a shared variable can be seen in the query father(terach,X),father(X,Y)?. On the one hand, it restricts the sons of terach to those who are themselves fathers. On the other hand, it considers individuals Y, whose fathers are sons of terach. There are several solutions, for example, {X=abraham,Y=isaac} and {X=haran,Y=lot}.

A conjunctive query is a logical consequence of a program P if all the goals in the conjunction are consequences of P, where shared variables are instantiated to the same values in different goals. A sufficient condition is that there be a ground instance of the query that is a consequence of P. This instance then deduces the conjuncts in the query via generalization.

The restriction to ground instances is unnecessary and will be lifted in Chapter 4 when we discuss the computation model of logic programs.

We employ this restriction in the meantime to simplify the discussion in the coming sections.

Operationally, to solve the conjunctive query $A_1,A_2,\ldots,A_n$? using a program P, find a substitution θ such that $A_1\theta$ and $\ldots$ and $A_n\theta$ are ground instances of facts in P. The same substitution applied to all the goals ensures that instances of variables are common throughout the query. For example, consider the query `father(haran,X),male(X)`? with respect to Program 1.1. Applying the substitution {X=lot} to the query gives the ground instance `father(haran,lot),male(lot)`?, which is a consequence of the program.

1.7   Rules

Interesting conjunctive queries are defining relationships in their own right. The query `father(haran,X),male(X)`? is asking for a son of Haran. The query `father(terach,X),father(X,Y)`? is asking about grandchildren of Terach. This brings us to the third and most important statement in logic programming, a rule, which enables us to define new relationships in terms of existing relationships.

Rules are statements of the form:

$A \leftarrow B_1,B_2,\ldots,B_n.$

where $n \geq 0$. The goal A is the *head* of the rule, and the conjunction of goals $B_1,\ldots,B_n$ is the *body* of the rule. Rules, facts, and queries are also called *Horn clauses*, or *clauses* for short. Note that a fact is just a special case of a rule when $n = 0$. Facts are also called *unit clauses*. We also have a special name for clauses with one goal in the body, namely, when $n = 1$. Such a clause is called an *iterative clause*. As for facts, variables appearing in rules are universally quantified, and their scope is the whole rule.

A rule expressing the son relationship is

`son(X,Y)  ← father(Y,X), male(X).`

Similarly one can define a rule for the daughter relationship:

`daughter(X,Y)  ← father(Y,X), female(X).`

A rule for the grandfather relationship is

grandfather(X,Y) ← father(X,Z), father(Z,Y).

Rules can be viewed in two ways. First, they are a means of expressing new or complex queries in terms of simple queries. A query son(X,haran)? to the program that contains the preceding rule for son is translated to the query father(haran,X),male(X)? according to the rule, and solved as before. A new query about the son relationship has been built from simple queries involving father and male relationships. Interpreting rules in this way is their *procedural* reading. The procedural reading for the grandfather rule is: "To answer a query *Is X the grandfather of Y?*, answer the conjunctive query *Is X the father of Z and Z the father of Y?*."

The second view of rules comes from interpreting the rule as a logical axiom. The backward arrow ←is used to denote logical implication. The son rule reads: "*X* is a son of *Y* if *Y* is the father of *X* and *X* is male." In this view, rules are a means of defining new or complex relationships using other, simpler relationships. The predicate son has been defined in terms of the predicates father and male. The associated reading of the rule is known as the *declarative* reading. The declarative reading of the grandfather rule is: "For all *X*, *Y*, and *Z*, *X* is the grandfather of *Y* if *X* is the father of *Z* and *Z* is the father of *Y*."

Although formally all variables in a clause are universally quantified, we will sometimes refer to variables that occur in the body of the clause, but not in its head, as if they are existentially quantified inside the body. For example, the grandfather rule can be read: "For all *X* and *Y*, *X* is the grandfather of *Y* if there exists a *Z* such that *X* is the father of *Z* and *Z* is the father of *Y*." The formal justification of this verbal transformation will not be given, and we treat it just as a convenience. Whenever it is a source of confusion, the reader can resort back to the formal reading of a clause, in which all variables are universally quantified from the outside.

To incorporate rules into our framework of logical deduction, we need the law of modus ponens. Modus ponens states that from *B* and *A* ← *B* we can deduce *A*.

Definition
The law of *universal modus ponens* says that from the rule

$$R = (A \leftarrow B_1, B_2, \ldots, B_n)$$

and the facts

$B'_1.$
$B'_2.$
.
.
.
$B'_n.$

   A' can be deduced if

$$A' \leftarrow B'_1,B'_2,\ldots,B'_n$$

is an instance of R.   ■

   Universal modus ponens includes identity and instantiation as special cases.

   We are now in a position to give a complete definition of the concept of a logic program and of its associated concept of logical consequence.

Definition
A *logic program* is a finite set of rules.   ■

Definition
An existentially quantified goal G is a logical consequence of a program P if there is a clause in P with a ground instance $A \leftarrow B_1,\ldots,B_n, n \geq 0$ such that $B_1,\ldots,B_n$ are logical consequences of P, and A is an instance of G.   ■

   Note that the goal G is a logical consequence of a program P if and only if G can be deduced from P by a finite number of applications of the rule of universal modus ponens.

   Consider the query `son(S,haran)?` with respect to Program 1.1 augmented by the rule for son. The substitution `{X=lot,Y=haran}` applied to the rule gives the instance `son(lot,haran)` `←father(haran,lot),` `male(lot)`. Both the goals in the body of this rule are facts in Program 1.1. Thus universal modus ponens implies the query with answer `{S=lot}`.

   Operationally, answering queries reflects the definition of logical consequence. Guess a ground instance of a goal, and a ground instance of a rule, and recursively answer the conjunctive query corresponding to the body of that rule. To solve a goal A with program P, choose a rule $A_1 \leftarrow B_1,B_2,\ldots,B_n$ in P, and guess substitution θ such that $A = A_1\theta$, and

$B_i\theta$ is ground for $1 \le i \le n$. Then recursively solve each $B_i\theta$. This procedure can involve arbitrarily long chains of reasoning. It is difficult in general to guess the correct ground instance and to choose the right rule. We show in Chapter 4 how the guessing of an instance can be removed.

The rule given for son is correct but is an incomplete specification of the relationship. For example, we cannot conclude that Isaac is the son of Sarah. What is missing is that a child can be the son of a mother as well as the son of a father. A new rule expressing this relationship can be added, namely,

```
son(X,Y) ← mother(Y,X), male(X).
```

To define the relationship grandparent correctly would take four rules to include both cases of father and mother:

```
grandparent(X,Y) ← father(X,Z), father(Z,Y).
grandparent(X,Y) ← father(X,Z), mother(Z,Y).
grandparent(X,Y) ← mother(X,Z), father(Z,Y).
grandparent(X,Y) ← mother(X,Z), mother(Z,Y).
```

There is a better, more compact, way of expressing these rules. We need to define the auxiliary relationship parent as being a father or a mother. Part of the art of logic programming is deciding on what intermediate predicates to define to achieve a complete, elegant axiomatization of a relationship. The rules defining parent are straightforward, capturing the definition of a parent being a father or a mother. Logic programs can incorporate alternative definitions, or more technically disjunction, by having alternative rules, as for parent:

```
parent(X,Y) ← father(X,Y).
parent(X,Y) ← mother(X,Y).
```

Rules for son and grandparent are now, respectively,

```
son(X,Y) ← parent(Y,X), male(X).
grandparent(X,Y) ← parent(X,Z), parent(Z,Y).
```

A collection of rules with the same predicate in the head, such as the pair of parent rules, is called a *procedure*. We shall see later that under the operational interpretation of these rules by Prolog, such a collection of rules is indeed the analogue of procedures or subroutines in conventional programming languages.

1.8   A Simple Abstract Interpreter

An operational procedure for answering queries has been informally described and progressively developed in the previous sections. In this section, the details are fleshed out into an abstract interpreter for logic programs. In keeping with the restriction of universal modus ponens to ground goals, the interpreter only answers ground queries.

The abstract interpreter performs yes/no computations. It takes as input a program and a goal, and answers *yes* if the goal is a logical consequence of the program and *no* otherwise. The interpreter is given in Figure 1.1. Note that the interpreter may fail to terminate if the goal is not deducible from the program, in which case no answer is given.

The current, usually conjunctive, goal at any stage of the computation is called the *resolvent*. A *trace* of the interpreter is the sequence of resolvents produced during the computation. Figure 1.2 is a trace of answering the query son(lot,haran)? with respect to Program 1.2, a subset of the facts of Program 1.1 together with rules defining son and daughter. For clarity, Figure 1.2 also explicitly states the choice of goal and clause made at each iteration of the abstract interpreter.

Each iteration of the *while* loop of the abstract interpreter corresponds to a single application of modus ponens. This is called a *reduction*.

Input: A ground goal G and a program P

Output: *yes* if G is a logical consequence of P,
                  no otherwise

Algorithm: Initialize the resolvent to G.
                  while the resolvent is not empty *do*
                      choose a goal A from the resolvent
                      choose a ground instance of a clause $A' \leftarrow B_1,\ldots,B_n$ from P
                          such that A and A' are identical
                          (if no such goal and clause exist, exit the while loop)
                      replace A by $B_1,\ldots,B_n$ in the resolvent
                  If the resolvent is empty, *then* output *yes*, *else* output *no*.

Figure 1.1   An abstract interpreter to answer ground queries with respect to logic programs

Input: son(lot,haran)? and Program 1.2
              Resolvent is son(lot,haran)
              Resolvent is not empty
                  choose son(lot,haran)   (the only choice)
                  choose son(lot,haran) ← father(haran,lot), male(lot).
                  new resolvent is father(haran,lot), male(lot)
              Resolvent is not empty
                  choose father(haran,lot)
                  choose father(haran,lot).
                  new resolvent is male(lot)
              Resolvent is not empty
                  choose male(lot)
                  choose male(lot).
                  new resolvent is empty

Output: *yes*

Figure 1.2   Tracing the interpreter

```
father(abraham,isaac).        male(isaac).
father(haran,lot).            male(lot).
father(haran,milcah).         female(milcah).
father(haran,yiscah).         female(yiscah).

son(X,Y) ← father(Y,X), male(X).
daughter(X,Y) ← father(Y,X), female(X).
```

Program 1.2   Biblical family relationships

Definition
A *reduction* of a goal *G* by a program *P* is the replacement of *G* by the
body of an instance of a clause in *P*, whose head is identical to the chosen
goal.   ■

A reduction is the basic computational step in logic programming. The
goal replaced in a reduction is *reduced*, and the new goals are *derived*.
In this chapter, we restrict ourselves to *ground reductions*, where the
goal and the instance of the clause are ground. Later, in Chapter 4, we
consider more general reductions where unification is used to choose the
instance of the clause and make the goal to be reduced and the head of
the clause identical.

The trace in Figure 1.2 contains three reductions. The first reduces the goal son(lot,haran) and produces two derived goals, father(haran, lot) and male(lot). The second reduction is of father(haran,lot) and produces no derived goals. The third reduction also produces no derived goals in reducing male(lot).

There are two unspecified choices in the interpreter in Figure 1.1. The first is the goal to reduce from the resolvent. The second choice is the clause (and an appropriate ground instance) to reduce the goal. These two choices have very different natures.

The selection of the goal to be reduced is arbitrary. In any given resolvent, all the goals must be reduced. It can be shown that the order of reductions is immaterial for answering the query.

In contrast, the choice of the clause and a suitable instance is critical. In general, there are several choices of a clause, and infinitely many ground instances. The choice is made nondeterministically. The concept of nondeterministic choice is used in the definition of many computation models, e.g., finite automata and Turing machines, and has proven to be a powerful theoretic concept. A nondeterministic choice is an unspecified choice from a number of alternatives, which is supposed to be made in a "clairvoyant" way. If only some of the alternatives lead to a successful computation, then one of them is chosen. Formally, the concept is defined as follows. A computation that contains nondeterministic choices *succeeds* if there is a sequence of choices that leads to success. Of course, no real machine can directly implement this definition. However, it can be approximated in a useful way, as done in Prolog. This is explained in Chapter 6.

The interpreter given in Figure 1.1 can be extended to answer nonground existential queries by an initial additional step. Guess a ground instance of the query. This is identical to the step in the interpreter of guessing ground instances of the rules. It is difficult in general to guess the correct ground instance, since that means knowing the result of the computation before performing it.

A new concept is needed to lift the restriction to ground instances and remove the burden of guessing them. In Chapter 4, we show how the guess of ground instances can be eliminated, and we introduce the computational model of logic programs more fully. Until then it is assumed that the correct choices can be made.

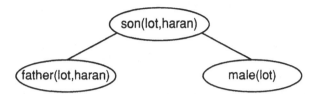

Figure 1.3 A simple proof tree

A trace of a query implicitly contains a proof that the query follows from the program. A more convenient representation of the proof is with a proof tree. A *proof tree* consists of nodes and edges that represent the goals reduced during the computation. The root of the proof tree for a simple query is the query itself. The nodes of the tree are goals that are reduced during the computation. There is a directed edge from a node to each node corresponding to a derived goal of the reduced goal. The proof tree for a conjunctive query is just the collection of proof trees for the individual goals in the conjunction. Figure 1.3 gives a proof tree for the program trace in Figure 1.2.

An important measure provided by proof trees is the number of nodes in the tree. It indicates how many reduction steps are performed in a computation. This measure is used as a basis of comparison between different programs in Chapter 3.

1.9   The Meaning of a Logic Program

How can we know if a logic program says what we wanted it to say? If it is correct, or incorrect? In order to answer such questions, we have to define what is the meaning of a logic program. Once defined, we can examine if the program means what we have intended it to mean.

Definition
The *meaning* of a logic program P, $M(P)$, is the set of ground goals deducible from P.   ■

From this definition it follows that the meaning of a logic program composed just of ground facts, such as Program 1.1, is the program itself. In other words, for simple programs, the program "means just what it says." Consider Program 1.1 augmented with the two rules defining the parent relationship. What is its meaning? It contains, in addition to the facts about fathers and mothers, mentioned explicitly in the program, all goals of the form parent(X,Y) for every pair X and Y such that father(X,Y) or mother(X,Y) is in the program. This example shows that the meaning of a program contains explicitly whatever the program states implicitly.

Assuming that we define the intended meaning of a program also to be a set of ground goals, we can ask what is the relation between the actual and the intended meanings of a program. We can check whether everything the program says is correct, or whether the program says everything we wanted it to say.

Informally, we say that a program is *correct* with respect to some intended meaning *M* if the meaning of *P*, *M(P)*, is a subset of *M*. That is, a correct program does not say things that were not intended. A program is *complete* with respect to *M* if *M* is a subset of *M(P)*. That is, a complete program says everything that is intended. It follows that a program *P* is correct and complete with respect to an intended meaning *M* if *M = M(P)*.

Throughout the book, when meaningful predicate and constant names are used, the intended meaning of the program is assumed to be the one intuitively implied by the choice of names.

For example, the program for the son relationship containing only the first axiom that uses father is incomplete with respect to the intuitively understood intended meaning of son, since it cannot deduce son(isaac,sarah). If we add to Program 1.1 the rule

```
son(X,Y) ← mother(X,Y), male(Y).
```

it would make the program incorrect with respect to the intended meaning, since it deduces son(sarah,isaac).

The notions of correctness and completeness of a logic program are studied further in Chapter 5.

Although the notion of truth is not defined fully here, we will say that a ground goal is *true* with respect to an intended meaning if it is a member of it, and *false* otherwise. We will say it is simply *true* if it is a member of the intended meaning implied by the names of the predicate and constant symbols appearing in the program.

1.10 Summary

We conclude this section with a summary of the constructs and concepts introduced, filling in the remaining necessary definitions.

The basic structure in logic programs is a term. A *term* is a constant, a variable, or a compound term. Constants denote particular individuals such as integers and atoms, while variables denote a single but unspecified individual. The symbol for an atom can be any sequence of characters, which is quoted if there is possibility of confusion with other symbols (such as variables or integers). Symbols for variables are distinguished by beginning with an uppercase letter.

A *compound term* comprises a functor (called the principal functor of the term) and a sequence of one or more terms called *arguments*. A *functor* is characterized by its *name*, which is an atom, and its *arity* or number of arguments. Constants are considered functors of arity 0. Syntactically, compound terms have the form $f(t_1,t_2,\ldots,t_n)$ where the functor has name f and is of arity n, and the t_i are the arguments. A functor f of arity n is denoted f/n. Functors with the same name but different arities are distinct. Terms are *ground* if they contain no variables; otherwise they are *nonground*. *Goals* are atoms or compound terms, and are generally nonground.

A *substitution* is a finite set (possibly empty) of pairs of the form $X = t$, where X is a variable and t is a term, with no variable on the left-hand side of a pair appearing on the right-hand side of another pair, and no two pairs having the same variable as left-hand side. For any substitution $\theta = \{X_1 = t_1, X_2 = t_2, \ldots, X_n = t_n\}$ and term s, the term $s\theta$ denotes the result of simultaneously replacing in s each occurrence of the variable X_i by t_i, $1 \le i \le n$; the term $s\theta$ is called an *instance* of s. More will be said on this restriction on substitutions in the background to Chapter 4.

A *logic program* is a finite set of clauses. A *clause* or *rule* is a universally quantified logical sentence of the form

$$A \leftarrow B_1, B_2, \ldots, B_k. \qquad k \ge 0,$$

where A and the B_i are goals. Such a sentence is read declaratively: "A is implied by the conjunction of the B_i," and is interpreted procedurally "To answer query A, answer the conjunctive query $B_1, B_2, \ldots, B_k$." A is called the clause's *head* and the conjunction of the B_i the clause's *body*. If $k = 0$, the clause is known as a *fact* or *unit clause* and written A., meaning A is true under the declarative reading, and goal A is satisfied under the procedural interpretation. If $k = 1$, the clause is known as an *iterative clause.*

A *query* is a conjunction of the form

$$A_1,\ldots,A_n?   \quad n > 0,$$

where the A_i are goals. Variables in a query are understood to be existentially quantified.

A *computation* of a logic program P finds an instance of a given query logically deducible from P. A goal G is deducible from a program P if there is an instance A of G where $A \leftarrow B_1,\ldots,B_n$, $n \geq 0$, is a ground instance of a clause in P, and the B_i are deducible from P. Deduction of a goal from an identical fact is a special case.

The *meaning* of a program P is inductively defined using logical deduction. The set of ground instances of facts in P are in the meaning. A ground goal G is in the meaning if there is a ground instance $G \leftarrow B_1,\ldots,B_n$ of a rule in P such that $B_1,\ldots,B_n$ are in the meaning. The meaning consists of the ground instances that are deducible from the program.

An intended meaning M of a program is also a set of ground unit goals. A program P is *correct* with respect to an intended meaning M if M(P) is a subset of M. It is *complete* with respect to M if M is a subset of M(P). Clearly, it is correct and complete with respect to its intended meaning, which is the desired situation, if $M = M(P)$.

A ground goal is *true* with respect to an intended meaning if it is a member of it, and *false* otherwise.

Logical deduction is defined syntactically here, and hence also the meaning of logic programs. In Chapter 5, alternative ways of describing the meaning of logic programs are presented, and their equivalence with the current definition is discussed.

2   Database Programming

There are two basic styles of using logic programs: defining a logical database, and manipulating data structures. This chapter discusses database programming. A logic database contains a set of facts and rules. We show how a set of facts can define relations, as in relational databases. We show how rules can define complex relational queries, as in relational algebra. A logic program composed of a set of facts and rules of a rather restricted format can express the functionalities associated with relational databases.

2.1 Simple Databases

We begin by revising Program 1.1, the biblical database, and its augmentation with rules expressing family relationships. The database itself had four basic predicates, father/2, mother/2, male/1, and female/1. We adopt a convention from database theory and give for each relation a *relation scheme* that specifies the role that each position in the relation (or argument in the goal) is intended to represent. Relation schemes for the four predicates here are, respectively, father(Father,Child), mother(Mother,Child), male(Person), and female(Person). The mnemonic names are intended to speak for themselves.

Variables are given mnemonic names in rules, but usually X or Y when discussing queries. Multiword names are handled differently for variables and predicates. Each new word in a variable starts with an uppercase letter, for example, NieceOrNephew, while words are delimited by underscores for predicate and function names, for example, schedule_conflict.

New relations are built from these basic relationships by defining suitable rules. Appropriate relation schemes for the relationships introduced in the previous chapter are son(Son,Parent), daughter(Daughter, Parent), parent(Parent,Child), and grandparent(Grandparent, Grandchild). From the logical viewpoint, it is unimportant which relationships are defined by facts and which by rules. For example, if the available database consisted of parent, male and female facts, the rules defining son and grandparent are still correct. New rules must be written for the relationships no longer defined by facts, namely, father and mother. Suitable rules are

```
father(Dad,Child) ← parent(Dad,Child), male(Dad).
mother(Mum,Child) ← parent(Mum,Child), female(Mum).
```

Interesting rules can be obtained by making relationships explicit that are present in the database only implicitly. For example, since we know the father and mother of a child, we know which couples produced offspring, or to use a Biblical term, procreated. This is not given explicitly in the database, but a simple rule can be written recovering the information. The relation scheme is procreated(Man,Woman).

```
procreated(Man,Woman) ←
    father(Man,Child), mother(Woman,Child).
```

This reads: "Man and Woman procreated if there is a Child such that Man is the father of Child and Woman is the mother of Child."

Another example of information that can be recovered from the simple information present is sibling relationships — brothers and sisters. We give a rule for brother(Brother,Sibling).

```
brother(Brother,Sib) ←
    parent(Parent,Brother), parent(Parent,Sib), male(Brother).
```

This reads: "Brother is the brother of Sib if Parent is a parent of both Brother and Sib, and Brother is male."

There is a problem with this definition of brother. The query brother(X,X)? is satisfied for any male child X, which is not our understanding of the brother relationship.

In order to preclude such cases from the meaning of the program,

```
abraham ≠ isaac.      abraham ≠ haran.      abraham ≠ lot.
abraham ≠ milcah.     abraham ≠ yiscah.     isaac ≠ haran.
isaac ≠ lot.          isaac ≠ milcah.       isaac ≠ yiscah.
haran ≠ lot.          haran ≠ milcah.       haran ≠ yiscah.
lot ≠ milcah.         lot ≠ yiscah.         milcah ≠ yiscah.
```

Figure 2.1   Defining inequality

```
uncle(Uncle,Person) ←
    brother(Uncle,Parent), parent(Parent,Person).
sibling(Sib1,Sib2) ←
    parent(Parent,Sib1), parent(Parent,Sib2), Sib1 ≠ Sib2.
cousin(Cousin1,Cousin2) ←
    parent(Parent1,Cousin1),
    parent(Parent2,Cousin2),
    sibling(Parent1,Parent2).
```

Program 2.1   Defining family relationships

we introduce a predicate ≠(Term1,Term2). It is convenient to write this predicate as an infix operator. Thus Term1 ≠ Term2 is true if Term1 and Term2 are different. For the present it is restricted to constant terms. It can be defined, in principle, by a table $X \neq Y$ for every two different individuals X and Y in the domain of interest. Figure 2.1 gives part of the appropriate table for Program 1.1.

The new brother rule is

```
brother(Brother,Sib) ←
    parent(Parent,Brother),
    parent(Parent,Sib),
    male(Brother),
    Brother ≠ Sib.
```

The more relationships that are present, the easier it is to define complicated relationships. Program 2.1 defines the relationships uncle(Uncle,Person), sibling(Sib1,Sib2), and cousin(Cousin1, Cousin2). The definition of uncle in Program 2.1 does not define the husband of a sister of a parent to be an uncle. This may or may not be the intended meaning. In general, different cultures define these family relationships differently. In any case, the logic makes clear exactly what the programmer means by these family relationships.

Another relationship implicit in the family database is whether a woman is a mother. This is determined by using the mother/2 relationship. The new relation scheme is mother(Woman), defined by the rule

mother(Woman) ← mother(Woman,Child).

This reads: "Woman is a mother if she is the mother of some Child." Note that we have used the same predicate name, mother, to describe two different mother relationships. The mother predicate takes a different number of arguments, i.e., has a different arity, in the two cases. In general, the same predicate name denotes a different relation when it has a different arity.

We change examples, lest the example of family relationships become incestuous, and consider describing simple logical circuits. A circuit can be viewed from two perspectives. The first is the topological layout of the physical components usually described in the circuit diagram. The second is the interaction of functional units. Both views are easily accommodated in a logic program. The circuit diagram is represented by a collection of facts, while rules describe the functional components.

Program 2.2 is a database giving a simplified view of the logical and-gate drawn in Figure 2.2. The facts are the connections of the particular resistors and transistors comprising the circuit. The relation scheme for resistors is resistor(End1,End2) and for transistors transistor(Gate,Source,Drain).

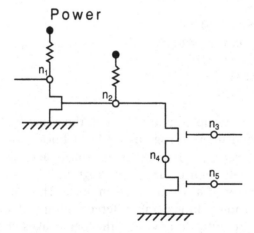

Figure 2.2 A logical circuit

```
resistor(power,n1).
resistor(power,n2).

transistor(n2,ground,n1).
transistor(n3,n4,n2).
transistor(n5,ground,n4).
```

inverter (Input,Output) ←
 Output is the inversion of *Input*.

```
inverter(Input,Output) ←
    transistor(Input,ground,Output),
    resistor(power,Output).
```

nand_gate(Input1,Input2,Output) ←
 Output is the logical nand of *Input1* and *Input2*.

```
nand_gate(Input1,Input2,Output) ←
    transistor(Input1,X,Output),
    transistor(Input2,ground,X),
    resistor(power,Output).
```

and_gate(Input1,Input2,Output) ←
 Output is the logical and of *Input1* and *Input2*.

```
and_gate(Input1,Input2,Output) ←
    nand_gate(Input1,Input2,X),
    inverter(X,Output).
```

Program 2.2 A circuit for a logical and-gate

The program demonstrates the style of commenting of logic programs we will follow throughout the book. Each interesting procedure is preceded by a relation scheme for the procedure, shown in italic font, and by English text defining the relation. We recommend this style of commenting, which emphasizes the declarative reading of programs, for Prolog programs as well.

Particular configurations of resistors and transistors fulfill roles captured via rules defining the functional components of the circuit. The circuit describes an and-gate, which takes two input signals and produces as output the logical *and* of these signals. One way of building an and-gate, and how this circuit is composed, is to connect a nand-gate with an inverter. Relation schemes for these three components are and_gate(Input1,Input2,Output), nand_gate(Input1,Input2,Output), and inverter(Input,Output).

To appreciate Program 2.2, let us read the inverter rule. This states that an inverter is built up from a transistor with the source connected to the ground, and a resistor with one end connected to the power source. The gate of the transistor is the input to the inverter, while the free end of the resistor must be connected to the drain of the transistor, which forms the output of the inverter. Sharing of variables is used to insist on the common connection.

Consider the query and_gate(In1,In2,Out)? to Program 2.2. It has the solution {In1=n3,In2=n5,Out=n1}. This solution confirms that the circuit described by the facts is an and-gate, and indicates the inputs and output.

2.1.1   Exercises for Section 2.1

(i)   Modify the rule for brother on page 21 to give a rule for sister, the rule for uncle in Program 2.1 to give a rule for niece, and the rule for sibling in Program 2.1 so that it only recognizes full siblings, i.e., those that have the same mother and father.

(ii)   Using a predicate married_couple(Wife,Husband), define the relationships mother_in_law, brother_in_law, and son_in_law.

(iii)   Describe the layout of objects in Figure 2.3 with facts using the predicates left_of(Object1,Object2) and above(Object1,Object2). Define predicates right_of(Object1,Object2) and below(Object1,Object2) in terms of left_of and above, respectively.

Figure 2.3   Still-life objects

2.2 Structured Data and Data Abstraction

A limitation of Program 2.2 for describing the and-gate is the treatment of the circuit as a black box. There is no indication of the structure of the circuit in the answer to the and_gate query, even though the structure has been implicitly used in finding the answer. The rules tell us that the circuit represents an and-gate, but the structure of the and-gate is present only implicitly. We remedy this by adding an extra argument to each of the goals in the database. For uniformity, the extra argument becomes the first argument. The base facts simply acquire an identifier. Proceeding from left to right in the diagram of Figure 2.2, we label the resistors r1 and r2, and the transistors t1, t2, and t3.

Names of the functional components should reflect their structure. An inverter is composed of a transistor and a resistor. To represent this, we need structured data. The technique is to use a compound term, inv(T,R), where T and R are the respective names of the inverter's component transistor and resistor. Analogously, the name of a nand-gate will be nand(T1,T2,R), where T1, T2, and R name the two transistors and resistor that comprise a nand-gate. Finally, an and-gate can be named in terms of an inverter and a nand-gate. The modified code containing the names appears in Program 2.3.

The query and_gate(G,In1,In2,Out)? has solution {G=and(nand(t2, t3,r2),inv(t1,r1)),In1=n3,In2=n5,Out=n1}. In1, In2, and Out have their previous values. The complicated structure for G reflects accurately the functional composition of the and-gate.

Structuring data is important in programming in general and in logic programming in particular. It is used to organize data in a meaningful way. Rules can be written more abstractly, ignoring irrelevant details. More modular programs can be achieved this way, because a change of data representation need not mean a change in the whole program, as shown by the following example.

Consider the following two ways of representing a fact about a lecture course on complexity given on Monday from 9 to 11 by David Harel in the Feinberg building, room A:

```
course(complexity,monday,9,11,david,harel,feinberg,a).
```

and

resistor(R,Node1,Node2) ←
   R is a resistor between *Node1* and *Node2*.

```
resistor(r1,power,n1).
resistor(r2,power,n2).
```

transistor(T,Gate,Source,Drain) ←
   T is a transistor whose gate is *Gate*,
   source is *Source*, and drain is *Drain*.

```
transistor(t1,n2,ground,n1).
transistor(t2,n3,n4,n2).
transistor(t3,n5,ground,n4).
```

inverter(I,Input,Output) ←
   I is an inverter that inverts *Input* to *Output*.

```
inverter(inv(T,R),Input,Output) ←
   transistor(T,Input,ground,Output),
   resistor(R,power,Output).
```

nand_gate(Nand,Input1,Input2,Output) ←
   Nand is a gate forming the logical nand, *Output*,
   of *Input1* and *Input2*.

```
nand_gate(nand(T1,T2,R),Input1,Input2,Output) ←
   transistor(T1,Input1,X,Output),
   transistor(T2,Input2,ground,X),
   resistor(R,power,Output).
```

and_gate(And,Input1,Input2,Output) ←
   And is a gate forming the logical and, *Output*,
   of *Input1* and *Input2*.

```
and_gate(and(N,I),Input1,Input2,Output) ←
   nand_gate(N,Input1,Input2,X),
   inverter(I,X,Output).
```

Program 2.3 The circuit database with names

```
course(complexity,time(monday,9,11),lecturer(david,harel),
    location(feinberg,a)).
```

The first fact represents course as a relation between eight items — a course name, a day, a starting hour, a finishing hour, a lecturer's first name, a lecturer's surname, a building, and a room. The second fact makes course a relation between four items — a name, a time, a lecturer, and a location with further qualification. The time is composed of a day, a starting time, and a finishing time; lecturers have a first name and a surname; and locations are specified by a building and a room. The second fact reflects more elegantly the relations that hold.

The four-argument version of course enables more concise rules to be written by abstracting the details that are irrelevant to the query. Program 2.4 contains examples. The occupied rule assumes a predicate less than or equal, represented as a binary infix operator ≤.

Rules not using the particular values of a structured argument need not "know" how the argument is structured. For example, the rules for duration and teaches represent time explicitly as time(Day,Start, Finish) because the Day or Start or Finish times of the course are desired. In contrast, the rule for lecturer does not. This leads to greater modularity, because the representation of time can be changed without affecting the rules that do not inspect it.

We offer no definitive advice on when to use structured data. Not using structured data allows a uniform representation where all the data are simple. The advantages of structured data are compactness of representation, which more accurately reflects our perspective of a situation, and

```
lecturer(Lecturer,Course) ←
    course(Course,Time,Lecturer,Location).

duration(Course,Length) ←
    course(Course,time(Day,Start,Finish),Lecturer,Location),
    plus(Start,Length,Finish).

teaches(Lecturer,Day) ←
    course(Course,time(Day,Start,Finish),Lecturer,Location).

occupied(Room,Day,Time) ←
    course(Course,time(Day,Start,Finish),Lecturer,Room),
    Start ≤ Time, Time ≤ Finish.
```

Program 2.4   Course rules

modularity. We can relate the discussion to conventional programming languages. Facts are the counterpart of tables, while structured data correspond to records with aggregate fields.

We believe that the appearance of a program is important, particularly when attempting difficult problems. A good structuring of data can make a difference when programming complex problems.

Some of the rules in Program 2.4 are recovering relations between two individuals, *binary* relations, from the single, more complicated one. All the course information could have been written in terms of binary relations as follows:

```
day(complexity,monday).
start_time(complexity,9).
finish_time(complexity,11).
lecturer(complexity,harel).
building(complexity,feinberg).
room(complexity,a).
```

Rules would then be expressed differently, reverting to the previous style of making implicit connections explicit. For example,

```
teaches(Lecturer,Day) ←
    lecturer(Course,Lecturer), day(Course,Day).
```

2.2.1 Exercises for Section 2.2

(i)   Add rules defining the relations location(Course,Building), busy(Lecturer,Time), and cannot_meet(Lecturer1,Lecturer2). Test with your own course facts.

(ii)   Possibly using relations from Exercise (i), define the relation schedule_conflict(Time,Place,Course1,Course2).

(iii) Write a program to check if a student has met the requirements for a college degree. Facts will be used to represent the courses that the student has taken and the grades obtained, and rules will be used to enforce the college requirements.

(iv)   Design a small database for an application of your own choice. Use a single predicate to express the information, and invent suitable rules.

2.3   Recursive Rules

The rules described so far define new relationships in terms of existing ones. An interesting extension is recursive definitions of relationships that define relationships in terms of themselves. One way of viewing recursive rules is as generalization of a set of nonrecursive rules.

Consider a series of rules defining ancestors — grandparents, great-grandparents, etc:

```
grandparent(Ancestor,Descendant) ←
    parent(Ancestor,Person), parent(Person,Descendant).
greatgrandparent(Ancestor,Descendant) ←
    parent(Ancestor,Person), grandparent(Person,Descendant).
greatgreatgrandparent(Ancestor,Descendant) ←
    parent(Ancestor,Person), greatgrandparent(Person,
                                              Descendant).
```

A clear pattern can be seen, which can be expressed in a rule defining the relationship ancestor(Ancestor,Descendant):

```
ancestor(Ancestor,Descendant) ←
    parent(Ancestor,Person), ancestor(Person,Descendant).
```

This rule is a generalization of the previous rules.

A logic program for ancestor also requires a nonrecursive rule, the choice of which affects the meaning of the program. If the fact ancestor(X,X) is used, defining the ancestor relationship to be reflexive, people will be considered to be their own ancestors. This is not the intuitive meaning of ancestor. Program 2.5 is a logic program defining the ancestor relationship, where parents are considered ancestors.

```
ancestor(Ancestor,Descendant) ←
    Ancestor is an ancestor of Descendant.
```
```
ancestor(Ancestor,Descendant) ←
    parent(Ancestor,Descendant).
ancestor(Ancestor,Descendant) ←
    parent(Ancestor,Person), ancestor(Person,Descendant).
```

Program 2.5   The ancestor relationship

The `ancestor` relationship is the transitive closure of the `parent` relationship. In general, finding the transitive closure of a relationship is easily done in a logic program by using a recursive rule.

Program 2.5 defining `ancestor` is an example of a linear recursive program. A program is *linear recursive* if there is only one recursive goal in the body of the recursive clause. The linearity can be easily seen from considering the complexity of proof trees solving `ancestor` queries. A proof tree establishing that two individuals are *n* generations apart given Program 2.5 and a collection of parent facts has $2 \cdot n$ nodes.

There are many alternative ways of defining ancestors. The declarative content of the recursive rule in Program 2.5 is that `Ancestor` is an ancestor of `Descendant` if `Ancestor` is a parent of an ancestor of `Descendant`. Another way of expressing the recursion is by observing that `Ancestor` would be an ancestor of `Descendant` if `Ancestor` is an ancestor of a parent of `Descendant`. The relevant rule is

```
ancestor(Ancestor,Descendant) ←
    ancestor(Ancestor,Person), parent(Person,Descendant).
```

Another version of defining ancestors is not linear recursive. A program identical in meaning to Program 2.5 but with two recursive goals in the recursive clause is

```
ancestor(Ancestor,Descendant) ←
    parent(Ancestor,Descendant).
ancestor(Ancestor,Descendant) ←
    ancestor(Ancestor,Person), ancestor(Person,Descendant).
```

Consider the problem of testing connectivity in a directed graph. A directed graph can be represented as a logic program by a collection of facts. A fact `edge(Node1,Node2)` is present in the program if there is an edge from `Node1` to `Node2` in the graph. Figure 2.4 shows a graph; Program 2.6 is its description as a logic program.

Two nodes are connected if there is a series of edges that can be traversed to get from the first node to the second. That is, the relation `connected(Node1,Node2)`, which is true if `Node1` and `Node2` are connected, is the transitive closure of the `edge` relation. For example, *a* and *e* are connected in the graph in Figure 2.4, but *b* and *f* are not. Program 2.7 defines the relation. The meaning of the program is the set of goals con-

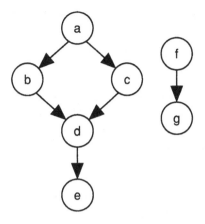

Figure 2.4   A simple graph

```
edge(a,b).     edge(a,c).     edge(b,d).
edge(c,d).     edge(d,e).     edge(f,g).
```

Program 2.6   A directed graph

connected(Node1,Node2) ←
   Node1 is connected to *Node2* in the
   graph defined by the *edge/2* relation.

```
connected(Node,Node).
connected(Node1,Node2) ←  edge(Node1,Link), connected(Link,Node2).
```

Program 2.7   The transitive closure of the edge relation

nected(X,Y), where X and Y are connected. Note that connected is a transitive reflexive relation because of the choice of base fact.

2.3.1   Exercises for Section 2.3

(i)   A stack of blocks can be described by a collection of facts on (Block1,Block2), which is true if Block1 is on Block2. Define a predicate above(Block1,Block2) that is true if Block1 is above Block2 in the stack. (Hint: above is the transitive closure of on.)

(ii)   Add recursive rules for `left_of` and above from Exercise 2.1(iii) on p. 34. Define `higher(Object1,Object2)`, which is true if `Object1` is on a line higher than `Object2` in Figure 2.3. For example, the bicycle is higher than the fish in the figure.

(iii)   How many nodes are there in the proof tree for `connected(a,e)` using Programs 2.6 and 2.7? In general, using Program 2.6 and a collection of `edge/2` facts, how many nodes are there in a proof tree establishing that two nodes are connected by a path containing n intermediate nodes?

2.4   Logic Programs and the Relational Database Model

Logic programs can be viewed as a powerful extension to the relational database model, the extra power coming from the ability to specify rules. Many of the concepts introduced have meaningful analogues in terms of databases. The converse is also true. The basic operations of the relational algebra are easily expressed within logic programming.

Procedures composed solely of facts correspond to relations, the arity of the relation being the arity of the procedure. Five basic operations define the relational algebra: union, set difference, Cartesian product, projection, and selection. We show how each is translated into a logic program.

The union operation creates a relation of arity n from two relations `r` and `s`, both of arity n. The new relation, denoted here `r_union_s`, is the union of `r` and `s`. It is defined directly as a logic program by two rules:

```
r_union_s(X₁, ... ,Xₙ)  ←  r(X₁, ... ,Xₙ).
r_union_s(X₁, ... ,Xₙ)  ←  s(X₁, ... ,Xₙ).
```

Set difference involves negation. We assume a predicate `not`. Intuitively, a goal `not G` is true with respect to a program P if `G` is not a logical consequence of P. Negation in logic programs is discussed in Chapter 5, where limitations of the intuitive definition are indicated. The definition is correct, however, if we deal only with ground facts, as is the case with relational databases.

The definition of `r_diff_s` of arity n, where `r` and `s` are of arity n, is

```
r_diff_s(X₁, ... ,Xₙ) ← r(X₁, ... ,Xₙ), not s(X₁, ... ,Xₙ).
```

Cartesian product can be defined in a single rule. If r is a relation of arity m, and s is a relation of arity n, then r_x_s is a relation of arity $m + n$ defined by

```
r_x_s(X₁, ... ,Xₘ,Xₘ₊₁, ... ,Xₘ₊ₙ) ←
    r(X₁, ... ,Xₘ), s(Xₘ₊₁, ... ,Xₘ₊ₙ).
```

Projection involves forming a new relation comprising only some of the attributes of an existing relation. This is straightforward for any particular case. For example, the projection r13 selecting the first and third arguments of a relation r of arity 3 is

```
r13(X₁,X₃) ← r(X₁,X₂,X₃).
```

Selection is similarly straightforward for any particular case. Consider a relation consisting of tuples whose third components are greater than their second, and a relation where the first component is Smith or Jones. In both cases a relation r of arity 3 is used to illustrate. The first example creates a relation r1:

```
r1(X₁,X₂,X₃) ← r(X₁,X₂,X₃),X₃ > X₂.
```

The second example creates a relation r2, which requires a disjunctive relationship, smith_or_jones:

```
r2(X₁,X₂,X₃) ← r(X₁,X₂,X₃), smith_or_jones(X₁).
smith_or_jones(smith).
smith_or_jones(jones).
```

Some of the derived operations of the relational algebra are more closely related to the constructs of logic programming. We mention two, intersection and the natural join. If r and s are relations of arity n, the intersection, r_meet_s is also of arity n and is defined in a single rule.

```
r_meet_s(X₁, ... ,Xₙ) ← r(X₁, ... ,Xₙ), s(X₁, ... ,Xₙ).
```

A natural join is precisely a conjunctive query with shared variables.

2.5 Background

Readers interested in pursuing the connection between logic programming and database theory are referred to the many papers that have been written on the subject. A good starting place is the review paper by Gallaire et al. (1984). There are earlier papers on logic and databases in Gallaire and Minker (1978). Another interesting book is about the implementation of a database query language in Prolog (Li, 1984). Our discussion of relational databases follows Ullman (1982). Another good account of relational databases can be found in Maier (1983).

In the seven years between the appearance of the first edition and the second edition of this book, the database community has accepted logic programs as extensions of relational databases. The term used for a database extended with logical rules is *logic database* or *deductive database*. There is now a wealth of material about logic databases. The rewritten version of Ullman's text (1989) discusses logic databases and gives pointers to the important literature.

Perhaps the major difference between logic databases as taught from a database perspective and the view presented here is the way of evaluating queries. Here we implicitly assume that the interpreter from Figure 4.2 will be used, a top-down approach. The database community prefers a bottom-up evaluation mechanism. Various bottom-up strategies for answering a query with respect to a logic database are given in Ullman (1989).

In general, an n-ary relation can be replaced by $n + 1$ binary relations, as shown by Kowalski (1979a). If one of the arguments forms a key for the relation, as does the course name in the example in Section 2.2, n binary relations suffice.

The addition of an extra argument to each predicate in the circuit, as discussed at the beginning of Section 2.2, is an example of an *enhancement* of a logic program. The technique of developing programs by enhancement is of growing importance. More will be said about this in Chapter 13.

3   Recursive Programming

The programs of the previous chapter essentially retrieve information from, and manipulate, finite data structures. In general, mathematical power is gained by considering infinite or potentially infinite structures. Finite instances then follow as special cases. Logic programs harness this power by using recursive data types.

Logical terms can be classified into types. A *type* is a (possibly infinite) set of terms. Some types are conveniently defined by unary relations. A relation p/1 defines the type p to be the set of X's such that p(X).

For example, the male/1 and female/1 predicates used previously define the male and female types.

More complex types can be defined by recursive logic programs. Such types are called *recursive types*. Types defined by unary recursive programs are called *simple recursive types*. A program defining a type is called a *type definition*.

In this chapter, we show logic programs defining relations over simple recursive types, such as integers, lists, and binary trees, and also programs over more complex types, such as polynomials.

3.1   Arithmetic

The simplest recursive data type, natural numbers, arises from the foundations of mathematics. Arithmetic is based on the natural numbers. This section gives logic programs for performing arithmetic.

In fact, Prolog programs for performing arithmetic differ considerably from their logical counterparts, as we will see in later chapters. However, it is useful to spend time discussing the logic programs. There are

natural_number(X) ←
    X is a natural number.

```
natural_number(0).
natural_number(s(X)) ← natural_number(X).
```

Program 3.1 Defining the natural numbers

two main reasons. First, the operations of arithmetic are usually thought of functionally rather than relationally. Presenting examples for such a familiar area emphasizes the change in thinking necessary for composing logic programs. Second, it is more natural to discuss the underlying mathematical issues, such as correctness and completeness of programs.

The natural numbers are built from two constructs, the constant symbol 0 and the successor function s of arity 1. All the natural numbers are then recursively given as 0, s(0), s(s(0)), s(s(s(0))), ... We adopt the convention that $s^n(0)$ denotes the integer *n*, that is, *n* applications of the successor function to 0.

As in Chapter 2, we give a relation scheme for each predicate, together with the intended meaning of the predicate. Recall that a program *P* is *correct* with respect to an intended meaning *M* if the meaning of *P* is a subset of *M*. It is *complete* if *M* is a subset of the meaning of *P*. It is correct and complete if its meaning is identical to *M*. Proving correctness establishes that everything deducible from the program is intended. Proving completeness establishes that everything intended is deducible from the program. Two correctness and completeness proofs are given in this section.

The simple type definition of natural numbers is neatly encapsulated in the logic program, shown as Program 3.1. The relation scheme used is `natural_number(X)`, with intended meaning that X is a natural number. The program consists of one unit clause and one iterative clause (a clause with a single goal in the body). Such a program is called *minimal recursive*.

Proposition
Program 3.1 is correct and complete with respect to the set of goals `natural_number`($s^i(0)$), for $i \geq 0$.

Proof (1) Completeness. Let *n* be a natural number. We show that the goal `natural_number(n)` is deducible from the program by giving an explicit proof tree. Either n is 0 or of the form $s^n(0)$. The proof tree for the goal `natural_number(0)` is trivial. The proof tree for the goal

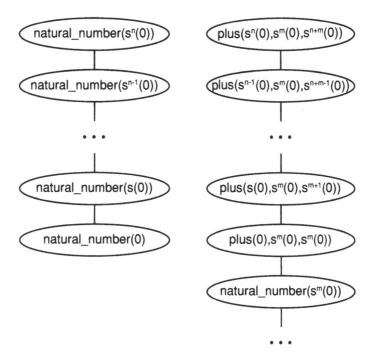

Figure 3.1 Proof trees establishing completeness of programs

`natural_number(s(...s(0)...))` contains n reductions, using the rule in Program 3.1, to reach the fact `natural_number(0)`, as shown in the left half of Figure 3.1.

(2) Correctness. Suppose that `natural_number(X)` is deducible from Program 3.1, in n deductions. We prove that `natural_number(X)` is in the intended meaning of the program by induction on n. If $n = 0$, then the goal must have been proved using a unit clause, which implies that X = 0. If $n > 0$, then the goal must be of the form `natural_number(s(X'))`, since it is deducible from the program, and further, `natural_number(X')` is deducible in $n - 1$ deductions. By the induction hypothesis, X' is in the intended meaning of the program, i.e., $X'=s^k(0)$ for some $k \geq 0$.   ∎

The natural numbers have a natural order. Program 3.2 is a logic program defining the relation less than or equal to according to the order. We denote the relation with a binary infix symbol, or *operator*, ≤, according to mathematical usage. The goal $0 \leq X$ has predicate symbol ≤ of arity 2, has arguments 0 and X, and is syntactically identical to '≤'(0,X).

$X \leq Y \leftarrow$
   X and Y are natural numbers,
   such that X is less than or equal to Y.

```
0 ≤ X ← natural_number(X).
s(X) ≤ s(Y) ← X ≤ Y.
```

natural_number(X) ← See Program 3.1 .

Program 3.2   The less than or equal relation

The relation scheme is $N_1 \leq N_2$. The intended meaning of Program 3.2 is all ground facts X ≤ Y, where X and Y are natural numbers and X is less than or equal to Y. Exercise (ii) at the end of this section is to prove the correctness and completeness of Program 3.2.

The recursive definition of ≤ is not computationally efficient. The proof tree establishing that a particular N is less than a particular M has $M + 2$ nodes. We usually think of testing whether one number is less than another as a unit operation, independent of the size of the numbers. Indeed, Prolog does not define arithmetic according to the axioms presented in this section but uses the underlying arithmetic capabilities of the computer directly.

Addition is a basic operation defining a relation between two natural numbers and their sum. In Section 1.1, a table of the plus relation was assumed for all relevant natural numbers. A recursive program captures the relation elegantly and more compactly, and is given as Program 3.3. The intended meaning of Program 3.3 is the set of facts plus(X,Y,Z), where X, Y, and Z are natural numbers and X+Y=Z.

Proposition
Programs 3.1 and 3.3 constitute a correct and complete axiomatization of addition with respect to the standard intended meaning of plus/3.

Proof   (1) Completeness. Let X, Y, and Z be natural numbers such that X+Y=Z. We give a proof tree for the goal plus(X,Y,Z). If X equals 0, then Y equals Z. Since Program 3.1 is a complete axiomatization of the natural numbers, there is a proof tree for natural_number(Y), which is easily extended to a proof tree for plus(0,Y,Y). Otherwise, X equals $s^n(0)$ for some n. If Y equals $s^m(0)$, then Z equals $s^{n+m}(0)$. The proof tree in the right half of Figure 3.1 establishes completeness.

plus(*X,Y,Z*) ←
      X, *Y* , and *Z* are natural numbers
      such that *Z* is the sum of *X* and *Y*.

```
plus(0,X,X) ← natural_number(X).
plus(s(X),Y,s(Z)) ← plus(X,Y,Z).
```

natural_number(X) ← See Program 3.1 .

Program 3.3   Addition

(2) Correctness. Let plus(X,Y,Z) be in the meaning. A simple inductive argument on the size of X, similar to the one used in the previous proposition, establishes that X+Y=Z.   ∎

Addition is usually considered to be a function of two arguments rather than a relation of arity 3. Generally, logic programs corresponding to functions of n arguments define relations of arity $n + 1$. Computing the value of a function is achieved by posing a query with n arguments instantiated and the argument place corresponding to the value of the function uninstantiated. The solution to the query is the value of the function with the given arguments. To make the analogy clearer, we give a functional definition of addition corresponding to the logic program:

```
0+X = X.
s(X)+Y = s(X+Y).
```

One advantage that relational programs have over functional programs is the multiple uses that can be made of the program. For example, the query plus(s(0),s(0),s(s(0)))? means checking whether $1 + 1 = 2$. (We feel free to use the more readable decimal notation when mentioning numbers.) As for ≤, the program for plus is not efficient. The proof tree confirming that the sum of N and M is $N + M$ has $N + M + 2$ nodes.

Posing the query plus(s(0),s(0),X)?, an example of the standard use, calculates the sum of 1 and 1. However, the program can just as easily be used for subtraction by posing a query such as plus(s(0),X,s(s(s(0))))?. The computed value of X is the difference between 3 and 1, namely, 2. Similarly, asking a query with the first argument uninstantiated, and the second and third instantiated, also performs subtraction.

A more novel use exploits the possibility of a query having *multiple solutions*. Consider the query plus(X,Y,s(s(s(0))))?. It reads: "Do there exist numbers X and Y that add up to 3." In other words, find a partition of the number 3 into the sum of two numbers, X and Y. There are several solutions.

A query with multiple solutions becomes more interesting when the properties of the variables in the query are restricted. There are two forms of restriction: using extra conjuncts in the query, and instantiating variables in the query. We saw examples of this when querying a database. Exercise (ii) at the end of this section requires to define a predicate even(X), which is true if X is an even number. Assuming such a predicate, the query plus(X,Y,N),even(X),even(Y)? gives a partition of N into two even numbers. The second type of restriction is exemplified by the query plus(s(s(X)),s(s(Y)),N)?, which insists that each of the numbers adding up to N is strictly greater than 1.

Almost all logic programs have multiple uses. Consider Program 3.2 for ≤, for example. The query s(0)≤s(s(0))? checks whether 1 is less than or equal to 2. The query X ≤ s(s(0))? finds numbers X less than or equal to 2. The query X ≤ Y? computes pairs of numbers less than or equal to each other.

Program 3.3 defining addition is not unique. For example, the logic program

```
plus(X,0,X) ← natural_number(X).
plus(X,s(Y),s(Z)) ← plus(X,Y,Z).
```

has precisely the same meaning as Program 3.3 for plus. Two programs are to be expected because of the symmetry between the first two arguments. A proof of correctness and completeness given for Program 3.3 applies to this program by reversing the roles of the symmetric arguments.

The meaning of the program for plus would not change even if it consisted of the two programs combined. This composite program is undesirable, however. There are several different proof trees for the same goal. It is important both for runtime efficiency and for textual conciseness that axiomatizations of logic programs be minimal.

We define a *type condition* to be a call to the predicate defining the type. For natural numbers, a type condition is any goal of the form natural_number(X).

In practice, both Programs 3.2 and 3.3 are simplified by omitting the body of the base rule, natural_number(X). Without this test, facts such

times(*X,Y,Z*) ←
    X, *Y*, and *Z* are natural numbers
    such that *Z* is the product of *X* and *Y*.

```
times(0,X,0).
times(s(X),Y,Z) ← times(X,Y,XY), plus(XY,Y,Z).
```

plus(X,Y,Z) ← See Program 3.3 .

Program 3.4 Multiplication as repeated addition

exp(*N,X,Y*) ←
    N, *X*, and *Y* are natural numbers
    such that *Y* equals *X* raised to the power *N*.

```
exp(s(X),0,0).
exp(0,s(X),s(0)).
exp(s(N),X,Y) ← exp(N,X,Z), times(Z,X,Y).
```

times(X,Y,Z) ← See Program 3.4 .

Program 3.5 Exponentiation as repeated multiplication

as $0 \leq a$ and plus(0,a,a), where a is an arbitrary constant, will be in the programs' meanings. Type conditions are necessary for correct programs. However, type conditions distract from the simplicity of the programs and affect the size of the proof trees. Hence in the following we might omit explicit type conditions from the example programs, Programs 3.4-3.7.

The basic programs shown are the building blocks for more complicated relations. A typical example is defining multiplication as repeated addition. Program 3.4 reflects this relation. The relation scheme is times(X,Y,Z), meaning X times Y equals Z.

Exponentiation is defined as repeated multiplication. Program 3.5 for exp(N,X,Y) expresses the relation that X^N=Y. It is analogous to Program 3.4 for times(X,Y,Z), with exp and times replacing times and plus, respectively. The base cases for exponentiation are X^0=1 for all positive values of X, and 0^N=0 for positive values of N.

A definition of the factorial function uses the definition of multiplication. Recall that $N! = N \cdot N - 1 \cdots 2 \cdot 1$. The predicate factorial(N,F) relates a number N to its factorial F. Program 3.6 is its axiomatization.

factorial(*N,F*) ←
    F equals *N* factorial.

```
factorial(0,s(0)).
factorial(s(N),F) ← factorial(N,F1), times(s(N),F1,F).
```

`times(X,Y,Z)` ← See Program 3.4 .

Program 3.6 Computing factorials

minimum(*N1,N2,Min*) ←
    The minimum of the natural numbers *N1* and *N2* is *Min*.

```
minimum(N1,N2,N1) ← N1 ≤ N2.
minimum(N1,N2,N2) ← N2 ≤ N1.
```

`N1 ≤ N2` ← See Program 3.2 .

Program 3.7 The minimum of two numbers

Not all relations concerning natural numbers are defined recursively. Relations can also be defined in the style of programs in Chapter 2. An example is Program 3.7 determining the minimum of two numbers via the relation `minimum(N1,N2,Min)`.

Composing a program to determine the remainder after integer division reveals an interesting phenomenon—different mathematical definitions of the same concept are translated into different logic programs. Programs 3.8a and 3.8b give two definitions of the relation `mod(X,Y,Z)`, which is true if Z is the value of X modulo Y, or in other words, Z is the remainder of X divided by Y. The programs assume a relation < as specified in Exercise (i) at the end of this section.

Program 3.8a illustrates the direct translation of a mathematical definition, which is a logical statement, into a logic program. The program corresponds to an existential definition of the integer remainder: "Z is the value of X mod Y if Z is strictly less than Y, and there exists a number Q such that $X = Q \cdot Y + Z$. In general, mathematical definitions are easily translated to logic programs.

We can relate Program 3.8a to constructive mathematics. Although seemingly an existential definition, it is also constructive, because of the constructive nature of <, `plus`, and `times`. The number Q, for example, proposed in the definition will be explicitly computed by `times` in any use of `mod`.

mod(*X,Y,Z*) ←
    Z is the remainder of the integer division of *X* by *Y*.

```
mod(X,Y,Z) ← Z < Y, times(Y,Q,QY), plus(QY,Z,X).
```

Program 3.8a A nonrecursive definition of modulus

mod(*X,Y,Z*) ←
    Z is the remainder of the integer division of *X* by *Y*.

```
mod(X,Y,X) ← X < Y.
mod(X,Y,Z) ← plus(X1,Y,X), mod(X1,Y,Z).
```

Program 3.8b A recursive definition of modulus

In contrast to Program 3.8a, Program 3.8b is defined recursively. It constitutes an algorithm for finding the integer remainder based on repeated subtraction. The first rule says that X mod Y is X if X is strictly less than Y. The second rule says that the value of X mod Y is the same as $X - Y$ mod Y. The effect of any computation to determine the modulus is to repeatedly subtract Y from X until it becomes less than Y and hence is the correct value.

The mathematical function X mod Y is not defined when Y is zero. Neither Program 3.8a nor Program 3.8b has goal mod(X,0,Z) in its meaning for any values of X or Z. The test of < guarantees that.

The computational model gives a way of distinguishing between the two programs for mod. Given a particular X, Y, and Z satisfying mod, we can compare the sizes of their proof trees. In general, proof trees produced with Program 3.8b will be smaller than those produced with Program 3.8a. In that sense Program 3.8b is more efficient. We defer more rigorous discussions of efficiency till the discussions on lists, where the insights gained will carry over to Prolog programs.

Another example of translating a mathematical definition directly into a logic program is writing a program that defines Ackermann's function. Ackermann's function is the simplest example of a recursive function that is not primitive recursive. It is a function of two arguments, defined by three cases:

ackermann(0, N) = N + 1.

ackermann(M, 0) = *ackermann*(M − 1, 1).

ackermann(M, N) = *ackermann*(M − 1, *ackermann*(M, N − 1)).

ackermann(*X,Y,A*) ←
    A is the value of Ackermann's
    function for the natural numbers *X* and *Y*.

```
ackermann(0,N,s(N)).
ackermann(s(M),0,Val) ← ackermann(M,s(0),Val).
ackermann(s(M),s(N),Val) ←
    ackermann(s(M),N,Val1), ackermann(M,Val1,Val).
```

Program 3.9   Ackermann's function

gcd(*X,Y,Z*) ←
    Z is the greatest common divisor of
    the natural numbers *X* and *Y*.

```
gcd(X,Y,Gcd) ← mod(X,Y,Z), gcd(Y,Z,Gcd).
gcd(X,0,X)← X > 0.
```

Program 3.10   The Euclidean algorithm

Program 3.9 is a translation of the functional definition into a logic program. The predicate `ackermann(M,N,A)` denotes that `A=ackermann(M,N)`. The third rule involves two calls to Ackermann's function, one to compute the value of the second argument.

The functional definition of Ackermann's function is clearer than the relational one given in Program 3.9. In general, functional notation is more readable for pure functional definitions, such as Ackermann's function and the factorial function (Program 3.6). Expressing constraints can also be awkward with relational logic programs. For example, Program 3.8a says less directly that $X = Q \cdot Y + Z$.

The final example in this section is the Euclidean algorithm for finding the greatest common divisor of two natural numbers, recast as a logic program. Like Program 3.8b, it is a recursive program not based on the recursive structure of numbers. The relation scheme is `gcd(X,Y,Z)`, with intended meaning that `Z` is the greatest common divisor (or gcd) of two natural numbers `X` and `Y`. It uses either of the two programs, 3.8a or 3.8b, for `mod`.

The first rule in Program 3.10 is the logical essence of the Euclidean algorithm. The gcd of *X* and *Y* is the same as the gcd of *Y* and *X* mod *Y*. A proof that Program 3.10 is correct depends on the correctness of the above mathematical statement about greatest common divisors. The proof that the Euclidean algorithm is correct similarly rests on this result.

The second fact in Program 3.10 is the base fact. It must be specified that X is greater than 0 to preclude gcd(0,0,0) from being in the meaning. The gcd of 0 and 0 is not well defined.

3.1.1   Exercises for Section 3.1

(i)   Modify Program 3.2 for $\leq$ to axiomatize the relations $<$, $>$, and $\geq$. Discuss multiple uses of these programs.

(ii)   Prove that Program 3.2 is a correct and complete axiomatization of $\leq$.

(iii)   Prove that a proof tree for the query $s^n(0) \leq s^m(0)$ using Program 3.2 has $m + 2$ nodes.

(iv)   Define predicates even(X) and odd(X) for determining if a natural number is even or odd. (Hint: Modify Program 3.1 for natural_number.)

(v)   Write a logic program defining the relation fib(N,F) to determine the Nth Fibonacci number F.

(vi)   The predicate times can be used for computing exact quotients with queries such as times(s(s(0)),X,s(s(s(s(0)))))? to find the result of 4 divided by 2. The query times(s(s(0)),X,s(s(s (0))))? to find 3/2 has no solution. Many applications require the use of integer division that would calculate 3/2 to be 1. Write a program to compute integer quotients. (Hint: Use repeated subtraction.)

(vii)   Modify Program 3.10 for finding the gcd of two integers so that it performs repeated subtraction directly rather than use the mod function. (Hint: The program repeatedly subtracts the smaller number from the larger number until the two numbers are equal.)

(viii) Rewrite the logic programs in Section 3.1 using a different representation of natural numbers, namely as a sum of 1's. For example, the modified version of Program 3.1 would be

```
natural_number(1).
natural_number(1+X) ← natural_number(X).
```

Note that + is used as a binary operator, and 0 is not defined to be a natural number.

3.2   Lists

The basic structure for arithmetic is the unary successor functor. Although complicated recursive functions such as Ackermann's function can be defined, the use of a unary recursive structure is limited. This section discusses the binary structure, the *list*.

The first argument of a list holds an *element*, and the second argument is recursively the rest of the list. Lists are sufficient for most computations — attested to by the success of the programming language Lisp, which has lists as its basic compound data structure. Arbitrarily complex structures can be represented with lists, though it is more convenient to use different structures when appropriate.

For lists, as for numbers, a constant symbol is necessary to terminate recursion. This "empty list," referred to as nil, will be denoted here by the symbol [ ]. We also need a functor of arity 2. Historically, the usual functor for lists is "." (pronounced dot), which overloads the use of the period. It is convenient to define a separate, special syntax. The term .(X,Y) is denoted [X|Y]. Its components have special names: X is called the *head* and Y is called the *tail*.

The term [X|Y] corresponds to a cons pair in Lisp. The corresponding words for head and tail are, respectively, *car* and *cdr*.

Figure 3.2 illustrates the relation between lists written with different syntaxes. The first column writes lists with the dot functor, and is the way lists are considered as terms in logic programs. The second column gives the square bracket equivalent of the dot syntax. The third column is an improvement upon the syntax of the second column, essentially hiding the recursive structure of lists. In this syntax, lists are written as a sequence of elements enclosed in square brackets and separated by commas. The empty list used to terminate the recursive structure is suppressed. Note the use of "cons pair notation" in the third column when the list has a variable tail.

Formal object	Cons pair syntax	Element syntax
.(a,[ ])	[a|[ ]]	[a]
.(a,.(b,[ ]))	[a|[b|[ ]]]	[a,b]
.(a,.(b,.(c,[ ])))	[a|[b|[c |[ ]]]]	[a,b,c]
.(a,X)	[a|X]	[a|X]
.(a,.(b,X))	[a|[b|X]]	[a,b|X]

Figure 3.2   Equivalent forms of lists

list (*Xs*) ←
     Xs is a list.
```
list([ ]).
list([X|Xs])  ←  list(Xs).
```

Program 3.11   Defining a list

Terms built with the dot functor are more general than lists. Program 3.11 defines a list precisely. Declaratively it reads: "A list is either the empty list or a cons pair whose tail is a list." The program is analogous to Program 3.1 defining natural numbers, and is the simple type definition of lists.

Figure 3.3 gives a proof tree for the goal list([a,b,c]). Implicit in the proof tree are ground instances of rules in Program 3.11, for example, list([a,b,c]) ← list([b,c]). We specify the particular instance here explicitly, as instances of lists in cons pair notation can be confusing. [a,b,c] is an instance of [X|Xs] under the substitution {X=a,Xs=[b,c]}.

Because lists are richer data structures than numbers, a great variety of interesting relations can be specified with them. Perhaps the most basic operation with lists is determining whether a particular element is in a list. The predicate expressing this relation is member(Element,List). Program 3.12 is a recursive definition of member/2.

Declaratively, the reading of Program 3.12 is straightforward. X is an element of a list if it is the head of the list by the first clause, or if it is a member of the tail of the list by the second clause. The meaning of the program is the set of all ground instances member(X,Xs), where

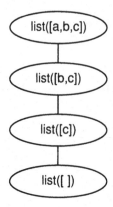

Figure 3.3 Proof tree verifying a list

member(Element,List) ←
    Element is an element of the list *List*.

```
member(X,[X|Xs]).
member(X,[Y|Ys]) ← member(X,Ys).
```

Program 3.12 Membership of a list

X is an element of Xs. We omit the type condition in the first clause. Alternatively, it would be written

```
member(X,[X|Xs]) ← list(Xs).
```

This program has many interesting applications, to be revealed throughout the book. Its basic uses are checking whether an element is in a list with a query such as member(b,[a,b,c])?, finding an element of a list with a query such as member(X,[a,b,c])?, and finding a list containing an element with a query such as member(b,X)?. This last query may seem strange, but there are programs that are based on this use of member.

We use the following conventions wherever possible when naming variables in programs involving lists. If X is used to denote the head of a list, then Xs will denote its tail. More generally, plural variable names will denote lists of elements, and singular names will denote individual elements. Numerical suffixes will denote variants of lists. Relation schemes will still contain mnemonic names.

prefix(Prefix,List) ←
    Prefix is a prefix of *List*.

```
prefix([ ],Ys).
prefix([X|Xs],[X|Ys]) ← prefix(Xs,Ys).
```

suffix(Suffix,List) ←
    Suffix is a suffix of *List*.

```
suffix(Xs,Xs).
suffix(Xs,[Y|Ys]) ← suffix(Xs,Ys).
```

Program 3.13   Prefixes and suffixes of a list

Our next example is a predicate sublist(Sub,List) for determining whether Sub is a sublist of List. A sublist needs the elements to be consecutive: [b,c] is a sublist of [a,b,c,d], whereas [a,c] is not.

It is convenient to define two special cases of sublists to make the definition of sublist easier. It is good style when composing logic programs to define meaningful relations as auxiliary predicates. The two cases considered are initial sublists, or prefixes, of a list, and terminal sublists, or suffixes, of a list. The programs are interesting in their own right.

The predicate prefix(Prefix,List) is true if Prefix is an initial sublist of List, for example, prefix([a,b],[a,b,c]) is true. The companion predicate to prefix is suffix(Suffix,List), determining if Suffix is a terminal sublist of List. For example, suffix([b,c],[a,b,c]) is true. Both predicates are defined in Program 3.13. A type condition expressing that the variables in the base facts are lists should be added to the base fact in each predicate to give the correct meaning.

An arbitrary sublist can be specified in terms of prefixes and suffixes: namely, as a suffix of a prefix, or as a prefix of a suffix. Program 3.14a expresses the logical rule that Xs is a sublist of Ys if there exists *Ps* such that *Ps* is a prefix of Ys and Xs is a suffix of *Ps*. Program 3.14b is the dual definition of a sublist as a prefix of a suffix.

The predicate prefix can also be used as the basis of a recursive definition of sublist. This is given as Program 3.14c. The base rule reads that a prefix of a list is a sublist of a list. The recursive rule reads that the sublist of a tail of a list is a sublist of the list itself.

The predicate member can be viewed as a special case of sublist defined by the rule

```
member(X,Xs) ← sublist([X],Xs).
```

sublist(Sub,List) ←
    Sub is a sublist of *List*.

a: Suffix of a prefix

```
sublist(Xs,Ys) ← prefix(Ps,Ys), suffix(Xs,Ps).
```

b: Prefix of a suffix

```
sublist(Xs,Ys) ← prefix(Xs,Ss), suffix(Ss,Ys).
```

c: Recursive definition of a sublist

```
sublist(Xs,Ys) ← prefix(Xs,Ys).
sublist(Xs,[Y|Ys]) ← sublist(Xs,Ys).
```

d: Prefix of a suffix, using append

```
sublist(Xs,AsXsBs) ←
    append(As,XsBs,AsXsBs), append(Xs,Bs,XsBs).
```

e: Suffix of a prefix, using append

```
sublist(Xs,AsXsBs) ←
    append(AsXs,Bs,AsXsBs), append(As,Xs,AsXs).
```

Program 3.14   Determining sublists of lists

append(Xs,Ys,XsYs) ←
    XsYs is the result of concatenating
    the lists *Xs* and *Ys*.

```
append([ ],Ys,Ys).
append([X|Xs],Ys,[X|Zs]) ← append(Xs,Ys,Zs).
```

Program 3.15   Appending two lists

The basic operation with lists is concatenating two lists to give a third list. This defines a relation, append(Xs,Ys,Zs), between two lists Xs, Ys and the result Zs of joining them together. The code for append, Program 3.15, is identical in structure to the basic program for combining two numbers, Program 3.3 for plus.

Figure 3.4 gives a proof tree for the goal append([a,b],[c,d],[a,b, c,d]). The tree structure suggests that its size is linear in the size of the first list. In general, if Xs is a list of n elements, the proof tree for append(Xs,Ys,Zs) has $n + 1$ nodes.

There are multiple uses for append similar to the multiple uses for plus. The basic use is to concatenate two lists by posing a query such

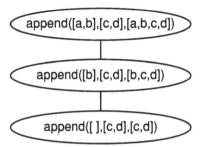

Figure 3.4   Proof tree for appending two lists

as append([a,b,c],[d,e],Xs)? with answer Xs=[a,b,c,d,e]. A query such as append(Xs,[c,d],[a,b,c,d])? finds the difference Xs=[a,b] between the lists [c,d] and [a,b,c,d]. Unlike plus, append is not symmetric in its first two arguments, and thus there are two distinct versions of finding the difference between two lists.

The analogous process to partitioning a number is splitting a list. The query append(As,Bs,[a,b,c,d])?, for example, asks for lists As and Bs such that appending Bs to As gives the list [a,b,c,d]. Queries about splitting lists are made more interesting by partially specifying the nature of the split lists. The predicates member, sublist, prefix, and suffix, introduced previously, can all be defined in terms of append by viewing the process as splitting a list.

The most straightforward definitions are for prefix and suffix, which just specify which of the two split pieces are of interest:

```
prefix(Xs,Ys) ← append(Xs,As,Ys).
suffix(Xs,Ys) ← append(As,Xs,Ys).
```

Sublist can be written using two append goals. There are two distinct variants, given as Programs 3.14d and 3.14e. These two programs are obtained from Programs 3.14a and 3.14b, respectively, where prefix and suffix are replaced by append goals.

Member can be defined using append, as follows:

```
member(X,Ys) ← append(As,[X|Xs],Ys).
```

This says that X is a member of Ys if Ys can be split into two lists where X is the head of the second list.

reverse(List,Tsil) ←
     Tsil is the result of reversing the list *List*.

a: Naive reverse

```
reverse([ ],[ ]).
reverse([X|Xs],Zs) ← reverse(Xs,Ys), append(Ys,[X],Zs).
```

b: Reverse-accumulate

```
reverse(Xs,Ys) ← reverse(Xs,[ ],Ys).

reverse([X|Xs],Acc,Ys) ← reverse(Xs,[X|Acc],Ys).
reverse([ ],Ys,Ys).
```

Program 3.16   Reversing a list

A similar rule can be written to express the relation adjacent(X,Y,Zs) that two elements X and Y are adjacent in a list Zs:

```
adjacent(X,Y,Zs) ← append(As,[X,Y|Ys],Zs).
```

Another relation easily expressed through append is determining the last element of a list. The desired pattern of the second argument to append, a list with one element, is built into the rule:

```
last(X,Xs) ← append(As,[X],Xs).
```

Repeated applications of append can be used to define a predicate reverse(List,Tsil). The intended meaning of reverse is that Tsil is a list containing the elements in the list List in reverse order to how they appear in List. An example of a goal in the meaning of the program is reverse([a,b,c],[c,b,a]). The naive version, given as Program 3.16a, is the logical equivalent of the recursive formulation in any language: recursively reverse the tail of the list, and then add the first element at the back of the reversed tail.

There is an alternative way of defining reverse without calling append directly. We define an auxiliary predicate reverse(Xs,Ys,Zs), which is true if Zs is the result of appending Ys to the elements of Xs reversed. It is defined in Program 3.16b. The predicate reverse/3 is related to reverse/2 by the first clause in Program 3.16b.

Program 3.16b is more efficient than Program 3.16a. Consider Figure 3.5, showing proof trees for the goal reverse([a,b,c],[c,b,a]) using both programs. In general, the size of the proof tree of Program 3.16a

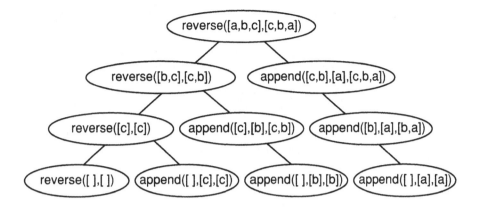

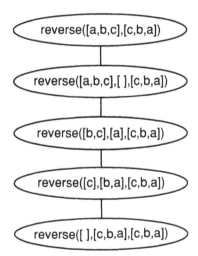

Figure 3.5   Proof trees for reversing a list

length(Xs,N) ←
    The list *Xs* has *N* elements.

```
length([ ],0).
length([X|Xs],s(N)) ← length(Xs,N).
```

Program 3.17 Determining the length of a list

is quadratic in the number of elements in the list to be reversed, while that of Program 3.16b is linear.

    The insight in Program 3.16b is the use of a better data structure for representing the sequence of elements, which we discuss in more detail in Chapters 7 and 15.

    The final program in this section, Program 3.17, expresses a relation between numbers and lists, using the recursive structure of each. The predicate length(Xs,N) is true if Xs is a list of length N, that is, contains N elements, where N is a natural number. For example, length([a,b],s(s(0))), indicating that [a,b] has two elements, is in the program's meaning.

    Let us consider the multiple uses of Program 3.17. The query length ([a,b],X)? computes the length, 2, of a list [a,b]. In this way, length is regarded as a function of a list, with the functional definition

```
length([ ]) = 0
length([X|Xs]) = s(length(Xs)).
```

    The query length([a,b],s(s(0)))? checks whether the list [a,b] has length 2. The query length(Xs,s(s(0)))? generates a list of length 2 with variables for elements.

3.2.1 Exercises for Section 3.2

(i)   A variant of Program 3.14 for sublist is defined by the following three rules:

```
subsequence([X|Xs],[X|Ys]) ← subsequence(Xs,Ys).
subsequence(Xs,[Y|Ys]) ← subsequence(Xs,Ys).
subsequence([ ],Ys).
```

Explain why this program has a different meaning from Program 3.14.

(ii)   Write recursive programs for `adjacent` and `last` that have the same meaning as the predicates defined in the text in terms of `append`.

(iii)   Write a program for `double(List,ListList)`, where every element in List appears twice in ListList, e.g., `double([1,2,3],[1,1,2,2,3,3])` is true.

(iv)   Compute the size of the proof tree as a function of the size of the input list for Programs 3.16a and 3.16b defining `reverse`.

(v)   Define the relation `sum(ListOfIntegers,Sum)`, which holds if `Sum` is the sum of the `ListOfIntegers`,

(a) Using `plus/3`;

(b) Without using any auxiliary predicate.

(Hint: Three axioms are enough.)

3.3   Composing Recursive Programs

No explanation has been given so far about how the example logic programs have been composed. The composition of logic programs is a skill that can be learned by apprenticeship or osmosis, and most definitely by practice. For simple relations, the best axiomatizations have an aesthetic elegance that look obviously correct when written down. Through solving the exercises, the reader may find, however, that there is a difference between recognizing and constructing elegant logic programs.

This section gives more example programs involving lists. Their presentation, however, places more emphasis on how the programs might be composed. Two principles are illustrated: how to blend procedural and declarative thinking, and how to develop a program top-down.

We have shown the dual reading of clauses: declarative and procedural. How do they interrelate when composing logic programs? Pragmatically, one thinks procedurally when programming. However, one thinks declaratively when considering issues of truth and meaning. One way to blend them in logic programming is to compose procedurally and then interpret the result as a declarative statement. Construct a program with a given use in mind; then consider if the alternative uses make declarative sense. We apply this to a program for deleting elements from a list.

The first, and most important, step is to specify the intended meaning of the relation. Clearly, three arguments are involved when deleting elements from a list: an element X to be deleted, a list L1 that might have occurrences of X, and a list L2 with all occurrences of X deleted. An appropriate relation scheme is delete(L1,X,L2). The natural meaning is all ground instances where L2 is the list L1 with all occurrences of X removed.

When composing the program, it is easiest to think of one specific use. Consider the query delete([a,b,c,b],b,X)?, a typical example of finding the result of deleting an element from a list. The answer here is X=[a,c]. The program will be recursive on the first argument. Let's don our procedural thinking caps.

We begin with the recursive part. The usual form of the recursive argument for lists is [X|Xs]. There are two possibilities to consider, one where X is the element to be deleted, and one where it is not. In the first case, the result of recursively deleting X from Xs is the desired answer to the query. The appropriate rule is

delete([X|Xs],X,Ys) ← delete(Xs,X,Ys).

Switching hats, the declarative reading of this rule is: "The deletion of X from [X|Xs] is Ys if the deletion of X from Xs is Ys." The condition that the head of the list and the element to be deleted are the same is specified by the shared variable in the head of the rule.

The second case where the element to be deleted is different from X, the head of the list, is similar. The result required is a list whose head is X and whose tail is the result of recursively deleting the element. The rule is

delete([X|Xs],Z,[X|Ys]) ← X ≠ Z, delete(Xs,Z,Ys).

The rule's declarative reading is: "The deletion of Z from [X|Xs] is [X|Ys] if Z is different from X and the deletion of Z from Xs is Ys." In contrast to the previous rule, the condition that the head of the list and the element to be deleted are different is made explicit in the body of the rule.

The base case is straightforward. No elements can be deleted from the empty list, and the required result is also the empty list. This gives the

delete(List,X,HasNoXs) ←
    The list *HasNoXs* is the result of removing all
    occurrences of *X* from the list *List*.

```
delete([X|Xs],X,Ys) ← delete(Xs,X,Ys).
delete([X|Xs],Z,[X|Ys]) ← X≠Z, delete(Xs,Z,Ys).
delete([ ],X,[ ]).
```

Program 3.18   Deleting all occurrences of an element from a list

select(X,HasXs,OneLessXs) ←
    The list *OneLessXs* is the result of removing
    one occurrence of *X* from the list *HasXs*.

```
select(X,[X|Xs],Xs).
select(X,[Y|Ys],[Y|Zs]) ← select(X,Ys,Zs).
```

Program 3.19   Selecting an element from a list

fact `delete([ ],X,[ ])`. The complete program is collected together as
Program 3.18.

Let us review the program we have written, and consider alternative
formulations. Omitting the condition X≠Z from the second rule in Program 3.18 gives a variant of `delete`. This variant has a less natural meaning, since any number of occurrences of an element may be deleted. For
example,   `delete([a,b,c,b],b,[a,c])`,   `delete([a,b,c,b],b,[a,c,
b])`, `delete([a,b,c,b],b,[a,b,c])`, and `delete([a,b,c,b],b,[a,b,
c,b])` are all in the meaning of the variant.

Both Program 3.18 and the variant include in their meaning instances
where the element to be deleted does not appear in either list, for example, `delete([a],b,[a])` is true. There are applications where this is
not desired. Program 3.19 defines `select(X,L1,L2)`, a relation that has
a different approach to elements not appearing in the list. The meaning
of `select(X,L1,L2)` is all ground instances where L2 is the list L1 where
exactly one occurrence of X has been removed. The declarative reading
of Program 3.19 is: "X is selected from [X|Xs] to give Xs; or X is selected
from [Y|Ys] to give [Y|Zs] if X is selected from Ys to give Zs."

A major thrust in programming has been the emphasis on a top-down
design methodology, together with stepwise refinement. Loosely, the

methodology is to state the general problem, break it down into subproblems, and then solve the pieces. A top-down programming style is one natural way for composing logic programs. Our description of programs throughout the book will be mostly top-down. The rest of this section describes the composition of two programs for sorting a list: permutation sort and quicksort. Their top-down development is stressed.

A logical specification of sorting a list is finding an ordered permutation of a list. This can be written down immediately as a logic program. The basic relation scheme is sort(Xs,Ys), where Ys is a list containing the elements in Xs sorted in ascending order:

```
sort(Xs,Ys) ← permutation(Xs,Ys), ordered(Ys).
```

The top-level goal of sorting has been decomposed. We must now define permutation and ordered.

Testing whether a list is ordered ascendingly can be expressed in the two clauses that follow. The fact says that a list with a single element is necessarily ordered. The rule says that a list is ordered if the first element is less than or equal to the second, and if the rest of the list, beginning from the second element, is ordered:

```
ordered([X]).
ordered([X,Y|Ys]) ← X ≤ Y, ordered([Y|Ys]).
```

A program for permutation is more delicate. One view of the process of permuting a list is selecting an element nondeterministically to be the first element of the permuted list, then recursively permuting the rest of the list. We translate this view into a logic program for permutation, using Program 3.19 for select. The base fact says that the empty list is its own unique permutation:

```
permutation(Xs,[Z|Zs]) ← select(Z,Xs,Ys), permutation(Ys,Zs).
permutation([ ],[ ]).
```

Another procedural view of generating permutations of lists is recursively permuting the tail of the list and inserting the head in an arbitrary position. This view also can be encoded immediately. The base part is identical to the previous version:

```
permutation([X|Xs],Zs) ← permutation(Xs,Ys), insert(X,Ys,Zs).
permutation([ ],[ ]).
```

sort(Xs,Ys) ←

> The list *Ys* is an ordered permutation of the list *Xs.*

```
sort(Xs,Ys) ← permutation(Xs,Ys), ordered(Ys).

permutation(Xs,[Z|Zs]) ← select(Z,Xs,Ys), permutation(Ys,Zs).
permutation([ ],[ ]).

ordered([ ]).
ordered([X]).
ordered([X,Y|Ys]) ← X ≤ Y, ordered([Y|Ys]).
```

Program 3.20   Permutation sort

The predicate `insert` can be defined in terms of Program 3.19 for select:

```
insert(X,Ys,Zs) ← select(X,Zs,Ys).
```

Both procedural versions of `permutation` have clear declarative readings.

The "naive" sorting program, which we call permutation sort, is collected together as Program 3.20. It is an example of the generate-and-test paradigm, discussed fully in Chapter 14. Note the addition of the extra base case for `ordered` so that the program behaves correctly for empty lists.

The problem of sorting lists is well studied. Permutation sort is not a good method for sorting lists in practice. Much better algorithms come from applying a "divide and conquer" strategy to the task of sorting. The insight is to sort a list by dividing it into two pieces, recursively sorting the pieces, and then joining the two pieces together to give the sorted list. The methods for dividing and joining the lists must be specified. There are two extreme positions. The first is to make the dividing hard, and the joining easy. This approach is taken by the quicksort algorithm. The second position is making the joining hard, but the dividing easy. This is the approach of merge sort, which is posed as Exercise (v) at the end of this section, and insertion sort, shown in Program 3.21.

In insertion sort, one element (typically the first) is removed from the list. The rest of the list is sorted recursively; then the element is inserted, preserving the orderedness of the list.

The insight in quicksort is to divide the list by choosing an arbitrary element in it, and then to split the list into the elements smaller than the

sort(*Xs*,*Ys*) ←

The list *Ys* is an ordered permutation of the list *Xs*.

```
sort([X|Xs],Ys) ← sort(Xs,Zs), insert(X,Zs,Ys).
sort([ ],[ ]).

insert(X,[ ],[X]).
insert(X,[Y|Ys],[Y|Zs]) ← X > Y, insert(X,Ys,Zs).
insert(X,[Y|Ys],[X,Y|Ys]) ← X ≤ Y.
```

Program 3.21   Insertion sort

quicksort(*Xs*,*Ys*) ←

The list *Ys* is an ordered permutation of the list *Xs*.

```
quicksort([X|Xs],Ys) ←
    partition(Xs,X,Littles,Bigs),
    quicksort(Littles,Ls),
    quicksort(Bigs,Bs),
    append(Ls,[X|Bs],Ys).
quicksort([ ],[ ]).

partition([X|Xs],Y,[X|Ls],Bs) ← X ≤ Y, partition(Xs,Y,Ls,Bs).
partition([X|Xs],Y,Ls,[X|Bs]) ← X > Y, partition(Xs,Y,Ls,Bs).
partition([ ],Y,[ ],[ ]).
```

Program 3.22   Quicksort

chosen element and the elements larger than the chosen element. The sorted list is composed of the smaller elements, followed by the chosen element, and then the larger elements. The program we describe chooses the first element of the list as the basis of partition.

Program 3.22 defines the quicksort algorithm. The recursive rule for quicksort reads: "Ys is a sorted version of [X|Xs] if Littles and Bigs are a result of partitioning Xs according to X; Ls and Bs are the result of sorting Littles and Bigs recursively; and Ys is the result of appending [X|Bs] to Ls."

Partitioning a list is straightforward, and is similar to the program for deleting elements. There are two cases to consider: when the current head of the list is smaller than the element being used for the partitioning, and when the head is larger than the partitioning element. The declarative reading of the first partition clause is: "Partitioning a list whose head is X and whose tail is Xs according to an element Y gives the lists [X|Littles] and Bigs if X is less than or equal to Y, and partitioning Xs according to Y gives the lists Littles and Bigs." The second clause for partition has a similar reading. The base case is that the empty list is partitioned into two empty lists.

3.3.1 Exercises for Section 3.3

(i)   Write a program for substitute(X,Y,L1,L2), where L2 is the result of substituting Y for all occurrences of X in L1, e.g., substitute(a,x,[a,b,a,c],[x,b,x,c]) is true, whereas substitute(a,x,[a,b,a,c],[a,b,x,c]) is false.

(ii) What is the meaning of the variant of select:

```
select(X,[X|Xs],Xs).
select(X,[Y|Ys],[Y|Zs]) ← X ≠ Y,
select(X,Ys,Zs).
```

(iii) Write a program for no_doubles(L1,L2), where L2 is the result of removing all duplicate elements from L1, e.g., no_doubles([a,b,c,b],[a,c,b]) is true. (Hint: Use member.)

(iv) Write programs for even_permutation(Xs,Ys) and odd_permutation(Xs,Ys) that find Ys, the even and odd permutations, respectively, of a list Xs. For example, even_permutation([1,2,3],[2,3,1]) and odd_permutation([1,2,3],[2,1,3]) are true.

(v)   Write a program for merge sort.

(vi) Write a logic program for kth_largest(Xs,K) that implements the linear algorithm for finding the *k*th largest element K of a list Xs. The algorithm has the following steps:

Break the list into groups of five elements.
Efficiently find the median of each of the groups, which can be done with a fixed number of comparisons.
Recursively find the median of the medians.
Partition the original list with respect to the median of medians.
Recursively find the *k*th largest element in the appropriate smaller list.

(vii) Write a program for the relation better_poker_hand(Hand1, Hand2,Hand) that succeeds if Hand is the better poker hand between Hand1 and Hand2. For those unfamiliar with this card game, here are some rules of poker necessary for answering this exercise:

(a) The order of cards is 2, 3, 4, 5, 6, 7, 8, 9, 10, jack, queen, king, ace.

(b) Each hand consists of five cards.

(c) The rank of hands in ascending order is no pairs < one pair < two pairs < three of a kind < flush < straight < full house < four of a kind < straight flush.

(d) Where two cards have the same rank, the higher denomination wins, for example, a pair of kings beats a pair of 7's.

(Hints: (1) Represent a poker hand by a list of terms of the form card(Suit,Value). For example a hand consisting of the 2 of clubs, the 5 of spades, the queen of hearts, the queen of diamonds, and the 7 of spades would be represented by the list [card (clubs,2),card(spades,5),card(hearts,queen),card(diamonds, queen),card(spades,7)]. (2) It may be helpful to define relations such as has_flush(Hand), which is true if all the cards in Hand are of the same suit; has_full_house(Hand), which is true if Hand has three cards with the same value but in different suits, and the other two cards have the same different value; and has_straight(Hand), which is true if Hand has cards with consecutive values. (3) The number of cases to consider is reduced if the hand is first sorted.)

3.4 Binary Trees

We next consider binary trees, another recursive data type. These structures have an important place in many algorithms.

Binary trees are represented by the ternary functor tree(Element, Left,Right), where Element is the element at the node, and Left and Right are the left and right subtrees respectively. The empty tree is represented by the atom void. For example, the tree

```
    a
   / \
  b   c
```

would be represented as

```
tree(a,tree(b,void,void),tree(c,void,void)).
```

Logic programs manipulating binary trees are similar to those manipulating lists. As with natural numbers and lists, we start with the type definition of binary trees. It is given as Program 3.23. Note that the program is *doubly recursive*; that is, there are two goals in the body of the recursive rule with the same predicate as the head of the rule. This results from the doubly recursive nature of binary trees and will be seen also in the rest of the programs of this section.

Let us write some tree-processing programs. Our first example tests whether an element appears in a tree. The relation scheme is tree_member(Element,Tree). The relation is true if Element is one of the nodes in the tree. Program 3.24 contains the definition. The declarative reading of the program is: "X is a member of a tree if it is the element at the node (by the fact) or if it is a member of the left or right subtree (by the two recursive rules)."

The two branches of a binary tree are distinguishable, but for many applications the distinction is not relevant. Consequently, a useful concept

binary_tree(Tree) ←
　　　Tree is a binary tree.

```
binary_tree(void).
binary_tree(tree(Element,Left,Right)) ←
    binary_tree(Left), binary_tree(Right).
```

Program 3.23　Defining binary trees

tree_member(Element,Tree) ←
　　　Element is an element of the binary tree *Tree*.

```
tree_member(X,tree(X,Left,Right)).
tree_member(X,tree(Y,Left,Right)) ← tree_member(X,Left).
tree_member(X,tree(Y,Left,Right)) ← tree_member(X,Right).
```

Program 3.24　Testing tree membership

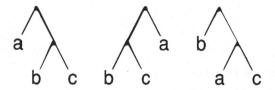

Figure 3.6   Comparing trees for isomorphism

isotree(Tree1,Tree2) ←
    Tree1 and *Tree2* are isomorphic binary trees.

```
isotree(void,void).
isotree(tree(X,Left1,Right1),tree(X,Left2,Right2)) ←
    isotree(Left1,Left2), isotree(Right1,Right2).
isotree(tree(X,Left1,Right1),tree(X,Left2,Right2)) ←
    isotree(Left1,Right2), isotree(Right1,Left2).
```

Program 3.25   Determining when trees are isomorphic

is isomorphism, which defines when unordered trees are essentially the same. Two binary trees T1 and T2 are *isomorphic* if T2 can be obtained by reordering the branches of the subtrees of T1. Figure 3.6 shows three simple binary trees. The first two are isomorphic; the first and third are not.

Isomorphism is an equivalence relation with a simple recursive definition. Two empty trees are isomorphic. Otherwise, two trees are isomorphic if they have identical elements at the node and either both the left subtrees and the right subtrees are isomorphic; or the left subtree of one is isomorphic with the right subtree of the other and the two other subtrees are isomorphic.

Program 3.25 defines a predicate `isotree(Tree1,Tree2)`, which is true if `Tree1` and `Tree2` are isomorphic. The predicate is symmetric in its arguments.

Programs related to binary trees involve double recursion, one for each branch of the tree. The double recursion can be manifest in two ways. Programs can have two separate cases to consider, as in Program 3.24 for `tree_member`. In contrast, Program 3.12 testing membership of a list has only one recursive case. Alternatively, the body of the recursive clause has two recursive calls, as in each of the recursive rules for `isotree` in Program 3.25.

substitute(X,Y,TreeX,TreeY) ←
    The binary tree *TreeY* is the result of replacing all
    occurrences of *X* in the binary tree *TreeX* by *Y*.

```
substitute(X,Y,void,void).
substitute(X,Y,tree(Node,Left,Right),tree(Node1,Left1,Right1)) ←
    replace(X,Y,Node,Node1),
    substitute(X,Y,Left,Left1),
    substitute(X,Y,Right,Right1).

replace(X,Y,X,Y).
replace(X,Y,Z,Z) ← X ≠ Z.
```

Program 3.26 Substituting for a term in a tree

The task in Exercise 3.3(i) is to write a program for substituting for elements in lists. An analogous program can be written for substituting elements in binary trees. The predicate substitute(X,Y,OldTree, NewTree) is true if NewTree is the result of replacing all occurrences of X by Y in OldTree. An axiomatization of substitute/4 is given as Program 3.26.

Many applications involving trees require access to the elements appearing as nodes. Central is the idea of a tree *traversal*, which is a sequence of the nodes of the tree in some predefined order. There are three possibilities for the linear order of traversal: *preorder*, where the value of the node is first, then the nodes in the left subtree, followed by the nodes in the right subtree; *inorder*, where the left nodes come first followed by the node itself and then the right nodes; and *postorder*, where the node comes after the left and right subtrees.

A definition of each of the three traversals is given in Program 3.27. The recursive structure is identical; the only difference between the programs is the order in which the elements are composed by the various append goals.

The final example in this section shows interesting manipulation of trees. A binary tree satisfies the *heap property* if the value at each node is at least as large as the value at its children (if they exist). Heaps, a class of binary trees that satisfy the heap property, are a useful data structure and can be used to implement priority queues efficiently.

It is possible to *heapify* any binary tree containing values for which an ordering exists. That is, the values in the tree are moved around so that

preorder(*Tree,Pre*) ←

   Pre is a preorder traversal of the binary tree *Tree*.

```
preorder(tree(X,L,R),Xs) ←
    preorder(L,Ls), preorder(R,Rs), append([X|Ls],Rs,Xs).
preorder(void,[ ]).
```

inorder(*Tree,In*) ←

   In is an inorder traversal of the binary tree *Tree*.

```
inorder(tree(X,L,R),Xs) ←
    inorder(L,Ls), inorder(R,Rs), append(Ls,[X|Rs],Xs).
inorder(void,[ ]).
```

postorder(*Tree,Post*) ←

   Post is a postorder traversal of the binary tree *Tree*.

```
postorder(tree(X,L,R),Xs) ←
    postorder(L,Ls),
    postorder(R,Rs),
    append(Rs,[X],Rs1),
    append(Ls,Rs1,Xs).
postorder(void,[ ]).
```

Program 3.27   Traversals of a binary tree

the shape of the tree is preserved and the heap property is satisfied. An example tree and its heapified equivalent are shown in Figure 3.7.

An algorithm for heapifying the elements of a binary tree so that the heap property is satisfied is easily stated recursively. Heapify the left and right subtrees so that they both satisfy the heap property and then adjust the element at the root appropriately. Program 3.28 embodies this algorithm. The relation `heapify/2` lays out the doubly recursive program structure, and `adjust(X,HeapL,HeapR,Heap)` produces the final tree `Heap` satisfying the heap property from the root value `X` and the left and right subtrees `HeapL` and `HeapR` satisfying the heap property.

There are three cases for `adjust/4` depending on the values. If the root value is larger than the root values of the left and right subtrees, then the heap is `tree(X,HeapL,HeapR)`. This is indicated in the first `adjust` clause in Program 3.28. The second clause handles the case where the root node in the left heap is larger than the root node and the root of the right heap. In that case, the adjustment proceeds recursively on the left heap. The third clause handles the symmetric case where the root node of the right heap is the largest. The code is simplified by relegating the concern whether the subtree is empty to the predicate `greater/2`.

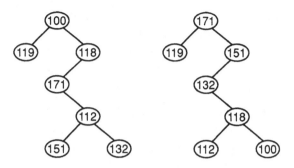

Figure 3.7   A binary tree and a heap that preserves the tree's shape

heapify(Tree,Heap) ←
    The elements of the complete binary tree *Tree* have been adjusted
    to form the binary tree *Heap*, which has the same shape as *Tree* and
    satisfies the heap property that the value of each parent node is
    greater than or equal to the values of its children.

```
heapify(void,void).
heapify(tree(X,L,R),Heap) ←
    heapify(L,HeapL), heapify(R,HeapR), adjust(X,HeapL,HeapR,Heap).

adjust(X,HeapL,HeapR,tree(X,HeapL,HeapR)) ←
    greater(X,HeapL), greater(X,HeapR).
adjust(X,tree(X1,L,R),HeapR,tree(X1,HeapL,HeapR)) ←
    X < X1, greater(X1,HeapR), adjust(X,L,R,HeapL).
adjust(X,HeapL,tree(X1,L,R),tree(X1,HeapL,HeapR)) ←
    X < X1, greater(X1,HeapL), adjust(X,L,R,HeapR).

greater(X,void).
greater(X,tree(X1,L,R)) ← X ≥ X1.
```

Program 3.28   Adjusting a binary tree to satisfy the heap property

3.4.1   Exercises for Section 3.4

(i)   Define a program for subtree(S,T), where S is a subtree of T.

(ii)   Define the relation sum_tree(TreeOfIntegers,Sum), which holds
        if Sum is the sum of the integer elements in TreeOfIntegers.

(iii)   Define the relation ordered(TreeOfIntegers), which holds if Tree
        is an ordered tree of integers, that is, for each node in the tree
        the elements in the left subtree are smaller than the element in

the node, and the elements in the right subtree are larger than the element in the node. (Hint: Define two auxiliary relations, ordered_left(X,Tree) and ordered_right(X,Tree), which hold if both Tree is ordered and X is larger (respectively, smaller) than the largest (smallest) node of Tree.)

(iv) Define the relation tree_insert(X,Tree,Tree1), which holds if Tree1 is an ordered tree resulting from inserting X into the ordered tree Tree. If X already occurs in Tree, then Tree and Tree1 are identical. (Hint: Four axioms suffice.)

(v) Write a logic program for the relation path(X,Tree,Path), where Path is the path from the root of the tree Tree to X.

3.5 Manipulating Symbolic Expressions

The logic programs illustrated so far in this chapter have manipulated natural numbers, lists, and binary trees. The programming style is applicable more generally. This section gives four examples of recursive programming — a program for defining polynomials, a program for symbolic differentiation, a program for solving the Towers of Hanoi problem, and a program for testing the satisfiability of Boolean formulae.

The first example is a program for recognizing polynomials in some term X. Polynomials are defined inductively. X itself is a polynomial in X, as is any constant. Sums, differences, and products of polynomials in X are polynomials in X. So too are polynomials raised to the power of a natural number, and the quotient of a polynomial by a constant.

An example of a polynomial in the term x is $x^2 - 3x + 2$. This follows from its being the sum of the polynomials, $x^2 - 3x$ and 2, where $x^2 - 3x$ is recognized recursively.

A logic program for recognizing polynomials is obtained by expressing the preceding informal rules in the correct form. Program 3.29 defines the relation polynomial(Expression,X), which is true if Expression is a polynomial in X. We give a declarative reading of two rules from the program.

The fact polynomial(X,X) says that a term X is a polynomial in itself. The rule

polynomial(Expression,X) ←
    Expression is a polynomial in *X*.

```
polynomial(X,X).
polynomial(Term,X) ←
    constant(Term).
polynomial(Term1+Term2,X) ←
    polynomial(Term1,X), polynomial(Term2,X).
polynomial(Term1−Term2,X) ←
    polynomial(Term1,X), polynomial(Term2,X).
polynomial(Term1*Term2,X) ←
    polynomial(Term1,X), polynomial(Term2,X).
polynomial(Term1/Term2,X) ←
    polynomial(Term1,X), constant(Term2).
polynomial(Term↑N,X) ←
    natural_number(N), polynomial(Term,X).
```

Program 3.29 Recognizing polynomials

```
polynomial(Term1+Term2,X) ←
    polynomial(Term1,X), polynomial(Term2,X).
```

says that the sum Term1+Term2 is a polynomial in X if both Term1 and
Term2 are polynomials in X.

Other conventions used in Program 3.29 are the use of the unary predicate constant for recognizing constants, and the binary functor ↑ to
denote exponentiation. The term X↑Y denotes X^Y.

The next example is a program for taking derivatives. The relation
scheme is derivative(Expression,X,DifferentiatedExpression).
The intended meaning of derivative is that DifferentiatedExpres-
sion is the derivative of Expression with respect to X.

As for Program 3.29 for recognizing polynomials, a logic program for
differentiation is just a collection of the relevant differentiation rules,
written in the correct syntax. For example, the fact

```
derivative(X,X,s(0)).
```

expresses that the derivative of X with respect to itself is *1*. The fact

```
derivative(sin(X),X,cos(X)).
```

derivative(Expression,X,DifferentiatedExpression) ←
    DifferentiatedExpression is the derivative of
    Expression with respect to *X*.

```
derivative(X,X,s(0)).
derivative(X↑s(N),X,s(N)*X↑N).
derivative(sin(X),X,cos(X)).
derivative(cos(X),X,-sin(X)).
derivative(e↑X,X,e↑X).
derivative(log(X),X,1/X).

derivative(F+G,X,DF+DG) ←
    derivative(F,X,DF), derivative(G,X,DG).
derivative(F-G,X,DF-DG) ←
    derivative(F,X,DF), derivative(G,X,DG).
derivative(F*G,X,F*DG+DF*G) ←
    derivative(F,X,DF), derivative(G,X,DG).
derivative(1/F,X,-DF/(F*F)) ←
    derivative(F,X,DF).
derivative(F/G,X,(G*DF-F*DG)/(G*G)) ←
    derivative(F,X,DF), derivative(G,X,DG).
```

Program 3.30 Derivative rules

reads: "The derivative of `sin(X)` with respect to X is `cos(X)`." Natural
mathematical notation can be used. A representative sample of functions
and their derivatives is given in Program 3.30.

Sums and products of terms are differentiated using the sum rule and
product rule, respectively. The sum rule states that the derivative of a
sum is the sum of derivatives. The appropriate clause is

```
derivative(F+G,X,DF+DG) ←
    derivative(F,X,DF), derivative(G,X,DG).
```

The product rule is a little more complicated, but the logical clause is
just the mathematical definition:

```
derivative(F*G,X,F*DG+DF*G) ←
    derivative(F,X,DF), derivative(G,X,DG).
```

Program 3.30 also contains the reciprocal and quotient rules.

The chain rule is a little more delicate. It states that the derivative of
$f(g(x))$ with respect to x is the derivative of $f(g(x))$ with respect to $g(x)$
times the derivative of $g(x)$ with respect to x. As stated, it involves quan-

tification over functions, and is outside the scope of the logic programs we have presented.

Nonetheless, a version of the chain rule is possible for each particular function. For example, we give the rule for differentiating X^N and sin(X):

```
derivative(U↑s(N),X,s(N)*U↑N*DU) ←
derivative(U,X,DU).
derivative(sin(U),X,cos(U)*DU) ← derivative(U,X,DU).
```

The difficulty of expressing the chain rule for differentiation arises from our choice of representation of terms. Both Programs 3.29 and 3.30 use the "natural" representation from mathematics where terms represent themselves. A term such as sin(X) is represented using a unary structure sin. If a different representation were used, for example, unary_term(sin,X) where the name of the structure is made accessible, then the problem with the chain rule disappears. The chain rule can then be formulated as

```
derivative(unary_term(F,U),X,DF*DU) ←
    derivative(unary_term(F,U),U,DF), derivative(U,X,DU).
```

Note that all the rules in Program 3.30 would have to be reformulated in terms of this new representation and would appear less natural.

People take for granted the automatic simplification of expressions when differentiating expressions. Simplification is missing from Program 3.30. The answer to the query derivative(3*x+2,x,D)? is D=(3*1+0*x)+0. We would immediately simplify D to 3, but it is not specified in the logic program.

The next example is a solution to the Towers of Hanoi problem, a standard introductory example in the use of recursion. The problem is to move a tower of n disks from one peg to another with the help of an auxiliary peg. There are two rules. Only one disk can be moved at a time, and a larger disk can never be placed on top of a smaller disk.

There is a legend associated with the game. Somewhere hidden in the surroundings of Hanoi, an obscure Far Eastern village when the legend was first told, is a monastery. The monks there are performing a task assigned to them by God when the world was created — solving the preceding problem with three golden pegs and 64 golden disks. At the moment they complete their task, the world will collapse into dust. Since the optimal solution to the problem with n disks takes $2^n - 1$ moves, we

```
hanoi(N,A,B,C,Moves) ←
```
    Moves is a sequence of moves for solving the Towers of
    Hanoi puzzle with *N* disks and three pegs, *A*, *B*, and *C*.

```
hanoi(s(0),A,B,C,[A to B]).
hanoi(s(N),A,B,C,Moves) ←
    hanoi(N,A,C,B,Ms1),
    hanoi(N,C,B,A,Ms2),
    append(Ms1,[A to B|Ms2],Moves).
```

Program 3.31   Towers of Hanoi

need not lose any sleep over this possibility. The number 2^{64} is comfortingly big.

The relation scheme for solving the problem is hanoi(N,A,B,C, Moves). It is true if Moves is the sequence of moves for moving a tower of N disks from peg A to peg B using peg C as the auxiliary peg. This is an extension to usual solutions that do not calculate the sequence of moves but rather perform them. The representation of the moves uses a binary functor *to*, written as an infix operator. The term *X to Y* denotes that the top disk on peg *X* is moved to peg *Y*. The program for solving the problem is given in Program 3.31.

The declarative reading of the heart of the solution, the recursive rule in Program 3.31, is: "Moves is the sequence of moves of s(N) disks from peg A to peg B using peg C as an auxiliary, if Ms1 is the solution for moving N disks from A to C using B, Ms2 is the solution for moving N disks from C to B using A, and Moves is the result of appending [A to B|Ms2] to Ms1."

The recursion terminates with moving one disk. A slightly neater, but less intuitive, base for the recursion is moving no disks. The appropriate fact is

```
hanoi(0,A,B,C,[ ]).
```

The final example concerns Boolean formulae.

A *Boolean formula* is a term defined as follows: The constants *true* and *false* are Boolean formulae; if *X* and *Y* are Boolean formulae, so are *X*∨*Y*, *X*∧*Y*, and *~X*, where ∨ and ∧ are binary infix operators for disjunction and conjunction, respectively, and ~ is a unary prefix operator for negation.

satisfiable(*Formula*) ←

    There is a true instance of the Boolean formula *Formula*.

```
satisfiable(true).
satisfiable(X∧Y) ← satisfiable(X), satisfiable(Y).
satisfiable(X∨Y) ← satisfiable(X).
satisfiable(X∨Y) ← satisfiable(Y).
satisfiable(~X) ← invalid(X).
```

invalid(*Formula*) ←

    There is a false instance of the Boolean formula *Formula*.

```
invalid(false).
invalid(X∨Y) ← invalid(X), invalid(Y).
invalid(X∧Y) ← invalid(X).
invalid(X∧Y) ← invalid(Y).
invalid(~Y) ← satisfiable(Y).
```

Program 3.32 Satisfiability of Boolean formulae

A Boolean formula F is *true* if

F = 'true'.
F = $X \wedge Y$, and both X and Y are true.
F = $X \vee Y$, and either X or Y (or both) are true.
F = $\sim X$, and X is false.

A Boolean formula F is *false* if

F = 'false'.
F = $X \wedge Y$, and either X or Y (or both) are false.
F = $X \vee Y$, and both X and Y are false.
F = $\sim X$, and X is true.

Program 3.32 is a logic program for determining the truth or falsity of a Boolean formula. Since it can be applied to Boolean formulae with variables, it is actually more powerful than it seems. A Boolean formula with variables is satisfiable if it has a true instance. It is invalid if it has a false instance. These are the relations computed by the program.

3.5.1 Exercises for Section 3.5

(i)   Write a program to recognize if an arithmetic sum is normalized, that is, has the form *A* + *B*, where *A* is a constant and *B* is a normalized sum.

(ii)   Write a type definition for Boolean formulae.

(iii) Write a program for recognizing whether a logical formula is in conjunctive normal form, namely, is a conjunction of disjunctions of literals, where a literal is an atomic formula or its negation.

(iv)   Write a program for the relation `negation_inwards(F1,F2)`, which is true if F2 is the logical formula resulting from moving all negation operators occurring in the formula F1 inside conjunctions and disjunctions.

(v)   Write a program for converting a logical formula into conjunctive normal form, that is, a conjunction of disjunctions.

(vi)   Consider the following representation of a bag, that is, a list of elements with multiplicities. The function symbol `bag(Element, Multiplicity,RestOfBag)` should be used. The atom `void` can be used as an empty bag. For example, the term `bag(a,3,bag(b,2, void))` represents a list of three copies of an element a, and two copies of an element b. Write logic programs to

(a) Take the union of two bags;

(b) Take the intersection of two bags;

(c) Substitute for an element in a bag;

(d) Convert a list into a bag;

(e) Convert a binary tree into a bag.

3.6   Background

Many of the programs in this chapter have been floating around the logic programming community, and their origins have become obscure. For example, several appear in Clocksin and Mellish (1984) and in the uneven collection of short Prolog programs, *How to Solve It in Prolog* by Coelho et al. (1980).

The latter book has been updated as Coelho and Cotta (1988) and is a source for other simple examples. The exercise on describing poker hands is due to Ken Bowen.

The classic reference for binary trees is Knuth (1968) and for sorting Knuth (1973).

A discussion of the linear algorithm for the kth largest algorithms can be found in most textbooks on algorithms, for example, Horowitz and Sahni (1978). The discussion of the heap property is taken from Horowitz and Sahni (1978).

Many of the basic programs for arithmetic and list processing have a simple structure that allows many correctness theorems to be proved automatically, see, for example, Boyer and Moore (1979) and Sterling and Bundy (1982).

Ackermann's function is discussed by Peter (1967).

4   The Computation Model of Logic Programs

The computation model used in the first three chapters of the book has a severe restriction. All goals appearing in the proof trees are ground. All rule instances used to derive the goals in the proof trees are also ground. The abstract interpreter described assumes that the substitutions giving the desired ground instances can be guessed correctly. In fact, the correct substitutions can be computed rather than guessed.

This chapter presents a general computation model of logic programs. The first section presents a unification algorithm that removes the guesswork in determining instances of terms. The second section presents an appropriately modified abstract interpreter and gives example computations of logic programs.

The computation model of logic programming we present is especially well suited to sequential languages such as Prolog. Our model can be used to describe parallel logic programming languages. However, developers of these languages have often used other models, such as state transitions or dynamic tree creation and destruction (see Section 4.3).

4.1   Unification

The heart of our computation model of logic programs is unification. Unification is the basis of most work in automated deduction and of the use of logical inference in artificial intelligence.

Necessary terminology for describing the algorithm is repeated from Chapter 1, and new definitions are introduced as needed.

Recall that a term t is a common instance of two terms, t_1 and t_2, if there exist substitutions θ_1 and θ_2 such that t equals $t_1\theta_1$ and $t_2\theta_2$. A term s is *more general* than a term t if t is an instance of s but s is not an instance of t. A term s is an *alphabetic variant* of a term t if both s is an instance of t and t is an instance of s. Alphabetic variants are related by the renaming of variables that occur in the terms. For example, `member(X,tree(Left,X,Right))` and `member(Y,tree(Left,Y,Z))` are alphabetic variants.

A *unifier* of two terms is a substitution making the terms identical. If two terms have a unifier, we say they *unify*. There is a close relation between unifiers and common instances. Any unifier determines a common instance, and conversely, any common instance determines a unifier.

For example, `append([1,2,3],[3,4],List)` and `append([X|Xs],Ys, [X|Zs])` unify. A unifying substitution is `{X=1,Xs=[2,3], Ys=[3,4], List=[1|Zs]}`. Their common instance, determined by this unifying substitution, is `append([1,2,3],[3,4],[1|Zs])`.

A *most general unifier*, or *mgu*, of two terms is a unifier such that the associated common instance is most general. It can be shown that if two terms unify, all mgus are equivalent. Making that statement precise is beyond the scope of this book, but we give pointers in Section 4.3. We proceed by giving an algorithm that computes a most general unifier of two terms if one exists.

The algorithm for unification presented here is based on solving equations. The input for the algorithm is two terms, T_1 and T_2. The output of the algorithm is an mgu of the two terms if they unify, or *failure* if the terms do not unify. The algorithm uses a pushdown stack for storing the equations that need to be solved and a location, θ, for collecting the substitution comprising the output.

The location θ is initially empty, and the stack is initialized to contain the equation $T_1 = T_2$. The algorithm consists of a loop of popping an equation from the stack and processing it. The loop terminates when the stack becomes empty or if failure occurs in processing an invalid equation.

We consider the possible actions for dealing with a popped equation $S = T$. The simplest case is if S and T are identical constants or variables. This equation is correct, and nothing further needs to be done. The computation continues by popping the next equation from the stack.

If *S* is a variable, and *T* is a term not containing *S*, the following happens. The stack is searched for all occurrences of *S*, which are replaced by *T*. Similarly, all occurrences of *S* in θ are replaced by *T*. Then the substitution *S* = *T* is added to θ. It is significant that *S* does not occur in *T*. The test embodied by the phrase "not containing" is known as the *occurs check*.

If *T* is a variable, and *S* is a term not containing *T*, i.e., *T* satisfies the occurs check with respect to *S*, the symmetric sequence of actions happens.

Equations are added to the stack if *S* and *T* are compound terms with the same principal functor and arity, $f(S_1,\ldots,S_n)$ and $f(T_1,\ldots,T_n)$, say. For the terms to unify, each of the argument pairs must simultaneously unify. This is achieved by pushing the *n* equations, $S_i = T_i$, onto the stack.

In any other case, *failure* is reported, and the algorithm terminates. If the stack is emptied, the terms unify, and the unifier can be found in θ. The complete algorithm is given as Figure 4.1. The occurs check is embodied in the phrase "that does not occur in."

We do not prove the correctness of this algorithm, nor analyze its complexity. The interested reader is referred to the literature in Section 4.3.

Consider attempting to unify the terms append([a,b],[c,d],Ls) and append([X|Xs],Ys;[X|Zs]). The stack is initialized to the equation

append([a,b],[c,d],Ls) = append([X|Xs],Ys,[X|Zs]).

These two terms have the same functor, append, and arity, 3, so we add the three equations relating the subterms of the two terms. These are [a,b]=[X|Xs], [c,d]=Ys, and Ls=[X|Zs].

The next equation, [a,b]=[X|Xs], is popped from the stack. These two compound terms have the same functor, ".", and arity, 2, so two equations, a=X and [b]=X, are added to the stack. Continuing, the equation a=X is popped. This is covered by the second case in Figure 4.1. X is a variable not occurring in the constant, a. All occurrences of X in the stack are replaced by a. One equation is affected, namely Ls=[X|Zs], which becomes Ls=[a|Zs]. The equation X=a is added to the initially empty substitution, and the algorithm continues.

The next equation to be popped is [b]=Xs. Again this is covered by the second case. Xs=[b] is added to the set of substitutions, and the stack is checked for occurrences of Xs. There are none, and the next equation is popped.

Input: Two terms T_1 and T_2 to be unified

Output: θ, the mgu of T_1 and T_2, or *failure*

Algorithm: Initialize the substitution θ to be empty,
                 the stack to contain the equation $T_1 = T_2$,
                 and failure to *false*.

> *while* stack not empty and no failure *do*
>
>> pop $X = Y$ from the stack
>>
>> *case*
>>
>>> X is a variable that does not occur in Y:
>>>> substitute Y for X in the stack and in θ
>>>> add $X = Y$ to θ
>>>
>>> Y is a variable that does not occur in X:
>>>> substitute X for Y in the stack and in θ
>>>> add $Y = X$ to θ
>>>
>>> X and Y are identical constants or variables:
>>>> continue
>>>
>>> X is $f(X_1,\ldots,X_n)$ and Y is $f(Y_1,\ldots,Y_n)$
>>>> for some functor f and $n > 0$:
>>>> push $X_i = Y_i, i = 1 \ldots n$, on the stack
>>>
>>> otherwise:
>>>> failure is *true*
>
> *If* failure, *then* output *failure else* output θ.

Figure 4.1   A unification algorithm

The second case also covers [c,d]=Ys. Another substitution, Ys=[c, d], is added to the collection, and the final equation, Ls=[a|Zs], is popped. This is handled by the symmetric first case. Ls does not occur in [a|Zs], so the equation is added as is to the unifier, and the algorithm terminates successfully. The unifier is {X=a,Xs=[b], Ys=[c,d], Ls=[a|Zs]}. The common instance produced by the unifier is append([a,b],[c,d],[a|Zs]). Note that in this unification, the substitutions were not updated.

The occurs check is necessary to prevent the unification of terms such as s(X) and X. There is no finite common instance of these terms. However, most Prolog implementations omit the occurs check from the unification algorithm, for pragmatic reasons.

When implementing this unification algorithm for a particular logic programming language, the explicit substitution in both the equations on the stack and the unifier is avoided. Instead, logical variables and other terms are represented by memory cells with different values, and variable binding is implemented by assigning to the memory cell representing a logical variable a reference to the cell containing the representation of the term the variable is bound to. Therefore,

Substitute Y for X in stack and in θ.
Add $X = Y$ to substitutions.

is replaced by

Make X a reference to Y.

4.1.1   Exercises for Section 4.1

(i)   Use the algorithm in Figure 4.1 to compute an mgu of append([b], [c,d],L) and append([X|Xs],Ys,[X|Zs]).

(ii)   Use the algorithm in Figure 4.1 to compute an mgu of hanoi(s(N), A,B,C,Ms) and hanoi(s(s(0)),a,b,c,Xs).

4.2   An Abstract Interpreter for Logic Programs

We revise the abstract interpreter of Section 1.8 in the light of the unification algorithm. The result is our full computation model of logic programs. All the concepts introduced previously, such as goal reductions and computation traces, have their analogues in the full model.

A computation of a logic program can be described informally as follows. It starts from some initial (possibly conjunctive) query G and, if it terminates, has one of two results: success or failure. If a computation succeeds, the instance of G proved is conceived of as the output of the computation. A given query can have several successful computations, each resulting in a different output. In addition, it may have nonterminating computations, to which we associate no result.

The computation progresses via *goal reduction*. At each stage, there is some resolvent, a conjunction of goals to be proved. A goal in the resolvent and clause in the logic program are chosen such that the clause's head unifies with the goal. The computation proceeds with a new resolvent, obtained by replacing the chosen goal by the body of the chosen clause in the resolvent and then applying the most general unifier of the head of the clause and the goal. The computation terminates when the resolvent is empty. In this case, we say the goal is solved by the program.

To describe computations more formally, we introduce some useful concepts. A *computation* of a goal $Q = Q_0$ by a program P is a (possibly infinite) sequence of triples $\langle Q_i, G_i, C_i \rangle$. Q_i is a (conjunctive) goal, G_i is a goal occurring in Q_i, and C_i is a clause $A \leftarrow B_1, \ldots, B_k$ in P renamed so that it contains new variable symbols not occurring in Q_j, $0 \leq j \leq i$. For all $i > 0$, Q_{i+1} is the result of replacing G_i by the body of C_i in Q_i, and applying the substitution θ_i, the most general unifier of G_i and A_i, the head of C_i; or the constant *true* if G_i is the only goal in Q_i and the body of C_i is empty; or the constant *fail* if G_i and the head of C_i do not unify.

The goals $B_i \theta_i$ are said to be *derived* from G_j and C_j. A goal $G_j = B_{ik} \theta$, where B_{ik} occurs in the body of clause C_i, is said to be *invoked* by G_i and C_i. G_i is the *parent* of any goal it invokes. Two goals with the same parent goal are *sibling goals*.

A *trace* of a computation of a logic program $\langle Q_i, G_i, C_i \rangle$ is the sequence of pairs $\langle G_i, \theta_i' \rangle$, where θ_i' is the subset of the mgu θ_i computed at the *i*th reduction, restricted to variables in G_i.

We present an abstract interpreter for logic programs. It is an adaptation of the interpreter for ground goals (Figure 1.1). The restriction to using ground instances of clauses to effect reductions is lifted. Instead, the unification algorithm is applied to the chosen goal and head of the chosen clause to find the correct substitution to apply to the new resolvent.

Care needs to be taken with the variables in rules to avoid name clashes. Variables are local to a clause. Hence variables in different clauses that have the same name are, in fact, different. This is ensured by renaming the variables appearing in a clause each time the clause is chosen to effect a reduction. The new names must not include any of the variable names used previously in the computation.

The revised version of the interpreter is given as Figure 4.2. It solves a query G with respect to a program P. The output of the interpreter is an

Input:	A goal G and a program P
Output:	An instance of G that is a logical consequence of P, or *no* otherwise
Algorithm:	Initialize the resolvent to G.

      while the resolvent is not empty *do*

            choose a goal A from the resolvent

            choose a (renamed) clause $A' \leftarrow B_1,\ldots,B_n$ from P

                such that A and A' unify with mgu θ

                    (if no such goal and clause exist, exit the *while* loop)

            replace A by $B_1,\ldots,B_n$ in the resolvent

            apply θ to the resolvent and to G

      If the resolvent is empty, *then* output G, *else* output *no*.

Figure 4.2   An abstract interpreter for logic programs

instance of G if a proof of such an instance is found, or *no* if a failure has occurred during the computation. Note that the interpreter may also fail to terminate.

An instance of a query for which a proof is found is called a *solution* to the query.

The policy for adding and removing goals from the resolvent is called the *scheduling policy* of the interpreter. The abstract interpreter leaves the scheduling policy unspecified.

Consider solving the query append([a,b],[c,d],Ls)? by Program 3.15 for append using the abstract interpreter of Figure 4.2. The resolvent is initialized to be append([a,b],[c,d],Ls). It is chosen as the goal to reduce, being the only one. The rule chosen from the program is

append([X|Xs],Ys,[X|Zs]) ← append(Xs,Ys,Zs).

The unifier of the goal and the head of the rule is {X=a,Xs=[b], Ys=[c,d], Ls=[a|Zs]}. A detailed calculation of this unifier appeared in the previous section. The new resolvent is the instance of append(Xs,Ys,Zs) under the unifier, namely, append([b],[c,d],Zs). This goal is chosen in the next iteration of the loop. The same clause for append is chosen, but variables must be renamed to avoid a clash of variable names. The version chosen is

append([X1|Xs1],Ys1,[X1|Zs1]) ← append(Xs1,Ys1,Zs1).

```
append([a,b],[c,d],Ls)          Ls=[a|Zs]
  append([b],[c,d],Zs)          Zs=[b|Zs1]
    append([ ],[c,d],Zs1)       Zs1=[c,d]
      true
        Output: Ls=[a,b,c,d]
```

Figure 4.3   Tracing the appending of two lists

The unifier of the head and goal is {X1=b, Xs1=[ ], Ys1=[c,d], Zs=[b|Zs1]}. The new resolvent is append([ ],[c,d],Zs1). This time the fact append([ ],Zs2,Zs2) is chosen; we again rename variables as necessary. The unifier this time is {Zs2=[c,d], Zs1=[c,d]}. The new resolvent is empty and the computation terminates.

To compute the result of the computation, we apply the relevant part of the mgu's calculated during the computation. The first unification instantiated Ls to [a|Zs]. Zs was instantiated to [b|Zs1] in the second unification, and Zs1 further became [c,d]. Putting it together, Ls has the value [a|[b|[c,d]]], or more simply, [a,b,c,d].

The computation can be represented by a trace. The trace of the foregoing append computation is presented in Figure 4.3. To make the traces clearer, goals are indented according to the indentation of their parent. A goal has an indentation depth of d+1 if its parent has indentation depth d.

As another example, consider solving the query son(S,haran)? by Program 1.2. It is reduced using the clause son(X,Y) ← father(Y,X), male(X). A most general unifier is {X=S,Y=haran}. Applying the substitution gives the new resolvent father(haran,S), male(S). This is a conjunctive goal. There are two choices for the next goal to reduce. Choosing the goal father(haran,S) leads to the following computation. The goal unifies with the fact father(haran,lot) in the program, and the computation continues with S instantiated to lot. The new resolvent is male(lot), which is reduced by a fact in the program, and the computation terminates. This is illustrated in the left trace in Figure 4.4.

The other possibility for computing S=haran is choosing to reduce the goal male(S) before father(haran,S). This goal is reduced by the fact male(lot) with S instantiated to lot. The new resolvent is father(haran,lot), which is reduced to the empty goal by the corresponding fact. This is the right trace in Figure 4.4.

```
son(S,haran)                              son(S,haran)
   father(haran,S)      S=lot                male(S)                S=lot
   male(lot)                                 father(haran,lot)
      true                                      true
```

Figure 4.4   Different traces of the same solution

Solutions to a query obtained using the abstract interpreter may contain variables. Consider the query member(a,Xs)? with respect to Program 3.12 for member. This can be interpreted as asking what list Xs has the element a as a member. One solution computed by the abstract interpreter is Xs=[a|Ys], namely, a list with a as its head and an unspecified tail. Solutions that contain variables denote an infinity of solutions—all their ground instances.

There are two choices in the interpreter of Figure 4.2: choosing the goal to reduce, and choosing the clause to effect the reduction. These must be resolved in any realization of the computation model. The nature of the choices is fundamentally different.

The choice of goal to reduce is arbitrary; it does not matter which is chosen for the computation to succeed. If there is a successful computation by choosing a given goal, then there is a successful computation by choosing any other goal. The two traces in Figure 4.4 illustrate two successful computations, where the choice of goal to reduce at the second step of the computation differs.

The choice of the clause to effect the reduction is nondeterministic. Not every choice will lead to a successful computation. For example, in both traces in Figure 4.4, we could have gone wrong. If we had chosen to reduce the goal father(haran,S) with the fact father(haran,yiscah), we would not have been able to reduce the invoked goal male(yiscah). For the second computation, had we chosen to reduce male(S) with male(isaac), the invoked goal father(haran,isaac) could not have been reduced.

For some computations, for example, the computation illustrated in Figure 4.3, there is only one clause from the program that can reduce each goal. Such a computation is called *deterministic*. Deterministic computations mean that we do not have to exercise our nondeterministic imagination.

The alternative choices that can be made by the abstract interpreter when trying to prove a goal implicitly define a search tree, as described more fully in Section 5.4. The interpreter "guesses" a successful path in this search tree, corresponding to a proof of the goal, if one exists. However, dumber interpreters, without guessing abilities, can also be built, with the same power as our abstract interpreter. One possibility is to search this tree breadth-first, that is, to explore all possible choices in parallel. This will guarantee that if there is a finite proof of the goal (i.e., a finite successful path in the search tree), it will be found.

Another possibility would be to explore the abstract search tree depth-first. In contrast to the breadth-first search strategy, the depth-first one does not guarantee finding a proof even if one exists, since the search tree may have infinite paths, corresponding to potentially infinite computations of the nondeterministic interpreter. A depth-first search of the tree might get lost in an infinite path, never finding a finite successful path, even if one exists.

In technical terms, the breadth-first search strategy defines a *complete* proof procedure for logic programs, whereas the depth-first one is *incomplete*. In spite of its incompleteness, depth-first search is the one incorporated in Prolog, for practical reasons, as explained in Chapter 6.

Let us give a trace of a longer computation, solving the Towers of Hanoi problem with three disks, using Program 3.31. It is a deterministic computation, given as Figure 4.5. The final append goal is given without unifications. It is straightforward to fill them in.

Computations such as that in Figure 4.5 can be compared to computations in more conventional languages. Unification can be seen to subsume many of the mechanisms of conventional languages: record allocation, assignment of and access to fields in records, parameter passing, and more. We defer the subject until the computation model for Prolog is introduced in Chapter 6.

A computation of G by P *terminates* if G_n = *true* or *fail* for some $n \geq 0$. Such a computation is finite and of length n. Successful computations correspond to terminating computations that end in *true*. Failing computations end in *fail*. All the traces given so far have been of successful computations.

Recursive programs admit the possibility of nonterminating computations. The query append(Xs,[c,d],Ys)? with respect to append can be reduced arbitrarily many times using the rule for append. In the process, Xs becomes a list of arbitrary length. This corresponds to solutions of the query appending [c,d] to an arbitrarily long list. The nonterminating computation is illustrated in Figure 4.6.

```
hanoi(s(s(s(0))),a,b,c,Ms)
    hanoi(s(s(0)),a,c,b,Ms1)
        hanoi(s(0),a,b,c,Ms11)              Ms11=[a to b]
        hanoi(s(0),b,c,a,Ms12)              Ms12=[b to c]
        append([a to b],[a to c,b to c],Ms1)   Ms1=[a to b|Xs]
            append([ ],[a to c,b to c],Xs)      Xs=[a to c,b to c]
    hanoi(s(s(0)),c,b,a,Ms2)
        hanoi(s(0),c,a,b,Ms21)              Ms21=[c to a]
        hanoi(s(0),a,b,c,Ms22)              Ms22=[a to b]
        append([c to a],[c to b,a to b],Ms2)   Ms2=[c to a|Ys]
            append([ ],[c to b,a to b],Ys)      Ys=[c to b,a to b]
    append([c to a,c to b,a to b],[a to b,c to a,
                    c to b,a to b],Ms)         Ms=[c to a|Zs]
        append([c to b,a to b],[a to b,c to a,
                        c to b,a to b],Zs)       Zs=[c to b|Zs1]
            append([a to b],[a to b,c to a,
                        c to b,a to b],Zs1)       Zs1=[a to b|Zs2]
                append([ ],[a to b,c to a,
                        c to b,a to b],Zs2)       Zs2=[a to b,c to a,
                                                   c to b,a to b]
```

Figure 4.5　Solving the Towers of Hanoi

```
append(Xs,[c,d],Ys)             Xs=[X|Xs1], Ys=[X|Ys1]
    append(Xs1,[c,d],Ys1)        Xs1=[X1|Xs2], Ys1=[X1|Ys2]
        append(Xs2,[c,d],Ys2)     Xs2=[X2|Xs3], Ys2=[X2|Ys3]
            append(Xs3,[c,d],Ys3)  Xs3=[X3|Xs4], Ys3=[X3|Ys4]
                    ⋮                      ⋮
```

Figure 4.6　A nonterminating computation

All the traces presented so far have an important feature in common. If two goals G_i and G_j are invoked from the same parent, and G_i appears before G_j in the trace, then all goals invoked by G_i will appear before G_j in the trace. This scheduling policy makes traces easier to follow, by solving queries depth-first.

The scheduling policy has another important effect: instantiating variables before their values are needed for other parts of the computation. A good ordering can mean the difference between a computation being deterministic or not.

Consider the computation traced in Figure 4.5. The goal

```
hanoi(s(s(s(0))),a,b,c,Ms)
```

is reduced to the following conjunction

```
hanoi(s(s(0)),a,c,b,Ms1),
    hanoi(s(s(0)),c,b,a,Ms2),
    append(Ms1,[a to b|Ms2],Ms).
```

If the append goal is now chosen, the append fact could be used (incorrectly) to reduce the goal. By reducing the two hanoi goals first, and all the goals they invoke, the append goal has the correct values for Ms1 and Ms2.

4.2.1   Exercises for Section 4.2

(i)   Trace the query sort([3,1,2],Xs)? using the permutation sort (3.20), insertion sort (3.21), and quicksort (3.22) programs in turn.

(ii)   Give a trace for the goal derivative(3*sin(x)-4*cos(x),x,D) using Program 3.30 for derivative.

(iii)   Practice tracing your favorite computations.

4.3   Background

Unification plays a central role in automated deduction and in the use of logical inference in artificial intelligence. It was first described in the landmark paper of Robinson (1965). Algorithms for unification have been the subject of much investigation: see, for example, Martelli and Montanari (1982), Paterson and Wegman (1978), and Dwork et al. (1984). Typical textbook descriptions appear in Bundy (1983) and Nilsson (1980).

The definition of unification presented here is nonstandard. Readers wishing to learn more about unifiers are referred to the definitive discussion on unification in Lassez, Maher, and Marriott (1988). This paper points out inconsistencies of the various definitions of unifiers that have been proposed in the literature, including the version in this book. Essentially, we have explained unifiers based on terms to avoid technical issues of composition of substitutions, which are not needed for our description of logic programming computations.

The computation model we have presented has a sequential bias and is influenced by the computation model for Prolog given in Chapter 6. Nonetheless, the model has potential for parallelism by selecting several goals or several rules at a time, and for elaborate control by selecting complicated computation rules. References for reading about different computation models for logic programming are given in Section 6.3.

Another bias of our computation model is the central place of unification. An exciting development within logic programming has been the realization that unification is just one instance of constraint solving. New computation models have been presented where the solution of equality constraints, i.e., unification, in the abstract interpreter of Figure 4.2 is replaced by solving other constraints. Good starting places to read about the new constraint-based models are Colmerauer (1990), Jaffar and Lassez (1987), and Lassez (1991).

A proof that the choice of goal to reduce from the resolvent is arbitrary can be found in Apt and van Emden (1982) or in the text of Lloyd (1987).

A method for replacing the runtime occurs check with compile-time analysis was suggested by Plaisted (1984).

Attempts have been made to make unification without the occurs check more than a necessary expedient for practical implementations of Prolog. In particular, Colmerauer (1982b) proposes a theoretical model for such unifications that incorporates computing with infinite terms.

A novel use of unification without the occurs check appears in Eggert and Chow (1983), where Escher-like drawings that gracefully tend to infinity are constructed.

5 Theory of Logic Programs

A major underlying theme of this book, laid out in the introduction, is that logic programming is attractive as a basis for computation because of its basis in mathematical logic, which has a well-understood, well-developed theory. In this chapter, we sketch some of the growing theory of logic programming, which merges the theory inherited from mathematical logic with experience from computer science and engineering. Giving a complete account is way beyond the scope of this book. In this chapter, we present some results to direct the reader in important directions. The first section, on semantics, gives definitions and suggests why the model-theoretic and proof-theoretic semantics give the same result. The main issue in the second section, on program correctness, is termination. Complexity of logic programs is discussed in the third section. The most important section for the rest of the book is Section 4, which discusses search trees. Search trees are vital to understanding Prolog's behavior. Finally, we introduce negation in logic programming.

5.1 Semantics

Semantics assigns meanings to programs. Discussing semantics allows us to describe more formally the relation a program computes. Chapter 1 informally describes the meaning of a logic program P as the set of ground instances that are deducible from P via a finite number of applications of the rule of universal modus ponens. This section considers more formal approaches.

```
parent(terach,abraham).    parent(abraham,isaac).
parent(isaac,jacob).       parent(jacob,benjamin).

ancestor(X,Y) ← parent(X,Y).
ancestor(X,Z) ← parent(X,Y), ancestor(Y,Z).
```

Program 5.1   Yet another family example

The *operational* semantics is a way of describing procedurally the meaning of a program. The operational meaning of a logic program P is the set of ground goals that are instances of queries solved by P using the abstract interpreter given in Figure 4.2. This is an alternative formulation of the previous semantics, which defined meaning in terms of logical deduction.

The *declarative* semantics of logic programs is based on the standard model-theoretic semantics of first-order logic. In order to define it, some new terminology is needed.

Definition

Let P be a logic program. The *Herbrand universe* of P, denoted $U(P)$, is the set of all ground terms that can be formed from the constants and function symbols appearing in P.   ∎

In this section, we use two running examples—yet another family database example, given as Program 5.1; and Program 3.1 defining the natural numbers, repeated here:

```
natural_number(0).
natural_number(s(X)) ← natural_number(X).
```

The Herbrand universe of Program 5.1 is the set of all constants appearing in the program, namely, {terach,abraham,isaac,jacob,benjamin}. If there are no function symbols, the Herbrand universe is finite. In Program 3.1, there is one constant symbol, 0, and one unary function symbol, s. The Herbrand universe of Program 3.1 is {0,s(0),s(s(0)), ... }. If no constants appear in a program, one is arbitrarily chosen.

Definition

The *Herbrand base*, denoted $B(P)$, is the set of all ground goals that can be formed from the predicates in P and the terms in the Herbrand universe.   ∎

There are two predicates, parent/2 and ancestor/2, in Program 5.1. The Herbrand base of Program 5.1 consists of 25 goals for each predicate, where each constant appears as each argument:

{parent(terach,terach), parent(terach,abraham),
parent(terach,isaac), parent(terach,jacob),
parent(terach,benjamin), parent(abraham,terach),
parent(abraham,abraham), parent(abraham,isaac),
parent(abraham,jacob), parent(abraham,benjamin),
parent(isaac,terach), parent(isaac,abraham),
parent(isaac,isaac), parent(isaac,jacob),
parent(isaac,benjamin), parent(jacob,terach),
parent(jacob,abraham), parent(jacob,isaac),
parent(jacob,jacob), parent(jacob,benjamin),
parent(benjamin,terach), parent(benjamin,abraham),
parent(benjamin,isaac), parent(benjamin,jacob),
parent(benjamin,benjamin), ancestor(terach,terach),
ancestor(terach,abraham), ancestor(terach,isaac),
ancestor(terach,jacob), ancestor(terach,benjamin),
ancestor(abraham,terach), ancestor(abraham,abraham),
ancestor(abraham,isaac), ancestor(abraham,jacob),
ancestor(abraham,benjamin), ancestor(isaac,terach),
ancestor(isaac,abraham), ancestor(isaac,isaac),
ancestor(isaac,jacob), ancestor(isaac,benjamin),
ancestor(jacob,terach), ancestor(jacob,abraham),
ancestor(jacob,isaac), ancestor(jacob,jacob),
ancestor(jacob,benjamin), ancestor(benjamin,terach),
ancestor(benjamin,abraham), ancestor(benjamin,isaac),
ancestor(benjamin,jacob), ancestor(benjamin,benjamin)}.

The Herbrand base is infinite if the Herbrand universe is. For Program 3.1, there is one predicate, natural_number. The Herbrand base equals {natural_number(0),natural_number(s(0)), ... }.

Definition
An *interpretation* for a logic program is a subset of the Herbrand base. ∎

An interpretation assigns truth and falsity to the elements of the Herbrand base. A goal in the Herbrand base is *true* with respect to an interpretation if it is a member of it, *false* otherwise.

Definition

An interpretation *I* is a *model* for a logic program if for each ground instance of a clause in the program $A \leftarrow B_1, \ldots, B_n$, *A* is in *I* if $B_1, \ldots, B_n$ are in *I*.   ∎

Intuitively, models are interpretations that respect the declarative reading of the clauses of a program.

For Program 3.1, `natural_number(0)` must be in every model, and `natural_number(s(X))` is in the model if `natural_number(X)` is. Any model of Program 3.1 thus includes the whole Herbrand base.

For Program 5.1, the facts `parent(terach,abraham)`, `parent(abraham,isaac)`, `parent(isaac,jacob)`, and `parent(jacob,benjamin)` must be in every model. A ground instance of the goal `ancestor(X,Y)` is in the model if the corresponding instance of `parent(X,Y)` is, by the first clause. So, for example, `ancestor(terach,abraham)` is in every model. By the second clause, `ancestor(X,Z)` is in the model if `parent(X,Y)` and `ancestor(Y,Z)` are.

It is easy to see that the intersection of two models for a logic program *P* is again a model. This property allows the definition of the intersection of all models.

Definition

The model obtained as the intersection of all models is known as the *minimal model* and denoted *M(P)*. The minimal model is the *declarative meaning* of a logic program.   ∎

The declarative meaning of the program for `natural_number`, its minimal model, is the complete Herbrand base {`natural_number(0)`,`natural_number(s(0))`,`natural_number(s(s(0)))`, ... }.

The declarative meaning of Program 5.1 is {`parent(terach,abraham)`, `parent(abraham,isaac)`, `parent(isaac,jacob)`, `parent(jacob,benjamin)`, `ancestor(terach,abraham)`, `ancestor(abraham,isaac)`, `ancestor(isaac,jacob)`, `ancestor(jacob,benjamin)`, `ancestor(terach,isaac)`, `ancestor(terach,jacob)`, `ancestor(terach,benjamin)`, `ancestor(abraham,jacob)`, `ancestor(abraham,benjamin)`, `ancestor(isaac,benjamin)`}.

Let us consider the declarative meaning of append, defined as Program 3.15 and repeated here:

```
append([X|Xs],Ys,[X|Zs]) ← append(Xs,Ys,Zs).
append([ ],Ys,Ys).
```

The Herbrand universe is [ ],[[ ]],[[ ],[ ]], . . . , namely, all lists that can be built using the constant [ ]. The Herbrand base is all combinations of lists with the append predicate. The declarative meaning is all ground instances of append([ ],Xs,Xs), that is, append([ ],[ ],[ ]), append([ ],[[ ]],[[ ]]), . . . , together with goals such as append ([[ ]],[ ],[[ ]]), which are logically implied by application(s) of the rule. This is only a subset of the Herbrand base. For example, append([ ],[ ],[[ ]]) is not in the meaning of append but is in the Herbrand base.

Denotational semantics assigns meanings to programs based on associating with the program a function over the domain computed by the program. The meaning of the program is defined as the least fixpoint of the function, if it exists. The domain of computations of logic programs is interpretations.

Definition

Given a logic program P, there is a natural mapping T_P from interpretations to interpretations, defined as follows:

$$T_P(I) = \{A \text{ in } B(P): A \leftarrow B_1, B_2, \ldots, B_n, n \geq 0, \text{ is a ground instance of}$$
$$\text{a clause in } P, \text{ and } B_1, \ldots, B_n \text{ are in } I\}. \qquad \blacksquare$$

The mapping is *monotonic*, since whenever an interpretation I is contained in an interpretation J, then $T_P(I)$ is contained in $T_P(J)$.

This mapping gives an alternative way of characterizing models. An interpretation I is a model if and only if $T_P(I)$ is contained in I.

Besides being monotonic, the transformation is also *continuous*, a notion that will not be defined here. These two properties ensure that for every logic program P, the transformation T_P has a least fixpoint, which is the meaning assigned to P by its denotational semantics.

Happily, all the different definitions of semantics are actually describing the same object. The operational, denotational, and declarative semantics have been demonstrated to be equivalent. This allows us to define the *meaning* of a logic program as its minimal model.

5.2 Program Correctness

Every logic program has a well-defined meaning, as discussed in Section 5.1. This meaning is neither correct nor incorrect.

The meaning of the program, however, may or may not be what was intended by the programmer. Discussions of correctness must therefore take into consideration the intended meaning of the program. Our previous discussion of proving correctness and completeness similarly was with respect to an intended meaning of a program.

We recall the definitions from Chapter 1. An *intended meaning* of a program *P* is a set of ground goals. We use intended meanings to denote the set of goals intended by the programmer for the program to compute. A program *P* is *correct* with respect to an intended meaning *M* if *M(P)* is contained in *M*. A program *P* is *complete* with respect to an intended meaning if *M* is contained in *M(P)*. A program is thus correct and complete with respect to an intended meaning if the two meanings coincide exactly.

Another important aspect of a logic program is whether it terminates.

Definition

A *domain* is a set of goals, not necessarily ground, closed under the instance relation. That is, if *A* is in *D* and *A′* is an instance of *A*, then *A′* is in *D* as well.   ■

Definition

A *termination domain* of a program *P* is a domain *D* such that every computation of *P* on every goal in *D* terminates.   ■

Usually, a useful program should have a termination domain that includes its intended meaning. However, since the computation model of logic programs is liberal in the order in which goals in the resolvent can be reduced, most interesting logic programs will not have interesting termination domains. This situation will improve when we switch to Prolog. The restrictive model of Prolog allows the programmer to compose nontrivial programs that terminate over useful domains.

Consider Program 3.1 defining the natural numbers. This program is terminating over its Herbrand base. However, the program is nonterminating over the domain {natural_number(X)}. This is caused by the possibility of the nonterminating computation depicted in the trace in Figure 5.1.

For any logic program, it is useful to find domains over which it is terminating. This is usually difficult for recursive logic programs. We

```
natural_number(X)                X=s(X1)
   natural_number(X1)            X1=s(X2)
      natural_number(X2)         X2=s(X3)
         .                          .
         .                          .
         .                          .
```

Figure 5.1 A nonterminating computation

need to describe recursive data types in a way that allows us to discuss termination.

Recall that a type, introduced in Chapter 3, is a set of terms.

Definition

A type is *complete* if the set is closed under the instance relation. With every complete type T we can associate an *incomplete type IT*, which is the set of terms that have instances in T and instances not in T. ∎

We illustrate the use of these definitions to find termination domains for the recursive programs using recursive data types in Chapter 3. Specific instances of the definitions of complete and incomplete types are given for natural numbers and lists. A (complete) natural number is either the constant 0, or a term of the form $s^n(X)$. An incomplete natural number is either a variable, X, or a term of the form $s^n(0)$, where X is a variable. Program 3.2 for $\leq$ is terminating for the domain consisting of goals where the first and/or second argument is a complete natural number.

Definition

A list is *complete* if every instance satisfies the definition given in Program 3.11. A list is *incomplete* if there are instances that satisfy this definition and instances that do not. ∎

For example, the list [a,b,c] is complete (proved in Figure 3.3), while the variable X is incomplete. Two more interesting examples: [a,X,c] is a complete list, although not ground, whereas [a,b|Xs] is incomplete.

A termination domain for append is the set of goals where the first and/or the third argument is a complete list. We discuss domains for other list-processing programs in Section 7.2, on termination of Prolog programs.

5.2.1 Exercises for Section 5.2

(i)   Give a domain over which Program 3.3 for plus is terminating.

(ii) Define complete and incomplete binary trees by analogy with the definitions for complete and incomplete lists.

5.3 Complexity

We have analyzed informally the complexity of several logic programs, for example, ≤ and plus (Programs 3.2 and 3.3) in the section on arithmetic, and append and the two versions of *reverse* in the section on lists (Programs 3.15 and 3.16). In this section, we briefly describe more formal complexity measures.

The multiple uses of logic programs slightly change the nature of complexity measures. Instead of looking at a particular use and specifying complexity in terms of the sizes of the inputs, we look at goals in the meaning and see how they were derived. A natural measure of the complexity of a logic program is the length of the proofs it generates for goals in its meaning.

Definition
The *size* of a term is the number of symbols in its textual representation.

∎

Constants and variables, consisting of a single symbol, have size 1. The size of a compound term is 1 more than the sum of the sizes of its arguments. For example, the list [b] has size 3, [a,b] has size 5, and the goal append([a,b],[c,d],Xs) has size 12. In general, a list of n elements has size $2 \cdot n + 1$.

Definition
A program P is of *length complexity* $L(n)$ if for any goal G in the meaning of P of size n there is a proof of G with respect to P of length less than equal to $L(n)$.

∎

Length complexity is related to the usual complexity measures in computer science. For sequential realizations of the computation model, it corresponds to time complexity. Program 3.15 for append has linear length complexity. This is demonstrated in Exercise (i) at the end of this section.

The applicability of this measure to Prolog programs, as opposed to logic programs, depends on using a unification algorithm without an occurs check. Consider the runtime of the straightforward program for appending two lists. Appending two lists, as shown in Figure 4.3, involves several unifications of append goals with the head of the append rule append([X|Xs],Ys,[X|Zs]). At least three unifications, matching variables against (possibly incomplete) lists, will be necessary. If the occurs check must be performed for each, the argument lists must be searched. This is directly proportional to the size of the input goal. However, if the occurs check is omitted, the unification time will be bounded by a constant. The overall complexity of append becomes quadratic in the size of the input lists with the occurs check, but only linear without it.

We introduce other useful measures related to proofs. Let R be a proof. We define the *depth* of R to be the deepest invocation of a goal in the associated reduction. The *goal-size* of R is the maximum size of any goal reduced.

Definition

A logic program P is of *goal-size complexity* $G(n)$ if for any goal A in the meaning of P of size n, there is a proof of A with respect to P of goal-size less than or equal to $G(n)$. ∎

Definition

A logic program P is of *depth-complexity* $D(n)$ if for any goal A in the meaning of P of size n, there is a proof of G with respect to P of depth $\leq D(n)$. ∎

Goal-size complexity relates to space. Depth-complexity relates to space of what needs to be remembered for sequential realizations, and to space and time complexity for parallel realizations.

5.3.1 Exercises for Section 5.3

(i)   Show that the size of a goal in the meaning of append joining a list of length n to one of length m to give a list of length $n + m$ is $4 \cdot n + 4 \cdot m + 4$. Show that a proof tree has $m + 1$ nodes. Hence show that `append` has linear complexity. Would the complexity be altered if the type condition were added?

(ii)   Show that Program 3.3 for `plus` has linear complexity.

(iii)   Discuss the complexity of other logic programs.

5.4   Search Trees

Computations of logic programs given so far resolve the issue of nondeterminism by always making the correct choice. For example, the complexity measures, based on proof trees, assume that the correct clause can be chosen from the program to effect the reduction. Another way of computationally modeling nondeterminism is by developing all possible reductions in parallel. In this section, we discuss search trees, a formalism for considering all possible computation paths.

Definition

A *search tree* of a goal *G* with respect to a program *P* is defined as follows. The root of the tree is *G*. Nodes of the tree are (possibly conjunctive) goals with one goal selected. There is an edge leading from a node *N* for each clause in the program whose head unifies with the selected goal. Each branch in the tree from the root is a computation of *G* by *P*. Leaves of the tree are *success nodes*, where the empty goal has been reached, or *failure nodes*, where the selected goal at the node cannot be further reduced. Success nodes correspond to solutions of the root of the tree.   ∎

There are in general many search trees for a given goal with respect to a program. Figure 5.2 shows two search trees for the query `son(S,haran)?` with respect to Program 1.2. The two possibilities correspond to the two choices of goal to reduce from the resolvent `father(haran,S),male(S)`. The trees are quite distinct, but both have a single success branch corresponding to the solution of the query `S=lot`. The respective success branches are given as traces in Figure 4.4.

We adopt some conventions when drawing search trees. The leftmost goal of a node is always the selected one. This implies that the goals in derived goals may be permuted so that the new goal to be selected for

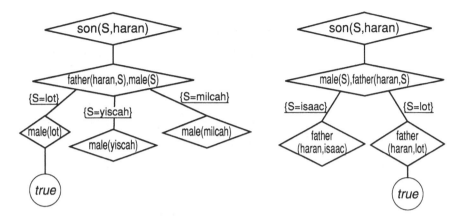

Figure 5.2   Two search trees

reduction is the first goal. The edges are labeled with substitutions that are applied to the variables in the leftmost goal. These substitutions are computed as part of the unification algorithm.

Search trees correspond closely to traces for deterministic computations. The traces for the append query and hanoi query given, respectively, in Figures 4.3 and 4.5 can be easily made into search trees. This is Exercise (i) at the end of this section.

Search trees contain multiple success nodes if the query has multiple solutions. Figure 5.3 contains the search tree for the query append(As,Bs,[a,b,c])? with respect to Program 3.15 for append, asking to split the list [a,b,c] into two. The solutions for As and Bs are found by collecting the labels of the edges in the branch leading to the success node. For example, in the figure, following the leftmost branch gives the solution {As=[a,b,c],Bs=[ ]}.

The number of success nodes is the same for any search tree of a given goal with respect to a program.

Search trees can have infinite branches, which correspond to nonterminating computations. Consider the goal append(Xs,[c,d],Ys) with respect to the standard program for append. The search tree is given in Figure 5.4. The infinite branch is the nonterminating computation given in Figure 4.6.

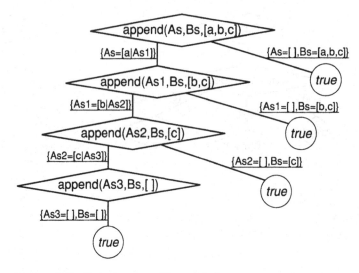

Figure 5.3 Search tree with multiple success nodes

Complexity measures can also be defined in terms of search trees. Prolog programs perform a depth-first traversal of the search tree. Therefore, measures based on the size of the search tree will be a more realistic measure of the complexity of Prolog programs than those based on the complexity of the proof tree. However, the complexity of the search tree is much harder to analyze.

There is a deeper point lurking. The relation between proof trees and search trees is the relation between nondeterministic computations and deterministic computations. Whether the complexity classes defined via proof trees are equivalent to complexity classes defined via search trees is a reformulation of the classic P=NP question in terms of logic programming.

5.4.1 Exercises for Section 5.4

(i)   Transform the traces of Figure 4.3 and 4.5 into search trees.

(ii) Draw a search tree for the query sort([2,4,1],Xs)? using permutation sort.

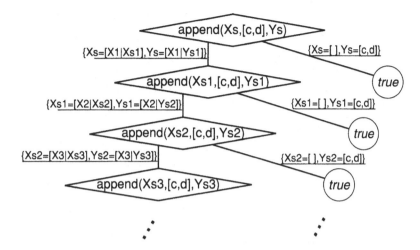

Figure 5.4   Search tree with an infinite branch

5.5 Negation in Logic Programming

Logic programs are collections of rules and facts describing what is true. Untrue facts are not expressed explicitly; they are omitted. When writing rules, it is often natural to include negative conditions. For example, defining a bachelor as an unmarried male could be written as

```
bachelor(X) ← male(X), not married(X).
```

if negation were allowed. In this section, we describe an extension to the logic programming computation model that allows a limited form of negation.

Researchers have investigated other extensions to logic programming to allow disjunction, and indeed, arbitrary first-order formulae. Discussing them is beyond the scope of this book. The most useful of the extensions is definitely negation.

We define a relation not G and give a semantics. The essence of logic programming is that there is an efficient procedural semantics. There is a natural way to adapt the procedural semantics to negation, namely by negation as failure. A goal G fails, (not G succeeds), if G cannot be derived by the procedural semantics.

The relation not G is only a partial form of negation from first-order logic. The relation *not* uses the *negation as failure* rule. A goal not G will be assumed to be a consequence of a program P if G is not a consequence of P.

Negation as failure can be characterized in terms of search trees.

Definition

A search tree of a goal *G* with respect to a program *P* is *finitely failed* if it has no success nodes or infinite branches. The *finite failure set* of a logic program *P* is the set of goals *G* such that *G* has a finitely failed search tree with respect to *P*.   ∎

A goal *not G* is implied by a program *P* by the "negation as failure" rule if *G* is in the finite failure set of *P*.

Let us see a simple example. Consider the program consisting of two facts:

```
likes(abraham,pomegranates).
likes(isaac,pomegranates).
```

The goal not likes(sarah,pomegranates) follows from the program by negation as failure. The search tree for the goal likes(sarah,pomegranates) has a single failure node.

Using negation as failure allows easy definition of many relations. For example, a declarative definition of the relation disjoint(Xs,Ys) that two lists, Xs and Ys, have no elements in common is possible as follows.

```
disjoint(Xs,Ys) ← not (member(X,Xs), member(X,Ys)).
```

This reads: "Xs is disjoint from Ys if there is no element X that is a member of both Xs and Ys."

An intuitive understanding of negation as failure is fine for the programs in this book using negation. There are semantic problems, however, especially when integrated with other issues such as completeness and termination. Pointers to the literature are given in Section 5.6, and Prolog's implementation of negation as failure is discussed in Chapter 11.

5.6 Background

The classic paper on the semantics of logic programs is of van Emden and Kowalski (1976). Important extensions were given by Apt and van Emden (1982). In particular, they showed that the choice of goal to reduce from the resolvent is arbitrary by showing that the number of success nodes is an invariant for the search trees. Textbook accounts of the theory of logic programming discussing the equivalence between the declarative and procedural semantics can be found in Apt (1990), Deville (1990), and Lloyd (1987).

In Shapiro (1984), complexity measures for logic programs are compared with the complexity of computations of alternating Turing machines. It is shown that goal-size is linearly related to alternating space, the product of length and goal-size is linearly related to alternating tree-size, and the product of depth and goal-size is linearly related to alternating time.

The classic name for search trees in the literature is SLD trees. The name SLD was coined by research in automatic theorem proving, which preceded the birth of logic programming. SLD resolution is a particular refinement of the resolution principle introduced in Robinson (1965). Computations of logic programs can be interpreted as a series of resolution steps, and in fact, SLD resolution steps, and are still commonly described thus in the literature. The acronym SLD stands for Selecting a literal, using a Linear strategy, restricted to Definite clauses.

The first proof of the correctness and completeness of SLD resolution, albeit under the name LUSH-resolution, was given by Hill (1974).

The subject of negation has received a large amount of attention and interest since the inception of logic programming. The fundamental work on the semantics of negation as failure is by Clark (1978). Clark's results, establishing soundness, were extended by Jaffar et al. (1983), who proved the completeness of the rule.

The concept of negation as failure is a restricted version of the closed world assumption as discussed in the database world. For more information see Reiter (1978). There has been extensive research on characterizing negation in logic programming that has not stabilized at this time. The reader should look up the latest logic programming conference proceedings to find current thinking. A good place to start reading to understand the issue is Kunen (1989).

Leonardo Da Vinci. Portrait of the Florentine poet *Bernardo Bellincioni*, engaged at the Court of Ludovico Sforza. Woodcut, based on a drawing by Leonardo. From Bellincioni's *Rime*. Milan 1493.

II The Prolog Language

In order to implement a practical programming language based on the computation model of logic programming, three issues need attention. The first concerns resolving the choices remaining in the abstract interpreter for logic programs, defined in Chapter 4. The second concerns enhancing the expressiveness of the pure computation model of logic programs by adding meta-logical and extra-logical facilities. Finally, access to some of the capabilities of the underlying computer, such as fast arithmetic and input/output, must be provided. This part discusses how Prolog, the most developed language based on logic programming, handles each of these issues.

6 Pure Prolog

A pure Prolog program is a logic program, in which an order is defined both for clauses in the program and for goals in the body of the clause. The abstract interpreter for logic programs is specialized to take advantage of this ordering information. This chapter discusses the execution model of Prolog programs in contrast to logic programs, and compares Prolog to more conventional languages.

The relation between logic programming and Prolog is reminiscent of the relation between the lambda-calculus and Lisp. Both are concrete realizations of abstract computation models. Logic programs that execute with Prolog's execution mechanism are referred to as *pure Prolog*. Pure Prolog is an approximate realization of the logic programming computation model on a sequential machine. It is certainly not the only possible such realization. However, it is a realization with excellent practical choices, which balance preserving the properties of the abstract model with catering for efficient implementation.

6.1 The Execution Model of Prolog

Two major decisions must be taken to convert the abstract interpreter for logic programs into a form suitable for a concrete programming language. First, the arbitrary choice of which goal in the resolvent to reduce, namely, the scheduling policy, must be specified. Second, the nondeterministic choice of the clause from the program to effect the reduction must be implemented.

Several logic programming languages exist, reflecting different choices. Prolog and its extensions (Prolog-II, IC-Prolog, and MU-Prolog, for example) are based on sequential execution. Other languages, such as PAR-LOG, Concurrent Prolog, GHC, Aurora-Prolog, and Andorra-Prolog, are based on parallel execution. The treatment of nondeterminism distinguishes between sequential and parallel languages. The distinction between Prolog and its extensions is in the choice of goal to reduce.

Prolog's execution mechanism is obtained from the abstract interpreter by choosing the leftmost goal instead of an arbitrary one and replacing the non-deterministic choice of a clause by sequential search for a unifiable clause and backtracking.

In other words, Prolog adopts a stack scheduling policy. It maintains the resolvent as a stack: pops the top goal for reduction, and pushes the derived goals onto the resolvent stack.

In addition to the stack policy, Prolog simulates the nondeterministic choice of reducing clause by sequential search and backtracking. When attempting to reduce a goal, the first clause whose head unifies with the goal is chosen. If no unifiable clause is found for the popped goal, the computation is unwound to the last choice made, and the next unifiable clause is chosen.

A *computation* of a goal G with respect to a Prolog program P is the generation of *all* solutions of G with respect to P. In terms of logic programming concepts, a Prolog computation of a goal G is a complete depth-first traversal of the particular search tree of G obtained by always choosing the leftmost goal.

Many different Prolog implementations exist with differing syntax and programming facilities. Recently, there has been an attempt to reach a Prolog standard based on the Edinburgh dialect of Prolog. At the time of writing, the standard has not been finalized. However a complete draft exists, which we essentially follow. We refer to the Prolog described in that document as *Standard Prolog*. The syntax of logic programs that we have been using fits within Standard Prolog except that we use some characters not available on a standard keyboard. We give the standard equivalent of our special characters. Thus :- should be used instead of ← in Prolog programs to separate the head of a clause from its body. All the programs in this book run (possibly with minor changes) in all Edinburgh-compatible Prologs.

A *trace* of a Prolog computation is an extension of the trace of a computation of a logic program under the abstract interpreter as described

```
father(abraham,isaac).    male(isaac).
father(haran,lot).        male(lot).
father(haran,milcah).     female(yiscah).
father(haran,yiscah).     female(milcah).
son(X,Y)  ←  father(Y,X), male(X).
daughter(X,Y)  ←  father(Y,X), female(X).

son(X,haran)?
    father(haran,X)                          X=lot
    male(lot)
            true
      Output:  X=lot
        ;
    father(haran,X)                          X=milcah
    male(milcah)         f
    father(haran,X)                          X=yiscah
    male(yiscah)         f
                    no (more) solutions
```

Figure 6.1 Tracing a simple Prolog computation

in Section 4.2. We revise the computations of Chapters 4 and 5, indicating the similarities and differences. Consider the query son(X,haran)? with respect to Program 1.2, biblical family relationships, repeated at the top of Figure 6.1. The computation is given in the bulk of Figure 6.1. It corresponds to a depth-first traversal of the first of the search trees in Figure 5.2. It is an extension of the first trace in Figure 4.4, since the whole search tree is searched.

The notation previously used for traces must be extended to handle failure and backtracking. An f after a goal denotes that a goal fails, that is there is no clause whose head unifies with the goal. The next goal after a failed goal is where the computation continues on backtracking. It already appears as a previous goal in the trace at the same depth of indentation and can be identified by the variable names. We adopt the Edinburgh Prolog convention that a ";" typed after a solution denotes a continuation of the computation to search for more solutions. Unifications are indicated as previously.

Trace facilities and answers provided by particular Prolog implementations vary from our description. For example, some Prolog implementations always give all solutions, while others wait for a user response after each solution.

```
append([X|Xs],Ys,[X|Zs]) ← append(Xs,Ys,Zs).
append([ ],Ys,Ys).
```

```
append(Xs,Ys,[a,b,c])                          Xs=[a|Xs1]
    append(Xs1,Ys,[b,c])                       Xs1=[b|Xs2]
        append(Xs2,Ys,[c])                     Xs2=[c|Xs3]
            append(Xs3,Ys,[ ])                 Xs3=[ ],Ys=[ ]
                true
              Output: (Xs=[a,b,c],Ys=[ ])
                                ;
        append(Xs2,Ys,[c])                     Xs2=[ ],Ys=[c]
                true
          Output: (Xs=[a,b],Ys=[c] )
                            ;
    append(Xs1,Ys,[b,c])                       Xs1=[ ],Ys=[b,c]
            true
      Output: (Xs=[a],Ys=[b,c])
                        ;
append(Xs,Ys,[a,b,c])                          Xs=[ ],Ys=[a,b,c]
        true
  Output: (Xs=[ ],Ys=[a,b,c])
                    ;
              no (more) solutions
```

Figure 6.2 Multiple solutions for splitting a list

The trace of append([a,b],[c,d],Ls)? giving the answer Ls=[a,b,c,d] is precisely the trace given in Figure 4.3. Figure 4.5, giving the trace for solving the Towers of Hanoi with three disks, is also a trace of the hanoi program considered as a Prolog program solving the query hanoi(s(s(s(0))),a,b,c,Ms)?. The trace of a deterministic computation is the same when considered as a logic program or a Prolog program, provided the order of goals is preserved.

The next example is answering the query append(Xs,Ys,[a,b,c])? with respect to Program 3.15 for append. There are several solutions of the query. The search tree for this goal was given as Figure 5.3. Figure 6.2 gives the Prolog trace.

Tracing computations is a good way to gain understanding of the execution model of Prolog. We give a slightly larger example, sorting a list with the quicksort program (Program 3.22, reproduced at the top of Figure 6.3). Computations using quicksort are essentially deterministic and show the algorithmic behavior of a Prolog program. Figure 6.3 gives a trace of the query quicksort([2,1,3],Xs)?. Arithmetic comparisons

```
quicksort([X|Xs],Ys) ←
    partition(Xs,X,Littles,Bigs),
    quicksort(Littles,Ls),
    quicksort(Bigs,Bs),
    append(Ls,[X|Bs],Ys).
quicksort([ ],[ ]).
partition([X|Xs],Y,[X|Ls],Bs) ←
    X ≤ Y, partition(Xs,Y,Ls,Bs).
partition([X|Xs],Y,Ls,[X|Bs]) ←
    X > Y, partition(Xs,Y,Ls,Bs).
partition([ ],Y,[ ],[ ]).
```

```
quicksort([2,1,3],Qs)
    partition([1,3],2,Ls,Bs)              Ls=[1|Ls1]
        1 ≤ 2
        partition([3],2,Ls1,Bs)           Ls1=[3|Ls2]
            3 ≤ 2      f
        partition([3],2,Ls1,Bs)           Bs=[3|Bs1]
            3 > 2
            partition([ ],2,Ls1,Bs1)      Ls1=[ ]=Bs1
    quicksort([1],Qs1)
        partition([ ],1,Ls2,Bs2)          Ls2=[ ]=Bs2
        quicksort([ ],Qs2)                Qs2=[ ]
        quicksort([ ],Qs3)                Qs3=[ ]
        append([ ],[1],Qs1)               Qs1=[1]
    quicksort([3],Qs4)
        partition([ ],3,Ls3,Bs3)          Ls3=[ ]=Bs3
        quicksort([ ],Qs5)                Qs5=[ ]
        quicksort([ ],Qs6)                Qs6=[ ]
        append([ ],[3],Qs4)               Qs4=[3]
    append([1],[2,3],Qs)                  Qs=[1|Ys]
        append([ ],[2,3],Ys)              Ys=[2,3]
                true
            Output:  (Qs=[1,2,3])
```

Figure 6.3 Tracing a quicksort computation

are assumed to be unit operations, and the standard program for append is used.

We introduce a distinction between *shallow* and *deep* backtracking. Shallow backtracking occurs when the unification of a goal and a clause fails, and an alternative clause is tried. Deep backtracking occurs when the unification of the last clause of a procedure with a goal fails, and control returns to another goal in the computation tree.

It is sometimes convenient to include, for the purpose of this definition, test predicates that occur first in the body of the clause as part of unification, and to classify the backtracking that occurs as a result of their failure as shallow. An example in Figure 6.3 is the choice of a new clause for the goal partition([3],2,Ls1,Bs).

6.1.1 Exercises for Section 6.1

(i)   Trace the execution of daughter(X,haran)? with respect to Program 1.2.

(ii) Trace the execution of sort([3,1,2],Xs)? with respect to Program 3.21.

(iii) Trace the execution of sort([3,1,2],Xs)? with respect to Program 3.20.

6.2 Comparison to Conventional Programming Languages

A programming language is characterized by its control and data manipulation mechanisms. Prolog, as a general-purpose programming language, can be discussed in these terms, as are conventional languages. In this section, we compare the control flow and data manipulation of Prolog to that of Algol-like languages.

The control in Prolog programs is like that in conventional procedural languages as long as the computation progresses forward. Goal invocation corresponds to procedure invocation, and the ordering of goals in the body of clauses corresponds to sequencing of statements. Specifically, the clause $A \leftarrow B_1,...,B_n$ can be viewed as the definition of a procedure A as follows:

```
procedure A
    call B₁,
    call B₂,
        .
        .
    call Bₙ,
end.
```

Recursive goal invocation in Prolog is similar in behavior and implementation to that of conventional recursive languages. The differences show when backtracking occurs. In a conventional language, if a computation cannot proceed (e.g., all branches of a case statement are false), a runtime error occurs. In Prolog, the computation is simply undone to the last choice made, and a different computation path is attempted.

The data structures manipulated by logic programs, terms, correspond to general record structures in conventional programming languages. The handling of data structures is very flexible in Prolog. Like Lisp, Prolog is a declaration-free, typeless language.

The major differences between Prolog and conventional languages in the use of data structures arise from the nature of logical variables. Logical variables refer to individuals rather than to memory locations. Consequently, having once beed specified to refer to a particular individual, a variable cannot be made to refer to another individual. In other words, logic programming does not support destructive assignment where the contents of an initialized variable can change.

Data manipulation in logic programs is achieved entirely via the unification algorithm. Unification subsumes

- Single assignment
- Parameter passing
- Record allocation
- Read/write-once field-access in records

We discuss the trace of the quicksort program in Figure 6.3, pointing out the various uses of unification. The unification of the initial goal quicksort([2,1,3],Qs) with the head of the procedure definition quicksort([X|Xs],Ys) illustrates several features. The unification of [2,1,3] with the term [X|Xs] achieves record access to the list and also selection of its two fields, the head and tail.

The unification of [1,3] with Xs achieves parameter passing to the partition procedure, because of the sharing of the variables. This gives the first argument of partition. Similarly, the unification of 2 with X passes the value of the second parameter to partition.

Record creation can be seen with the unification of the goal partition([1,3],2,Ls,Bs) with the head of the partition procedure partition([X|Xs],Z,[X|Ls1],Bs1). As a result, Ls is instantiated to [1|Ls1]. Specifically, Ls is made into a list and its head is assigned the value 1, namely, record creation and field assignment via unification.

The recursive algorithm embodied by the quicksort program can be easily coded in a conventional programming language using linked lists and pointer manipulation. As discussed, unification is achieving the effect of the necessary pointer manipulations. Indeed, the manipulation of logical variables via unification can be viewed as an abstraction of low-level manipulation of pointers to complex data structures.

These analogies may provide hints on how to implement Prolog efficiently on a von Neumann machine. Indeed, the basic idea of compilation of Prolog is to translate special cases of unification to conventional memory manipulation operations, as specified previously.

Conventional languages typically incorporate error-handling or exception-handling mechanisms of various degrees of sophistication. Pure Prolog does not have an error or exception mechanism built into its definition. The pure Prolog counterparts of nonfatal errors in conventional programs, e.g., a missing case in a case statement, or dividing by zero, cause failure in pure Prolog.

Full Prolog, introduced in the following chapters, includes system predicates, such as arithmetic and I/O, which may cause errors. Current Prolog implementations do not have sophisticated error-handling mechanisms. Typically, on an error condition, a system predicate prints an error message and either fails or aborts the computation.

This brief discussion of Prolog's different way of manipulating data does not help with the more interesting question: How does programming in Prolog compare with programming in conventional programming languages? That is the major underlying topic of the rest of this book.

6.3 Background

The origins of Prolog are shrouded in mystery. All that is known is that the two founders, Robert Kowalski, then at Edinburgh, and Alain Colmerauer at Marseilles worked on similar ideas during the early 1970s, and even worked together one summer. The results were the formulation of the logic programming philosophy and computation model by Kowalski (1974), and the design and implementation of the first logic programming language Prolog, by Colmerauer and his colleagues (1973). Three recent articles giving many more details about the beginnings of Prolog and logic programming are Cohen (1988), Kowalski (1988), and Colmerauer and Roussel (1993).

A major force behind the realization that logic can be the basis of a practical programming language has been the development of efficient implementation techniques, as pioneered by Warren (1977). Warren's compiler identified special cases of unification and translated them into efficient sequences of conventional memory operations. Good accounts of techniques for Prolog implementation, both interpretation and compilation, can be found in Maier and Warren (1988) and Ait-Kaci (1991).

Variations of Prolog with extra control features, such as IC-Prolog (Clark and McCabe, 1979), have been developed but have proved too costly in runtime overhead to be seriously considered as alternatives to Prolog. We will refer to particular interesting variations that have been proposed in the appropriate sections.

Another breed of logic programming languages, which indirectly emerged from IC-Prolog, was concurrent logic languages. The first was the Relational Language (Clark and Gregory, 1981), followed by Concurrent Prolog (Shapiro, 1983b), PARLOG (Clark and Gregory, 1984), GHC (Ueda, 1985), and a few other proposals.

References for the variations mentioned in the text are, for Prolog-II (van Caneghem, 1982), IC-Prolog (Clark et al., 1982), and MU-Prolog (Naish, 1986). Aurora-Prolog is described in Disz et al. (1987), while a starting place for reading about AKL, a language emerging from Andorra-Prolog is Janson and Haridi (1991).

The syntax of Prolog stems from the clausal form of logic due to Kowalski (1974). The original Marseilles interpreter used the terminology of positive and negative literals from resolution theory. The clause $A \leftarrow B_1, \ldots, B_n$ was written $+A - B_1 \cdots - B_n$.

David H. D. Warren adapted Marseilles Prolog for the DEC-10 at the University of Edinburgh, with help from Fernando Pereira. Their decisions have been very influential. Many systems adopted most of the conventions of Prolog-10 (Warren et al., 1979), which has become known more generically as Edinburgh Prolog. Its essential features are described in the widespread primer on Prolog (Clocksin and Mellish, 1984). This book follows the description of Standard Prolog existing as Scowen (1991).

A paper by Cohen (1985) delves further into the relation between Prolog and conventional languages.

7 Programming in Pure Prolog

A major aim of logic programming is to enable the programmer to program at a higher level. Ideally one should write axioms that define the desired relations, maintaining ignorance of the way they are going to be used by the execution mechanism. Current logic programming languages, Prolog in particular, are still far away from allowing this ideal of declarative programming. The specific, well-defined choices of how their execution mechanisms approximate the abstract interpreter cannot be ignored. Effective logic programming requires knowing and utilizing these choices.

This chapter discusses the consequences of Prolog's execution model for the logic programmer. New aspects of the programming task are introduced. Not only must programmers come up with a correct and complete axiomatization of a relation but they must also consider its execution according to the model.

7.1 Rule Order

Two syntactic issues, irrelevant for logic programs, are important to consider when composing Prolog programs. The *rule order*, or *clause order*, of clauses in each procedure must be decided. Also the *goal order* of goals in the bodies of each clause must be determined. The consequences of these decisions can be immense. There can be orders of magnitude of difference in efficiency in the performance of Prolog programs. In extreme though quite common cases, correct logic programs will fail to give solutions because of nontermination.

```
parent(terach,abraham).        parent(abraham,isaac).
parent(isaac,jacob).           parent(jacob,benjamin).

ancestor(X,Y) ← parent(X,Y).
ancestor(X,Z) ← parent(X,Y), ancestor(Y,Z).
```

Program 7.1 Yet another family example

The rule order determines the order in which solutions are found.

Changing the order of rules in a procedure permutes the branches in any search tree for a goal using that procedure. The search tree is traversed depth-first. So permuting the branches causes a different order of traversal of the search tree, and a different order of finding solutions. The effect is clearly seen when using facts to answer an existential query. With our biblical database and a query such as father(X,Y)?, changing the order of facts will change the order of solutions found by Prolog. Deciding how to order facts is not very important.

The order of solutions of queries solved by recursive programs is also determined by the clause order. Consider Program 5.1, a simple biblical database together with a program for the relationship ancestor, repeated here as Program 7.1.

For the query ancestor(terach,X)? with respect to Program 7.1, the solutions will be given in the order, X=abraham, X=isaac, X=jacob, and X=benjamin. If the rules defining ancestor are swapped, the solutions will appear in a different order, namely, X=benjamin, X=jacob, X=isaac, and X=abraham.

The different order of ancestor clauses changes the order of searching the implicit family tree. In one order, Prolog outputs solutions as it goes along. With the other order, Prolog travels to the end of the family tree and gives solutions on the way back. The desired order of solutions is determined by the application, and the rule order of ancestor is chosen accordingly.

Changing the order of clauses for the member predicate (Program 3.12) also changes the order of search. As written, the program searches the list until the desired element is found. If the order of the clauses is reversed, the program always searches to the end of the list. The order of solutions will also be affected, for example, responding to the query member(X,[1,2,3])?. In the standard order, the order of solutions is intuitive: X=1, X=2, X=3. With the rules swapped, the order is X=3, X=2, X=1. The order of Program 3.12 is more intuitive and hence preferable.

When the search tree for a given goal has an infinite branch, the order of clauses can determine if any solutions are given at all. Consider the query append(Xs,[c,d],Ys)? with respect to append. As can be seen from the search tree in Figure 5.4, no solutions would be given. If, however, the append fact appeared before the append rule, an infinite number of pairs Xs,Ys satisfying the query would be given.

There is no consensus as to how to order the clauses of a Prolog procedure. Clearly, the standard dictated in more conventional languages, of testing for the termination condition before proceeding with the iteration or recursion is not mandatory in Prolog. This is demonstrated in Program 3.15 for append as well as in other programs in this book. The reason is that the recursive or iterative clause tests its applicability by unification. This test is done explicitly and independently of the other clauses in the procedure.

Clause order is more important for general Prolog programs than it is for pure Prolog programs. Other control features, notably the cut to be discussed in Chapter 11, depend significantly on the clause order. When such constructs are used, clauses lose their independence and modularity, and clause order becomes significant.

In this chapter, for the most part, the convention that the recursive clauses precede the base clauses is adopted.

7.1.1 Exercises for Section 7.1

(i)   Verify the order of solutions for the query ancestor(abraham,X)? with respect to Program 7.1, and its variant with different rule order for ancestor, claimed in the text.

(ii) What is the order of solutions for the query ancestor(X,benjamin)? with respect to Program 7.1? What if the rule order for ancestor were swapped?

7.2   Termination

Prolog's depth-first traversal of search trees has a serious problem. If the search tree of a goal with respect to a program contains an infinite branch, the computation will not terminate. Prolog may fail to find a solution to a goal, even though the goal has a finite computation.

Nontermination arises with recursive rules. Consider adding a relationship married(Male,Female) to our database of family relationships. A sample fact from the biblical situation is married(abraham,sarah). A user querying the married relationship should not care whether males or females are first, as the relationship is commutative. The "obvious" way of overcoming the commutativity is adding a recursive rule married(X,Y) ← married(Y,X). If this is added to the program, no computation involving married would ever terminate. For example, the trace of the query married(abraham,sarah)? is given in Figure 7.1.

Recursive rules that have the recursive goal as the first goal in the body are known as *left recursive* rules. The problematic married axiom is an example. Left recursive rules are inherently troublesome in Prolog. They cause nonterminating computations if called with inappropriate arguments.

The best solution to the problem of left recursion is avoidance. The married relationship used a left recursive rule to express commutativity. Commutative relationships are best handled differently, by defining a new predicate that has a clause for each permutation of the arguments of the relationship. For the relationship married, a new predicate, are_married(Person1,Person2), say, would be defined using two rules:

```
are_married(X,Y) ← married(X,Y).
are_married(X,Y) ← married(Y,X).
```

Unfortunately, it is not generally possible to remove all occurrences of left recursion. All the elegant minimal recursive logic programs shown in Chapter 3 are left recursive, and can cause nontermination. However,

```
married(X,Y) ← married(Y,X).
married(abraham,sarah).

married(abraham,sarah)
  married(sarah,abraham)
    married(abraham,sarah)
      married(sarah,abraham)
        ⋮
```

Figure 7.1 A nonterminating computation

the appropriate analysis, using the concepts of domains and complete structures introduced in Section 5.2, can determine which queries will terminate with respect to recursive programs.

Let us consider an example, Program 3.15 for appending two lists. The program for append is everywhere terminating for the set of goals whose first and/or last argument is a complete list. Any append query whose first argument is a complete list will terminate. Similarly, all queries where the third argument is a complete list will terminate. The program will also terminate if the first and/or third argument is a ground term that is not a list. The behavior of append is best summed up by considering the queries that do not terminate, namely, when both the first and third arguments are incomplete lists that are unifiable.

The condition for when a query to Program 3.12 for member terminates is also stated in terms of incomplete lists. A query does not terminate if the second argument is an incomplete list. If the second argument of a query to member is a complete list, the query terminates.

Another guaranteed means of generating nonterminating computations, easy to overlook, is circular definitions. Consider the pair of rules

```
parent(X,Y) ← child(Y,X).
child(X,Y) ← parent(Y,X).
```

Any computation involving parent or child, for example, parent (haran,lot)?, will not terminate. The search tree necessarily contains an infinite branch, because of the circularity.

7.2.1 Exercises for Section 7.2

(i)   Discuss the termination behavior of both programs in Program 3.13 determining prefixes and suffixes of lists.

(ii) Discuss the termination of Program 3.14c for sublist.

7.3 Goal Order

Goal order is more significant than clause order. It is the principal means of specifying sequential flow of control in Prolog programs. The programs for sorting lists, e.g., Program 3.22 for quicksort, exploit goal order to indicate the sequence of steps in the sorting algorithms.

We first discuss goal order from the perspective of database programming. The order of goals can affect the order of solutions. Consider the query daughter(X,haran)? with respect to a variant of Program 1.2, where the order of the facts female(milcah) and female(yiscah) is interchanged. The two solutions are given in the order X=milcah, X=yiscah. If the goal order of the daughter rule were changed to be daughter(X,Y) ← female(X),father(Y,X)., the order of the solutions to the query, given the same database, would be X=yiscah, X=milcah.

The reason that the order of goals in the body of a clause affects the order of solutions to a query is different from the reason that the order of rules in a procedure affects the solution order. Changing rule order does not change the search tree that must be traversed for a given query. The tree is just traversed in a different order. Changing goal order changes the search tree.

Goal order determines the search tree.

Goal order affects the amount of searching the program does in solving a query by determining which search tree is traversed. Consider the two search trees for the query son(X,haran)?, given in Figure 5.2. They represent two different ways of finding a solution. In the first case, solutions are found by searching for children of haran and checking if they are male. The second case corresponds to the rule for son being written with the order of the goals in its body swapped, namely, son(X,Y) ← male(X), parent(Y,X). Now the query is solved by searching through all the males in the program and checking if they are children of haran. If there were many male facts in the program, more search would be involved. For other queries, for example, son(sarah,X)?, the reverse order has advantages. Since sarah is not male, the query would fail more quickly.

The optimal goal order of Prolog programs varies with different uses. Consider the definition of grandparent. There are two possible rules:

```
grandparent(X,Z) ← parent(X,Y), parent(Y,Z).
grandparent(X,Z) ← parent(Y,Z), parent(X,Y).
```

If you wish to find someone's grandson with the grandfather relationship with a query such as grandparent(abraham,X)?, the first of the rules searches more directly. If looking for someone's grandparent with a query such as grandparent(X,isaac)?, the second rule finds the solution more directly. If efficiency is important, then it is advisable to have two distinct relationships, grandparent and grandchild, to be used appropriately at the user's discretion.

In contrast to rule order, goal order can determine whether computations terminate. Consider the recursive rule for ancestor:

ancestor(X,Y) ← parent(X,Z), ancestor(Z,Y).

If the goals in the body are swapped, the ancestor program becomes left recursive, and all Prolog computations with ancestor are nonterminating.

The goal order is also important in the recursive clause of the quicksort algorithm in Program 3.22:

```
quicksort([X|Xs],Ys) ←
    partition(Xs,X,Littles,Bigs),
    quicksort(Littles,Ls),
    quicksort(Bigs,Bs),
    append(Ls,[X|Bs],Ys).
```

The list should be partitioned into its two smaller pieces before recursively sorting the pieces. If, for example, the order of the partition goal and the recursive sorting goal is swapped, no computations terminate.

We next consider Program 3.16a for reversing a list:

```
reverse([ ],[ ]).
reverse([X|Xs],Zs) ← reverse(Xs,Ys), append(Ys,[X],Zs).
```

The goal order is significant. As written, the program terminates with goals where the first argument is a complete list. Goals where the first argument is an incomplete list give nonterminating computations. If the goals in the recursive rule are swapped, the determining factor of the termination of reverse goals is the second argument. Calls to reverse with the second argument a complete list terminate. They do not terminate if the second argument is an incomplete list.

A subtler example comes from the definition of the predicate sublist in terms of two append goals, specifying the sublist as a suffix of a prefix, as given in Program 3.14e. Consider the query sublist([2,3],[1,2,3,4])? with respect to the program. The query is reduced to append(AsXs,Bs,[1,2,3,4]), append(As,[2,3],AsXs)?.

This has a finite search tree, and the initial query succeeds. If Program 3.14e had its goals reversed, the initial query would be reduced to `append(As,[2,3],AsXs),append(AsXs,Bs,[1,2,3,4])?`. This leads to a nonterminating computation because of the first goal, as illustrated in Figure 5.4.

A useful heuristic for goal order can be given for recursive programs with tests such as arithmetic comparisons, or determining whether two constants are different. The heuristic is to place the tests as early as possible. An example comes in the program for `partition`, which is part of Program 3.22. The first recursive rule is

`partition([X|Xs],Y,[X|Ls],Bs) ← X ≤ Y, partition(Xs,Y,Ls,Bs).`

The test $X \leq Y$ should go before the recursive call. This leads to a smaller search tree.

In Prolog programming (in contrast, perhaps, to life in general) our goal is to fail as quickly as possible. Failing early prunes the search tree and brings us to the right solution sooner.

7.3.1 Exercises for Section 7.3

(i)   Consider the goal order for Program 3.14e defining a sublist of a list as a suffix of a prefix. Why is the order of the append goals in Program 3.14e preferable? (Hint: Consider the query `sublist(Xs,[a,b,c])?`.)

(ii)   Discuss the clause order, goal order, and termination behavior for `substitute`, posed as Exercise 3.3(i).

7.4 Redundant Solutions

An important issue when composing Prolog programs, irrelevant for logic programs, is the redundancy of solutions to queries. The meaning of a logic program is the set of ground goals deducible from it. No distinction is made between whether a goal in the meaning could be deduced uniquely from the program, or whether it could be deduced in several distinct ways. This distinction is important for Prolog when considering the efficiency of searching for solutions. Each possible deduction means an extra branch in the search tree. The bigger the search tree, the longer a computation will take. It is desirable in general to keep the size of the search tree as small as possible.

Having a redundant program may cause, in an extreme case, exponential increase in runtime, in the event of backtracking. If a conjunction of n goals is solved, and each goal has one redundant solution, then in the event of backtracking, the conjunction may generate 2^n solutions, thus possibly changing a polynomial-time program (or even a linear one) to be exponential.

One way for redundancy to occur in Prolog programs is by covering the same case with several rules. Consider the following two clauses defining the relation minimum.

```
minimum(X,Y,X) ← X ≤ Y.
minimum(X,Y,Y) ← Y ≤ X.
```

The query minimum(2,2,M)? with respect to these two clauses has a unique solution M=2, which is given twice; one is redundant.

Careful specification of the cases can avoid the problem. The second clause can be changed to

```
minimum(X,Y,Y) ← Y < X.
```

Now only the first rule covers the case when the two numbers have equal values.

Similar care is necessary with the definition of partition as part of Program 3.22 for quicksort. The programmer must ensure that only one of the recursive clauses for partition covers the case when the number being compared is the same as the number being used to split the list.

Another way redundancy appears in programs is by having too many special cases. Some of these can be motivated by efficiency. An extra fact can be added to Program 3.15 for append, namely, append(Xs,[ ],Xs), to save recursive computations when the second argument is an empty list. In order to remove redundancy, each of the other clauses for append would have to cover only lists with at least one element as their second argument.

We illustrate these points when composing Program 7.2 for the relation merge(Xs,Ys,Zs), which is true if Xs and Ys are lists of integers sorted in ascending order and Zs is the ordered list resulting from merging them.

merge(Xs,Ys,Zs) ←
    Zs is an ordered list of integers obtained from
    merging the ordered lists of integers *Xs* and *Ys*.

```
merge([X|Xs],[Y|Ys],[X|Zs]) ←
    X < Y, merge(Xs,[Y|Ys],Zs).
merge([X|Xs],[Y|Ys],[X,X|Zs]) ←
    X =:= Y, merge(Xs,Ys,Zs).
merge([X|Xs],[Y|Ys],[Y|Zs]) ←
    X > Y, merge([X|Xs],Ys,Zs).
merge([ ],[X|Xs],[X|Xs]).
merge(Xs,[ ],Xs).
```

Program 7.2 Merging ordered lists

There are three separate recursive clauses. They cover the three possible cases: when the head of the first list is less than, equal to, or greater than the head of the second list. We discuss the predicates <, =:=, and > in Chapter 8. Two cases are needed when the elements in either list have been exhausted. Note that we have been careful that the goal `merge([ ],[ ],[ ])` is covered by only one fact, the bottom one.

Redundant computations occur when using `member` to find whether a particular element occurs in a particular list, and there are multiple occurrences of the particular element being checked for in the list. For example, the search tree for the query `member(a,[a,b,a,c])` would have two success nodes.

The redundancy of previous programs was removed by a careful consideration of the logic. In this case, the `member` program is correct. If we want a different behavior, the solution is to compose a modified version of `member`.

Program 7.3 defines the relation `member_check(X,Xs)` which checks whether an element X is a member of a list Xs. The program is a variant of Program 3.12 for `member` that adds a test to the recursive clause. It has the same meaning but, as a Prolog program, it behaves differently. Figure 7.2 shows the difference between the search trees for the identical query to the two programs. The left tree is for the goal `member(a,[a,b,a,c])` with respect to Program 3.12. Note there are two success nodes. The right tree is for the goal `member_check(a,[a,b,a,c])` with respect to Program 7.3. It has only one success node.

member_check(X,Xs) ←
  X is a member of the list *Xs*.

```
member_check(X,[X|Xs]).
member_check(X,[Y|Ys]) ← X ≠ Y, member_check(X,Ys).
```

Program 7.3   Checking for list membership

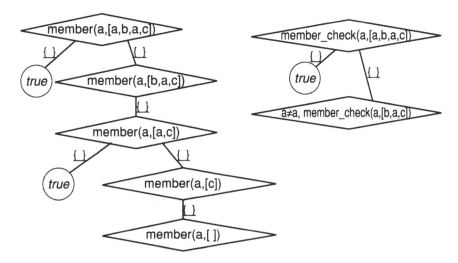

Figure 7.2   Variant search trees

We restrict use of Program 7.3 to queries where both arguments are ground. This is because of the way ≠ is implemented in Prolog, discussed in Section 11.3.

7.5   Recursive Programming in Pure Prolog

Lists are a very useful data structure for many applications written in Prolog. In this section, we revise several logic programs of Sections 3.2 and 3.3 concerned with list processing. The chosen clause and goal orders are explained, and their termination behavior presented. The section also discusses some new examples. Their properties are analyzed, and a reconstruction offered of how they are composed.

select_first (X,Xs,Ys) ←
> *Ys* is the list obtained by removing the
> first occurrence of *X* from the list *Xs*.

```
select_first(X,[X|Xs],Xs).
select_first(X,[Y|Ys],[Y|Zs]) ←
    X ≠ Y, select_first(X,Ys,Zs).
```

Program 7.4   Selecting the first occurrence of an element from a list

Programs 3.12 and 3.15 for member and append, respectively, are correct Prolog programs as written. They are both minimal recursive programs, so there is no issue of goal order. They are in their preferred clause order, the reasons for which have been discussed earlier in this chapter. The termination of the programs was discussed in Section 7.2.

Program 3.19 for select is analogous to the program for member:

```
select(X,[X|Xs],Xs).
select(X,[Y|Ys],[Y|Zs]) ← select(X,Ys,Zs).
```

The analysis of select is similar to the analysis of member. There is no issue of goal order because the program is minimal recursive. The clause order is chosen to reflect the intuitive order of solutions to queries such as select(X,[a,b,c],Xs), namely, {X=a,Xs=[b,c]}, {X=b,Xs=[a,c]}, {X=c,Xs=[a,b]}. The first solution is the result of choosing the first element, and so forth. The program terminates unless both the second and third arguments are incomplete lists.

A variant of select is obtained by adding the test X ≠ Y in the recursive clause. As before, we assume that ≠ is only defined for ground arguments. The variant is given as Program 7.4 defining the relation select_first(X,Xs,Ys). Programs 3.12 and 7.3 defining member and member_check have the same meaning. Program 7.4, in contrast, has a different meaning from Program 3.19. The goal select(a,[a,b,a,c],[a,b,c]) is in the meaning of select, whereas select_first(a,[a,b,a,c],[a,b,c]) is not in the meaning of select_first.

The next program considered is Program 3.20 for permutation. The order of clauses, analogously to the clause order for append, reflects the more likely mode of use:

```
permutation(Xs,[X|Ys]) ← select(X,Xs,Zs), permutation(Zs,Ys).
permutation([ ],[ ]).
```

nonmember(X,Xs) ←

    X is not a member of the list *Xs*.

```
nonmember(X,[Y|Ys]) ← X ≠ Y, nonmember(X,Ys).
nonmember(X,[ ]).
```

Program 7.5   Nonmembership of a list

The goal order and the termination behavior of `permutation` are closely related. Computations of `permutation` goals where the first argument is a complete list will terminate. The query calls `select` with its second argument a complete list, which terminates generating a complete list as its third argument. Thus there is a complete list for the recursive `permutation` goal. If the first argument is an incomplete list, the `permutation` query will not terminate, because it calls a `select` goal that will not terminate. If the order of the goals in the recursive rule for `permutation` is swapped, the second argument of a `permutation` query becomes the significant one for determining termination. If it is an incomplete list, the computation will not terminate; otherwise it will.

A useful predicate using ≠ is `nonmember(X,Ys)` which is true if X is not a member of a list Ys. Declaratively the definition is straightforward: An element is a nonmember of a list if it is not the head and is a nonmember of the tail. The base case is that any element is a nonmember of the empty list. This program is given as Program 7.5.

Because of the use of ≠, `nonmember` is restricted to ground instances. This is sensible intuitively. There are arbitrarily many elements that are not elements of a given list, and also arbitrarily many lists not containing a given element. Thus the behavior of Program 7.5 with respect to these queries is largely irrelevant.

The clause order of `nonmember` follows the convention of the recursive clause preceding the fact. The goal order uses the heuristic of putting the test before the recursive goal.

We reconstruct the composition of two programs concerned with the subset relation. Program 7.6 defines a relation based on Program 3.12 for `member`, and Program 7.7 defines a relation based on Program 3.19 for `select`. Both consider the occurrences of the elements of one list in a second list.

members(Xs,Ys) ←
    Each element of the list *Xs* is a member of the list *Ys*.

```
members([X|Xs],Ys) ← member(X,Ys), members(Xs,Ys).
members([ ],Ys).
```

Program 7.6   Testing for a subset

selects(Xs,Ys) ←
    The list *Xs* is a subset of the list *Ys*.

```
selects([X|Xs],Ys) ← select(X,Ys,Ys1), selects(Xs,Ys1).
selects([ ],Ys).
```

```
select(X,Ys,Zs) ← See Program 3.19.
```

Program 7.7   Testing for a subset

Program 7.6 defining members(Xs,Ys) ignores the multiplicity of elements in the lists. For example, members([b,b],[a,b,c]) is in the meaning of the program. There are two occurrences of b in the first list, but only one in the second.

Program 7.6 is also restrictive with respect to termination. If either the first or the second argument of a members query is an incomplete list, the program will not terminate. The second argument must be a complete list because of the call to member, while the first argument must also be complete, since that is providing the recursive control. The query members(Xs,[1,2,3])? asking for subsets of a given set does not terminate. Since multiple copies of elements are allowed in Xs, there are an infinite number of solutions, and hence the query should not terminate.

Both these limitations are avoided by Program 7.7. The revised relation is selects(Xs,Ys). Goals in the meaning of Program 7.7 have at most as many copies of an element in the first list as appear in the second. Related to this property, Program 7.7 terminates whenever the second argument is a complete list. A query such as selects(Xs,[a,b,c]) has as solution all the subsets of a given set.

We now consider a different example: translating a list of English words, word for word, into a list of French words. The relation is translate(Words,Mots), where Words is a list of English words and Mots the corresponding list of French words. Program 7.8 performs the trans-

translate(Words,Mots) ←
    Mots is a list of French words that is the
    translation of the list of English words *Words*.

```
translate([Word|Words],[Mot|Mots]) ←
    dict(Word,Mot), translate(Words,Mots).
translate([ ],[ ]).
```

```
dict(the,le).          dict(dog,chien).
dict(chases,chasse).   dict(cat,chat).
```

Program 7.8 Translating word for word

lation. It assumes a dictionary of pairs of corresponding English and
French words, the relation scheme being dict(Word,Mot). The translation is very naive, ignoring issues of number, gender, subject-verb
agreement, and so on. Its range is solving a query such as trans-
late([the,dog,chases,the,cat]),X)? with solution X=[le,chien,
chasse,le,chat]. This program can be used in multiple ways. English
sentences can be translated to French, French ones to English, or two
sentences can be checked to see if they are correct mutual translations.

Program 7.8 is a typical program performing *mapping*, that is, converting one list to another by applying some function to each element of the
list. The clause order has the recursive rule(s) first, and the goal order
calls dict first, so as not to be left recursive.

We conclude this section with a discussion of the use of data structures
in Prolog programs. Data structures are handled somewhat differently in
Prolog than in conventional programming languages. Rather than having
a global structure, all parts of which are accessible, the programmer
specifies logical relations between various substructures of the data.

Taking a more procedural view, in order to build and modify structures, the Prolog programmer must pass the necessary fields of the structure to subprocedures. These fields are used and/or acquire values during the computation. Assignment of values to the structures happens via
unification.

Let us look more closely at a generic example — producing a single
output from some given input. Examples are the standard use of append, joining two lists together to get a third, and using Program 7.8 to
translate a list of English words into French. The computation proceeds
recursively. The initial call instantiates the output to be an incomplete

list [X|Xs]. The head X is instantiated by the call to the procedure, often in unification with the head of the clause. The tail Xs is progressively instantiated while solving the recursive call. The structure becomes fully instantiated with the solution of the base case and the termination of the computation.

Consider appending the list [c,d] to the list [a,b], as illustrated in Figure 4.3. The output Ls=[a,b,c,d] is constructed in stages, as Ls=[a|Zs], Zs=[b|Zs1], and finally Zs1=[c,d], when the base fact of append is used. Each recursive call partially instantiates the originally incomplete list. Note that the recursive calls to append do not have access to the list being computed. This is a *top-down construction* of recursive structures and is typical of programming in Prolog.

The top-down construction of recursive data structures has one limitation. Pieces of the global data structure cannot be referred to deeper in the computation. This is illustrated in a program for the relation no_doubles(XXs,Xs), which is true if Xs is a list of all the elements appearing in the list XXs with all duplicates removed.

Consider trying to compose no_doubles top-down. The head of the recursive clause will be

```
no_doubles([X|Xs],...) ←
```

where we need to fill in the blank. The blank is filled by calling no_doubles recursively on Xs with output Ys and integrating Ys with X. If X has not appeared in the output so far, then it should be added, and the blank will be [X|Ys]. If X has appeared, then it should not be added and the blank is Ys. This cannot be easily said. There is no way of knowing what the output is so far.

A program for no_doubles can be composed by thinking differently about the problem. Instead of determining whether an element has already appeared in the output, we can determine whether it will appear. Each element X is checked to see if it appears again in the tail of the list Xs. If X appears, then the result is Ys, the output of the recursive call to no_doubles. If X does not appear, then it is added to the recursive result. This version of no_doubles is given as Program 7.9. It uses Program 7.5 for nonmember.

A problem with Program 7.9 is that the list without duplicates may not have the elements in the desired order. For example, no_doubles([a,b, c,b],Xs)? has the solution Xs=[a,c,b], where the solution Xs=[a,b,c]

no_doubles(Xs,Ys) ←
    Ys is the list obtained by removing
    duplicate elements from the list *Xs*.

```
no_doubles([X|Xs],Ys) ←
    member(X,Xs), no_doubles(Xs,Ys).
no_doubles([X|Xs],[X|Ys]) ←
    nonmember(X,Xs), no_doubles(Xs,Ys).
no_doubles([ ],[ ]).
```

`nonmember(X,Xs)` ← See Program 7.5.

Program 7.9 Removing duplicates from a list

may be preferred. This latter result is possible if the program is rewritten. Each element is deleted from the remainder of the list as it is found. In terms of Program 7.9, this is done by replacing the two recursive calls by a rule

```
no_doubles([X|Xs],[X|Ys]) ←
    delete(X,Xs,Xs1), no_doubles(Xs1,Ys).
```

The new program builds the output top-down. However, it is inefficient for large lists, as will be discussed in Chapter 13. Briefly, each call to *delete* rebuilds the whole structure of the list.

The alternative to building structures top-down is building them bottom-up. A simple example of bottom-up construction of data structures is Program 3.16b for reversing a list:

```
reverse(Xs,Ys) ← reverse(Xs,[ ],Ys).

reverse([X|Xs],Revs,Ys) ← reverse(Xs,[X|Revs],Ys).
reverse([ ],Ys,Ys).
```

An extra argument is added to `reverse/2` and used to accumulate the values of the reversed list as the computation proceeds. This procedure for `reverse` builds the output list bottom-up rather than top-down. In the trace in Figure 7.3 solving the goal `reverse([a,b,c],Xs)`, the successive values of the middle argument of the calls to `reverse/3` `[ ]`, `[a]`, `[b,a]`, and `[c,b,a]` represent the structure being built.

A bottom-up construction of structures allows access to the partial results of the structure during the computation. Consider a relation `nd_reverse(Xs,Ys)` combining the effects of `no_doubles` and `reverse`. The

```
reverse([a,b,c],Xs)
  reverse([a,b,c],[ ],Xs)
    reverse([b,c],[a],Xs)
      reverse([c],[b,a],Xs)
        reverse([ ],[c,b,a],Xs)     Xs=[c,b,a]
          true
```

Figure 7.3 Tracing a reverse computation

nd_reverse(Xs,Ys) ←
        Ys is the reversal of the list obtained by
        removing duplicate elements from the list *Xs*.

```
nd_reverse(Xs,Ys) ← nd_reverse(Xs,[ ],Ys).

nd_reverse([X|Xs],Revs,Ys) ←
    member(X,Revs), nd_reverse(Xs,Revs,Ys).
nd_reverse([X|Xs],Revs,Ys) ←
    nonmember(X,Revs), nd_reverse(Xs,[X|Revs],Ys).
nd_reverse([ ],Ys,Ys).

nonmember(X,Xs) ← See Program 7.5.
```

Program 7.10 Reversing with no duplicates

meaning of nd_reverse is that Ys is a list of elements in Xs in reverse order and with duplicates removed. Analogously to reverse, nd_reverse calls nd_reverse/3 with an extra argument that builds the result bottom-up. This argument is checked to see whether a particular element appears, rather than checking the tail of the list as in Program 7.9 for no_doubles. The program is given as Program 7.10.

We emphasize the characteristics of bottom-up construction illustrated here. One argument behaves as an accumulator of the final data structure. It is augmented in the recursive call, so that the more complex version is in the body of the clause rather than in its head. This contrasts with top-down construction, where the more complex version of the data structure being built is in the head of the clause. Another argument is used solely for returning the output, namely, the final value of the accumulator. It is instantiated with the satisfaction of the base fact. The argument is explicitly carried unchanged in the recursive call.

The technique of adding an accumulator to a program can be generalized. It is used in Chapter 8 discussing Prolog programs for arithmetic.

Accumulators can also be viewed as a special case of incomplete data structures, as is discussed in Chapter 15.

7.5.1 Exercise for Section 7.5

(i)   Write Program 7.9 for `no_doubles`, building the structure bottom-up.

7.6 Background

Prolog was envisaged as a first approximation to logic programming, which would be superseded by further research. Its control has always been acknowledged as being limited and naive. An oft-cited slogan, credited to Kowalski (1979b), is "Algorithm = Logic + Control." The particular control provided in pure Prolog was intended as just one solution on the path to declarative programming and intelligent control. Time has shown otherwise. The control of Prolog has proven adequate for a large range of applications, and the language has not only endured but has blossomed.

Nonetheless, logic programming researchers have investigated other forms of control. For example, LOGLISP (Robinson and Sibert, 1982) has breadth-first traversal of the search tree, and IC-Prolog (Clark and McCabe, 1979) has co-routining. MU-Prolog (Naish, 1986) allows suspension to provide a correct implementation of negation and to prevent the computation from searching infinite branches in certain cases. Wait declarations are generated (Naish, 1985b) that are related to the conditions on termination of Prolog programs given in Section 7.2.

A methodology for systematically constructing simple Prolog programs is given in Deville (1990). Essential to Deville's methods are specifications, a subject touched upon in Section 13.3.

Analysis of Prolog programs, and logic programs more generally, has become a hot topic of research. Most analyses are based on some form of *abstract interpretation*, a topic beyond the scope of this book. The initial work in Prolog can be found in Mellish (1985), and a view of leading research groups can be found in a special issue of the *Journal of Logic Programming* (1993).

Extensive work has also appeared recently on analyzing termination of Prolog programs. A starting place for this topic is Plümer (1990).

8 Arithmetic

The logic programs for performing arithmetic presented in Section 3.1 are very elegant, but they are not practical. Any reasonable computer provides very efficient arithmetic operations directly in hardware, and practical logic programming languages cannot afford to ignore this feature. Computations such as addition take unit time on most computers independent of the size of the addends (as long as they are smaller than some large constant). The recursive logic program for plus (Program 3.3) takes time proportional to the first of the numbers being added. This could be improved by switching to binary or decimal notation but still won't compete with direct execution by dedicated hardware.

Every Prolog implementation reserves some predicate names for system-related procedures. Queries to these predicates, called *system predicates*, are handled by special code in the implementation in contrast to calls to predicates defined by pure Prolog programs. A Prolog implementor should build system predicates that complement pure Prolog naturally and elegantly. Other names for system predicates are *evaluable* predicates, *builtin* predicates, or *bips*, the latter two being referred to in the draft for Standard Prolog.

8.1 System Predicates for Arithmetic

The role of the system predicates for arithmetic introduced in Prolog is to provide an interface to the underlying arithmetic capabilities of the computer in a straightforward way. The price paid for this efficiency is that some of the machine-oriented arithmetic operations are not as general as their logical counterparts. The interface provided is an arithmetic evaluator, which uses the underlying arithmetic facilities of the computer. Standard Prolog has a system predicate `is(Value,Expression)` for arithmetic evaluation. Goals with the predicate `is` are usually written in binary infix form, taking advantage of the operator facility of Prolog, about which we now digress.

Operators are used in order to make programs more readable. People are very flexible and learn to adjust to strange surroundings—they can become accustomed to reading Lisp and Fortran programs, for example. We believe nonetheless that syntax is important; the power of a good notation is well known from mathematics. An integral part of a good syntax for Prolog is the ability to specify and use operators.

Operators, for example $\neq$ and $<$, have already been used in earlier chapters. Standard Prolog provides several operators, which we introduce as they arise. Programmers can also define their own operators using the built-in predicate `op/3`. An explanation of the mechanism for operator declarations, together with a list of pre-defined operators and their precedences is given in Appendix B.

Queries using the arithmetic evaluator provided by Prolog have the form `Value is Expression?`. Queries to the evaluator are interpreted as follows. The arithmetic expression `Expression` is evaluated and the result is unified with `Value`. Once arithmetic evaluation succeeds, the query succeeds or fails depending on whether unification succeeds or fails.

Here are some examples of simple addition, illustrating the use and behavior of the evaluator. The query `(X is 3+5)?` has the solution `X=8`. This is the standard use of the evaluator, instantiating a variable to the value of an arithmetic expression. The query `(8 is 3+5)?` succeeds. Having both arguments to `is` instantiated allows checking the value of an arithmetic expression. `(3+5 is 3+5)?` fails because the left-hand argument, 3+5, does not unify with 8, the result of evaluating the expression.

Standard Prolog specifies a range of arithmetic operations that should be supported by Prolog for both integers and reals represented as floating-point numbers. In particular, the evaluator provides for addition, subtraction, multiplication, and division (+, −, *, /) with their usual mathematical precedences. In this book, we restrict ourselves to integer arithmetic.

What happens if the term to be evaluated is not a valid arithmetic expression? An expression can be invalid for one of two reasons, which should be treated differently, at least conceptually. A term such as 3+x for a constant x cannot be evaluated. In contrast, a term 3+Y for a variable Y may or may not be evaluable, depending on the value of Y.

The semantics of any logic program is completely defined, and, in this sense, logic programs cannot have runtime "errors." For example, the goal X is 3+Y has solutions {X=3,Y=0}. However, when interfacing logic programs to a computer, the limitations of the machine should be taken into account. A runtime error occurs when the machine cannot determine the result of the computation because of insufficient information, that is, uninstantiated variables. This is distinct from goals that simply fail. Extensions to Prolog and other logic languages handle such "errors" by suspending until the values of the concerned variables are known. The execution model of Prolog as introduced does not permit suspension. Instead of simply failure, we say an error condition occurs.

The query (X is 3+x)? fails because the right-hand argument cannot be evaluated as an arithmetic expression. The query (X is 3+Y)? is an example of a query that would succeed if Y were instantiated to an arithmetic expression. Here an error condition should be reported.

A common misconception of beginning Prolog programmers is to regard is as taking the place of assignment as in conventional programming languages. It is tempting to write a goal such as (N is N+1). This is meaningless. The goal fails if N is instantiated, or causes an error if N is a variable.

Further system predicates for arithmetic are the comparison operators. Instead of the logically defined <, ≤ (written =<), >, ≥ (written >=), Prolog directly calls the underlying arithmetic operations. We describe the behavior of <; the others are virtually identical. To answer the query (A < B)?, A and B are evaluated as arithmetic expressions. The two resultant numbers are compared, and the goal succeeds if the result of evaluating A is less than the result of evaluating B. Again, if A or B is not an arithmetic expression, the goal will fail, and an error condition should result if A or B are not ground.

Here are some simple examples. The query (1 < 2)? succeeds, as does the query (3-2 < 2*3+1)?. On the other hand, (2 < 1)? fails, and (N < 1)? generates an error when N is a variable.

Tests for equality and inequality of values of arithmetic expressions are implemented via the builtin predicates =:= and =/=, which evaluate both of their arguments and compare the resulting values.

8.2 Arithmetic Logic Programs Revisited

Performing arithmetic via evaluation rather than logic demands a reconsideration of the logic programs for arithmetic presented in Section 3.1. Calculations can certainly be done more efficiently. For example, finding the minimum of two numbers can use the underlying arithmetic comparison. The program syntactically need not change from Program 3.7. Similarly, the greatest common divisor of two integers can be computed efficiently using the usual Euclidean algorithm, given as Program 8.1. Note that the explicit condition J > 0 is necessary to avoid multiple solutions when J equals 0 and errors from calling mod with a zero argument.

Two features of logic programs for arithmetic are missing from their Prolog counterparts. First, multiple uses of programs are restricted. Suppose we wanted a predicate plus(X,Y,Z) that performed as before, built using is. The obvious definition is

plus(X,Y,Z) ← Z is X+Y.

This works correctly if X and Y are instantiated to integers. However, we cannot use the same program for subtraction with a goal such as plus(3,X,8)?, which raises an error condition. Meta-logical tests are needed if the same program is to be used for both addition and subtraction. We defer this until meta-logical predicates are introduced in Chapter 10.

Programs effectively become specialized for a single use, and it is tricky to understand what happens when the program is used differently.

greatest_common_divisor(X,Y,Z) ←
   Z is the greatest common divisor of the integers *X* and *Y*.

```
greatest_common_divisor(I,0,I).
greatest_common_divisor(I,J,Gcd) ←
    J > 0, R is I mod J, greatest_common_divisor(J,R,Gcd).
```

Program 8.1 Computing the greatest common divisor of two integers

factorial(*N*,*F*) ←
   F is the integer *N* factorial.

```
factorial(N,F) ←
    N > 0, N1 is N-1, factorial(N1,F1), F is N*F1.
factorial(0,1).
```

Program 8.2   Computing the factorial of a number

Program 3.7 for `minimum`, for example, can be used reliably only for finding the minimum of two integers.

The other feature missing from Prolog programs for arithmetic is the recursive structure of numbers. In logic programs, the structure is used to determine which rule applies, and to guarantee termination of computations. Program 8.2 is a Prolog program for computing factorials closely corresponding to Program 3.6. The recursive rule is more clumsy than before. The first argument in the recursive call of `factorial` must be calculated explicitly rather than emerging as a result of unification. Furthermore, the explicit condition determining the applicability of the recursive rule, `N > 0`, must be given. This is to prevent nonterminating computations with goals such as `factorial(-1,N)`? or even `factorial(3,F)`?. Previously, in the logic program, unification with the recursive structure prevented nonterminating computations.

Program 8.2 corresponds to the standard recursive definition of the factorial function. Unlike Program 3.6, the program can be used only to calculate the factorial of a given number. A `factorial` query where the first argument is a variable will cause an error condition.

We must modify the concept of correctness of a Prolog program to accommodate behavior with respect to arithmetic tests. Other system predicates that generate runtime "errors" are handled similarly. A Prolog program is *totally correct* over a domain *D* of goals if for all goals in *D* the computation terminates, does not produce a runtime error, and has the correct meaning. Program 8.2 is totally correct over the domain of goals where the first argument is an integer.

8.2.1   Exercises for Section 8.2

(i)   The *N*th triangular number is the sum of the numbers up to and including *N*. Write a program for the relation `triangle(N,T)`, where T is the Nth triangular number. (Hint: Adapt Program 8.2.)

(ii)   Write a Prolog program for `power(X,N,V)`, where V equals X^N. Which way can it be used? (Hint: Model it on Program 3.5 for `exp`.)

(iii) Write Prolog programs for other logic programs for arithmetic given in the text and exercises in Section 3.1.

(iv)   Write a Prolog program to generate a Huffman encoding tree from a list of symbols and their relative frequencies.

8.3   Transforming Recursion into Iteration

In Prolog there are no iterative constructs as such, and a more general concept, namely recursion, is used to specify both recursive and iterative algorithms. The main advantage of iteration over recursion is efficiency, mostly space efficiency. In the implementation of recursion, a data structure (called a stack frame) has to be maintained for every recursive call that has not terminated yet. A recursive computation involving n recursive procedure calls would require, therefore, space linear in n. On the other hand, an iterative program typically uses only a constant amount of memory, independent of the number of iterations.

Nevertheless, there is a restricted class of recursive programs that corresponds quite closely to conventional iterative programs. Under some conditions, explained further in Section 11.2 on tail recursion optimization, such Prolog programs can be implemented with almost the same efficiency as iterative programs in conventional languages. For this reason, it is preferable to express a relation using an iterative program, if possible. In this section, we show how recursive programs can be made iterative using accumulators.

Recall that a pure Prolog clause is *iterative* if it has one recursive call in the body. We extend this notion to full Prolog, and allow zero or more calls to Prolog system predicates *before* the recursive call. A Prolog procedure is *iterative* if it contains only unit clauses and iterative clauses.

Most simple arithmetic calculations can be implemented by iterative programs.

Factorials can be computed, for example, in a loop where the numbers up to the desired factorial are multiplied together. A procedure in a

```
factorial(N);
    I is 0; T is 1;
    while I < N do
        I is I + 1; T is T * I  end;
    return T.
```

Figure 8.1 Computing factorials iteratively

factorial (*N,F*) ←
    F is the integer *N* factorial.

```
factorial(N,F) ← factorial(0,N,1,F).

factorial(I,N,T,F) ←
    I < N, I1 is I+1, T1 is T*I1, factorial(I1,N,T1,F).
factorial(N,N,F,F).
```

Program 8.3 An iterative *factorial*

Pascal-like language using a *while* loop is given in Figure 8.1. Its iterative behavior can be encoded directly in Prolog with an iterative program.

Prolog does not have storage variables, which can hold intermediate results of the computation and be modified as the computation progresses. Therefore, to implement iterative algorithms, which require the storage of intermediate results, Prolog procedures are augmented with additional arguments, called *accumulators*. Typically, one of the intermediate values constitutes the result of the computation upon termination of the iteration. This value is unified with the result variable using the unit clause of the procedure.

This technique is demonstrated by Program 8.3, which is a Prolog definition of factorial that mirrors the behavior of the *while* loop in Figure 8.1. It uses factorial(I,N,T,F), which is true if F is the value of N factorial, and I and T are the values of the corresponding loop variables before the (I+1)th iteration of the loop.

The basic iterative loop is performed by the iterative procedure factorial/4. Each reduction of a goal using factorial/4 corresponds to an iteration of the *while* loop. The call of factorial/4 by factorial/2 corresponds to the initialization stage. The first argument of factorial/4, the loop counter, is set to 0.

factorial(*N,F*) ←
    F is the integer *N* factorial.

```
factorial(N,F) ← factorial(N,1,F).

factorial(N,T,F) ←
    N > 0, T1 is T*N, N1 is N-1, factorial(N1,T1,F).
factorial(0,F,F).
```

Program 8.4   Another iterative *factorial*

The third argument of `factorial/4` is used as an accumulator of the running value of the product. It is initialized to 1 in the call to `factorial/4` by `factorial/2`. The handling of both accumulators in Program 8.3 is a typical programming technique in Prolog. It is closely related to the use of accumulators in Programs 3.16b and 7.10 for collecting elements in a list.

Accumulators are logical variables rather than locations in memory. The value is passed between iterations, not an address. Since logical variables are "write-once," the updated value, a new logical variable, is passed each time. Stylistically, we use variable names with the suffix 1, for example, `T1` and `I1`, to indicate updated values.

The computation terminates when the counter `I` equals `N`. The rule for `factorial/4` in Program 8.3 no longer applies, and the fact succeeds. With this successful reduction, the value of the factorial is returned. This happens as a result of the unification with the accumulator in the base clause. Note that the logical variable representing the solution, the final argument of `factorial/4`, had to be carried throughout the whole computation to be set on the final call of `factorial`. This passing of values in arguments is characteristic of Prolog programs and might seem strange to the newcomer.

Program 8.3 exactly mirrors the *while* loop for factorial given in Figure 8.1. Another iterative version of `factorial` can be written by counting down from `N` to 0, rather than up from 0 to `N`. The basic program structure remains the same and is given as Program 8.4. There is an initialization call that sets the value of the accumulator, and recursive and base clauses implementing the *while* loop.

Program 8.4 is marginally more efficient than Program 8.3. In general, the fewer arguments a procedure has, the more readable it becomes, and the faster it runs.

between(I,J,K) ←
   K is an integer between the integers *I* and *J* inclusive.
```
between(I,J,I) ← I ≤ J.
between(I,J,K) ← I < J, I1 is I+1, between(I1,J,K).
```

Program 8.5 Generating a range of integers

sumlist (Is,Sum) ←
   Sum is the sum of the list of integers *Is*.
```
sumlist([I|Is],Sum) ← sumlist(Is,IsSum), Sum is I+IsSum.
sumlist([ ],0).
```

Program 8.6a Summing a list of integers

sumlist (Is,Sum) ←
   Sum is the sum of the list of integers *Is*.
```
sumlist(Is,Sum) ← sumlist(Is,0,Sum).

sumlist([I|Is],Temp,Sum) ←
   Temp1 is Temp+I, sumlist(Is,Temp1,Sum).
sumlist([ ],Sum,Sum).
```

Program 8.6b Iterative version of summing a list of integers using an accumulator

A useful iterative predicate is between(I,J,K), which is true if K is an integer between I and J inclusive. It can be used to generate nondeterministically integer values within a range (see Program 8.5). This is useful in generate-and-test programs, explained in Section 14.1, and in failure-driven loops, explained in Section 12.5.

Iterative programs can be written for calculations over lists of integers as well. Consider the relation sumlist(IntegerList,Sum), where Sum is the sum of the integers in the list IntegerList. We present two programs for the relation. Program 8.6a is a recursive formulation. To sum a list of integers, sum the tail, and then add the head. Program 8.6b uses an accumulator to compute the progressive sum precisely as Program 8.3 for factorial uses an accumulator to compute a progressive product. An auxiliary predicate, sumlist/3, is introduced with an extra argument for the accumulator, whose starting value, 0, is set in the initial call to

inner_product (*Xs,Ys,Value*) ←
   Value is the inner product of the vectors
   represented by the lists of integers *Xs* and *Ys.*

```
inner_product([X|Xs],[Y|Ys],IP) ←
    inner_product(Xs,Ys,IP1), IP is X*Y+IP1.
inner_product([ ],[ ],0).
```

Program 8.7a   Computing inner products of vectors

inner_product (*Xs,Ys,Value*) ←
   Value is the inner product of the vectors
   represented by the lists of integers *Xs* and *Ys.*

```
inner_product(Xs,Ys,IP) ← inner_product(Xs,Ys,0,IP).

inner_product([X|Xs],[Y|Ys],Temp,IP) ←
    Temp1 is X*Y+Temp, inner_product(Xs,Ys,Temp1,IP).
inner_product([ ],[ ],IP,IP).
```

Program 8.7b   Computing inner products of vectors iteratively

`sumlist/3`. The sum is passed out in the final call by unification with the base fact. The only difference between Program 8.6b and the iterative versions of `factorial` is that the recursive structure of the list rather than a counter is used to control the iteration.

Let us consider another example. The inner product of two vectors X_i, Y_i is the sum $X_1 \cdot Y_1 + \cdots + X_n \cdot Y_n$. If we represent vectors as lists, it is straightforward to write a program for the relation `inner_product(Xs,Ys,IP)`, where IP is the inner product of Xs and Ys. Programs 8.7a and 8.7b are recursive and iterative versions, respectively. The iterative version of `inner_product` bears the same relation to the recursive `inner_product` that Program 8.6b for `sumlist` bears to Program 8.6a.

Both Programs 8.7a and 8.7b are correct for goals `inner_product(Xs, Ys,Zs)`, where Xs and Ys are lists of integers of the same length. There is a built-in check that the vectors are of the same length. The programs fail if Xs and Ys are of different lengths.

The similarity of the relations between Programs 8.6a and 8.6b, and Programs 8.7a and 8.7b, suggests that one may be automatically transformed to the other. The transformation of recursive programs to equiv-

area(Chain,Area) ←
>   *Area* is the area of the polygon enclosed by the list of points
>   *Chain*, where the coordinates of each point are represented by
>   a pair *(X,Y)* of integers.

```
area([Tuple],0).
area([(X1,Y1),(X2,Y2)|XYs],Area) ←
    area([(X2,Y2)|XYs],Area1),
    Area is (X1*Y2-Y1*X2)/2 + Area1.
```

Program 8.8   Computing the area of polygons

alent iterative programs is an interesting research question. Certainly it
can be done for the simple examples shown here.

The sophistication of a Prolog program depends on the underlying
logical relation it axiomatizes. Here is a very elegant example of a simple
Prolog program solving a complicated problem.

Consider the following problem: Given a closed planar polygon chain
$\{P_1,P_2,...,P_n\}$, compute the area of the enclosed polygon and the orientation of the chain. The area is computed by the line integral

1/2 ∫xdy-ydx,

where the integral is over the polygon chain.

The solution is given in Program 8.8, which defines the relation
`area(Chain,Area)`. Chain is given as a list of tuples, for example,
$[(4,6),(4,2),(0,8),(4,6)]$. The magnitude of Area is the area of the polygon bounded by the chain. The sign of Area is positive if the orientation
of the polygon is counterclockwise, and negative if it is clockwise.

The query `area([(4,6),(4,2),(0,8),(4,6)],Area)?` has the solution Area = -8. The polygon gains opposite orientation by reversing
the order of the tuples. The solution of the query `area([(4,6),(0,8),`
`(4,2),(4,6)],Area)?` is Area = 8.

The program shown is not iterative. Converting it to be iterative is the
subject of Exercise (v) at the end of the section.

An iterative program can be written to find the maximum of a list of
integers. The relation scheme is `maxlist(Xs,Max)`, and the program is
given as Program 8.9. An auxiliary predicate `maxlist(Xs,X,Max)` is used
for the relation that Max is the maximum of X and the elements in the
list Xs. The second argument of `maxlist/3` is initialized to be the first

maxlist(Xs,N) ←
    N is the maximum of the list of integers *Xs.*

```
maxlist([X|Xs],M) ← maxlist(Xs,X,M).

maxlist([X|Xs],Y,M) ← maximum(X,Y,Y1), maxlist(Xs,Y1,M).
maxlist([ ],M,M).

maximum(X,Y,Y) ← X ≤ Y.
maximum(X,Y,X) ← X > Y.
```

Program 8.9 Finding the maximum of a list of integers

length(Xs,N) ←
    Xs is a list of length *N.*

```
length([X|Xs],N) ← N > 0, N1 is N-1, length(Xs,N1).
length([ ],0).
```

Program 8.10 Checking the length of a list

element of the list. Note that the maximum of an empty list is not defined by this program.

The standard recursive program for finding the maximum of a list of integers constitutes a slightly different algorithm. The recursive formulation finds the maximum of the tail of the list and compares it to the head of the list to find the maximum element. In contrast, Program 8.9 keeps track of the running maximum as the list is traversed.

Program 3.17 for finding the length of a list is interesting, affording several ways of translating a logic program into Prolog, each of which has its separate features. One possibility is Program 8.10, which is iterative. Queries length(Xs,N)? are handled correctly if N is a natural number, testing if the length of a list is N, generating a list of N uninstantiated elements, or failing. The program is unsuitable, however, for finding the length of a list with a call such as length([1,2,3],N)?. This query generates an error.

The length of a list can be found using Program 8.11. This program cannot be used, however, to generate a list of N elements. In contrast to Program 8.10, the computation does not terminate if the first argument is an incomplete list. Different programs for length are needed for the different uses.

length(Xs,N) ←
    N is the length of the list *Xs.*

```
length([X|Xs],N) ← length(Xs,N1), N is N1+1.
length([ ],0).
```

Program 8.11   Finding the length of a list

range(M,N,Ns) ←
    Ns is the list of integers between *M* and *N* inclusive.

```
range(M,N,[M|Ns]) ← M < N, M1 is M+1, range(M1,N,Ns).
range(N,N,[N]).
```

Program 8.12   Generating a list of integers in a given range

Similar considerations about the intended use of a program occur when trying to define the relation range(M,N,Ns), where Ns is the list of integers between M and N inclusive. Program 8.12 has a specific use: generating a list of numbers in a desired range. The program is totally correct over all goals range(M,N,Ns) where M and N are instantiated. The program cannot be used, however, to find the upper and lower limits of a range of integers, because of the test M < N. Removing this test would allow the program to answer a query range(M,N,[1,2,3])?, but then it would not terminate for the intended use, solving queries such as range(1,3,Ns)?.

8.3.1   Exercises for Section 8.3

(i)   Write an iterative version for triangle(N,T), posed as Exercise 8.2(i).

(ii)   Write an iterative version for power(X,N,V), posed as Exercise 8.2(ii).

(iii) Rewrite Program 8.5 so that the successive integers are generated in descending order.

(iv)   Write an iterative program for the relation timeslist(Integer-List,Product) computing the product of a list of integers, analogous to Program 8.6b for sumlist.

(v)   Rewrite Program 8.8 for finding the area enclosed by a polygon so that it is iterative.

(vi)   Write a program to find the minimum of a list of integers.

(vii)   Rewrite Program 8.11 for finding the length of a list so that it is iterative. (Hint: Use a counter, as in Program 8.3.)

(viii) Rewrite Program 8.12 so that the range of integers is built bottom-up rather than top-down.

8.4   Background

The examples given in this chapter are small and do not especially exploit Prolog's features. Algorithms that are fundamentally recursive are more interesting in Prolog. A good example of such a program is the Fast Fourier Transform, for which efficient versions have been written in Prolog.

A good place for reading about Huffman encoding trees for Exercise 8.2(iv) is Abelson and Sussman (1985).

A program for transforming recursive programs to iterative ones, which handles the examples in the text, is described in Bloch (1984).

Program 8.8, computing the area of a polygon, was shown to us by Martin Nilsson.

9 Structure Inspection

Standard Prolog has several predicates related to the structure of terms. These predicates are used to recognize the different types of terms, to decompose terms into their functor and arguments, and to create new terms. This chapter discusses the use of predicates related to term structure.

9.1 Type Predicates

Type predicates are unary relations that distinguish between the different types of terms. System predicates exist that test whether a given term is a structure or a constant, and further, whether a constant is an atom, an integer or floating-point. Figure 9.1 gives the four basic type predicates in Standard Prolog, together with their intended meanings.

Each of the basic predicates in Figure 9.1 can be regarded as an infinite table of facts. The predicate integer/1 would consist of a table of integers:

```
integer(0).    integer(1).    integer(-1). ...
```

The predicate atom/1 would consist of a table of atoms in the program:

```
atom(foo).    atom(bar). ...
```

The predicate compound/1 would consist of a table of the function symbols in the program with variable arguments, etc.

```
compound(father(X,Y)).    compound(son(X,Y)). ...
```

```
integer(X) ← X is an integer.
atom(X) ← X is an atom.
real(X) ← X is a floating-point number.
compound(X) ← X is a compound term.
```

Figure 9.1 Basic system type predicates

Other type predicates can be built from the basic type predicates. For example, that a number is either an integer or floating-point can be represented by two clauses:

```
number(X) ← integer(X).
number(X) ← real(X).
```

Standard Prolog includes a predicate number/1 effectively defined in this way. It also includes a predicate atomic(X), which is true if X is an atom or a number. In this book, we prefer to call the predicate constant/1. To run under Standard Prolog, the following clause may be necessary:

```
constant(X) ← atomic(X).
```

To illustrate the use of type predicates, the query integer(3)? would succeed, but the query atom(3)? would fail. One might expect that a call to a type predicate with a variable argument, such as integer(X)?, would generate different integers on backtracking. This is not practical for implementation, however, and we would prefer that such a call report an error condition. In fact, Standard Prolog specifies that the call integer(X)? should fail.

The only terms not covered by the predicates in Figure 9.1 are variables. Prolog does provide system predicates relating to variables. The use of such predicates, however, is conceptually very different from the use of structure inspection predicates described in this chapter. Metalogical predicates (their technical name) are the subject of Chapter 10.

We give an example of the use of a type predicate as part of a program for flattening a list of lists. The relation flatten(Xs,Ys) is true if Ys is the list of elements occurring in the list of lists Xs. The elements of Xs can themselves be lists or elements, so elements can be arbitrarily deeply nested. An example of a goal in the meaning of flatten is flatten([[a],[b,[c,d]],e],[a,b,c,d,e]).

flatten(Xs,Ys) ←
    Ys is a list of the elements of *Xs*.

```
flatten([X|Xs],Ys) ←
    flatten(X,Ys1), flatten(Xs,Ys2), append(Ys1,Ys2,Ys).
flatten(X,[X]) ←
    constant(X), X≠[ ].
flatten([ ],[ ]).
```

Program 9.1a Flattening a list with double recursion

The simplest program for flattening uses double recursion. To flatten an arbitrary list [X|Xs], where X can itself be a list, flatten the head of the list X, flatten the tail of the list Xs, and concatenate the results:

```
flatten([X|Xs],Ys) ←
    flatten(X,Ys1), flatten(Xs,Ys2), append(Ys1,Ys2,Ys).
```

What are the base cases? The empty list is flattened to itself. A type predicate is necessary for the remaining case. The result of flattening a constant is a list containing the constant:

```
flatten(X,[X]) ← constant(X), X≠[ ].
```

The condition constant(X) is necessary to prevent the rule being used when X is a list. The complete program for flatten is given as Program 9.1a.

Program 9.1a, although very clear declaratively, is not the most efficient way of flattening a list. In the worst case, which is a left-linear tree, the program would require a number of reductions whose order is quadratic in the number of elements in the flattened list.

A program for flatten that constructs the flattened list top-down is a little more involved than the doubly recursive version. It uses an auxiliary predicate flatten(Xs,Stack,Ys), where Ys is a flattened list containing the elements in Xs and a stack Stack to keep track of what needs to be flattened. The stack is represented as a list.

The call of flatten/3 by flatten/2 initializes the stack to the empty list. We discuss the cases covered by flatten/3. The general case is flattening a list [X|Xs], where X is itself a list. In this case Xs is pushed onto the stack, and X is recursively flattened. The predicate list(X) is used to recognize a list. It is defined by the fact list([X|Xs]):

flatten(Xs,Ys) ←

    Ys is a list of the elements of *Xs*.

```
flatten(Xs,Ys) ← flatten(Xs,[ ],Ys).

flatten([X|Xs],S,Ys) ←
    list(X), flatten(X,[Xs|S],Ys).
flatten([X|Xs],S,[X|Ys]) ←
    constant(X), X≠[ ], flatten(Xs,S,Ys).
flatten([ ],[X|S],Ys) ←
    flatten(X,S,Ys).
flatten([ ],[ ],[ ]).

list([X|Xs]).
```

Program 9.1b Flattening a list using a stack

```
flatten([X|Xs],S,Ys) ← list(X), flatten(X,[Xs|S],Ys).
```

When the head of the list is a constant other then the empty list, it is added to the output, and the tail of the list is flattened recursively:

```
flatten([X|Xs],S,[X|Ys]) ←
    constant(X),X≠[ ], flatten(Xs,S,Ys).
```

When the end of the list is reached, there are two possibilities, depending on the state of the stack. If the stack is nonempty, the top element is popped, and the flattening continues:

```
flatten([ ],[X|S],Ys) ← flatten(X,S,Ys).
```

If the stack is empty, the computation terminates:

```
flatten([ ],[ ],[ ]).
```

The complete program is given as Program 9.1b.

    A general technique of using a stack is demonstrated in Program 9.1b. The stack is managed by unification. Items are pushed onto the stack by recursive calls to a consed list. Items are popped by unifying with the head of the list and recursive calls to the tail. Another application of stacks appears in Programs 17.3 and 17.4 simulating pushdown automata.

    Note that the stack parameter is an example of an accumulator.

    The reader can verify that the revised program requires a number of reductions linear in the size of the flattened list.

9.1.1 Exercise for Section 9.1

(i)   Rewrite Program 9.1a for `flatten(Xs,Ys)` to use an accumulator
       instead of the call to append, keeping it doubly recursive.

9.2 Accessing Compound Terms

Recognizing a term as compound is one aspect of structure inspection.
Another aspect is providing access to the functor name, arity, and arguments of a compound term. One system predicate for delving into compound terms is `functor(Term,F,Arity)`. This predicate is true if `Term` is
a term whose principal functor has name `F` and arity `Arity`. For example,
`functor(father(haran,lot),father,2)?` succeeds.

The functor predicate can be defined, analogously to the type predicates, by a table of facts of the form `functor(f(X`$_1$`,...,X`$_N$`),f,N)` for
each functor `f` of arity `N`, for example, `functor(father(X,Y),father,`
`2)`, `functor(son(X,Y),son,2)`, ... Standard Prolog considers constants
to be functors of arity 0, with the appropriate extension to the functor
table.

Calls to `functor` can fail for various reasons. A goal such as `func-`
`tor(father(X,Y),son,2)` does not unify with an appropriate fact in
the table. Also, there are type restrictions on the arguments of `func-`
`tor` goals. For example, the third argument of `functor`, the arity of the
term, cannot be an atom or a compound term. If these restrictions are
violated, the goal fails. A distinction can be made between calls that fail
and calls that should give an error because there are infinitely many solutions, such as `functor(X,Y,2)?`.

The predicate `functor` is commonly used in two ways, term decomposition and creation. The first use finds the functor name and arity of a
given term. For example, the query `functor(father(haran,lot),X,Y)?`
has the solution {X=father,Y=2}. The second use builds a term with a
particular functor name and arity. A sample query is `functor(T,father,`
`2)?` with solution T=father(X,Y).

The companion system predicate to `functor` is `arg(N,Term,Arg)`,
which accesses the arguments of a term rather than the functor name.

subterm(Sub,Term) ←
   Sub is a subterm of the ground term *Term*.

```
subterm(Term,Term).
subterm(Sub,Term) ←
    compound(Term), functor(Term,F,N), subterm(N,Sub,Term).

subterm(N,Sub,Term) ←
    N > 1, N1 is N-1, subterm(N1,Sub,Term).
subterm(N,Sub,Term) ←
    arg(N,Term,Arg), subterm(Sub,Arg).
```

Program 9.2 Finding subterms of a term

The goal `arg(N,Term,Arg)` is true if `Arg` is the Nth argument of `Term`. For example, `arg(1,father(haran,lot),haran)` is true.

Like `functor/3`, `arg/3` is commonly used in two ways. The term decomposition use finds a particular argument of a compound term. A query exemplifying this use is `arg(2,father(haran,lot),X)?` with solution `X=lot`. The term creation use instantiates a variable argument of a term. For example, the query `arg(1,father(X,lot),haran)?` succeeds, instantiating `X` to `haran`.

The predicate `arg` is also defined as if there is an infinite table of facts. A fragment of the table is

```
arg(1,father(X,Y),X).      arg(2,father(X,Y),Y).
arg(1,son(X,Y),X).         ... .
```

Calls to `arg` fail if the goal does not unify with the appropriate fact in the table, for example, `arg(1,father(haran,lot),abraham)`. They also fail if the type restrictions are violated, for example, if the first argument is an atom. An error is reported with a goal such as `arg(1,X,Y)`.

Let us consider an example of using `functor` and `arg` to inspect terms. Program 9.2 axiomatizes a relation `subterm(T1,T2)`, which is true if `T1` is a subterm of `T2`. For reasons that will become apparent later, we restrict `T1` and `T2` to be ground.

The first clause of Program 9.2 defining `subterm/2` states that any term is a subterm of itself. The second clause states that `Sub` is a subterm of a compound term `Term` if it is a subterm of one of the arguments. The number of arguments, i.e., the arity of the principal functor of the term, is found and used as a loop counter by the auxiliary subterm/3, which iteratively tests all the arguments.

The first clause of subterm/3 decrements the counter and recursively calls subterm. The second clause covers the case when Sub is a subterm of the Nth argument of the term.

The subterm procedure can be used in two ways: to test whether the first argument is indeed a subterm of the second; and to generate subterms of a given term. Note that the clause order determines the order in which subterms are generated. The order in Program 9.2 gives subterms of the first argument before subterms of the second argument, and so on. Swapping the order of the clauses changes the order of solutions.

Consider the query subterm(a,f(X,Y))?, where the second argument is not ground. Eventually the subgoal subterm(a,X) is reached. This succeeds by the first subterm rule, instantiating X to a. The subgoal also matches the second subterm rule, invoking the goal compound(X), which generates an error. This is undesirable behavior.

We defer the issues arising when performing structure inspection on nonground terms to Chapter 10, where meta-logical predicates with suitable expressive power are introduced. For the rest of this chapter, all programs are assumed to take only ground arguments unless otherwise stated.

Program 9.2 is typical code for programs that perform structure inspection. We look at another example, substituting for a subterm in a term.

The relation scheme for a general program for substituting subterms is substitute(Old,New,OldTerm,NewTerm), where NewTerm is the result of replacing all occurrences of Old in OldTerm by New. Program 9.3 implementing the relation generalizes substituting for elements in a list, posed as Exercise 3.3(i) and the logic program (Program 3.26) substituting for elements in binary trees.

Program 9.3 is a little more complicated than Program 9.2 for subterm but conforms to the same basic pattern. The clauses for substitute/4 cover three different cases. The last, handling compound terms, calls an auxiliary predicate substitute/5, which iteratively substitutes in the subterms. The arity of the principal functor of the term is used as the initial value of a loop counter that is successively decremented to control the iteration. We present a particular example to illustrate

substitute(Old,New,OldTerm,NewTerm) ←
    NewTerm is the result of replacing all occurrences of *Old*
    in *OldTerm* by *New*.

```
substitute(Old,New,Old,New).
substitute(Old,New,Term,Term) ←
    constant(Term), Term ≠ Old.
substitute(Old,New,Term,Term1) ←
    compound(Term),
    functor(Term,F,N),
    functor(Term1,F,N),
    substitute(N,Old,New,Term,Term1).

substitute(N,Old,New,Term,Term1) ←
    N > 0,
    arg(N,Term,Arg),
    substitute(Old,New,Arg,Arg1),
    arg(N,Term1,Arg1),
    N1 is N-1,
    substitute(N1,Old,New,Term,Term1).
substitute(0,Old,New,Term,Term1).
```

Program 9.3   A program for substituting in a term

the interesting points lurking in the code. A trace of the query `substitute(cat,dog,owns(jane,cat),X)`? is given in Figure 9.2.

The query fails to unify with the fact in Program 9.3. The second rule is also not applicable because `owns(jane,cat)` is not a constant.

The third `substitute` rule is applicable to the query. The second call of `functor` is interesting. `Name` and `Arity` have been instantiated to `owns` and 2, respectively, in the previous call of `functor`, so this call builds a term that serves as the answer template to be filled in as the computation progresses. This explicit term building has been achieved by implicit unification in previous Prolog programs. The call to `substitute/5` successively instantiates the arguments of `Term1`. In our example, the second argument of `owns(X1,X2)` is instantiated to `dog`, and then `X1` is instantiated to `jane`.

The two calls to `arg` serve different tasks in `substitute/5`. The first call selects an argument, while the second call of `arg` instantiates an argument.

Substitution in a term is typically done by destructive assignment in conventional languages. Destructive assignment is not possible directly

```
substitute(cat,dog,owns(jane,cat),X)                          X=owns(jane,
    constant(owns(jane,cat))         f                              cat)
substitute(cat,dog,owns(jane,cat),X)
    compound(owns(jane,cat))
    functor(owns(jane,cat),F,N)                               F=owns,N=2
    functor(X,owns,2)                                         X=owns(X1,X2)
    substitute(2,cat,dog,owns(jane,cat),owns(X1,X2))
        2 > 0
        arg(2,owns(jane,cat),Arg)                             Arg=cat
        substitute(cat,dog,cat,Arg1)                          Arg1=dog
        arg(2,owns(X1,X2),dog)                                X2=dog
        N1 is 2-1                                             N1=1
        substitute(1,cat,dog,owns(jane,cat), owns(X1,dog))
            1 > 0
            arg(1,owns(jane,cat),Arg2)                        Arg2=jane
            substitute(cat,dog,jane,Arg3)                     Arg3=jane
                constant(jane)
                jane ≠ cat
            arg(1,owns(X1,dog),jane)                          X1=jane
            N2 is 1-1                                         N2=0
            substitute(0,cat,dog,owns(jane,cat),owns(jane,dog))
                0 > 0                    f
            substitute(0,cat,dog,owns(jane,cat),owns(jane,dog))
                true
                    Output: (X=owns(jane,dog))
```

Figure 9.2   Tracing the substitute predicate

in Prolog. Program 9.3 typifies how Prolog handles changing data structures. The new term is recursively built as the old term is being traversed, by logically relating the corresponding subterms of the terms.

Note that the order of the second `arg` goal and the recursive call to `substitute/5` can be swapped. The modified clause for `substitute/5` is logically equivalent to the previous one and gives the same result in the context of Program 9.3. Procedurally, however, they are radically different.

Another system predicate for structure inspection is a binary operator `=..`, called, for historical reasons, `univ`. The goal `Term =.. List` succeeds if `List` is a list whose head is the functor name of the term `Term` and whose tail is the list of arguments of `Term`. For example, the query `(father(haran,lot) =.. [father,haran,lot])?` succeeds.

subterm(Sub,Term) ←
   Sub is a subterm of the ground term *Term*.

```
subterm(Term,Term).
subterm(Sub,Term) ←
    compound(Term), Term =.. [F|Args], subterm_list(Sub,Args).

subterm_list(Sub,[Arg|Args]) ←
    subterm(Sub,Arg).
subterm_list(Sub,[Arg|Args]) ←
    subterm_list(Sub,Args).
```

Program 9.4   Subterm defined using univ

Like `functor` and `arg`, `univ` has two uses. Either it builds a term given a list, for example, (X =.. [father,haran,lot])? with solution X=father(haran,lot), or it builds a list given a term, for example, (father(haran,lot) =.. Xs)? with solution Xs=[father,haran,lot].

In general, programs written using `functor` and `arg` can also be written with `univ`. Program 9.4 is an alternative definition of `subterm`, equivalent to Program 9.2. As in Program 9.2, an auxiliary predicate investigates the arguments; here it is `subterm_list`. Univ is used to access the list of arguments, `Args`, of which subterms are recursively found by `subterm_list`.

Programs using `univ` to inspect structures are usually simpler. However, programs written with `functor` and `arg` are in general more efficient than those using `univ`, since they avoid building intermediate structures.

A neat use of `univ` is formulating the chain rule for symbolic differentiation. The chain rule states that $d/dx\{f(g(x)\} = d/dg(x)\{f(g(x)\} \times d/dx\{g(x)\}$. In Section 3.5, we noted that this rule could not be expressed as a single clause of a logic program as part of Program 3.30. A Prolog rule encapsulating the chain rule is

```
derivative(F_G_X,X,DF*DG) ←
    F_G_X =.. [F,G_X],
    derivative(F_G_X,G_X,DF),
    derivative(G_X,X,DG).
```

The function F_G_X is split up by `univ` into its function F and argument G_X, checking that F is a function of arity 1 at the same time. The deriva-

Term =.. List ←
    List is a list containing the functor of *Term* followed
    by the arguments of *Term*.

```
Term =.. [F|Args] ←
    functor(Term,F,N), args(0,N,Term,Args).

args(I,N,Term,[Arg|Args]) ←
    I < N, I1 is I+1, arg(I1,Term,Arg), args(I1,N,Term,Args).
args(N,N,Term,[ ]).
```

Program 9.5a Constructing a list corresponding to a term

tive of F with respect to its argument is recursively calculated, as is the
derivative of G_X. These are combined to give the solution.

Univ can be defined in terms of functor and arg. Two different definitions are necessary, however, to cover both building lists from terms
and building terms from lists. One definition does not suffice, because of
errors caused by uninstantiated variables. Other system predicates are
similarly precluded from flexible use.

Program 9.5a behaves correctly for building a list from a term. The
functor F is found by the call to functor, and the arguments are recursively found by the predicate args. The first argument of args is a
counter that counts up, so that the arguments will appear in order in the
final list. If Program 9.5a is called with Term uninstantiated, an error will
be generated because of an incorrect call of functor.

Program 9.5b behaves correctly for constructing a term from a list. The
length of the list is used to determine the number of arguments. The
term template is built by the call to functor, and a different variant of
args is used to fill in the arguments. Program 9.5b results in an error
if used to build a list, because of the goal length(Args,N) being called
with uninstantiated arguments.

9.2.1 Exercises for Section 9.2

(i)   Define a predicate occurrences(Sub,Term,N), true if N is the num-
    ber of occurrences of subterm Sub in Term. Assume that Term is
    ground.

(ii)   Define a predicate position(Subterm,Term,Position), where Po-
    sition is a list of argument positions identifying Subterm within
    Term. For example, the position of X in $2 \cdot \sin(X)$ is [2,1], since

Term =.. List ←

> The functor of *Term* is the first element of the list *List*,
> and its arguments are the rest of *List*'s elements.

```
Term =.. [F|Args] ←
    length(Args,N), functor(Term,F,N), args(Args,Term,1).

args([Arg|Args],Term,N) ←
    arg(N,Term,Arg), N1 is N+1, args(Args,Term,N1).
args([ ],Term,N).

length(Xs,N) ← See Program 8.11.
```

Program 9.5b   Constructing a term corresponding to a list

> sin(X) is the second argument of the binary operator "·", and X
> is the first argument of sin(X). (Hint: Add an extra argument for
> Program 9.2 for subterm, and build the position list top-down.)

(iii)   Rewrite Program 9.5a so that it counts down. (Hint: Use an accumu-
    lator.)

(iv)   Define functor and arg in terms of univ. How can the programs be
    used?

(v)   Rewrite Program 9.3 for substitute so that it uses univ.

9.3   Background

Prolog does not distinguish between object-level and meta-level type
predicates. We have taken a different approach, by defining the type test
predicates to work only on instantiated terms and by treating the meta-
logical test predicates (e.g., var/1, discussed in Section 10.1) separately.
The predicates for accessing and constructing terms, functor, arg, and
=.., originate from the Edinburgh family. The origin of =.. is in the old
Prolog-10 syntax for lists, which used the operator ,.. instead of the
current | in lists, e.g., [a,b,c,..Xs] instead of [a,b,c|Xs]. The .. on
the right-hand side suggested or reminded that the right-hand side of
the equality is a list.

Several of the examples in this section were adapted from O'Keefe
(1983).

Exercises 9.2(i) and 9.2(ii) are used in the equation solver in Chapter 23.

10   Meta-Logical Predicates

A useful extension to the expressive power of logic programs is provided by the meta-logical predicates. These predicates are outside the scope of first-order logic, because they query the state of the proof, treat variables (rather than the terms they denote) as objects of the language, and allow the conversion of data structures to goals.

Meta-logical predicates allow us to overcome two difficulties involving the use of variables encountered in previous chapters. The first difficulty is the behavior of variables in system predicates. For example, evaluating an arithmetic expression with variables gives an error. So does calling type predicates with variable arguments. A consequence of this behavior is to restrict Prolog programs to have a single use in contrast to the multiple uses of the equivalent logic programs.

The second difficulty is the accidental instantiation of variables during structure inspection. Variables need to be considered as specific objects rather than standing for an arbitrary unspecified term. In Chapter 9 we handled the difficulty by restricting inspection to ground terms only.

This chapter has four sections, each for a different class of meta-logical predicates. The first section discusses type predicates that determine whether a term is a variable. The second section discusses term comparison. The next sections describe predicates enabling variables to be manipulated as objects. Finally, a facility is described for converting data into executable goals.

10.1   Meta-Logical Type Predicates

The basic meta-logical type predicate is var(Term), which tests whether a given term is at present an uninstantiated variable. Its behavior is similar to the type predicates discussed in Section 9.1. The query var(Term)? succeeds if Term is a variable and fails if Term is not a variable. For example, var(X)? succeeds, whereas both var(a)? and var([X|Xs])? fail.

The predicate var is an extension to pure Prolog programs. A table cannot be used to give all the variable names. A fact var(X) means that all instances of X are variables rather than that the letter X denotes a variable. Being able to refer to a variable name is outside the scope of first-order logic in general or pure Prolog in particular.

The predicate nonvar(Term) has the opposite behavior to var. The query nonvar(Term)? succeeds if Term is not a variable and fails if Term is a variable.

The meta-logical type predicates can be used to restore some flexibility to programs using system predicates and also to control goal order. We demonstrate this by revising some programs from earlier chapters.

Consider the relation plus(X,Y,Z). Program 10.1 is a version of plus that can be used for subtraction as well as addition. The idea is to check which arguments are instantiated before calling the arithmetic evaluator. For example, the second rule says that if the first and third arguments, X and Z, are not variables, the second argument, Y, can be determined as their difference. Note that if the arguments are not integers, the evaluation will fail, the desired behavior.

The behavior of Program 10.1 resembles that of Program 3.3, the logic program for plus. Further, it does not generate any errors. Nonetheless, it does not have the full flexibility of the recursive logic program: it cannot be used to partition a number into two smaller numbers, for

$plus(X,Y,Z)$ ←
    The sum of the numbers X and Y is Z.

```
plus(X,Y,Z) ← nonvar(X), nonvar(Y), Z is X+Y.
plus(X,Y,Z) ← nonvar(X), nonvar(Z), Y is Z-X.
plus(X,Y,Z) ← nonvar(Y), nonvar(Z), X is Z-Y.
```

Program 10.1   Multiple uses for plus

length(Xs,N) ←
  The list *Xs* has length *N*.

```
length(Xs,N) ← nonvar(Xs), length1(Xs,N).
length(Xs,N) ← var(Xs), nonvar(N), length2(Xs,N).

length1(Xs,N) ← See Program 8.11.
length2(Xs,N) ← See Program 8.10.
```

Program 10.2   A multipurpose length program

example. To partition a number involves generating numbers, for which a different program is needed. This is posed as Exercise (ii) at the end of this section.

Meta-logical goals placed initially in the body of a clause to decide which clause in a procedure should be used are called *meta-logical tests*. Program 10.1 for plus is controlled by meta-logical tests. These tests refer to the current state of the computation. Knowledge of the operational semantics of Prolog is required to understand them.

Standard Prolog in fact endows the type predicates with a meta-logical ability. For example, if X is a variable the goal integer(X) fails, rather than giving an error. This enables the rules from Program 10.1 to be written using the system predicate integer rather than nonvar, for example,

```
plus(X,Y,Z) ← integer(X), integer(Y), Z is X+Y.
```

We feel it is preferable to separate type checking, which is a perfectly legitimate first-order operation, from meta-logical tests, which are a much stronger tool.

Another relation that can have multiple uses restored is length(Xs,N) determining the length N of a list Xs. Separate Prolog programs (8.10 and 8.11) are needed to find the length of a given list and to generate an arbitrary list of a given length, despite the fact that one logic program (3.17) performs both functions. Program 10.2 uses meta-logical tests to define a single length relation. The program has an added virtue over Programs 8.10 and 8.11. It avoids the non-terminating behavior present in both, when both arguments are uninstantiated.

Meta-logical tests can also be used to make the best choice of the goal order of clauses in a program. Section 7.3 discusses the definition of grandparent:

grandparent(*X,Z*) ←
    X is the grandparent of *Z*.

```
grandparent(X,Z) ← nonvar(X), parent(X,Y), parent(Y,Z).
grandparent(X,Z) ← nonvar(Z), parent(Y,Z), parent(X,Y).
```

Program 10.3 A more efficient version of grandparent

ground(*Term*) ←
    Term is a ground term.

```
ground(Term) ←
    nonvar(Term), constant(Term).
ground(Term) ←
    nonvar(Term),
    compound(Term),
    functor(Term,F,N),
    ground(N,Term).

ground(N,Term) ←
    N > 0,
    arg(N,Term,Arg),
    ground(Arg),
    N1 is N-1,
    ground(N1,Term).
ground(0,Term).
```

Program 10.4 Testing if a term is ground

```
grandparent(X,Z) ← parent(X,Y), parent(Y,Z).
```

The optimum goal order changes depending on whether you are searching for the grandchildren of a given grandparent or the grandparents of
a given grandchild. Program 10.3 is a version of grandparent that will
search more efficiently.

    The basic meta-logical type predicates can be used to define more in-
volved meta-logical procedures. Consider a relation ground(Term), which
is true if Term is ground. Program 10.4 gives a definition.

    The program is in the style of the programs for structure inspection
given in Section 9.2, in particular Program 9.3 for substitute. The two
clauses for ground/1 are straightforward. In both cases, a meta-logical
test is used to ensure that no error is generated. The first clause says
that constant terms are ground. The second clause deals with structures.

It calls an auxiliary predicate ground/2, which iteratively checks that all the arguments of the structure are ground.

We look at a more elaborate example of using meta-logical type predicates; writing a unification algorithm. The necessity of Prolog to support unification for matching goals with clause heads means that explicit unification is readily available. Prolog's underlying unification can be used to give a trivial definition

```
unify(X,X).
```

which is the definition of the system predicate =/2, namely, X=X.

Note that this definition depends on Prolog's underlying mechanism for unification, and hence does not enforce the occurs check.

A more explicit definition of Prolog's unification is possible using meta-logical type predicates. Although more cumbersome and less efficient, this definition is useful as a basis for more elaborate unification algorithms. One example is unification with the occurs check, described in Section 10.2. Another example is unification in other logic programming languages that can be embedded in Prolog, such as read-only unification of Concurrent Prolog.

Program 10.5 is an explicit definition of unification. The relation unify(Term1,Term2) is true if Term1 unifies with Term2. The clauses of unify outline the possible cases. The first clause of the program says that two variables unify. The next clause is an encapsulation of the rule for unification that if X is a variable, then X unifies with Y.

The other case bearing discussion in Program 10.5 is unifying two compound terms, as given in the predicate term_unify(X,Y). This predicate checks that the two terms X and Y have the same principal functor and arity, and then checks that all the arguments unify, using unify_args, in a way similar to the structure inspection programs shown before.

10.1.1 Exercises for Section 10.1

(i)   Write a version of Program 8.12 for range that can be used in multiple ways.

(ii)   Write a version of Program 10.1 for plus that partitions a number as well as performing addition and subtraction. (Hint: Use between to generate numbers.)

unify(Term1,Term2) ←
    Term1 and *Term2* are unified, ignoring the occurs check.

```
unify(X,Y) ←
    var(X), var(Y), X=Y.
unify(X,Y) ←
    var(X), nonvar(Y), X=Y.
unify(X,Y) ←
    var(Y), nonvar(X), Y=X.
unify(X,Y) ←
    nonvar(X), nonvar(Y), constant(X), constant(Y), X=Y.
unify(X,Y) ←
    nonvar(X), nonvar(Y), compound(X), compound(Y), term_unify(X,Y).

term_unify(X,Y) ←
    functor(X,F,N), functor(Y,F,N), unify_args(N,X,Y).

unify_args(N,X,Y) ←
    N > 0, unify_arg(N,X,Y), N1 is N-1, unify_args(N1,X,Y).
unify_args(0,X,Y).

unify_arg(N,X,Y) ←
    arg(N,X,ArgX), arg(N,Y,ArgY), unify(ArgX,ArgY).
```

Program 10.5   Unification algorithm

10.2   Comparing Nonground Terms

Consider the problem of extending the explicit unification program, Program 10.5, to handle the occurs check. Recall that the occurs check is part of the formal definition of unification, which requires that a variable not be unified with a term containing this variable. In order to implement it in Prolog, we need to check whether two variables are identical (not just unifiable, as any two variables are). This is a meta-logical test.

Standard Prolog provides a system predicate, ==/2, for this purpose. The query X == Y? succeeds if X and Y are identical constants, identical variables, or both structures whose principal functors have the same name and arity, and recursively X_i == Y_i? succeeds for all corresponding arguments X_i and Y_i of X and Y. The goal fails otherwise. For example, X == 5? fails (in contrast to X = 5?).

There is also a system predicate that has the opposite behavior to ==. The query X \== Y? succeeds unless X and Y are identical terms.

unify(Term1,Term2) ←
    Term1 and *Term2* are unified with the occurs check.

```
unify(X,Y) ←
    var(X), var(Y), X=Y.
unify(X,Y) ←
    var(X), nonvar(Y), not_occurs_in(X,Y), X=Y.
unify(X,Y) ←
    var(Y), nonvar(X), not_occurs_in(Y,X), Y=X.
unify(X,Y) ←
    nonvar(X), nonvar(Y), constant(X), constant(Y), X=Y.
unify(X,Y) ←
    nonvar(X), nonvar(Y), compound(X), compound(Y), term_unify(X,Y).
```

not_occurs_in(X,Term) ←
    The variable *X* does not occur in *Term*.

```
not_occurs_in(X,Y) ←
    var(Y), X \== Y.
not_occurs_in(X,Y) ←
    nonvar(Y), constant(Y).
not_occurs_in(X,Y) ←
    nonvar(Y), compound(Y), functor(Y,F,N), not_occurs_in(N,X,Y).

not_occurs_in(N,X,Y) ←
    N>0, arg(N,Y,Arg), not_occurs_in(X,Arg), N1 is N-1,
        not_occurs_in(N1,X,Y).
not_occurs_in(0,X,Y).

term_unify(X,Y) ← See Program 10.5.
```

Program 10.6 Unification with the occurs check

The predicate \== can be used to define a predicate not_occurs_in(Sub,Term), which is true if Sub does not occur in Term, the relation that is needed in the unification algorithm with the occurs check. not_occurs_in(Sub,Term) is a meta-logical structure inspection predicate. It is used in Program 10.6, a variant of Program 10.5, to implement unification with the occurs check.

Note that the definition of not_occurs_in is not restricted to ground terms. Lifting the restriction on Program 9.2 for subterm is not as easy. Consider the query subterm(X,Y)?. This would succeed using Program 9.2, instantiating X to Y.

We define a meta-logical predicate occurs_in(Sub,Term) that has the desired behavior.

occurs_in(Sub,Term) ←
    Sub is a subterm of the (possibly nonground) term *Term*.

a: Using `==`

```
occurs_in(X,Term) ←
    subterm(Sub,Term), X == Sub.
```

b: Using `freeze`

```
occurs_in(X,Term) ←
    freeze(X,Xf), freeze(Term,Termf), subterm(Xf,Termf).
```

```
subterm(X,Term) ← See Program 9.2.
```

Program 10.7   Occurs in

The predicate `==` allows a definition of `occurs_in` based on Program 9.2 for `subterm`. All the subterms of the given term are generated on backtracking and tested to see if they are identical to the variable. The code is given in Program 10.7a.

As defined, `subterm` works properly only for ground terms. However, by adding meta-logical type tests, as in the definition of `not_occurs_in` in Program 10.6, this problem is easily rectified.

10.3 Variables as Objects

The delicate handling of variables needed to define `occurs_in` in Section 10.2 highlights a deficiency in the expressive power of Prolog. Variables are not easily manipulated. When trying to inspect, create, and reason about terms, variables can be unwittingly instantiated.

A similar concern occurs with Program 9.3 for `substitute`. Consider the goal `substitute(a,b,X,Y)`, substituting a for b in a variable X to give Y. There are two plausible behaviors for `substitute` in this case. Logically there is a solution when X is a and Y is b. This is the solution actually given by Program 9.3, achieved by unification with the base fact `substitute(Old,New,Old,New)`.

In practice, another behavior is usually preferred. The two terms X and a should be considered different, and Y should be instantiated to X. The other base case from Program 9.3,

```
substitute(Old,New,Term,Term) ← constant(Term), Term ≠ Old.
```

covers this behavior. However, the goal would fail because a variable is not a constant.

We can prevent the first (logical) solution by using a meta-logical test to ensure that the term being substituted in is ground. The unification implicit in the head of the clause is then only performed if the test succeeds, and so must be made explicit. The base fact becomes the rule

```
substitute(Old,New,Term,New) ← ground(Term), Old = Term.
```

Treating a variable as different from a constant is handled by a special rule, again relying on a meta-logical test:

```
substitute(Old,New,Var,Var) ← var(Var).
```

Adding the two preceding clauses to Program 9.3 for substitute and adding other meta-logical tests allows the program to handle nonground terms. However, the resultant program is inelegant. It is a mixture of procedural and declarative styles, and it demands of the reader an understanding of Prolog's control flow. To make a medical analogy, the symptoms have been treated (undesirable instantiation of variables), but not the disease (inability to refer to variables as objects). Additional meta-logical primitives are necessary to cure the problem.

The difficulty of mixing object-level and meta-level manipulation of terms stems from a theoretical problem. Strictly speaking, meta-level programs should view object-level variables as constants and be able to refer to them by name.

We suggest two system predicates, freeze(Term,Frozen) and melt(Frozen,Thawed), to allow explicit manipulation of variables. Freezing a term Term makes a copy of the term, Frozen, where all the uninstantiated variables in the term become unique constants. A frozen term looks like, and can be manipulated as, a ground term.

Frozen variables are regarded as ground atoms during unification. Two frozen variables unify if and only if they are identical. Similarly, if a frozen term and an uninstantiated variable are unified, they become an identical frozen term. The behavior of frozen variables in system predicates is the behavior of the constants. For example, arithmetic evaluation involving a frozen variable will fail.

The predicate freeze is meta-logical in a similar sense to var. It enables the state of a term during the computation to be manipulated directly.

The predicate `freeze` allows an alternative definition of `occurs_in` from the one given in Section 10.2. The idea is to freeze the term so that variables become ground objects. This makes Program 9.2 for `subterm`, which works correctly for ground terms, applicable. The definition is given as Program 10.7b.

Freezing gives the ability to tell whether two terms are identical. Two frozen terms, X and Y, unify if and only if their unfrozen versions are identical, that is, X `==` Y. This property is essential to the correct behavior of Program 10.7b.

The difference between a frozen term and a ground term is that the frozen term can be "melted back" into a nonground term. The companion predicate to `freeze` is `melt(Frozen,Thawed)`. The goal `melt(X,Y)` produces a copy Y of the term X where frozen variables become regular Prolog variables. Any instantiations to the variables in X during the time when X has been frozen are taken into account when melting Y.

The combination of `freeze` and `melt` allows us to write a variant of `substitute`, `non_ground_substitute`, where variables are not accidentally instantiated. The procedural view of `non_ground_substitute` is as follows. The term is frozen before substitution; the substitution is performed on the frozen term using the version of `substitute`, which works correctly on ground terms; and then the new term is melted:

```
non_ground_substitute(X,Y,Old,New) ←
    freeze(Old,Old1), substitute(X,Y,Old1,Old2),
    melt(Old2,New).
```

The frozen term can also be used as a template for making copies. The system predicate `melt_new(Frozen,Term)` makes a copy Term of the term Frozen, where frozen variables are replaced by new variables.

One use of `melt_new` is to copy a term. The predicate `copy(Term,Copy)` produces a new copy of a term. It can be defined in a single rule:

```
copy(Term,Copy) ← freeze(Term,Frozen), melt_new(Frozen,Copy).
```

Standard Prolog provides the predicate `copy_term(Term1,Term2)` for copying terms. It is true if and only if Term2 unifies with a term T that is a copy of Term1 except that all the variables of Term1 have been replaced by fresh variables.

Unfortunately, the predicates `freeze/2`, `melt/2`, and `melt_new/2` as described here are not present in existing Prolog implementations. They

numbervars(Term,N1,N2) ←
  The variables in *Term* are numbered from *N1* to *N2 − 1*.

```
numbervars('$VAR'(N),N,N1) ←
    N1 is N+1.
numbervars(Term,N,N) ←
    nonvar(Term), constant(Term).
numbervars(Term,N1,N2) ←
    nonvar(Term), compound(Term),
    functor(Term,Name,N),
    numbervars(0,N,Term,N1,N2).

numbervars(N,N,Term,N1,N1).
numbervars(I,N,Term,N1,N3) ←
    I < N
    I1 is I+1,
    arg(I1,Term,Arg),
    numbervars(Arg,N1,N2),
    numbervars(I1,N,Term,N2,N3).
```

Program 10.8 Numbering the variables in a term

will be useful nonetheless in expressing and explaining the behavior of extra-logical predicates, discussed in Chapter 12.

A useful approximation to freeze is the predicate numbervars(Term, N1,N2), which is provided in many Edinburgh Prolog libraries. A call to the predicate is true if the variables appearing in Term can be numbered from N1 to N2-1. The effect of the call is to replace each variable in the term by a term of the form '$VAR'(N) where N lies between N1 and N2. For example, the goal numbervars(append([X|Xs],Ys,[X|Zs]),1,N) succeeds with the substitution {X='$VAR(1)', Xs='$VAR'(2), Ys='$VAR' (3), Zs='$VAR'(4), N=5}. Code implementing numbervars is given as Program 10.8. It is in the same style as the structure inspection utilities given in Chapter 9.

10.4 The Meta-Variable Facility

A feature of Prolog is the equivalence of programs and data — both can be represented as logical terms. In order for this to be exploited, programs need to be treated as data, and data must be transformed into programs. In this section, we mention a facility that allows a term to be

$X ; Y \leftarrow$
    X or Y.

```
X ; Y ← X.
X ; Y ← Y.
```

Program 10.9 Logical disjunction

converted into a goal. The predicate `call(X)` calls the goal X for Prolog
to solve.

In practice, most Prolog implementations relax the restriction we have
imposed on logic programs, that the goals in the body of a clause must
be nonvariable terms. The *meta-variable facility* allows a variable to appear as a goal in a conjunctive goal or in the body of the clause. During
the computation, by the time it is called, the variable must be instantiated to a term. It will then be treated as usual. If the variable is not
instantiated when it comes to be called, an error is reported. The meta-
variable facility is a syntactic convenience for the system predicate `call`.

The meta-variable facility greatly facilitates meta-programming, in particular the construction of meta-interpreters and shells. Two important
examples to be discussed in later chapters are Program 12.6, a simple
shell, and Program 17.5, a meta-interpreter. It is also essential for defining negation (Program 11.6) and allowing the definition of higher-order
predicates to be described in Section 16.3.

We give an example of using the meta-variable facility with a definition
of logical disjunction, denoted by the binary infix operator ";". The goal
(X;Y) is true if X or Y is true. The definition is given as Program 10.9.

10.5 Background

An excellent discussion of meta-logical system predicates in DEC-10 Prolog, and how they are used, can be found in O'Keefe (1983).

The unification procedure for Concurrent Prolog, written in Prolog, is
in Shapiro (1983b).

The difficulty in correctly manipulating object-level variables in Prolog
at the meta-level has been raised by several people. The discussion first
extensive discussion is in Nakashima et al. (1984), where the predicates
`freeze`, `melt`, and `melt_new` are introduced. The name `freeze` was a little

unfortunate, as it has been suggested for other additions to pure Prolog. Most notable is Colmerauer's `geler` (Colmerauer, 1982a), which allows the suspension of a goal and gives the programmer more control over goal order. This predicate is provided by Sicstus Prolog as `freeze`. The discussion of Nakashima and colleagues, although publicized in the first editon of this book, was largely ignored, to be revived by Barklund (1989) musing over "What is a variable in Prolog?" and by attempts to do meta-programming in constraint logic programming languages, for example, Heintze et al. (1989) and Lim and Stuckey (1990).

The Gödel project (Hill and Lloyd, 1993) has advocated replacing Prolog by a language that facilitates explicit manipulation of variables at a meta-level. In Lloyd and Hill (1989), the terms ground and nonground representation are used. Prolog uses a nonground representation, and adding `freeze` and `numbervars` allows a ground representation.

11 Cuts and Negation

Prolog provides a single system predicate, called *cut*, for affecting the procedural behavior of programs. Its main function is to reduce the search space of Prolog computations by dynamically pruning the search tree. The cut can be used to prevent Prolog from following fruitless computation paths that the programmer knows could not produce solutions.

The cut can also be used, inadvertently or purposefully, to prune computation paths that do contain solutions. By doing so, a weak form of negation can be effected.

The use of cut is controversial. Many of its uses can only be interpreted procedurally, in contrast to the declarative style of programming we encourage. Used sparingly, however, it can improve the efficiency of programs without compromising their clarity.

11.1 Green Cuts: Expressing Determinism

Consider the program merge(Xs,Ys,Zs) (Program 11.1), which merges two sorted lists of numbers Xs and Ys into the combined sorted list Zs.

Merging two lists of sorted numbers is a deterministic operation. Only one of the five merge clauses applies for each nontrivial goal in a given computation. To be more specific, when comparing two numbers X and Y, for example, only one of the three tests X < Y, X =:= Y, and X > Y can be true. Once a test succeeds, there is no possibility that any other test will succeed.

merge(Xs,Ys,Zs) ←
    Zs is an ordered list of integers obtained from merging
    the ordered lists of integers *Xs* and *Ys*.

```
merge([X|Xs],[Y|Ys],[X|Zs]) ← X < Y, merge(Xs,[Y|Ys],Zs).
merge([X|Xs],[Y|Ys],[X,Y|Zs]) ← X=:=Y, merge(Xs,Ys,Zs).

merge([X|Xs],[Y|Ys],[Y|Zs]) ← X > Y, merge([X|Xs],Ys,Zs).
merge(Xs,[ ],Xs).
merge([ ],Ys,Ys).
```

Program 11.1   Merging ordered lists

The cut, denoted !, can be used to express the mutually exclusive
nature of the tests. It is placed after the arithmetic tests. For example,
the first merge clause is written

```
merge([X|Xs],[Y|Ys],[X|Zs]) ← X < Y, !, merge(Xs,[Y |Ys],Zs).
```

Operationally, the cut is handled as follows.
*The goal succeeds and commits Prolog to all the choices made since the
parent goal was unified with the head of the clause the cut occurs in.*

Although this definition is complete and precise, its ramifications and
implications are not always intuitively clear or apparent.

Misunderstandings concerning the effects of a cut are a major source
for bugs for experienced and inexperienced Prolog programmers alike.
The misunderstandings fall into two categories: assuming that the cut
prunes computation paths it does not, and assuming that it does not
prune solutions where it actually does.

The following implications may help clarify the foregoing terse definition:

- First, a cut prunes all clauses below it. A goal *p* unified with a clause
  containing a cut that succeeded would not be able to produce solutions
  using clauses that occur below that clause.

- Second, a cut prunes all alternative solutions to the conjunction of
  goals that appear to its left in the clause. For example, a conjunctive
  goal followed by a cut will produce at most one solution.

- On the other hand, the cut does not affect the goals to its right in
  the clause. They can produce more than one solution in the event of
  backtracking. However, once this conjunction fails, the search proceeds

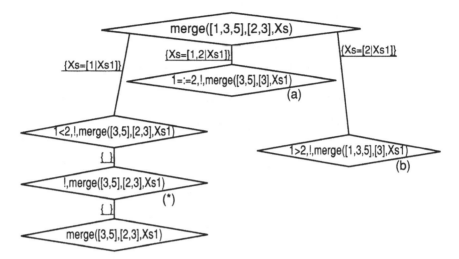

Figure 11.1   The effect of cut

from the last alternative prior to the choice of the clause containing the cut.

Let us consider a fragment of the search tree of the query merge([1,3, 5],[2,3],Xs)? with respect to Program 11.2, a version of merge with cuts added. The fragment is given as Figure 11.1. The query is first reduced to the conjunctive query 1 < 2,!,merge([3,5],[2,3],Xs1)?; the goal 1 < 2 is successfully solved, reaching the node marked (∗) in the search tree. The effect of executing the cut is to prune the branches marked (a) and (b).

Continuing discussion of Program 11.2, the placement of the cuts in the three recursive clauses of merge is after the test.[1] The two base cases of merge are also deterministic. The correct clause is chosen by unification, and thus a cut is placed as the first goal (and in fact the only goal) in the body of the rule. Note that the cuts eliminate the redundant solution to the goal merge([ ],[ ],Xs). Previously, this was accomplished more awkwardly, by specifying that Xs (or Ys) had at least one element.

---

1. The cut after the third merge clause is unnecessary in any practical sense. Procedurally, it will not cause any reduction of search. But it makes the program more symmetric, and like the old joke says about chicken soup, it doesn't hurt.

merge(Xs,Ys,Zs) ←
    Zs is an ordered list of integers obtained from merging
    the ordered lists of integers *Xs* and *Ys*.

```
merge([X|Xs],[Y|Ys],[X|Zs]) ←
    X < Y, !, merge(Xs,[Y|Ys],Zs).
merge([X|Xs],[Y|Ys],[X,Y|Zs]) ←
    X=:=Y, !, merge(Xs,Ys,Zs).
merge([X|Xs],[Y|Ys],[Y|Zs]) ←
    X > Y, !, merge([X|Xs],Ys,Zs).
merge(Xs,[ ],Xs) ← !.
merge([ ],Ys,Ys) ← !.
```

Program 11.2   Merging with cuts

We restate the effect of a cut in a general clause $C = A \leftarrow B_1,\ldots,B_k,!,$ $B_{k+2},\ldots,B_n$ in a procedure defining A. If the current goal G unifies with the head of C, and $B_1,\ldots,B_k$ further succeed, the cut has the following effect. The program is committed to the choice of C for reducing G; any alternative clauses for A that might unify with G are ignored. Further, should B_i fail for $i > k + 1$, backtracking goes back only as far as the !. Other choices remaining in the computation of B_i, $i \leq k$, are pruned from the search tree. If backtracking actually reaches the cut, then the cut fails, and the search proceeds from the last choice made before the choice of G to reduce C.

The cuts used in the merge program express that merge is deterministic. That is, only one of the clauses can be used successfully for proving an applicable goal. The cut commits the computation to a single clause, once the computation has progressed enough to determine that this is the only clause to be used.

The information conveyed by the cut prunes the search tree, and hence shortens the path traversed by Prolog, which reduces the computation time. In practice, using cuts in a program is even more important for saving space. Intuitively, knowing that a computation is deterministic means that less information needs to be kept for use in the event of backtracking. This can be exploited by Prolog implementations with tail recursion optimization, discussed in Section 11.2.

Let us consider some other examples. Cuts can be added to the program for computing the minimum of two numbers (Program 3.7) in precisely the same way as for merge. Once an arithmetic test succeeds, there

minimum(X,Y,Min) ←
   Min is the minimum of the numbers *X* and *Y*.

```
minimum(X,Y,X) ← X≤Y, !.
minimum(X,Y,Y) ← X > Y, !.
```

Program 11.3 minimum with cuts

polynomial(Term,X) ←
   Term is a polynomial in *X*.

```
polynomial(X,X) ← !.
polynomial(Term,X) ←
   constant(Term), !.
polynomial(Term1+Term2,X) ←
   !, polynomial(Term1,X), polynomial(Term2,X).
polynomial(Term1-Term2,X) ←
   !, polynomial(Term1,X), polynomial(Term2,X).
polynomial(Term1*Term2,X) ←
   !, polynomial(Term1,X), polynomial(Term2,X).
polynomial(Term1/Term2,X) ←
   !, polynomial(Term1,X), constant(Term2).
polynomial(Term↑N,X) ←
   !, integer(N), N ≥ 0, polynomial(Term,X).
```

Program 11.4 Recognizing polynomials

is no possibility for the other test succeeding. Program 11.3 is the appropriately modified version of minimum.

A more substantial example where cuts can be added to indicate that a program is deterministic is provided by Program 3.29. The program defines the relation polynomial(Term,X) for recognizing if Term is a polynomial in X. A typical rule is

```
polynomial(Term1+Term2,X)←
    polynomial(Term1,X), polynomial(Term2,X).
```

Once the term being tested has been recognized as a sum (by unifying with the head of the rule), it is known that none of the other polynomial rules will be applicable. Program 11.4 gives the complete polynomial program with cuts added. The result is a deterministic program that has a mixture of cuts after conditions and cuts after unification.

When discussing the Prolog programs for arithmetic, which use the underlying arithmetic capabilities of the computer rather than a recursive logic program, we argued that the increased efficiency is often achieved at the price of flexibility. The logic programs lost their multiple uses when expressed as Prolog programs. Prolog programs with cuts also have less flexibility than their cut-free equivalents. This is not a problem if the intended use of a program is one-way to begin with, as is often the case.

The examples so far have demonstrated pruning useless alternatives for the parent goal. We give an example where cuts greatly aid efficiency by removing redundant computations of sibling goals. Consider the recursive clause of an interchange sort program:

```
sort(Xs,Ys) ←
    append(As,[X,Y|Bs],Xs),
    X > Y,
    append(As,[Y,X|Bs],Xs1),
    sort(Xs1,Ys).
```

The program searches for a pair of adjacent elements that are out of order, swaps them, and continues until the list is ordered. The base clause is

```
sort(Xs,Xs) ← ordered(Xs).
```

Consider a goal sort([3,2,1],Xs). This is sorted by swapping 3 and 2, then 3 and 1, and finally 2 and 1 to produce the ordered list [1,2,3]. It could also be sorted by first swapping 2 and 1, then swapping 3 and 1, and finally swapping 3 and 2, to arrive at the same solution. We know there is only one sorted list. Consequently there is no point in searching for another alternative once an interchange is made. This can be indicated by placing the cut after the test X > Y. This is the earliest it is known that an interchange is necessary. The interchange sort program with cut is given as Program 11.5.

The addition of cuts to the programs described in this section does not alter their declarative meaning; all solutions to a given query are found. Conversely, removing the cuts should similarly not affect the meaning of the program. Unfortunately, this is not always the case. A distinction has been made in the literature between *green cuts* and *red cuts*. Green cuts have been considered in this section. The addition and removal of green cuts from a program do not affect the program's meaning. Green cuts

sort (*Xs*, *Ys*) ←
   Ys is an ordered permutation of the list of integers *Xs*.

```
sort(Xs,Ys) ←
    append(As,[X,Y|Bs],Xs),
    X > Y,
    !,
    append(As,[Y,X|Bs],Xs1),
    sort(Xs1,Ys).
sort(Xs,Xs) ←
    ordered(Xs),
    !.
```

```
ordered(Xs) ← See Program 3.20.
```

Program 11.5 Interchange sort

prune only computation paths that do not lead to new solutions. Cuts that are not green are *red*.

The cut interacts with system predicates such as `call` and `;`, introduced in Chapter 10, and with predicates such as `not`, introduced later in this chapter. The question is what *scope* should cut have, that is, which choice points should be affected. Since such tricky uses of cut are not presented or advocated in this book, we defer discussion of the scope of cut until Chapter 17 on interpreters.

Exercises for Section 11.1

(i)   Add cuts to the partition program from `quicksort`, Program 3.22.

(ii)   Add cuts to the differentiation program, Program 3.30.

(iii)   Add cuts to the insertion sort program, Program 3.21.

11.2   Tail Recursion Optimization

As noted in Section 8.3, the main difference from a performance point of view between recursion and iteration is that recursion requires, in general, space linear in the number of recursive calls to execute, whereas iteration can be executed in constant space, independent of the number of iterations performed.

Recursive programs defined free of side effects might be considered more elegant and pleasing than their iterative counterparts defined in terms of iteration and local variables. However, an order of magnitude in space complexity seems an unacceptable price for such aesthetic pleasures. Fortunately, there is a class of recursive programs, precisely those that can be translated directly into iterative ones, that can be executed in constant space.

The implementation technique that achieves this space saving is called *tail recursion optimization*, or more precisely, *last call optimization*. Intuitively, the idea of tail recursion optimization is to execute a recursive program as if it were an iterative one.

Consider the reduction of a goal A using the clause

$$A' \leftarrow B_1, B_2, \ldots, B_n.$$

with most general unifier θ. The optimization is potentially applicable to the last call in the body of a clause, B_n. It reuses the area allocated for the parent goal A for the new goal B_n.

The key precondition for this optimization to apply is that there be no choice points left from the time the parent goal A reduced to this clause to the time the last goal B_n is reduced. In other words, A has no alternative clauses for reduction left, and there are no choice points left in the computation of goals to the left of B_n, namely, the computation of the conjunctive goal $(B_1, B_2, \ldots, B_{n-1})\theta$, was deterministic.

Most implementations of tail recursion optimization can recognize to a limited extent at runtime whether this condition occurs, by comparing backtracking-related information associated with the goals B_n and A. Another implementation technique, clause indexing, also interacts closely with tail recursion optimization and enhances the ability of the implementation to detect that this precondition occurs. Indexing performs some analysis of the goal, to detect which clauses are applicable for reduction, before actually attempting to do the unifications. Typically, indexing is done on the type and value of the first argument of the goal.

Consider the append program:

```
append([X|Xs],Ys,[X|Zs]) ← append(Xs,Ys,Zs).
append([ ],Ys,Ys).
```

If it is used to append two complete lists, then by the time the recursive append goal is executed, the preconditions for tail recursion optimization hold. No other clause is applicable to the parent goal (if the first argument unifies with [X|Xs], it certainly won't unify with [ ], since we assumed that the first argument is a complete list). There are no other goals in the body besides append, so the second precondition holds vacuously.

However, for the implementation to know that the optimization applies, it needs to know that the second clause, although not tried yet, is not applicable. Here indexing comes into play. By analyzing the first argument of append, it is possible to know that the second clause would fail even before trying it, and to apply the optimization in the recursive call to append.

Not all implementations provide indexing, and not all cases of determinism can be detected by the indexing mechanisms available. Therefore it is in the interest of the programmer to help an implementation that supports tail recursion optimization to recognize that the preconditions for applying it hold.

There is a sledgehammer technique for doing so: Add a cut before the last goal of a clause, in which tail recursion optimization should always apply, as in

$$A_1 \leftarrow B_1, B_2, \ldots, !, B_n.$$

This cut prunes both alternative clauses left for the parent goal A, and any alternatives left for the computation of $(B_1, B_2, \ldots, B_{n-1})\theta$.

In general, it is not possible to answer if such a cut is green or red, and the programmer's judgment should be applied.

It should be noted that the effect of tail recursion optimization is enhanced greatly when accompanied with a good garbage collector. Stated negatively, the optimization is not very significant without garbage collection. The reason is that most tail recursive programs generate some data structures on each iteration. Most of these structures are temporary and can be reclaimed (see, for instance, the editor in Program 12.5). Together with a garbage collector, such programs can run, in principle, forever. Without it, although the stack space they consume would remain constant, the space allocated to the uncollected temporary data structures would overflow.

not X ←
   X is not provable.

```
not X ← X, !, fail.
not X.
```

Program 11.6 Negation as failure

11.3 Negation

The cut can be used to implement a version of negation as failure. Program 11.6 defines a predicate not(Goal), which succeeds if Goal fails. As well as using cut, the program uses the meta-variable facility described in Chapter 10, and a system predicate fail that always fails.

Standard Prolog provides a predicate fail_if(Goal), which has the same behavior as not/1. Other Prologs provide the same predicate under the name \+/1. The rationale for not calling the system predicate not is that the predicate does not implement true logical negation, and it is misleading to label it as such. We believe that the user easily learns how the predicate differs from true negation, as we will explain, and programmers are helped rather than misled by the name.

Let us consider the behavior of Program 11.6 in answering the query not G? The first rule applies, and G is called using the meta-variable facility. If G succeeds, the cut is encountered. The computation is then committed to the first rule, and not G fails. If the call to G fails, then the second rule of Program 11.6 is used, which succeeds. Thus not G fails if G succeeds and succeeds if G fails.

The rule order is essential for Program 11.6 to behave as intended. This introduces a new, not entirely desirable, dimension to Prolog programs. Previously, changing the rule order only changed the order of solutions. Now the meaning of the program can change. Procedures where the rule order is critical in this sense must be considered as a single unit rather than as a collection of individual clauses.

The termination of a goal not G depends on the termination of G. If G terminates, so does not G. If G does not terminate, then not G may or may not terminate depending on whether a success node is found in the search tree before an infinite branch. Consider the following nonterminating program:

```
married(abraham,sarah).
married(X,Y) ← married(Y,X).
```

The query not married(abraham,sarah)? terminates (with failure) even though married(abraham,sarah)? does not terminate.

Program 11.6 is incomplete as an implementation of negation by failure. The incompleteness arises from Prolog's incompleteness in realizing the computation model of logic programs. The definition of negation as failure for logic programs is in terms of a finitely failed search tree. A Prolog computation is not guaranteed to find one, even if it exists. There are goals that could fail by negation as failure, that do not terminate under Prolog's computation rule. For example, the query not(p(X),q(X))? does not terminate with respect to the program

```
p(s(X)) ← p(X).
q(a).
```

The query would succeed if the q(X) goal were selected first, since that gives a finitely failed search tree.

The incorrectness of Program 11.6 stems from the order of traversal of the search tree and arises when not is used in conjunction with other goals. Consider using not to define a relationship unmarried_student(X) for someone who is both not married and a student, as in the following program:

```
unmarried_student(X) ← not married(X), student(X).
student(bill).
married(joe).
```

The query unmarried_student(X)? fails with respect to the preceding data, ignoring that X=bill is a solution logically implied by the rule and two facts. The failure occurs in the goal not married(X), since there is a solution X=joe. The problem can be avoided here by swapping the order of the goals in the body of the rule.

A similar example is the query not (X=1), X=2?, which fails although there is a solution X=2.

The implementation of negation as failure is not guaranteed to work correctly for nonground goals, as the foregoing examples demonstrate. In most implementations of Prolog, it is the responsibility of the programmer to ensure that negated goals are ground before they are solved.

variants(Term1,Term2) ←
    Term1 and *Term2* are variants.

```
variants(Term1,Term2) ←
    verify((numbervars(Term1,0,N),
    numbervars(Term2,0,N),
    Term1=Term2)).
```

verify(Goal) ←
    Goal has a true instance. Verifying this is not done
    constructively, so variables are not instantiated in the process.

```
verify(Goal) ← not(not Goal).
```

`numbervars(Term,N,N1)` ← See Program 10.8.

Program 11.7   Testing if terms are variants

This can be done either by a static analysis of the program or by a run-time check, using the predicate ground defined in Program 10.4.

The predicate not is very useful. It allows us to define interesting concepts. For example, consider a predicate `disjoint(Xs,Ys)`, true if two lists Xs and Ys have no elements in common. It can be defined as

```
disjoint(Xs,Ys) ← not (member(Z,Xs), member(Z,Ys)).
```

Many other examples of using not will appear in the programs throughout this book.

An interesting property of `not(Goal)` is that it never instantiates the arguments in Goal. This is because of the explicit failure after the call to Goal succeeds, which undoes any bindings made. This property can be exploited to define a procedure `verify(Goal)`, given as part of Program 11.7, which determines whether a goal is true without affecting the current state of the variable bindings. Double negation provides the means.

We note in passing that negation as implemented in Prolog shares a feature with negation in natural language. A doubly negated statement is not the same as the equivalent affirmative statement.

The program for verify can be used in conjunction with Program 10.8 for numbervars to define a notion of equality intermediate between unifiability provided by =/2 and syntactic equality provided by ==/2. The predicate `variants(X,Y)` defined in Program 11.7 is true if two terms X and Y are variants. Recall from Chapter 4 that two terms are variants

$X \neq Y \leftarrow$
    X and Y are not unifiable.

```
X ≠ X ← !, fail.
X ≠ Y.
```

Program 11.8 Implementing $\neq$

if they are instances of each other. This can be achieved with the following trick, implemented in Program 11.7. Instantiate the variables using numbervars, test whether the terms unify, and undo the instantiation.

The three forms of comparison =/2, variant/2, and ==/2 are progressively stronger, with unifiability being the weakest and most general. Identical terms are variants, and variant terms are unifiable. The distinction between the different comparisons vanishes for ground terms; for ground terms all three comparisons return the same results.

The conjunction of cut and fail used in the first clause of not in Program 11.6 is known as the *cut-fail combination*. The cut-fail combination is a technique that can be used more generally. It allows early failure. A clause with a cut-fail combination says that the search need not (and will not) proceed.

Some cuts in a cut-fail combination are green cuts. That is, the program has the same meaning if the clause containing the cut-fail combination is removed. For example, consider Program 10.4 defining the predicate ground. An extra clause can be added, which can reduce the search without affecting the meaning:

```
ground(Term) ← var(Term), !, fail.
```

The use of cut in Program 11.6 implementing not is not green, but red. The program does not behave as intended if the cut is removed.

The cut-fail combination is used to implement other system predicates involving negation. For example, the predicate $\neq$ (written as \= in Standard Prolog) can be simply implemented via unification and cut-fail, rather than via an infinite table, with Program 11.8. This program is also only guaranteed to work correctly for ground goals.

With ingenuity, and a good understanding of unification and the execution mechanism of Prolog, interesting definitions can be found for many meta-logical predicates. A sense of the necessary contortions can be found in the program for same_var(X,Y), which succeeds if X and Y are the same variable and otherwise fails:

```
same_var(foo,Y) ← var(Y), !, fail.
same_var(X,Y) ← var(X), var(Y).
```

The argument for its correctness follows: "If the arguments to same_var are the same variable, binding X to foo will bind the second argument as well, so the first clause will fail, and the second clause will succeed. If either of the arguments is not a variable, both clauses will fail. If the arguments are different variables, the first clause will fail, but the cut stops the second clause from being considered."

Exercises for Section 11.3

(i)   Define the system predicate \== using == and the cut-fail combination.

(ii)   Define nonvar using var and the cut-fail combination.

11.4   Red Cuts: Omitting Explicit Conditions

Prolog's sequential choice of rules and its behavior in executing cut are the key features necessary to compose the program for not. The programmer can take into account that Prolog will only execute a part of the procedure if certain conditions hold. This suggests a new, and misguided, style of programming in Prolog, where the explicit conditions governing the use of a rule are omitted.

The prototypical (bad) example in the literature is a modified version of Program 11.3 for minimum. The comparison in the second clause of the program can be discarded to give the program

```
minimum(X,Y,X) ← X≤Y, !.
minimum(X,Y,Y).
```

The reasoning offered to justify the program is as follows: "If X is less than or equal to Y, then the minimum is X. Otherwise the minimum is Y, and another comparison between X and Y is unnecessary." Such a comparison is performed, however, by Program 11.3.

There is a severe flaw with this reasoning. The modified program has a different meaning from the standard program for minimum. It succeeds on the goal minimum(2,5,5). The modified program is a false logic program.

The incorrect minimum goal implied by the modified program can be avoided. It is necessary to make explicit the unification between the first and third arguments, which is implicit in the first rule. The modified rule is

minimum(X,Y,Z) ← X≤Y, !, Z=X.

This technique of using the cut to commit to a clause after part of the unification has been done is quite general. But for minimum the resultant code is contrived. It is far better to simply write the correct logic program, adding cuts if efficiency is important, as done in Program 11.3.

Using cut with the operational behavior of Prolog in mind is problematic. It allows the writing of Prolog programs that are false when read as logic programs, that is, have false conclusions but behave correctly because Prolog is unable to prove the false conclusions. For example, if minimum goals are of the form minimum(X,Y,Z), where X and Y are instantiated, but Z is not, the modified program behaves correctly.

The only effect of the green cuts presented in Section 11.1 is to prune from the search tree branches that are known to be useless. Cuts whose presence in a program changes the meaning of that program are called *red cuts*. The removal of a red cut from a program changes its meaning, i.e., the set of goals it can prove.

A standard Prolog programming technique using red cuts is the omission of explicit conditions. Knowledge of the behavior of Prolog, specifically the order in which rules are used in a program, is relied on to omit conditions that could be inferred to be true. This is sometimes essential in practical Prolog programming, since explicit conditions, especially negative ones, are cumbersome to specify and inefficient to run. But making such omissions is error-prone.

Omitting an explicit condition is possible if the failure of the previous clauses implies the condition. For example, the failure of the comparison X≤Y in the minimum code implies that X is greater than Y. Thus the test X > Y can be omitted. In general, the explicit condition is effectively the negation of the previous conditions. By using red cuts to omit conditions, negation is being expressed implicitly.

delete(Xs,X,Ys) ←
>   *Ys* is the result of deleting all occurrences of *X* from the list *Xs*.

```
delete([X|Xs],X,Ys) ← !, delete(Xs,X,Ys).
delete([X|Xs],Z,[X|Ys]) ← X ≠ Z, !, delete(Xs,Z,Ys).
delete([ ],X,[ ]).
```

Program 11.9a   Deleting elements from a list

delete(Xs,X,Ys) ←
>   *Ys* is the result of deleting all occurrences of *X* from the list *Xs*.

```
delete([X|Xs],X,Ys) ← !, delete(Xs,X,Ys).
delete([X|Xs],Z,[X|Ys]) ← !, delete(Xs,Z,Ys).
delete([ ],X,[ ]).
```

Program 11.9b   Deleting elements from a list

Consider Program 11.5 for interchange sort. The first (recursive) rule applies whenever there is an adjacent pair of elements in the list that are out of order. When the second sort rule is used, there are no such pairs and the list must be sorted. Thus the condition ordered(Xs) can be omitted, leaving the second rule as the fact sort(Xs,Xs). As with minimum, this is an incorrect logical statement.

Once the ordered condition is removed from the program, the cut changes from green to red. Removing the cut from the variant without the ordered condition leaves a program that gives false solutions.

Let us consider another example of omitting an explicit condition. Consider Program 3.18 for deleting elements in a list. The two recursive clauses cover distinct cases, corresponding to whether or not the head of the list is the element to be deleted. The distinct nature of the cases can be indicated with cuts, as shown in Program 11.9a.

By reasoning that the failure of the first clause implies that the head of the list is not the same as the element to be deleted, the explicit inequality test can be omitted from the second clause. The modified program is given as Program 11.9b. The cuts in Program 11.9a are green in comparison to the red cut in the first clause of Program 11.9b.

In general, omitting simple tests as in Program 11.9b is inadvisable. The efficiency gain by their omission is minimal compared to the loss of readability and modifiability of the code.

if_then_else(P,Q,R) ←
   Either *P* and *Q* , or not *P* and *R*.

```
if_then_else(P,Q,R) ← P, !, Q.
if_then_else(P,Q,R) ← R.
```

Program 11.10 If-then-else statement

Let us investigate the use of cut to express the if-then-else control structure. Program 11.10 defines the relation `if_then_else(P,Q,R)`. Declaratively, the relation is true if P and Q are true, or not P and R are true. Operationally, we prove P and, if successful, prove Q, else prove R.

The utility of a red cut to implement this solution is self-evident. The alternative to using a cut is to make explicit the condition under which R is run. The second clause would read

```
if_then_else(P,Q,R) ← not P, R.
```

This could be expensive computationally. The goal P will have to be computed a second time in the determination of `not`.

We have seen so far two kinds of red cuts. One kind is built into the program, as in the definitions of `not` and ≠. A second kind was a green cut that became red when conditions in the programs were removed. However, there is a third kind of red cut. A cut that is introduced into a program as a green cut that just improves efficiency can turn out to be a red cut that changes the program's meaning.

For example, consider trying to write an efficient version of `member` that does not succeed several times when there are multiple copies of an element in a list. Taking a procedural view, one might use a cut to avoid backtracking once an element is found to be a member of a list. The corresponding code is

```
member(X,[X|Xs]) ← !.
member(X,[Y|Ys]) ← member(X,Ys).
```

Adding the cut indeed changes the behavior of the program. However, it is now not an efficient variant of `member`, since, for example, the query `member(X,[1,2,3])`? gives only one solution, X=1. It is a variant of `member_check`, given as Program 7.3, with the explicit condition X ≠ Y omitted, and hence the cut is red.

Exercises for Section 11.4

(i)   Discuss where cuts could be placed in Program 9.3 for substitute. Consider whether a cut-fail combination would be useful, and whether explicit conditions can be omitted.

(ii)   Analyze the relation between Program 3.19 for select and the program obtained by adding a single cut:

```
select(X,[X|Xs],Xs) ← !.
select(X,[Y|Ys],[Y|Zs]) ← select(X,Ys,Zs).
```

(Hint: Consider variants of select.)

11.5   Default Rules

Logic programs with red cuts essentially consist of a series of special cases and a default rule. For example, Program 11.6 for not had a special case when the goal G succeeded and a default fact not G used otherwise. The second rule for if_then_else in Program 11.10 is

```
if_then_else(P,Q,R) ← R.
```

It is used by default if P fails.

Using cuts to achieve default behavior is in the logic programming folklore. We argue, using a simple example, that often it is better to compose an alternative logical formulation than to use cuts for default behavior.

Program 11.11a is a naive program for determining social welfare payments. The relation pension(Person,Pension) determines which pension, Pension, a person, Person, is entitled to. The first pension rule says that a person is entitled to an invalid's pension if he is an invalid. The second rule states that people over the age of 65 are entitled to an old age pension if they have contributed to a suitable pension scheme long enough, that is, they must be paid_up. People who are not paid up are still entitled to supplementary benefit if they are over 65.

Consider extending Program 11.11a to include the rule that people receive nothing if they do not qualify for one of the pensions. The procedural "solution" is to add cuts after each of the three rules, and an extra default fact

```
pension(X,nothing).
```

This version is given as Program 11.11b.

Program 11.11b behaves correctly on queries to determine the pension to which people are entitled, for example, `pension(mc_tavish,X)`?. The program is not correct, though. The query `pension(mc_tavish,nothing)`? succeeds, which `mc_tavish` wouldn't be too happy about, and `pension(X,old_age_pension)`? has the erroneous unique answer X=mc_tavish. The cuts prevent alternatives being found. Program 11.11b only works correctly to determine the pension to which a given person is entitled.

A better solution is to introduce a new relation `entitlement(X,Y)`, which is true if X is entitled to Y. It is defined with two rules and uses Program 11.11a for pension:

```
entitlement(X,Y)  ←  pension(X,Y).
entitlement(X,nothing)  ←  not pension(X,Y).
```

This program has all the advantages of Program 11.11b and neither of the disadvantages mentioned before. It shows that making a person

pension(Person,Pension) ←
    Pension is the type of pension received by *Person*.

```
pension(X,invalid_pension)  ←  invalid(X).
pension(X,old_age_pension)  ←  over_65(X), paid_up(X).
pension(X,supplementary_benefit)  ←  over_65(X).

invalid(mc_tavish).

over_65(mc_tavish).  over_65(mc_donald).  over_65(mc_duff).

paid_up(mc_tavish).  paid_up(mc_donald).
```

Program 11.11a   Determining welfare payments

pension(Person,Pension) ←
    Pension is the type of pension received by *Person*.

```
pension(X,invalid_pension)  ←  invalid(X), !.
pension(X,old_age_pension)  ←  over_65(X), paid_up(X), !.
pension(X,supplementary_benefit)  ←  over_65(X), !.
pension(X,nothing).
```

Program 11.11b   Determining welfare payments

entitled to nothing as the default rule is really a new concept and should be presented as such.

11.6   Cuts for Efficiency

Earlier in this chapter, we claimed that the efficiency of some Prolog programs could be improved through sparing use of the cut. This section explores the claim. Two issues are addressed. The first is the meaning of efficiency in the context of Prolog. The second is appropriate uses of cut.

Efficiency relates to utilization of resources. The resources used by computations are space and time. To understand Prolog's use of space and time, we need to consider Prolog implementation technology.

The two major areas of memory manipulated during a Prolog computation are the stack and the heap. The stack, called the local stack in many Edinburgh Prolog implementations, is used to govern control flow. The heap, called the global stack in many Edinburgh Prolog implementations, is used to construct data structures that are needed throughout the computation.

Let us relate stack management to the computation model of Prolog. Each time a goal is chosen for reduction, a stack frame is placed on the stack. Pointers are used to specify subsequent flow of control once the goal succeeds or fails. The pointers depend on whether other clauses can be used to reduce the chosen goal. Handling the stack frame is simplified considerably if it is known that only one clause is applicable. Technically, a *choice point* needs to be put on the stack if more than one clause is applicable.

Experience has shown that avoiding placing choice points on the stack has a large impact on efficiency. Indeed, Prolog implementation technology has advanced to the stage that deterministic code, i.e., without choice points, can be made to run almost as efficiently as conventional languages.

Cuts are one way that Prolog implementations know that only one clause is applicable. Another way is by the effective use of indexing. Whether a cut is needed to tell a particular Prolog implementation that only one clause is applicable depends on the particular indexing scheme.

In this book, we often use the first argument to differentiate between clauses. Indexing on the first argument is the most common among Prolog implementations. For effective use, consult your Prolog manual.

Efficient use of space is determined primarily by controlling the growth of the stack. Already we have discussed the advantages of iterative code and last call optimization. Too many frames placed on the stack can cause computations to abort. In practice this is a major concern. Running out of stack space is a common symptom of an infinite loop or running a highly recursive program. For example, Program 3.9 implementing Ackermann's function, when adapted for Prolog arithmetic, quickly exhausts an implementation's capacity.

Time complexity is approximated by number of reductions. Thus efficient use of time can be determined by analyzing the number of reductions a program makes. In Part I, we analyzed different logic programs by the size of proof trees. In Prolog, size of search tree is a better measure, but it becomes difficult to incorporate Prolog's nondeterminism.

Probably the most important approach to improving time performance is better algorithms. Although Prolog is a declarative language, the notion of an algorithm applies equally well to Prolog as to other languages. Examples of good and bad algorithms for the same problem, together with their Prolog implementations, have been given in previous chapters. Linear reverse using accumulators (Program 3.16b) is clearly more efficient than naive reverse (Program 3.16a). Quicksort (Program 3.22) is better than permutation sort (Program 3.20).

Besides coming up with better algorithms, several things can be done to influence the performance of Prolog programs. One is to choose a better implementation. An efficient implementation is characterized by its raw speed, its indexing capabilities, support for tail recursion optimization, and garbage collection. The speed of logic programming languages is usually measured in LIPS, or *logical inferences per second*. A logical inference corresponds to a reduction in a computation. Most Prolog implementations claim a LIPS rating. The standard benchmark, by no means ideal, is to time Program 3.16a, naive `reverse`, reversing a list. There are 496 reductions for a list of 30 elements.

Once the implementation is fixed, the programs themselves can be tuned by

- Good goal ordering, where the rule is "fail as early as possible"

- Exploitation of the indexing facility, by ordering arguments appropriately

- Elimination of nondeterminism using explicit conditions and cuts

Let us elaborate on the third item and discuss guidelines for using cut. As discussed, Prolog implementations will perform more efficiently if they know a predicate is deterministic. The appropriate sparing use of cut is primarily for saying that predicates are deterministic, not for controlling backtracking.

The two basic principles for using a cut are

- Make cuts as local as possible.

- Place a cut as soon as it is known that the correct clause has been chosen.

Let us illustrate the principles with the quicksort program, Program 3.22. The recursive clause is as follows

```
quicksort([X|Xs],Ys) ←
    partition(Xs,X,Littles,Bigs), quicksort(Littles,Ls),
    quicksort(Bigs,Bs), append(Ls,[X|Bs],Ys).
```

We know there is only one solution for the partition of the list. Rather than place a cut in the clause for quicksort, the partition predicate should be made deterministic. This is in accordance with the first principle.

One of the partition clauses is

```
partition([X|Xs],Y,[X|Ls],Bs) ←
    X ≤ Y, partition(Xs,Y,Ls,Bs).
```

If the clause succeeds, then no other will be applicable. But the cut should be placed before the recursive call to partition rather than after, according to the second principle.

Where and whether to place cuts can depend on the Prolog implementation being used. Cuts are needed only if Prolog does not know the determinism of a predicate. If, for example, indexing can determine that only one predicate is applicable, no cuts are needed. In a system without indexing, cuts would be needed for the same program.

Having discussed appropriate use of cuts, we stress that adding cuts to a program should typically be done *after* the program runs correctly.

A common misconception is that a program can be fixed from giving extraneous answers and behaving incorrectly by adding cuts. This is not so. Prolog code should be debugged as declaratively as possible, a topic we discuss in Chapter 13. Only when the logic is correct should efficiency be addressed.

The final factor that we consider in evaluating the efficiency of Prolog programs is the creation of intermediate data structures, which primarily affects use of the heap. Minimizing the number of data structures being generated is a subject that has not received much attention in the Prolog literature. We analyze two versions of the predicate sublist(Xs,Ys) to illustrate the type of reasoning possible.

The two versions of sublist that we consider involve Program 3.13 for calculating prefixes and suffixes of lists. We must also specify the comparison with respect to a particular use. The one chosen for the analysis is whether a given list is a sublist of a second given list. The first clause that follows denotes a sublist as a prefix of a suffix, and the second clause defines a sublist as a suffix of a prefix:

```
sublist(Xs,AsXsBs) ← suffix(XsBs,AsXsBs), prefix(Xs,XsBs).
sublist(Xs,AsXsBs) ← prefix(AsXs,AsXsBs), suffix(Xs,AsXs).
```

Although both programs have the same meaning, there is a difference in the performance of the two programs. If the two arguments to sublist are complete lists, the first clause simply goes down the second list, returning a suffix, then goes down the first list, checking if the suffix is a prefix of the first list. This execution does not generate any new intermediate data structures. On the other hand, the second clause creates a new list, which is a prefix of the second list, then checks if this list is a suffix of the first list. If the check fails, backtracking occurs, and a new prefix of the first list is created.

Even though, on the average, the number of reductions performed by the two clauses is the same, they are different in their efficiency. The first clause does not generate new structures (does not cons, in Lisp jargon). The second clause does. When analyzing Lisp programs, it is common to examine the consing performance in great detail, and whether a program conses or not is an important efficiency consideration. We feel that the issue is important for Prolog programs, but perhaps the state of the art of studying the performance of large Prolog programs has not matured enough to dictate such analyses.

11.7   Background

The cut was introduced in Marseilles Prolog (Colmerauer et al., 1973) and was perhaps one of the most influential design decisions in Prolog. Colmerauer experimented with several other constructs, which corresponded to special cases of the cut, before coming up with its full definition.

The terminology *green cuts* and *red cuts* was introduced by van Emden (1982), in order to try to distinguish between legitimate and illegitimate uses of cuts. Alternative control structures, which are more structured then the cut, are constantly being proposed, but the cut still remains the workhorse of the Prolog programmer. Some of the extensions are if-then-else constructs (O'Keefe, 1985) and notations for declaring that a relation is functional, or deterministic, as well as "weak-cuts," "snips," remote-cuts (Chikayama, 1984), and not itself, which, as currently implemented, can be viewed as a structured application of the cut.

The controversial nature of cut has not been emphasized in this book. A good starting place to read about some of cut's problems, and the variation in its implementation, is Moss (1986). Many of the difficulties arise from the scope of the cut, and how cuts interact with the system predicates for control such as conjunction, disjunction, and the meta-variable facility. For example, two versions of call have been suggested, one that blocks the cut and one that does not. Further discussion of cut can be found in O'Keefe (1990), including an exposition on when cut should be used.

Some Prologs provide if_then_else(P,Q,R) under the syntax P → Q; R and an abridged if-then form P → Q. Whether to include if-then-else in Standard Prolog has been a controversial issue. The trade-off is convenience for some programming tasks versus thorny semantic anomalies. This issue has been raised several times on the USENET newsgroup comp.lang.prolog. Relevant comments were collected in the May 1991 issue of the Newsletter of the Association for Logic Programming, Volume 4, No. 2.

The cut is also the ancestor of the commit operator of concurrent logic languages, which was first introduced by Clark and Gregory (1981) in their Relational Language. The commit cleans up one of the major drawbacks of the cut, which is destroying the modularity of clauses.

The cut is asymmetric, because it eliminates alternative clauses below the clause in which it appears, but not above. Hence a cut in one clause affects the meaning of other clauses. The commit, on the other hand, is symmetric and therefore cannot implement negation as failure; it does not destroy the modularity of clauses.

The pioneering work on Prolog implementation technology was in D.H.D. Warren's Ph.D. thesis (1977). Warren later added tail recursion optimization to his original DEC-10 compiler (1986). Tail recursion optimization was implemented concurrently by Bruynooghe (1982) in his Prolog system. A motley collection of papers on Prolog implementations can be found in Campbell (1984).

Most current compilers and implementation technology are based on the WAM (Warren Abstract Machine), published as a somewhat cryptic technical report (Warren, 1983). Readers seriously interested in program efficiency need to understand the WAM. The best places to start reading about the WAM are Maier and Warren (1988) and Aït-Kaci (1991).

References to negation in logic programming can be found in Section 5.6. Implementations of a sound negation as failure rule in dialects of Prolog can be found in Prolog-II (van Caneghem, 1982) and MU-Prolog (Naish, 1985a).

The program for `same_var` and its argument for correctness are due to O'Keefe (1983).

Program 11.11b for `pension` is a variant of an example due to Sam Steel for a Prolog course at the University of Edinburgh — hence the Scottish flavor. Needless to say, this is not intended as, nor is it an accurate expression, of the Scottish or British social welfare system.

12   Extra-Logical Predicates

There is a class of predicates in Prolog that lie outside the logic programming model, and are called *extra-logical predicates*. These predicates
achieve a side effect in the course of being satisfied as a logical goal.
There are basically three types of extra-logical system predicates: predicates concerned with I/O, predicates for accessing and manipulating the
program, and predicates for interfacing with the underlying operating
system. Prolog I/O and program manipulation predicates are discussed
in this chapter. The interface to the operating system is too system-
dependent to be discussed in this book.

12.1   Input/Output

A very important class of predicates that produces side effects is that
concerned with I/O. Any practical programming language must have a
mechanism for both input and output. The execution model of Prolog,
however, precludes the expression of I/O within the pure component of
the language.

The basic predicate for input is read(X). This goal reads a term from
the current input stream, usually from the terminal. The term that has
been read is unified with X, and read succeeds or fails depending on the
result of unification.

The basic predicate for output is write(X). This goal writes the term
X on the current output stream, as defined by the underlying operating
system, usually to the terminal. Neither read nor write give alternative
solutions on backtracking.

```
writeln([X|Xs]) ← write(X), writeln(Xs).
writeln([ ]) ← nl.
```

Program 12.1   Writing a list of terms

The normal use of read is with a variable argument X, which acquires the value of the first term in the current input stream. The instantiation of X to something outside the program lies outside the logical model, since each time the procedure is called, read(X) succeeds with a (possibly) different value for X.

Read attempts to parse the next term on the input stream. If it fails, it prints an error message on the terminal.

There is an asymmetry between the extra-logical nature of read and write. If all calls to write were replaced with the goal *true*, which always succeeded once, the semantics of the program would be unaffected. That is not true for read.

Early Prolog implementations did not concentrate on input and output facilities, providing the basic predicates read and write, or their equivalents, and little else. More recent Prolog implementations have a wider range of formatted I/O options, some of which have been adopted in Standard Prolog. In this book, the emphasis is not on I/O, and so we restrict outselves to basic predicates and some simple utilities described in the rest of this section. For more elaborate I/O, consult your particular Prolog manual.

A useful utility is a predicate writeln(Xs), analogous to the Pascal command, which writes the list of terms Xs as a line of output on the current output stream. It is defined in Program 12.1. The predicate writeln uses the builtin predicate nl, which causes the next output character to be on a new line. As an example of its use, executing the conjunctive goal (X=3, writeln(['The value of X is ',X]) produces the output

The value of X is 3.

Note the use of the quoted atom 'The value of X is '. Both read and write operate at the term level. A lower level for I/O is the character level. Edinburgh Prolog assumed that characters were represented by ASCII codes. Standard Prolog takes a broader perspective to support such character sets as Kanji. The basic output predicate is put_char(Char),

read_word_list(Words) ←
    Words is a list of words read from the input stream via side effects.

```
read_word_list(Words) ←
    get_char(FirstChar),
    read_words(FirstChar,Words).

read_words(Char,[Word|Words]) ←
    word_char(Char),
    read_word(Char,Word,NextChar),
    read_words(NextChar,Words).

read_words(Char,Words) ←
    fill_char(Char),
    get_char(NextChar),
    read_words(NextChar,Words).

read_words(Char,[ ]) ←
    end_of_words_char(Char).

read_word(Char,Word,NextChar) ←
    word_chars(Char,Chars,NextChar),
    atom_list(Word,Chars).

word_chars(Char,[Char|Chars],FinalChar) ←
    word_char(Char), !,
    get_char(NextChar),
    word_chars(NextChar,Chars,FinalChar).
word_chars(Char,[ ],Char) ←
    not word_char(Char).
```

Program 12.2   Reading in a list of words

which outputs the character Char on the current output stream. Standard Prolog allows you to specify the output stream, but we do not give examples here. The basic input predicate at the character level is get_char(Char), which reads a character C from the current input stream and then unifies C with Char.

Program 12.2 defines read_word_list(Words), a utility predicate for reading in a list of words, Words, from the current input, terminated by an end-of-words character, for example a period. Specific definitions of the predicates word_char/1, fill_char/1, and end_of_words_char/1 need to be added. It can be used to allow freer form input. In Program 12.2, words can be separated by arbitrarily many fill characters.

The predicate `read_word_list` reads a character, FirstChar, and calls `read_words(FirstChar,Words)`. This predicate does one of three actions, depending on what FirstChar is. If FirstChar is a word character, then the next word is found. Word characters in Standard Prolog are uppercase and lowercase letters, underscores, and digits. The second action is to ignore filling characters, and so the next character is read, and the program continues recursively. Finally, if the character denoting the end of the words is reached, the program terminates and returns the list of words.

It is important that the program must always read a character ahead and then test what it should do. If the character is useful, for example, a word character, it must be passed down to be part of the word. Otherwise characters can get lost when backtracking. Consider the following read and process loop:

```
process([ ]) ←
    get_char(C), end_of_words_char(C).
process([W|Words]) ←
    get_char(C), word_char(C), get_word(C,W), process(Words).
```

If the first character in a word is not an `end_of_words_char`, the first clause will fail, and the second clause will cause the reading of the next character.

Returning to Program 12.2, the predicate `read_word(Char,Word,NextChar)` reads a word Word given the current character Char and returns the next character after the word, NextChar. The list of characters composing the word is found by `word_chars/3` (with the same arguments as `read_word`). The word is created from the list of characters using the system predicate `atom_list/2`. In `word_chars` there is the same property of looking ahead one character, so that no character is lost.

Predicates such as `fill_char/1` and `word_char/1` exemplify data abstraction in Prolog.

Exercise for Section 12.1

(i)   Extend Program 12.2 to handle a wider range of inputs, for example, numbers.

12.2 Program Access and Manipulation

So far programs have been assumed to be resident in computer memory, without discussion of how they are represented or how they got there. Many applications depend on accessing the clauses in the program. Furthermore, if programs are to be modified at runtime, there must be a way of adding (and deleting) clauses.

The first Prologs, implemented as simple interpreted systems, classified predicates as builtin and static or user-defined and dynamic. The subsequent development of compilers and libraries require a more sophisticated classification.

Each user-defined predicate is either *dynamic* or *static*. The procedure of a dynamic predicate can be altered, whereas the procedure of a static predicate cannot. Builtin predicates are assumed to be static. The system predicates introduced in this section apply only to dynamic predicates and will probably cause error messages if applied to static predicates. In this book, we assume all predicates are dynamic unless otherwise specified. In many Prologs, declarations are needed to make a predicate dynamic.

The system predicate for accessing a program is clause(Head,Body). The goal clause(Head,Body) must be called with Head instantiated. The program is searched for the first clause whose head unifies with Head. The head and body of this clause are then unified with Head and Body. On backtracking, the goal succeeds once for each unifiable clause in the procedure. Note that clauses in the program cannot be accessed via their body.

Facts have the atom true as their body. Conjunctive goals are represented using the binary functor , . The actual representations can be easily abstracted away, however.

Consider Program 3.12 for member:

```
member(X,[X|Xs]).
member(X,[Y|Ys]) ← member(X,Ys).
```

The goal clause(member(X,Ys),Body) has two solutions: {Ys=[X|Xs], Body=true} and {Ys=[Y|Ys1],Body=member(X,Ys1)}. Note that a fresh copy of the variables appearing in the clause is made each time a unification is performed. In terms of the meta-logical primitives freeze and melt, the clause is stored in frozen form in the program. Each call to clause causes a new melt of the frozen clause. This is the logical counterpart of the classic notion of reentrant code.

System predicates are provided both to add clauses to the program and to remove clauses. The basic predicate for adding clauses is assertz(Clause), which adds Clause as the last clause of the corresponding procedure. For example, assertz(father(haran,lot))? adds the father fact to the program. When describing rules an extra level of brackets is needed for technical reasons concerning the precedence of terms. For example, assertz((parent(X,Y) ← father(X,Y))) is the correct syntax.

There is a variant of assertz, asserta, that adds the clause at the beginning of a procedure.

If Clause is uninstantiated (or if Clause has the form *H←B* with *H* uninstantiated), an error condition occurs.

The predicate retract(C) removes from the program the first clause in the program unifying with C. Note that to retract a clause such as a ← b,c,d, you need to specify retract((a ← C)). A call to retract may only mark a clause for removal, rather than physically removing it, and the actual removal would occur only when Prolog's top-level query is solved. This is for implementation reasons, but may lead to anomalous behavior in some Prologs.

Asserting a clause freezes the terms appearing in the clause. Retracting the same clause melts a new copy of the terms. In many Prologs this is exploited to be the easiest way of copying a term. Standard Prolog, however, provides a builtin predicate copy_term/2 for this purpose.

The predicates assert and retract introduce to Prolog the possibility of programming with side effects. Code depending on side effects for its successful execution is hard to read, hard to debug, and hard to reason about formally. Hence these predicates are somewhat controversial, and using them is sometimes a result of intellectual laziness or incompetence. They should be used as little as possible when programming. Many of the programs to be given in this book can be written using assert and retract, but the results are less clean and less efficient. Further, as Prolog compiler technology advances, the inefficiency in using assert and retract will become more apparent.

It is possible, however, to give logical justification for some limited uses of assert and retract. Asserting a clause is justified, for example, if the clause already logically follows from the program. In such a case, adding it will not affect the meaning of the program, since no new consequences can be derived. Perhaps program efficiency will improve, as some consequences could be derived faster. This use is exemplified in the lemma construct, introduced in Section 12.3.

Similarly, retracting a clause is justified if the clause is logically redundant. In this case, retracting constitutes a kind of logical garbage collection, whose purpose is to reduce the size of the program.

12.3 Memo-Functions

Memo-functions save the results of subcomputations to be used later in a computation. Remembering partial results is impossible within pure Prolog, so memo-functions are implemented using side effects to the program. Programming in this way can be considered bottom-up programming.

The prototypical memo-function is `lemma(Goal)`. Operationally, it attempts to prove the goal `Goal` and, if successful, stores the result of the proof as a lemma. It is implemented as

```
lemma(P) ← P, asserta((P ← !)).
```

The next time the goal P is attempted, the new solution will be used, and there will be no unnecessary recomputation. The cut is present to prevent the more general program being used. Its use is justified only if P does not have multiple solutions.

Using lemmas is demonstrated with Program 12.3 for solving the Towers of Hanoi problem. The performance of Program 3.31 in solving the problem is dramatically improved. It is well known that the solution of the Towers of Hanoi with N disks requires $2^N - 1$ moves. For example, ten disks require 1,023 moves, or in terms of Program 3.31, 1,023 calls of `hanoi(1,A,B,C,Xs)`. The overall number of general calls of `hanoi/5` is significantly more.

The solution to the Towers of Hanoi repeatedly solves subproblems moving the identical number of disks. A memo-function can be used to recall the moves made in solving each subproblem of moving a smaller

hanoi(*N,A,B,C,Moves*) ←
    Moves is the sequence of moves required to move *N* disks
    from peg *A* to peg *B* using peg *C* as an intermediary
    according to the rules of the Towers of Hanoi puzzle.

```
hanoi(1,A,B,C,[A to B]).
hanoi(N,A,B,C,Moves) ←
    N > 1,
    N1 is N-1,
    lemma(hanoi(N1,A,C,B,Ms1)),
    hanoi(N1,C,B,A,Ms2),
    append(Ms1,[A to B|Ms2],Moves).

lemma(P) ← P, asserta((P ← !)).
```

Testing

```
test_hanoi(N,Pegs,Moves) ←
    hanoi(N,A,B,C,Moves), Pegs = [A,B,C].
```

Program 12.3   Towers of Hanoi using a memo-function

number of disks. Later attempts to solve the subproblem can use the
computed sequence of moves rather than recomputing them.

The idea is seen with the recursive clause of `hanoi` in Program 12.3.
The first call to solve `hanoi` with *N* − 1 disks is remembered, and can be
used by the second call to `hanoi` with *N* − 1 disks.

The program is tested with the predicate `test_hanoi(N,Pegs,Moves)`.
`N` is the number of disks, `Pegs` is a list of the three peg names, and
`Moves` is the list of moves that must be made. Note that in order to take
advantage of the memo-functions, a general problem is solved first. Only
when the solution is complete, and all memo-functions have recorded
their results, are the peg names instantiated.

Exercise for Section 12.3

(i)   Two players take turns to say a number between 1 and 3 inclusive.
    A sum is kept of the numbers, and the player who brings the sum
    to 20 wins. Write a program to play the game to win, using memo-
    functions.

12.4 Interactive Programs

A common form of a program requiring side effects is an interactive loop. A command is read from the terminal, responded to, and the next command read. Interactive loops are implemented typically by *while* loops in conventional languages. Program 12.4 gives the basic skeleton of such programs, where a command is read, then echoed by being written on the screen.

The read/echo loop is invoked by the goal echo. The heart of the program is the relation echo(X), where X is the term to be echoed. The program assumes a user-defined predicate last_input/1, which succeeds if the argument satisfies the termination condition for input. If the termination condition is satisfied by the input, the loop terminates; otherwise the term is written and a new term is read.

Note that the testing of the term is separate from its reading. This is necessary to avoid losing a term: terms cannot be reread. The same phenomenon occurred in Program 12.2 for processing characters. The character was read and then separately processed.

Program 12.4 is iterative and deterministic. It can be run efficiently on a system with tail recursion optimization, always using the same small amount of space.

We give two examples of programs using the basic cycle of reading a term, and then processing it. The first is a line editor. The second interactive program is a shell for Prolog commands, which is essentially a top-level interpreter for Prolog in Prolog.

The first decision in writing a simple line editor in Prolog is how to represent the file. Each line in the file must be accessible, together with the cursor position, that is the current position within the file. We use a structure file(Before,After), where Before is a list of lines before the cursor, and After is a list of lines after the cursor. The cursor position is

```
echo  ← read(X), echo(X).

echo(X)  ← last_input(X), !.
echo(X)  ← write(X), nl, read(Y), !, echo(Y).
```

Program 12.4 Basic interactive loop

```
edit ← edit(file([ ],[ ])).

edit(File) ←
    write_prompt, read(Command), edit(File,Command).

edit(File,exit) ← !.
edit(File,Command) ←
    apply(Command,File,File1), !, edit(File1).
edit(File,Command) ←
    writeln([Command,' is not applicable']), !, edit(File).

apply(up,file([X|Xs],Ys),file(Xs,[X|Ys])).
apply(up(N),file(Xs,Ys),file(Xs1,Ys1)) ←
    N > 0, up(N,Xs,Ys,Xs1,Ys1).
apply(down,file(Xs,[Y|Ys]),file([Y|Xs],Ys)).
apply(insert(Line),file(Xs,Ys),file(Xs,[Line|Ys])).
apply(delete,file(Xs,[Y|Ys]),file(Xs,Ys)).
apply(print,file([X|Xs],Ys),file([X|Xs],Ys)) ←
    write(X), nl.
apply(print(*),file(Xs,Ys),file(Xs,Ys)) ←
    reverse(Xs,Xs1), write_file(Xs1), write_file(Ys).

up(N,[ ],Ys,[ ],Ys).
up(0,Xs,Ys,Xs,Ys).
up(N,[X|Xs],Ys,Xs1,Ys1) ←
    N > 0, N1 is N−1, up(N1,Xs,[X|Ys],Xs1,Ys1).

write_file([X|Xs]) ←
    write(X), nl, write_file(Xs).
write_file([ ]).

write_prompt ← write('≫'), nl.
```

Program 12.5   A line editor

restricted to be at the end of some line. The lines before the cursor will
be in reverse order to give easier access to the lines nearer the cursor.
The basic loop accepts a command from the keyboard and applies it to
produce a new version of the file. Program 12.5 is the editor.

An editing session is invoked by edit, which initializes the file being processed to the empty file, file([ ],[ ]). The interactive loop
is controlled by edit(File). It writes a prompt on the screen, using
write_prompt, then reads and processes a command. The processing uses the basic predicate edit(File,Command), which applies the
command to the file. The application is performed by the goal ap-
ply(Command,File,File1), where File1 is the new version of the file

after the command has been applied. The editing continues by calling edit/1 on File1. The third edit/2 clause handles the case when no command is applicable, indicated by the failure of apply. In this case, an appropriate message is printed on the screen and the editing continues. The editing session is terminated by the command exit, which is separately tested for by edit/2.

Let us look at a couple of apply clauses, to give the flavor of how commands are specified. Particularly simple are commands for moving the cursor. The clause

```
apply(up,file([X|Xs],Ys),file(Xs,[X|Ys])).
```

says that we move the cursor up by moving the line immediately above the cursor to be immediately below the cursor. The command fails if the cursor is at the top of the file. The command for moving the cursor down, also shown in Program 12.5, is analogous to moving the cursor up.

Moving the cursor up N lines rather than a single line involves using an auxiliary predicate up/5 to change the cursor position in the file. Issues of robustness surface in its definition. Note that apply tests that the argument to up is sensible, i.e., a positive number of lines, before up is invoked. The predicate up itself handles the case when the number of lines to be moved up is greater than the number of lines in the file. The command succeeds with the cursor placed at the top of the file. Extending the editor program to move a cursor down N lines is posed as an exercise at the end of this section.

Other commands given in Program 12.5 insert and delete lines. The command for insert, insert(Line), contains an argument, namely the line to be inserted. The command for delete is straightforward. It fails if the cursor is at the bottom of the screen. Also in the editor are commands for printing the line above the cursor, print, and for printing the whole file, print(*).

The editor commands are mutually exclusive. Only one apply clause is applicable for any command. As soon as an apply goal succeeds, there are no other possible alternatives. Prolog implementations that support indexing would find the correct clause immediately and leave no choice points. Imposing determinism via exploitation of indexing is a little different than adding explicit cuts, as described in Section 11.1, where the cuts would have been applied directly to the apply facts themselves. The difference between the two approaches is merely cosmetic. Note that a

```
shell ←
    shell_prompt, read(Goal), shell(Goal).
shell(exit) ← !.
shell(Goal) ←
    ground(Goal), !, shell_solve_ground(Goal), shell.
shell(Goal) ←
    shell_solve(Goal), shell.

shell_solve(Goal) ←
    Goal, write(Goal), nl, fail.
shell_solve(Goal) ←
    write('No (more) solutions'), nl.

shell_solve_ground(Goal) ←
    Goal, !, write('Yes'), nl.
shell_solve_ground(Goal) ←
    write('No'), nl.

shell_prompt ← write('Next command? ').
```

Program 12.6   An interactive shell

cut is still needed in the second `edit` clause to indicate that successful execution of a command and reporting of an error message are mutually exclusive.

A possible extension to the editor is to allow each command to handle its own error message. For example, suppose you wanted a more helpful message than "Command not applicable" when trying to move up when at the top of the file. This would be handled by extending the `apply` clause for moving up in the file.

We shift from editors to shells. A shell accepts commands from a terminal and executes them. We illustrate with an example of a shell for answering Prolog goals. This is presented as Program 12.6.

The shell is invoked by `shell`. The code is similar to the editor. The shell gives a prompt, using `shell_prompt`, then reads a goal and tries to solve it using `shell(Goal)`. A distinction is made between solving ground goals, where a yes/no answer is given, and solving nonground goals, where the answer is the appropriately instantiated goal. These two cases are handled by `shell_solve_ground` and `shell_solve`, respectively. The shell is terminated by the goal `exit`.

Both `shell_solve_ground` and `shell_solve` use the meta-variable facility to call the goal to be solved. The success or failure of the goal determines the output message. These predicates are the simplest examples of meta-interpreters, a subject discussed in Chapter 17.

The `shell_solve` procedure shows an interesting solve-write-fail combination, which is useful to elicit all solutions to a goal by forced backtracking. Since we do not wish the shell to fail, an alternative clause is provided, which succeeds when all solutions to the goal are exhausted. It is interesting to note that it is not possible to collect all solutions to goals in a straightforward way without using some sort of side effect. This is explained further in Chapter 16 on second-order programming.

The shell can be used as a basis for a logging facility to keep a record of a session with Prolog. Such a facility is given as Program 12.7. This new shell is invoked by `log`, which calls the basic interactive predicate `shell(Flag)` with Flag initialized to `log`. The flag takes one of two values, `log` or `nolog`, and indicates whether the output is currently being logged.

The logging facility is an extension of Program 12.6. The principal predicates take an extra argument, which indicates the current state of logging. Two extra commands are added, `log` and `nolog`, to turn logging on and off.

The flag is used by the predicates concerned with I/O. Each message written on the screen must also be written in the logging file. Also, each goal read is inserted in the log to increase the log's readability. Thus calls to `read` in Program 12.6 are replaced by a call to `shell_read`, and calls to `write` replaced by calls to `shell_write`.

The definition of `shell_write` specifies what must be done:

```
shell_write(X,nolog) ← write(X).
shell_write(X,log) ← write(X), file_write([X],'prolog.log').
```

If the flag is currently `nolog`, the output is written normally to the screen. If the flag is `log`, an extra copy is written to the file `prolog.log`. The predicate `file_write(X,File)` writes the line X to file File.

The remaining two predicates in Program 12.7, `file_write/2` and `close_logging_file`, involve interacting with the underlying file system. Appropriate commands from Standard Prolog are given, and the reader is referred to a Prolog manual for more information.

```
log ← shell(log).

shell(Flag) ←
    shell_prompt, shell_read(Goal,Flag), shell(Goal,Flag).

shell(exit,Flag) ←
    !, close_logging_file.
shell(nolog,Flag) ←
    !, shell(nolog).
shell(log,Flag) ←
    !, shell(log).
shell(Goal,Flag) ←
    ground(Goal), !, shell_solve_ground(Goal,Flag), shell(Flag).
shell(Goal,Flag) ←
    shell_solve(Goal,Flag), shell(Flag).

shell_solve(Goal,Flag) ←
    Goal, shell_write(Goal,Flag), nl, fail.
shell_solve(Goal,Flag) ←
    shell_write('No (more) solutions',Flag), nl.

shell_solve_ground(Goal,Flag) ←
    Goal, !, shell_write('Yes',Flag), nl.
shell_solve_ground(Goal,Flag) ←
    shell_write('No',Flag), nl.

shell_prompt ← write('Next command? ').

shell_read(X,log) ← read(X),
    file_write(['Next command? ',X],'prolog.log').
shell_read(X,nolog) ← read(X).

shell_write(X,nolog) ← write(X).
shell_write(X,log) ← write(X), file_write(X,'prolog.log').

file_write(X,File) ← write_term(File,Term,[ ]).

close_logging_file ← close('prolog.log').
```

Program 12.7 Logging a session

Exercises for Section 12.4

(i)   Extend Program 12.5, the editor, to handle the following commands:

(a) Move the cursor down N lines,

(b) Delete N lines,

(c) Move to a line containing a given term,

(d) Replace one term by another,

(e) Any command of your choice.

(ii) Modify the logging facility, Program 12.7, so that the user can specify the destination file of the logged output.

12.5   Failure-Driven Loops

The interactive programs in the previous section were all based on tail recursive loops. There is an alternative way of writing loops in Prolog that are analogous to repeat loops in conventional languages. These loops are driven by failure and are called *failure-driven loops*. These loops are useful only when used in conjunction with extra-logical predicates that cause side effects. Their behavior can be understood only from an operational point of view.

A simple example of a failure-driven loop is a query Goal, write (Goal), nl, fail?, which causes all solutions to a goal to be written on the screen. Such a loop is used in the shells of Programs 12.6 and 12.7.

A failure-driven loop can be used to define the system predicate tab(N) for printing N blanks on the screen. It uses Program 8.5 for between:

```
tab(N) ← between(1,N,I), put_char(' '), fail.
```

Each of the interactive programs in the previous section can be rewritten using a failure-driven loop. The new version of the basic interactive loop is given as Program 12.8. It is based on a nonterminating system

```
echo ← repeat, read(X), echo(X), !.
echo(X) ← last_input(X), !.
echo(X) ← write(X), nl, fail.
repeat.
repeat ← repeat.
```

Program 12.8   Basic interactive repeat loop

consult(*File*) ←

    The clauses of the program in the file *File* are read and asserted.

```
consult(File) ← open(File,read,DD), consult_loop(DD), close(DD).

consult_loop(DD) ← repeat, read(Clause), process(Clause,DD), !.

process(Clause,DD) ← at_end_of_stream(DD).
process(Clause,DD) ← assertz(Clause), fail.
```

Program 12.9   Consulting a file

predicate `repeat`, which can be defined by the minimal recursive procedure in Program 12.8. Unlike the Program 12.4 goal, the goal `echo(X)` fails unless the termination condition is satisfied. The failure causes backtracking to the `repeat` goal, which succeeds, and the next term is read and echoed. The cut in the definition of `echo` ensures that the repeat loop is not reentered later.

Failure-driven loops that use `repeat` are called *repeat loops* and are the analogue of repeat loops from conventional languages. Repeat loops are useful in Prolog for interacting with the outside system to repeatedly read and/or write. Repeat loops require a predicate that is guaranteed to fail, causing the iteration to continue, unless the loop should be terminated. The goal `echo(X)` in Program 12.8 serves that function, only succeeding when the last input is reached. A useful heuristic for building repeat loops is that there should be a cut in the body of the clause with the `repeat` goal, which prevents a nonterminating computation were the loop to be reentered via backtracking.

We use a repeat loop to define the system predicate `consult(File)` for reading in a file of clauses and asserting them. Program 12.9 contains its definition. The system predicates `open/3` and `close/1` are used for opening and closing an input file, respectively.

Tail recursive loops are preferable to repeat loops because the latter have no logical meaning. In practice, repeat loops are often necessary to run large computations, especially on Prolog implementations without tail recursion optimization or garbage collection. Explicit failure typically initiates some implementation-dependent reclamation of space.

Exercise for Section 12.5

(i)   Write your own version of the builtin predicate `abolish(F,N)` that retracts all the clauses for the procedure F of arity N.

12.6 Background

I/O has never really blended well with the rest of the language of Prolog. Its standard implementation, with side effects, relies solely on the procedural semantics of Prolog and has no connection to the underlying logic programming model. For example, if an output is issued on a failing branch of a computation, it is not undone upon backtracking. If an input term is read, it is lost on backtracking, as the input stream is not backtrackable.

Concurrent logic languages attempt to remedy the problem and to integrate I/O better with the logic programming model by identifying the I/O streams of devices with the logical streams in the language (Shapiro, 1986). Perpetual recursive processes can produce or consume incrementally those potentially unbounded streams.

Self-modifying programs are a bygone concept in computer science. Modern programming languages preclude this ability, and good assembly language practice also avoids such programming tricks. It is ironic that a programming language attempting to open a new era in computer programming opens the front door to such arcane techniques, using the predicates `assert` and `retract`.

These program manipulation predicates of Prolog were devised initially as a low-level mechanism for loading and reloading programs, implemented in DEC-10 Prolog by the `consult` and `reconsult` predicates. However, like any other feature of a language, they ended up being used for tasks that, we believe, were not intended by their original designers.

Reluctantly, we must acknowledge that `assert` and `retract` are part of Prolog, and clarify the anomalies. Attempts have been made in this direction. Inconsistencies between different Prolog implementations are discussed in Moss (1986). The best way of handling retracts seems to be the logical update view presented in Lindholm and O'Keefe (1987).

The discussion of static and dynamic predicates comes from the Standard Prolog draft (Scowen, 1991).

The program for the Towers of Hanoi was shown to us by Shmuel Safra. Memo-functions in the context of artificial intelligence were proposed by Donald Michie (1968).

The line editor is originally due to Warren (1982b).

13   Program Development

Software engineering considerations are as relevant for programming in logic programming languages as in procedural languages. Prolog is no different from any other language in its need for a methodology to build and maintain large programs. A good programming style is important, as is a good program development methodology. This chapter discusses programming style and layout and program development, and introduces a method called stepwise enhancement for systematic construction of Prolog programs.

13.1   Programming Style and Layout

One basic concern in composing the programs in this book has been to make them as declarative as possible to increase program clarity and readability. A program must be considered as a whole. Its readability is determined by its physical layout and by the choice of names appearing in it. This section discusses the guidelines we use when composing programs.

An important influence in making programs easy to read is the naming of the various objects in the program. The choice of all predicate names, variable names, constants, and structures appearing in the program affect readability. The aim is to emphasize the declarative reading of the program.

We choose predicate names to be a word (or several words) that names relations between objects in the program rather than describing what the program is doing. Coining a good declarative name for a procedure does not come easily.

The activity of programming is procedural. It is often easier to name procedurally than declaratively (and programs with procedural names usually run faster :-). Once the program works, however, we often revise the predicate names to be declarative. Composing a program is a cyclic activity in which names are constantly being reworked to reflect our improved understanding of our creation, and to enhance readability by us and others.

Mnemonic variable names also have an effect on program readability. A name can be a meaningful word (or words) or a standard variable form such as Xs for lists.

Variables that appear only once in a clause can be handled separately. They are in effect *anonymous*, and from an implementation viewpoint need not be named. Standard Prolog supports a special syntactic convention, a single underscore, for referring to anonymous variables. Using this convention, Program 3.12 for member would be written

```
member(X,[X|_]).
member(X,[_|Ys]) ← member(X,Ys).
```

The advantage of the convention is to highlight the significant variables for unification. The disadvantage is related; the reading of clauses becomes procedural rather than declarative.

We use different syntactic conventions for separating multiple words in variable names and predicate functors. For variables, composite words are run together, each new word starting with a capital letter. Multiple words in predicate names are linked with underscores. Syntactic conventions are a matter of taste, but it is preferable to have a consistent style.

The layout of individual clauses also has an effect on how easily programs can be understood. We have found the most helpful style to be

```
foo(⟨Arguments⟩) ←
    bar₁(⟨Arguments₁⟩),
    bar₂(⟨Arguments₂⟩),
    ⋮
    barₙ(⟨Argumentsₙ⟩).
```

The heads of all clauses are aligned, the goals in the body of a clause are indented and occupy a separate line each. A blank line is inserted between procedures, but there is no space between individual clauses of a procedure.

Layout in a book and the typography used are not entirely consistent with actual programs. If all the goals in the body of a clause are short, then have them on one line. Occasionally we have tables of facts with more than one fact per line.

A program can be self-documenting if sufficient care is taken with these two factors and the program is sufficiently simple. Given the natural aversion of programmers to comments and documentation, this is very desirable.

In practice, code is rarely self-documenting and comments are needed. One important part of the documentation is the relation scheme, which can be presented before the clauses defining that relation, augmented with further explanations if necessary. The explanations used in this book define the relation a procedure computes. It is not always easy to come up with a precise, declarative, natural language description of a relation computed by a logic program. However, the inability to do so usually indicates that the programmer does not fully understand the creation, even if the creation actually works. Hence we encourage the use of the declarative documentation conventions adopted in this book. They are a good means of communicating to others what a program defines as well as a discipline of thought, enabling programmers to think about and reflect on their own creations.

13.2   Reflections on Program Development

Since programming in pure Prolog is as close to writing specifications as any practical programming language has gotten, one might hope that pure Prolog programs would be bug-free. This, of course, is not the case. Even when axiomatizing one's concepts and algorithms, a wide spectrum of bugs, quite similar to ones found in conventional languages, can be encountered.

Stating it differently, for any formalism there are sufficiently complex problems for which there are no self-evidently correct formulations of solutions. The difference between low-level and high-level languages, then, is only the threshold after which simple examination of the program is insufficient to determine its correctness.

There are two schools of thought on what to do on such an occasion. The "verification" school suggests that such complex programs be verified by proving that they behave correctly with respect to an abstract specification. It is not clear how to apply this approach to logic programs, since the distance between the abstract specification and the program is much smaller then in other languages. If the Prolog axiomatization is not self-evident, there is very little hope that the specification, no matter in what language it is written, would be.

One might suggest using full first-order logic as a specification formalism for Prolog. It is the authors' experience that very rarely is a specification in full first-order logic shorter, simpler, or more readable then the simplest Prolog program defining the relation.

Given this situation, there are weaker alternatives. One is to prove that one Prolog program, perhaps more efficient though more complex, is equivalent to a simpler Prolog program, which, though less efficient, could serve as a specification for the first. Another is to prove that a program satisfies some constraint, such as a "loop invariant," which, though not guaranteeing the program's correctness, increases our confidence in it.

In some sense, Prolog programs are executable specifications. The alternative to staring at them, trying to convince ourselves that they are correct, is to execute them, and see if they behave in the way we want. This is the standard testing and debugging activity, carried out in program development in any other programming language. All the classical methods, approaches, and common wisdom concerning program testing and debugging apply equally well to Prolog.

What is the difference, then, between program development in conventional, even symbolic languages and Prolog?

One answer is that although Prolog programming is "just" programming, there is some improvement in ease of expression and speed of debugging compared to other lower-level formalisms — we hope the reader has already had a glimpse of it.

Another answer is that declarative programming clears your mind. Said less dramatically, programming one's ideas in general, and programming in a declarative and high-level language in particular, clarifies one's thoughts and concepts. For experienced Prolog programmers, Prolog is not just a formalism for coding a computer, but also a formalism in which ideas can be expressed and evaluated — a tool for thinking.

A third answer is that the properties of the high-level formalism of logic may eventually lead to practical program development tools that are an order of magnitude more powerful then the tools used today. Examples of such tools are automatic program transformers, partial-evaluators, type inference programs, and algorithmic debuggers. The latter are addressed in Section 17.3, where program diagnosis algorithms and their implementation in Prolog are described.

Unfortunately, practical Prolog programming environments incorporating these novel ideas are not yet widely available. In the meantime, a simple tracer, such as explained in Section 17.2, is most of what one can expect. Nevertheless, large and sophisticated Prolog programs can be developed even using the current Prolog environments, perhaps with greater ease than in other available languages.

The current tools and systems do not dictate or support a specific program development methodology. However, as with other symbolic programming languages, rapid prototyping is perhaps the most natural development strategy. In this strategy, one has an evolving, usable prototype of the system in most stages of the development. Development proceeds by either rewriting the prototype program or extending it. Another alternative, or complementary, approach to program development is "think top-down, implement bottom-up." Although the design of a system should be top-down and goal-driven, its implementation proceeds best if done bottom-up. In bottom-up programming each piece of code written can be debugged immediately. Global decisions, such as representation, can be tested in practice on small sections of the system, and cleaned up and made more robust before most of the programming has been done. Also, experience with one subsystem may lead to changes in the design of other subsystems.

The size of the chunks of code that should be written and debugged as a whole varies and grows as the experience of the programmer grows. Experienced Prolog programmers can write programs consisting of several pages of code, knowing that what is left after writing is done is mostly simple and mundane debugging. Less experienced programmers might find it hard to grasp the functionality and interaction of more then a few procedures at a time.

We would like to conclude this section with a few moralistic statements. For every programming language, no matter how clean, elegant, and high-level, one can find programmers who will use it to write dirty, contorted, and unreadable programs. Prolog is no exception. However, we feel that for most problems that have an elegant solution, there is an elegant expression of that solution in Prolog. It is a goal of this book to convey both this belief and the tools to realize it in concrete cases, by showing that aesthetics and practicality are not necessarily opposed or conflicting goals. Put even more strongly, elegance is not optional.

13.3   Systematizing Program Construction

The pedagogic style of this book is to present well-constructed programs illustrating the important Prolog programming techniques. The examples are explained in sufficient detail so that readers can apply the techniques to construct similar programs to meet their own programming needs. Implicitly, we are saying that Prolog programming is a skill that can be learned by observing good examples and abstracting the principles.

Learning by apprenticeship, observing other programs, is not the only way. As experience with programming in Prolog accumulates, more systematic methods of teaching Prolog programming are emerging. The emergence of systematic methods is analogous to the emergence of structured programming and stepwise refinement in the early 1970s after sufficient experience had accumulated in writing programs in the computer languages of the 1950s and 1960s.

In this section, we sketch a method to develop Prolog programs. The reader is invited to reconstruct for herself how this method could be applied to develop the programs in Parts III and IV of this book. Underlying the method is a desire to provide more structure to Prolog programs so that software components can be reused and large applications can be routinely maintained and extended.

Central to the method is identifying the essential flow of control of a program. A program embodying a control flow is called a *skeleton*. Extra goals and arguments can be attached to a skeleton. The extra goals and arguments are entwined around the central flow of control and perform additional computations. The program containing the extra arguments and goals is called an *enhancement* of the skeleton. Building an enhancement from a skeleton will be called *applying a technique*.

For example, consider Program 8.6a for summing a list of numbers, reproduced here:

```
sumlist([X|Xs],Sum) ← sumlist(Xs,XsSum), Sum is X+XsSum.
sumlist([ ],0).
```

The control flow embodied in the `sumlist` program is traversing the list of numbers. The skeleton is obtained by dropping the second argument completely, restricting to a predicate with one argument, and removing goals that only pertain to the second argument. This gives the following program, which should be identifiable as Program 3.11 defining a list.

```
list([X|Xs]) ← list(Xs).
list([ ]).
```

The extra argument of the `sumlist` program calculates the sum of the numbers in the list. This form of calculation is very common and appeared in several of the examples in Chapter 8.

Another enhancement of the `list` program is Program 8.11 calculating the length of a list. There is a clear similarity between the programs for `length` and `sumlist`. Both use a similar technique for calculating a number, in one case the sum of the numbers in the list, in the second the length of the list.

```
length([X|Xs],N) ← length(Xs,N1), N is N1+1.
length([ ],0).
```

Multiple techniques can be applied to a skeleton. For example, we can apply both summing elements and counting elements in one pass to get the program `sum_length`:

```
sum_length([X|Xs],Sum,N) ←
    sumlist(Xs,XsSum,N1), Sum is X+XsSum, N is N1+1.
sum_length([ ],0,0).
```

Intuitively, it is straightforward to create the `sum_length` program from the programs for `sumlist` and `length`. The arguments are taken directly and combined to give a new program. We call this operation *composition*. In Chapter 18, a program for composition is presented.

Another example of a technique is adding a pair of arguments as an accumulator and a final result. The technique is informally described in Section 7.5. Applying the appropriate version of the technique to the list skeleton can generate Program 8.6b for sumlist or the iterative version of length, which is the solution to Exercise 8.3(vii).

Identifying control flows of programs may seem contradictory to the ideal of declarative programming espoused in the previous section. However, at some level programming is a procedural activity, and describing well-written chunks of code is fine. It is our belief that recognizing patterns of programs makes it easier for people to develop good style. Declarativeness is preserved by ensuring wherever possible that each enhancement produced be given a declarative reading.

The programming method called *stepwise enhancement* consists of three steps:

1. Identify the skeleton program constituting the control flow.

2. Create enhancements using standard programming techniques.

3. Compose the separate enhancements to give the final program.

We illustrate stepwise enhancement for a simple example — calculating the union and intersection of two lists of elements. For simplicity we assume that there are no duplicate elements in the two lists and that we do not care about the order of elements in the answer.

A skeleton for this program follows. The appropriate control flow is to traverse the first list, checking whether each element is a member or not of the second list. There will be two cases:

```
skel([X|Xs],Ys) ← member(X,Ys), skel(Xs,Ys).
skel([X|Xs],Ys) ← nonmember(X,Ys), skel(Xs,Ys).
skel([ ],Ys).
```

To calculate the union, we need a third argument, which can be built top-down in the style discussed in Section 7.5. We consider each clause in turn. When an element in the first list is a member of the second list, it is not included in the union. When an element in the first list is not a member of the second list, it is included in the union. When the first list is empty, the union is the second list. The enhancement for union is given as Program 13.1.

union(Xs,Ys,Us) ←
　　Us is the union of the elements in *Xs* and *Ys*.

```
union([X|Xs],Ys,Us) ← member(X,Ys), union(Xs,Ys,Us).
union([X|Xs],Ys,[X|Us]) ← nonmember(X,Ys), union(Xs,Ys,Us).
union([ ],Ys,Ys).
```

Program 13.1　Finding the union of two lists

intersect(Xs,Ys,Is) ←
　　Is is the intersection of the elements in *Xs* and *Ys*.

```
intersect([X|Xs],Ys,[X|Is]) ← member(X,Ys), intersect(Xs,Ys,Is).
intersect([X|Xs],Ys,Is) ← nonmember(X,Ys), intersect(Xs,Ys,Is).
intersect([ ],Ys,[ ]).
```

Program 13.2　Finding the intersection of two lists

union_intersect(Xs,Ys,Us,Is) ←
　　Us and *Is* are the union and intersection, respectively, of the
　　elements in *Xs* and *Ys*.

```
union_intersect([X|Xs],Ys,Us,[X|Is]) ←
    member(X,Ys), union_intersect(Xs,Ys,Us,Is).
union_intersect([X|Xs],Ys,[X|Us],Is) ←
    nonmember(X,Ys), union_intersect(Xs,Ys,Us,Is).
union_intersect([ ],Ys,Ys,[ ]).
```

Program 13.3　Finding the union and intersection of two lists

The intersection, given as Program 13.2, is determined with a similar technique. We again consider each clause in turn. When an element in the first list is a member of the second list, it is included in the intersection. When an element in the first list is not a member of the second list, it is not included in the intersection. When the first list is empty, so is the intersection.

Calculating both the union and the intersection can be determined in a single traversal of the first list by composing the two enhancements. This program is given as Program 13.3.

Developing a program is typically straightforward once the skeleton has been decided. Knowing what skeleton to use is less straightforward and is learned by experience. Experience is necessary for any design task. By splitting up the program development into three steps, however, the design process is simplified and given structure.

A motivation behind giving programs structure, as is done by stepwise enhancement, is to facilitate program maintenance. It is easy to extend a program by adding new techniques to a skeleton, and it is possible to improve programs by changing skeletons while maintaining techniques. Further, the structure makes it easy to explain a program.

Skeletons and techniques can be considered as constituting reusable software components. This will be illustrated in Chapter 17, where the same skeleton meta-interpreter is useful both for program debugging and for expert system shells.

Having raised software engineering issues such as maintainability and reusability, we conclude this chapter by examining two other issues that must be addressed if Prolog is to be routinely used for large software projects. The place of specifications should be clarified, and modules are necessary if code is to be developed in pieces.

It is clear from the previous section that we do not advocate using first-order logic as a specification language. Still, it is necessary to have a specification, that is, a document explaining the behavior of a program sufficiently so that the program can be used without the code having to be read. We believe that a specification should be the primary form of documentation and be given for each procedure in a program.

A suggested form for a specification is given in Figure 13.1. It consists of a procedure declaration, effectively giving the name and arity of the predicate; a series of type declarations about the arguments; a relation scheme; and other important information such as modes of use of the predicate and multiplicities of solutions in each mode of use. We discuss each component in turn.

Types are emerging as important in Prolog programs. An untyped language facilitates rapid prototyping and interactive development, but for more systematic projects, imposing types is probably worthwhile.

The relation scheme is a precise statement in English that explains the relation computed by the program. All the programs in this book have a relation scheme. It should be stressed that relation schemes must be precise statements. We believe that proving properties of programs will proceed in the way of mathematics, where proofs are given by precise statements in an informal language.

```
procedure p(T₁,T₂, ... ,Tₙ)
```

Types: T_1: type 1
         T_2: type 2
            ⋮
         T_n: type n

Relation scheme:

Modes of use:

Multiplicities of solution:

Figure 13.1   Template for a specification

Prolog programs inherit from logic programs the possibility of being multi-use. In practice, multi-use is rare. A specification should state which uses are guaranteed to be correct. That is the purpose of the modes of use component in Figure 13.1. Modes of use are specified by the instantiation state of arguments before and after calls to the predicate.

For example, the most common mode of use of Program 3.15 for append(Xs,Ys,Zs) for concatenating two lists Xs and Ys to produce a list Zs is as follows. Xs and Ys are instantiated at the time of call, whereas Zs is not, and all three arguments are instantiated after the goal succeeds. Calling append/3 with all three arguments instantiated is a different mode of use. A common convention, taken from DEC-10 Prolog is to use + for an instantiated argument, – for an uninstantiated argument, and ? for either. The modes for the preceding use of append are append(+, +, –) before the call and append(+, +, +) after the call.

More precise statements can be made by combining modes with types. The mode of use of the current example becomes the following: Before the call the first two arguments are complete lists and the third a variable; after the call all three arguments are complete lists.

Multiplicities are the number of solutions of the predicate, and should be specified for each mode of use of the program. It is useful to give both the minimum and maximum number of solutions of a predicate. The multiplicities can be used to reason about properties of the program.

Modules are primarily needed to allow several people to work on a project. Several programmers should be able to develop separate components of a large system without worrying about undesirable interactions such as conflict of predicate names. What is needed is a mechanism for specifying what is local to a module and which predicates are imported and exported.

Current Prolog systems provide primitive facilities for handling modules. The current systems are either atom-based or predicate-based, depending on what is made local to the module. Directives are provided for specifying imports and exports. Experience is growing in using existing module facilities, which will be translated into standards for modules that will ultimately be incorporated into Standard Prolog. The current draft on modules in Standard Prolog is in too much flux to describe here. The user needing modules should consult the relevant Prolog manual.

Exercises for Section 13.3

(i)   Enhance Program 13.3 to build the list of elements contained in the first list but not in the second list.

(ii)   Write a program to solve the following problem. Given a binary tree T with positive integers as values, build a tree that has the same structure as T but with every node replaced by the maximum value in the tree. It can be accomplished with one traversal of the tree. (Hint: Use Program 3.23 as a skeleton.)

(iii) Write a program to calculate the mean and mode of an ordered list of numbers in one pass of the list.

13.4   Background

Commenting on Prolog programming style has become more prevalent in recent Prolog textbooks. There are useful discussions in both Ross (1989) and O'Keefe (1990). The latter book also introduces program schemas, which have parallels with skeletons and techniques.

Stepwise enhancement has emerged from ongoing work at Case Western Reserve University, first in the COMPOSERS group and more recently in the ProSE group. Examples of decomposing Prolog programs into skeletons and techniques are given in Sterling and Kirschenbaum (1993) and presented in tutorial form in Deville, Sterling, and Deransart (1991).

Underlying theory is given in Power and Sterling (1990) and Kirschenbaum, Sterling, and Jain (1993). An application of structuring Prolog programs using skeletons and techniques to the inductive inference of Prolog programs can be found in Kirschenbaum and Sterling (1991).

Automatic incorporation of techniques into skeletons via partial evaluation has been described in Lakhotia (1989).

The discussion on specifications for Prolog programs is strongly influenced by Deville (1990).

Exercise 13.3(ii) was suggested by Gilles Kahn. The example is originally due to Bird. Exercise 13.3(iii) emerged through interaction with Marc Kirschenbaum. Solutions to both exercises are given in Deville, Sterling, and Deransart (1991).

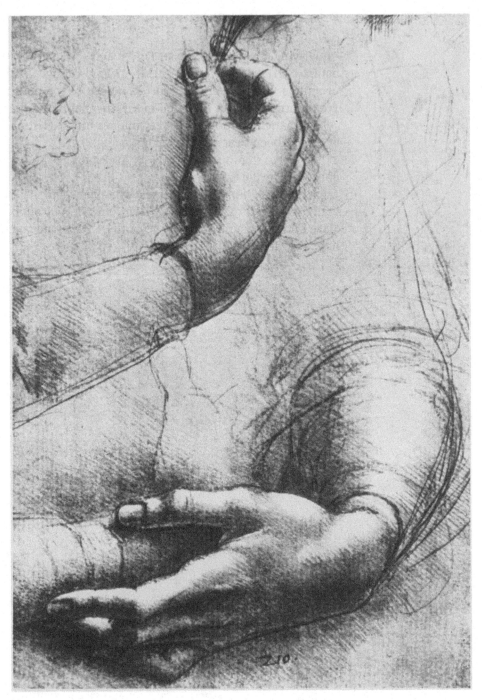

Leonardo Da Vinci. *Study of a Woman's Hands folded over her Breast*. Silver-point on pink prepared paper, heightened with white. About 1478. Windsor Castle, Royal Library.

III Advanced Prolog Programming Techniques

The expressive power and high-level nature of logic programming can be exploited to write programs that are not easily expressed in conventional programming languages. Different problem-solving paradigms can be supported, and alternative data construction and access mechanisms can be used.

The simple Prolog programs of the previous part are examples of the use of basic programming techniques, reinterpreted in the context of logic programming. This part collects more advanced techniques that have evolved in the logic programming community and exploit the special features of logic programs. We show how they can be used to advantage.

14   Nondeterministic Programming

One feature of the logic programming computation model lacking in conventional programming models is nondeterminism. Nondeterminism is a technical concept used to define, in a concise way, abstract computation models. However, in addition to being a powerful theoretical concept, nondeterminism is also useful for defining and implementing algorithms. This chapter shows how, by thinking nondeterministically, one can construct concise and efficient programs.

Intuitively, a nondeterministic machine can choose its next operation correctly when faced with several alternatives. True nondeterministic machines cannot be realized but can be simulated or approximated. In particular, the Prolog interpreter approximates the nondeterministic behavior of the abstract interpreter of logic programs by sequential search and backtracking, as explained in Chapter 6. However, the fact that nondeterminism is only simulated without being "really present" can be abstracted away in many cases in favor of nondeterministic thinking in much the same way as pointer manipulation details involved in unification can be abstracted away in favor of symbolic thinking.

14.1   Generate-and-Test

Generate-and-test is a common technique in algorithm design and programming. Here is how generate-and-test works for problem solving. One process or routine generates candidate solutions to the problem, and another process or routine tests the candidates, trying to find one or all candidates that actually solve the problem.

It is easy to write logic programs that, under the execution model of Prolog, implement the generate-and-test technique. Such programs typically have a conjunction of two goals, in which one acts as the generator and the other tests whether the solution is acceptable, as in the following clause:

```
find(X) ← generate(X), test(X).
```

This Prolog program would actually behave like a conventional, procedural, generate-and-test program. When called with find(X)?, generate(X) succeeds, returning some X, with which test(X) is called. If the test goal fails, execution backtracks to generate(X), which generates the next element. This continues iteratively until the tester successfully finds a solution with the distinguishing property or until the generator has exhausted all alternative solutions.

The programmer, however, need not be concerned with the generate-and-test cycle and can view this technique more abstractly, as an instance of nondeterministic programming. In this nondeterministic program the generator guesses correctly an element in the domain of possible solutions, and the tester simply verifies that the guess of the generator is correct.

A good example of a program with multiple solutions and commonly used as a generator is Program 3.12 for member. The query member(X,[a,b,c])? will yield the solutions X=a, X=b, and X=c successively as required. Thus member can be used to nondeterministically choose the correct element of a list in a generate-and-test program.

Program 14.1 is a simple example of generate-and-test using member as a generator. The program identifies parts of speech of a sentence. We assume that a sentence is represented as a list of words and that there is a database of facts giving the parts of speech of particular words. Each part of speech is a unary predicate whose argument is a word, for example, noun(man) indicates that man is a noun. The relation verb(Sentence,Word) is true if Word is a verb in sentence Sentence. The analogous meanings are intended for noun/2 and article/2. The query verb([a,man,loves,a,woman],V)? finds the verb V=loves in the sentence using generate-and-test. Words in the sentence are generated by member and tested to see if they are verbs.

verb(Sentence,Verb) ←
    Verb is a verb in the list of words *Sentence*.

```
verb(Sentence,Word) ← member(Word,Sentence), verb(Word).
noun(Sentence,Word) ← member(Word,Sentence), noun(Word).
article(Sentence,Word) ← member(Word,Sentence), article(Word).
```

Vocabulary

```
noun(man).      noun(woman).
article(a).     verb(loves).

member(X,Xs) ← See Program 3.12.
```

Program 14.1 Finding parts of speech in a sentence

Another simple example is testing whether two lists have an element in common. Consider the predicate `intersect(Xs,Ys)`, which is true if Xs and Ys have an element in common:

```
intersect(Xs,Ys) ← member(X,Xs), member(X,Ys).
```

The first `member` goal in the body of the clause generates members of the first list, which are then tested to see whether they are in the second list by the second `member` goal. Thinking nondeterministically, the first goal guesses an X in Xs, and the second verifies that the guess is a member of Ys.

Note that when executed as a Prolog program, this clause effectively implements two nested loops. The outer loop iterates over the elements of the first list, and the inner loop checks whether the chosen element is a member of the second list. Hence this nondeterministic logic program achieves, under the execution model of Prolog, a behavior very similar to the standard solution one would compose for this problem in Fortran, Pascal, or Lisp.

The definition of `member` in terms of append,

```
member(X,Xs) ← append(As,[X|Bs],Xs).
```

is itself essentially a generate-and-test program. The two stages, however, are amalgamated by the use of unification. The append goal generates splits of the list, and immediately a test is made whether the first element of the second list is X.

Typically, generate-and-test programs are easier to construct than programs that compute the solution directly, but they are also less efficient.

A standard technique for optimizing generate-and-test programs is to "push" the tester inside the generator as deeply as possible. Ultimately, the tester is completely intertwined with the generator, and only correct solutions are generated.

Let us consider optimizing generate-and-test programs by pushing the tester into the generator. Program 3.20 for permutation sort is another example of a generate-and-test program. The top level is as follows:

```
sort(Xs,Ys) ← permutation(Xs,Ys), ordered(Ys).
```

Abstractly, this program guesses nondeterministically the correct permutation via `permutation(Xs,Ys)`, and `ordered` checks that the permutation is actually ordered.

Operationally, the behavior is as follows. A query involving `sort` is reduced to a query involving `permutation` and `ordered`. A failure-driven loop ensues. A permutation of the list is generated by `permutation` and tested by `ordered`. If the permuted list is not ordered, the execution backtracks to the `permutation` goal, which generates another permutation to be tested. Eventually an ordered permutation is generated and the computation terminates.

Permutation sort is a highly inefficient sorting algorithm, requiring time super-exponential in the size of the list to be sorted. Pushing the tester into the generator, however, leads to a reasonable algorithm. The generator for permutation sort, `permutation`, selects an arbitrary element and recursively permutes the rest of the list. The tester, `ordered`, verifies that the first two elements of the permutation are in order, then recursively checks the rest. If we view the combined recursive `permutation` and `ordered` goals as a recursive sorting process, we have the basis for insertion sort, Program 3.21. To sort a list, sort the tail of the list and insert the head of the list into its correct place in the order. The arbitrary selection of an element has been replaced by choosing the first element.

Another example of the advantage of intertwining generating and testing can be seen with programs solving the N queens problem.

The N queens problem requires the placement of N pieces on an N-by-N rectangular board so that no two pieces are on the same line: horizontal, vertical, or diagonal. The original formulation called for 8 queens to be placed on a chessboard, and the criterion of not being on the same line corresponds to two queens not attacking each other under the rules of chess. Hence the problem's name.

Figure 14.1   A solution to the 4 queens problem

queens(N,Queens) ←
    Queens is a placement that solves the *N* queens problem,
    represented as a permutation of the list of numbers $[1, 2, \ldots, N]$.

```
queens(N,Qs) ←
    range(1,N,Ns), permutation(Ns,Qs), safe(Qs).
```

safe(Qs) ←
    The placement *Qs* is safe.

```
safe([Q|Qs]) ← safe(Qs), not attack(Q,Qs).
safe([ ]).

attack(X,Xs) ← attack(X,1,Xs).

attack(X,N,[Y|Ys]) ← X is Y+N ; X is Y-N.
attack(X,N,[Y|Ys]) ← N1 is N+1, attack(X,N1,Ys).
```

```
permutation(Xs,Ys) ← See Program 3.20.
```

```
range(M,N,Ns) ← See Program 8.12.
```

Program 14.2   Naive generate-and-test program solving *N* queens

The program has been well studied in the recreational mathematics literature. There is no solution for $N = 2$ and $N = 3$, and a unique solution up to reflection for $N = 4$, shown in Figure 14.1. There are 88 solutions for $N = 8$, or 92, depending on strictness with symmetries.

Program 14.2 is a simplistic program solving the *N* queens problem. The relation queen(N,Qs) is true if Qs is a solution to the *N* queens problem. Solutions are specified as a permutation of the list of the numbers 1 to *N*. The first element of the list is the row number to place the queen in the first column, the second element indicates the row number to place the queen in the second column, etc. Figure 14.1 indicates the solution [2,4,1,3] to the 4 queens problem. This specification of solutions, and the program generating them, has implicitly incorporated the observation that any solution to the N queens problem will have a queen on each row and a queen on each column.

The program behaves as follows. The predicate range creates a list Ns of the numbers from 1 to N. Then a generate-and-test cycle begins. The permutation predicate generates a permutation Qs of Ns, which is tested to see whether it is a solution to the problem with the predicate safe(Qs). This predicate is true if Qs is a correct placement of the queens. Since two queens are not placed on the same row or column, the predicate need only check whether two queens attack each other along a diagonal. Safe is defined recursively. A list of queens is safe if the queens represented by the tail of the list are safe and the queen represented by the head of the list does not attack any of the other queens. The definition of attack(Q,Qs) uses a neat encapsulation of the interaction of diagonals. A queen is on the same diagonal as a second queen N columns away if the second queen's row number is N units greater than, or N units less than, the first queen's row number. This is expressed by the first clause of attack/3 in Program 14.2. The meaning of attack(Q,Qs) is that queen Q attacks some queen in Qs. The diagonals are tested iteratively until the end of the board is reached.

Program 14.2 cannot recognize when solutions are symmetric. The program gives two solutions to the query queens(4,Qs)?, namely Qs=[2,4,1,3] and Qs=[3,1,4,2].

Although it is a well-written logic program, Program 14.2 behaves inefficiently. Many permutations are generated that have no chance of being solutions. As with permutation sort, we improve the program by pushing the tester, in this case safe, into the generator.

Instead of testing the complete permutation, that is, placing all the queens, each queen can be checked as it is being placed. Program 14.3 computes solutions to the N queens problem by placing the queens one at a time. It also proceeds by generating and testing, in contrast to insertion sort, which became a deterministic algorithm by the transformation. The generator in the program is select and the tester is attack, or more precisely its negation.

The positions of the previously placed queens are necessary to test whether a new queen is safe. Therefore the final solution is built upward using an accumulator. This is an application of the basic technique described in Section 7.5. A consequence of using an accumulator is that the queens are placed on the right-hand edge of the board. The two solu-

queens(N,Queens) ←

   Queens is a placement that solves the *N* queens problem,
   represented as a permutation of the list of numbers [1, 2, ..., *N*].

```
queens(N,Qs) ← range(1,N,Ns), queens(Ns,[ ],Qs).

queens(UnplacedQs,SafeQs,Qs) ←
    select(Q,UnplacedQs,UnplacedQs1),
    not attack(Q,SafeQs),
    queens(UnplacedQs1,[Q|SafeQs],Qs).
queens([ ],Qs,Qs).

select(X,Xs,Ys) ← See Program 3.19.

attack(X,Xs) ← See Program 14.2.
```

Program 14.3   Placing one queen at a time

Figure 14.2   A map requiring four colors

tions to the query queens(4,Qs)? are given in the opposite order to the
solutions given by Program 14.2.

   The next problem is to color a planar map so that no two adjoining regions have the same color. A famous conjecture, an open question for a
hundred years, was proved in 1976, showing that four colors are sufficient to color any planar map. Figure 14.2 gives a simple map requiring
four colors to be colored correctly. This can be proved by enumeration of
the possibilities. Hence four colors are both necessary and sufficient.

   Program 14.4, which solves the map-coloring problem, uses the
generate-and-test programming technique extensively. The program implements the following nondeterministic iterative algorithm:

For each region of the map,
   choose a color,
   choose (or verify) colors for the neighboring regions from the
      remaining colors.

color_map(Map,Colors) ←
   Map is colored with *Colors* so that no two neighbors have the same
   color. The map is represented as an adjacency-list of regions
   region(Name,Color,Neighbors), where *Name* is the name of the
   region, *Color* is its color, and *Neighbors* are the colors of its
   neighbors.

```
color_map([Region|Regions],Colors) ←
    color_region(Region,Colors),
    color_map(Regions,Colors).
color_map([ ],Colors).
```

color_region(Region,Colors) ←
   Region and its neighbors are colored using *Colors* so that the
   region's color is different from the color of any of its neighbors.

```
color_region(region(Name,Color,Neighbors),Colors) ←
    select(Color,Colors,Colors1),
    members(Neighbors,Colors1).
```

`select(X,Xs,Ys)` ← See Program 3.19.

`members(Xs,Ys)` ← See Program 7.6.

Program 14.4   Map coloring

A data structure is needed to support the algorithm. The map is represented as a list of regions. Each region has a name, a color, and a list of
colors of the adjoining regions. The map in Figure 14.2, for example, is
represented as

```
[region(a,A,[B,C,D]),region(b,B,[A,C,E]),
    region(c,C,[A,B,D,E,F]),region(d,D,[A,C,F]),
    region(e,E,[B,C,F]),region(f,F,[C,D,E])].
```

The sharing of variables is used to ensure that the same region is not
colored with two different colors by different iterations of the algorithm.
   The top-level relation is `color_map(Map,Colors)`, where Map is represented as before, and Colors is a list of colors used to color the map.
Our colors are red, yellow, blue, and white. The heart of the algorithm is
the definition of `color_region(Region,Colors)`:

```
color_region(region(Name,Color,Neighbors),Colors) ←
    select(Color,Colors,Colors1), members(Neighbors,Colors1).
```

Test data

```
test_color(Name,Map) ←
    map(Name,Map),
    colors(Name,Colors),
    color_map(Map,Colors).

map(test,[region(a,A,[B,C,D]),region(b,B,[A,C,E]),
    region(c,C,[A,B,D,E,F]),region(d,D,[A,C,F]),
    region(e,E,[B,C,F]),region(f,F,[C,D,E])]).

map(west_europe,[region(portugal,P,[E]), region(spain,E,[F,P]),
    region(france,F,[E,I,S,B,WG,L]), region(belgium,B,[F,H,L,WG]),
    region(holland,H,[B,WG]), region(west_germany,WG,[F,A,S,H,B,L]),
    region(luxembourg,L,[F,B,WG]), region(italy,I,[F,A,S]),
    region(switzerland,S,[F,I,A,WG]), region(austria,A,[I,S,WG])]).

colors(X,[red,yellow,blue,white]).
```

Program 14.5   Test data for map coloring

Both the select and members goals can act as generators or testers, depending on whether their arguments are instantiated.

Overall, the effect of the program is to instantiate a data structure, the map. The calls to select and members can be viewed as specifying local constraints. The predicates either generate by instantiating arguments in the structure or test whether instantiated values satisfy local constraints. Program 14.5 tests the map coloring solution.

Instantiating a data structure designed especially for a problem is a particularly effective means of implementing generate-and-test solutions. Unification and failure to unify control the building of the final solution structure, avoiding creation of unnecessary intermediate data structures. Since unification is supported well by Prolog implementations, solutions are found quickly. Exercise 14.1(iv) assigns the task of designing a data structure that can be instantiated to solve the N queens problem. The resulting program solves the N queens problem much more quickly than Program 14.3.

Our final example is solving a logic puzzle. The behavior of the program is similar to the map-coloring program. The logic puzzle consists of some facts about some small number of objects that have various attributes. The minimum number of facts is given about the objects and attributes, to yield a unique way of assigning attributes to objects.

Here is an example that we use to describe the technique of solving logic puzzles.

Three friends came first, second, and third in a programming competition. Each of the three has a different first name, likes a different sport, and has a different nationality.

Michael likes basketball and did better than the American. Simon, the Israeli, did better than the tennis player. The cricket player came first.

Who is the Australian? What sport does Richard play?

Logic puzzles such as this one are elegantly solved by instantiating the values of a suitable data structure and extracting the solution values. Each clue is translated into a fact about the data structure. This can be done before the exact form of the data structure is determined using data abstraction. Let us analyze the first clue: "Michael likes basketball and did better than the American." Two distinct people are referred to. One is named Michael, whose sport is basketball, and the other is American. Further, Michael did better than the American. If we assume the structure to be instantiated is `Friends`, then the clue is expressed as the conjunction of goals

```
did_better(Man1,Man2,Friends), first_name(Man1,michael),
sport(Man1,basketball), nationality(Man2,american),
```

Similarly, the second clue can be translated to the conditions

```
did_better(Man1,Man2,Friends), first_name(Man1,simon),
nationality(Man1,israeli), sport(Man2,tennis),
```

and the third clue to the conditions

```
first(Friends,Man), sport(Man,cricket).
```

A framework for solving puzzles is given as Program 14.6. The relation computed is `solve_puzzle(Puzzle,Solution)`, where `Solution` is the solution to `Puzzle`. The puzzle is represented by the structure `puzzle(Clues,Queries,Solution)`, where the data structure being instantiated is incorporated into the clues and queries, and the values to be extracted are given by `Solution`.

The code for `solve_puzzle` is trivial. All it does is successively solve each clue and query, which are expressed as Prolog goals and are executed with the meta-variable facility.

The clues and queries for our example puzzle are given in Program 14.7. We describe the structure assumed by the clues to solve the puzzle.

solve_puzzle(Puzzle,Solution) ←
    Solution is a solution of *Puzzle*,
    where *Puzzle* is *puzzle(Clues,Queries,Solution)*.

```
solve_puzzle(puzzle(Clues,Queries,Solution),Solution) ←
    solve(Clues),
    solve(Queries).

solve([Clue|Clues]) ←
    Clue, solve(Clues).
solve([ ]).
```

Program 14.6 A puzzle solver

Each person has three attributes and can be represented by the structure `friend(Name,Country,Sport)`. There are three friends whose order in the programming competition is significant. This suggests an ordered sequence of three elements as the structure for the problem, i.e., the list

```
[friend(N1,C1,S1),friend(N2,C2,S2),friend(N3,C3,S3)].
```

The programs defining the conditions `did_better`, `first_name`, `nationality`, `sport`, and `first` are straightforward, and are given in Program 14.7.

The combination of Programs 14.6 and 14.7 works as a giant generate-and-test. Each of the `did_better` and `member` goals access people, and the remaining goals access attributes of the people. Whether they are generators or testers depends on whether the arguments are instantiated or not. The answer to the complete puzzle, for the curious, is that Michael is the Australian, and Richard plays tennis.

The puzzle given in Program 14.7 is simple. An interesting question is how well does the framework of Program 14.6 scale. A good example of a larger puzzle is given in Exercise 14.1(vi). Is the framework adequate for such a puzzle?

The short answer is yes. Prolog is an excellent language for solving logic puzzles. However, care must be taken when formulating the clues and queries. For example, the predicate `member` is often essential to specify individuals, as is done to formulate the query in Program 14.7. It may be tempting to become systematic and begin the puzzle solution by specifying all individuals by `member` goals. This can lead to very inefficient programs because too many choice-points are set up. In general, implicit checking of a condition is usually more efficient. Another observation is

Test data

```
test_puzzle(Name,Solution) ←
    structure(Name,Structure),
    clues(Name,Structure,Clues),
    queries(Name,Structure,Queries,Solution),
    solve_puzzle(puzzle(Clues,Queries,Solution),Solution).

structure(test,[friend(N1,C1,S1),friend(N2,C2,S2),friend(N3,C3,S3)]).

clues(test,Friends,
    [(did_better(Man1Clue1,Man2Clue1,Friends),          % Clue 1
    first_name(Man1Clue1,michael), sport(Man1Clue1,basketball),
    nationality(Man2Clue1,american)),
    (did_better(Man1Clue2,Man2Clue2,Friends),           % Clue 2
    first_name(Man1Clue2,simon), nationality(Man1Clue2,israeli),
    sport(Man2Clue2,tennis)),
    (first(Friends,ManClue3), sport(ManClue3,cricket))  % Clue 3
    ]).

queries(test, Friends,
    [ member(Q1,Friends),
      first_name(Q1,Name),
      nationality(Q1,australian),                       % Query 1
      member(Q2,Friends),
      first_name(Q2,richard),
      sport(Q2,Sport)                                   % Query 2
    ],
    [['The Australian is ', Name],['Richard plays ', Sport]]
).

did_better(A,B,[A,B,C]).
did_better(A,C,[A,B,C]).
did_better(B,C,[A,B,C]).

first_name(friend(A,B,C),A).
nationality(friend(A,B,C),B).
sport(friend(A,B,C),C).

first([X|Xs],X).
```

Program 14.7 A description of a puzzle

that the order of the goals in the queries can significantly affect running time. It is best to worry about this once the problem formulation is correct. Determining appropriate goal order is a skill easily learned by experience.

Another tip concerns negative clues, such as "John is not the tailor." These clues are best regarded as specifying two separate individuals, John and the tailor, rather than as setting up a negative condition about one individual. The predicate `select` can be used instead of `member` to guarantee that individuals are different.

Exercises for Section 14.1

(i)   Write a program to compute the integer square root of a natural number N defined to be the number I such that $I^2 \leq N$, but $(I + 1)^2 > N$. Use the predicate `between/3`, Program 8.5, to generate successive natural numbers on backtracking.

(ii)   Write a program to solve the stable marriage problem (Sedgewick, 1983), stated as follows:

Suppose there are N *men and* N *women who want to get married. Each man has a list of all the women in his preferred order, and each woman has a list of all the men in her preferred order. The problem is to find a set of marriages that is stable.*
A pair of marriages is unstable *if there are a man and woman who prefer each other to their spouses. For example, consider the pair of marriages where David is married to Paula, and Jeremy is married to Judy. If David prefers Judy to Paula, and Judy prefers David to Jeremy, the pair of marriages is unstable. This pair would also be unstable if Jeremy preferred Paula to Judy, and Paula preferred Jeremy to David. A set of marriages is* stable *if there is no pair of unstable marriages.*

Your program should have as input lists of preferences, and produce as output a stable set of marriages. It is a theorem from graph theory that this is always possible. Test the program on the following five men and five women with their associated preferences:

avraham: chana tamar zvia ruth sarah
binyamin: zvia chana ruth sarah tamar
chaim: chana ruth tamar sarah zvia
david: zvia ruth chana sarah tamar
elazar: tamar ruth chana zvia sarah

zvia:	elazar avraham david binyamin chaim
chana:	david elazar binyamin avraham chaim
ruth:	avraham david binyamin chaim elazar
sarah:	chaim binyamin david avraham elazar
tamar:	david binyamin chaim elazar avraham

(iii) Use Program 14.4 to color the map of Western Europe. The countries are given in Program 14.5.

(iv) Design a data structure for solving the *N* queens problem by instantiation. Write a program that solves the problem by instantiating the structure.

(v) Explain why the following program solves the *N* queens problem:

```
queens(N,Qs) ←
    gen_list(N,Qs), place_queens(N,Qs,Ups,Downs).
gen_list(0,[ ]).
gen_list(N,[Q|L]) ← N > 0, N1 is N-1, gen_list(N1,L).

place_queens(0,Qs,Ups,Downs).
place_queens(I,Qs,Ups,[D|Downs]) ←
    I > 0, I1 is I-1,
    place_queens(I1,Qs,[U|Ups],Downs),
    place_queen(I,Qs,Ups,Downs).

place_queen(Q,[Q|Qs],[Q|Ups],[Q|Downs]).
place_queen(Q,[Q1|Qs],[U|Ups],[D|Downs] ←
    place_queen(Q,Qs,Ups,Downs).
```

(vi) Write a program to solve the following logic puzzle. There are five houses, each of a different color and inhabited by a man of a different nationality, with a different pet, drink, and brand of cigarettes.

(a) The Englishman lives in the red house.

(b) The Spaniard owns the dog.

(c) Coffee is drunk in the green house.

(d) The Ukrainian drinks tea.

(e) The green house is immediately to the right (your right) of the ivory house.

(f) The Winston smoker owns snails.

(g) Kools are smoked in the yellow house.

(h) Milk is drunk in the middle house.

(i) The Norwegian lives in the first house on the left.

(j) The man who smokes Chesterfields lives in the house next to the man with the fox.

(k) Kools are smoked in the house next to the house where the horse is kept.

(l) The Lucky Strike smoker drinks orange juice.

(m) The Japanese smokes Parliaments.

(n) The Norwegian lives next to the blue house.

Who owns the Zebra? Who drinks water?

(vii) Write a program to test whether a graph is planar using the algorithm of Hopcroft and Tarjan (Deo, 1974; Even, 1979).

14.2 Don't-Care and Don't-Know Nondeterminism

Two forms of nondeterminism are distinguished in the logic programming literature. They differ in the nature of the choice that must be made among alternatives. For *don't-care nondeterminism*, the choice can be made arbitrarily. In terms of the logic programming computation model, any goal reduction will lead to a solution, and it does not matter which particular solution is found. For *don't-know nondeterminism*, the choice matters but the correct one is not known at the time the choice is made.

Most examples of don't-care nondeterminism are not relevant for the Prolog programmer. A prototypical example is the code for `minimum`. Program 3.7 is the standard, incorporating a limited amount of don't-care nondeterminism, namely, when X and Y are the same:

```
minimum(X,Y,X) ← X ≤ Y.
minimum(X,Y,Y) ← Y ≤ X.
```

In Section 7.4, we termed this redundancy and advised against its use.

On the other hand, programs exhibiting don't-know nondeterminism are common. Consider the program for testing whether two binary trees are isomorphic (Program 3.25, reproduced here). Each clause is independently correct, but given two isomorphic binary trees, we don't know which of the two recursive clauses should be used to prove the isomorphism. Operationally, only when the computation terminates successfully do we know the correct choice:

```
isotree(void,void).
isotree(tree(X,L1,R1),tree(X,L2,R2)) ←
    isotree(L1,L2), isotree(R1,R2).
isotree(tree(X,L1,R1),tree(X,L2,R2)) ←
    isotree(L1,R2), isotree(L2,R1).
```

Composing Prolog programs exhibiting either form of nondeterminism can be indistinguishable from composing deterministic programs. Each clause is written independently. Whether inputs match only one clause or several is irrelevant to the programmer. Indeed this is seen from the multiple uses that can be made of Prolog programs. With arguments instantiated in one way, the program is deterministic; with another pattern of instantiation, the program is nondeterministic. For example, append/3 is deterministic if called with its first two arguments instantiated, while it is generally nondeterministic if called with the third argument instantiated and the first two arguments uninstantiated.

The behavior of Prolog programs seemingly having don't-know nondeterminism such as isotree is known. A given logic program and a query determine a search tree, as discussed in Chapter 5, which is searched depth-first by Prolog. Writing a program possessing don't-know nondeterminism is really specifying a depth-first search algorithm for solving the problem.

We consider this viewpoint in a little more detail with a particular example: finding whether two nodes in a graph are connected. Figure 14.3 contains two graphs that will be used to test our ideas. The left-hand one is a tree, while the right-hand one is not, containing a cycle. Trees, or more generally, directed acyclic graphs (DAGs), behave better than graphs with cycles, as we will see in our example programs.

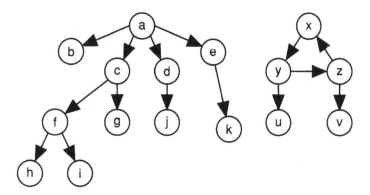

Figure 14.3 Directed graphs

connected(X,Y) ←
    Node *X* is connected to node *Y,*
    given an *edge/2* relation describing a DAG.

```
connected(X,X).
connected(X,Y) ← edge(X,N), connected(N,Y).
```

Data

```
edge(a,b).    edge(a,c).    edge(a,d).    edge(a,e).    edge(d,j).
edge(c,f).    edge(c,g).    edge(f,h).    edge(e,k).    edge(f,i).
edge(x,y).    edge(y,z).    edge(z,x).    edge(y,u).    edge(z,v).
```

Program 14.8 Connectivity in a finite DAG

Our first program is a small modification of a logic program of Section 2.3. Program 14.8 defines the relation connected(X,Y), which is true if two nodes in a graph, X and Y, are connected. Edges are directed; the fact edge(X,Y) states that a directed edge exists from X to Y. Declaratively the program is a concise, recursive specification of what it means for nodes in a graph to be connected. Interpreted operationally as a Prolog program, it is the implementation of an algorithm to find whether two nodes are connected using depth-first search.

The solutions to the query connected(a,X)? using the data from the left-hand graph in Figure 14.3 gives as values for X, a, b, c, f, h, i, g, d, j, e, k. Their order constitutes a depth-first traversal of the tree.

Program 14.9 is an extension of this simple program that finds a path between two nodes. The predicate path(X,Y,Path) is true if Path is

path(X,Y,Path) ←
    Path is a path between two nodes *X* and *Y*
    in the DAG defined by the relation *edge/2*.

```
path(X,X,[X]).
path(X,Y,[X|P]) ← edge(X,N), path(N,Y,P).
```

Program 14.9   Finding a path by depth-first search

connected (X,Y) ←
    Node *X* is connected to node *Y* in the graph defined by *edge/2*.

```
connected(X,Y) ← connected(X,Y,[X]).

connected(X,X,Visited).
connected(X,Y,Visited) ←
    edge(X,N), not member(N,Visited), connected(N,Y,[N|Visited]).
```

Program 14.10   Connectivity in a graph

a path from the node X to the node Y in a graph. Both endpoints are included in the path. The path is built downward, which fits well with the recursive specification of the connected relation. The ease of computing the path is a direct consequence of the depth-first traversal. Extending a breadth-first traversal to find the path is much more difficult. Sections 16.2 and 20.1 show how it can be done.

Depth-first search, *dfs*, correctly traverses any finite tree or DAG (directed acyclic graph). There is a problem, however, with traversing a graph with cycles. The computation can become lost in an infinite loop around one of the cycles. For example, the query connected(x,Node)?, referring to the right-hand graph of Figure 14.3 gives solutions Node=y, Node=z, and Node=x repeatedly without reaching *u* or *v*.

The problem is overcome by modifying connected. An extra argument is added that accumulates the nodes visited so far. A test is made to avoid visiting the same node twice. This is shown in Program 14.10.

Program 14.10 successfully traverses a finite directed graph depth-first. The pure Prolog program needed for searching finite DAGs must be extended by negation in order to work correctly. Adding an accumulator of paths visited to avoid entering loops effectively breaks the cycles in the graph by preventing traversal of an edge that would complete a cycle.

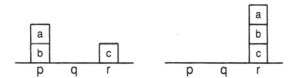

Figure 14.4   Initial and final states of a blocks world problem

The program is not guaranteed to reach every node of an infinite graph. To do so, breadth-first search is necessary. This is discussed further in Section 16.2.

This section is completed with a program for building simple plans in the blocks world. The program is written nondeterministically, essentially performing a depth-first search. It combines the two extensions mentioned before — keeping an accumulator of what has been traversed, and computing a path.

The problem is to form a plan in the blocks world, that is, to specify a sequence of actions for restacking blocks to achieve a particular configuration. Figure 14.4 gives the initial state and the desired final state of a blocks world problem. There are three blocks, *a*, *b*, and *c*, and three places, *p*, *q*, and *r*. The actions allowed are moving a block from the top of a block to a place and moving a block from one block to another. For an action to succeed, the top of the moved block must be clear, and also the place or block to which it is being moved must be clear.

The top-level procedure of Program 14.11 solving the problem is `transform(State1,State2,Plan)`. A plan of actions, `Plan`, is produced that transforms `State1` into `State2` when executed.

States are represented by a list of relations of the form `on(X,Y)`, where `X` is a block and `Y` is a block or place. They represent the facts that are true in the state. For example, the initial and final states in Figure 14.4 are, respectively, `[on(a,b),on(b,p),on(c,r)]` and `[on(a,b),on(b,c),on(c,r)]`. The state descriptions are ordered in the sense that the on relation for a precedes that of b, which precedes the on relation for c. The state descriptions allow easy testing of whether a block or place X is clear in a given state by checking that there is no relation of the form `on(A,X)`. The predicates `clear/2` and `on/3` in Program 14.11 take advantage of this representation.

transform(State1,State2,Plan) ←
    Plan is a plan of actions to transform *State1* into *State2*.

```
transform(State1,State2,Plan) ←
    transform(State1,State2,[State1],Plan).

transform(State,State,Visited,[ ]).
transform(State1,State2,Visited,[Action|Actions]) ←
    legal_action(Action,State1),
    update(Action,State1,State),
    not member(State,Visited),
    transform(State,State2,[State|Visited],Actions).

legal_action(to_place(Block,Y,Place),State) ←
    on(Block,Y,State), clear(Block,State),
    place(Place), clear(Place,State).
legal_action(to_block(Block1,Y,Block2),State) ←
    on(Block1,Y,State), clear(Block1,State), block(Block2),
    Block1 ≠ Block2, clear(Block2,State).

clear(X,State) ← not member(on(A,X),State).

on(X,Y,State) ← member(on(X,Y),State).

update(to_block(X,Y,Z),State,State1) ←
    substitute(on(X,Y),on(X,Z),State,State1).
update(to_place(X,Y,Z),State,State1) ←
    substitute(on(X,Y),on(X,Z),State,State1).

substitute(X,Y,Xs,Ys) ← See Exercise 3.3(i).
```

Program 14.11 A depth-first planner

The nondeterministic algorithm used by the planner is given by the recursive clause of `transform/4` in the program:

While the desired state is not reached,
    find a legal action,
    update the current state,
    check that it has not been visited before.

There are two possible actions, moving to a block and moving to a place. For each, the conditions for which it is legal must be specified, and a method given for updating the state as a result of performing the action.

Program 14.11 successfully solves the simple problem given as Program 14.12. The first plan it produces is horrendous, however:

```
[to_place(a,b,q),to_block(a,q,c),to_place(b,p,q),to_place(a,c,p),
 to_block(a,p,b),to_place(c,r,p),to_place(a,b,r),to_block(a,r,c),
 to_place(b,q,r),to_place(a,c,q),to_block(a,q,b),to_place(c,p,q),
 to_place(a,b,p),to_block(a,p,c),to_place(b,r,p),to_place(a,c,r),
 to_block(b,p,a),to_place(c,q,p),to_block(b,a,c),to_place(a,r,q),
 to_block(b,c,a),to_place(c,p,r),to_block(b,a,c),to_place(a,q,p),
 to_block(a,p,b)].
```

Block a is first moved to q, then to c. After that, block b is moved to q, block a is moved to p and b, and after 20 more random moves, the final configuration is reached.

It is easy to incorporate a little more intelligence by first trying to achieve one of the goal states. The predicate legal_action can be replaced by a predicate choose_action(Action,State1,State2). A simple definition suffices to produce intelligent behavior in our example problem:

```
choose_action(Action,State1,State2) ←
    suggest(Action,State2), legal_action(Action,State1).
choose_action(Action,State1,State2) ←
    legal_action(Action,State1).

suggest(to_place(X,Y,Z),State) ←
    member(on(X,Z),State), place(Z).
suggest(to_block(X,Y,Z),State) ←
    member(on(X,Z),State), block(Z).
```

The first plan now produced is [to_place(a,b,q),to_block(b,p,c), to_block(a,q,b)].

Testing and data

```
test_plan(Name,Plan) ←
    initial_state(Name,I), final_state(Name,F), transform(I,F,Plan).

initial_state(test,[on(a,b),on(b,p),on(c,r)]).
final_state(test,[on(a,b),on(b,c),on(c,r)]).

block(a).    block(b).    block(c).
place(p).    place(q).    place(r).
```

Program 14.12 Testing the depth-first planner

Exercises for Section 14.2

(i)   Apply Program 14.11 to solve another simple blocks world problem.

(ii)   Modify Program 14.11 to solve the following planning problem.

Consider a simplified computer consisting of a single accumulator and a large number of general purpose registers. There are four instructions: *load*, *store*, *add* and *subtract*. From the initial state where the accumulator is empty, *register1* contains the value *c1*, *register2* contains *c2*, *register3* contains *c3* and *register4* contains *c4*, achieve a final state where the accumulator contains

(a) $(c1 - c2) + (c3 - c4)$

(b) $(c1 - c2) + (c1 - c2)$

(c) *c1*, and *register1* contains $c1 + (c2 - c3)$, and *register2* contains $c2 - c3$.

14.3   Artificial Intelligence Classics: ANALOGY, ELIZA, and McSAM

"The best way to learn a subject is to teach it" is a cliche commonly repeated to new teachers. An appropriate analogue for new programmers is that the best way to understand a program is to rewrite or extend it. In this spirit, we present logical reconstructions of three AI programs. Each is clear, understandable, and easily extended. The exercises at the end of the section encourage the reader to add new facts and rules to the programs.

The three programs chosen are the ANALOGY program of Evans for solving geometric analogy questions from intelligence tests; the ELIZA program of Weizenbaum, which simulates or rather parodies conversation; and McSAM, a microversion of SAM, a program for "understanding" stories from the Yale language group. Each logical reconstruction is expressed very simply. The nondeterminism of Prolog allows the programmer to ignore the issues of search.

Consider the task of solving the geometric analogy problems typically used in intelligence tests. Several diagrams are presented in a prototypi-

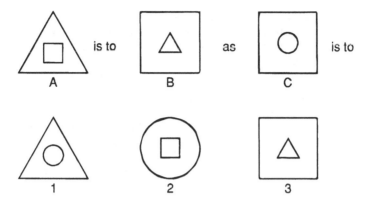

Figure 14.5   A geometric analogy problem

cal problem. Diagrams A, B, and C are singled out from a list of possible answers and the following question is posed: "A is to B as C is to which one of the 'answer' diagrams?" Figure 14.5 gives a simple problem of this type.

Here is an intuitive algorithm for solving the problem, where terms such as *find*, *apply*, and *operation* are left unspecified:

Find an operation that relates A to B.
Apply the operation to C to give a diagram X.
Find X, or its nearest equivalent, among the answers.

In the problem in Figure 14.5, the positions of the square and triangle are swapped (with appropriate scaling) between diagrams A and B. The "obvious" answer is to swap the square and the circle in diagram C. The resultant diagram appears as no. 2 in the possible answers.

Program 14.13 is a simple program for solving analogy problems. The basic relation is analogy(Pair1,Pair2,Answers), where each Pair is of the form X is_to Y. To parse the program, is_to must be declared as an infix operator. The two elements in Pair1 bear the same relation as the two elements in Pair2, and the second element in Pair2 appears in Answers. The definition of analogy implements the intuitive algorithm:

```
analogy(A is_to B,C is_to X,Answers) ← match(A,B,Operation),
    match(C,X,Operation), member(X,Answers).
```

analogy(Pair1,Pair2,Answers) ←
    An analogy holds between the pairs of figures *Pair1* and *Pair2*.
    The second element of *Pair2* is one of the possible *Answers*.

```
analogy(A is_to B,C is_to X,Answers) ←
    match(A,B,Operation),
    match(C,X,Operation),
    member(X,Answers).

match(inside(Figure1,Figure2),inside(Figure2,Figure1),invert).
match(above(Figure1,Figure2),above(Figure2,Figure1),invert).
```

Program 14.13 A program solving geometric analogies

A fundamental decision is how the figures in the problem should be represented. In Program 14.13, figures are represented as Prolog terms. Diagram A in Figure 14.5 is a square inside a triangle and is represented as the term `inside(square,triangle)`.

The relation between two diagrams is found by the predicate `match (A,B,Operation)`. This relation is true if `Operation` matches A and B. The operation `invert` is used to solve our example problem. The behavior of `invert` is to swap its arguments.

The predicate `match` is used in two distinct ways in this program. The first time it produces an operation matching two given diagrams. The second time it produces a second diagram given an operation and a diagram. These details are, however, irrelevant from the nondeterministic viewpoint. Finding the answer is implemented simply, checking whether a given diagram appears in the list of answers. Note that the second `match` goal and the `member` goal can be swapped. The behavior then becomes guessing an answer using `member` as a generator, and verifying that the guess has the same relation to diagram C as A does to B. Program 14.14 tests the analogy program.

Exercise 14.3(i) poses three additional problems to be solved by analogy, which can be expressed within the framework of Program 14.13. The representation of pictures by terms, and the description of operations becomes increasingly ad hoc. Indeed, much of the "intelligence" of the program is embedded in the representation. The original ANALOGY program did not assume as much knowledge. It took a line drawing and tried to recognize the objects. Triangles, squares, and so on, were not assumed to be the primitives.

Testing and data

```
test_analogy(Name,X) ←
    figures(Name,A,B,C),
    answers(Name,Answers),
    analogy(A is_to B,C is_to X,Answers).

figures(test1,inside(square,triangle),inside(triangle,square),
    inside(circle,square)).
answers(test1,[inside(circle,triangle),inside(square,circle),
    inside(triangle,square)]).
```

Program 14.14   Testing ANALOGY

	I am unhappy.
> >	How long have you been unhappy?
	Six months. Can you help me.
> >	What makes you think I help you?
	You remind me of my father and brother.
> >	Please tell me more about father.
	I like teasing father.
> >	Does anyone else in your family like teasing father?
	No, only me.
> >	Please go on.

Figure 14.6   Sample conversation with ELIZA

The next AI classic considered is a simplified version of ELIZA. The program aims to simulate a conversation. A user types in a sentence, and ELIZA responds with an appropriate question or comment. ELIZA does not understand in any real sense, responding to its input by recognizing word patterns and replying by using a corresponding response pattern. To make the patterns of responses more credible, a psychiatrist setting is adopted. A sample interaction with ELIZA is given in Figure 14.6. Computer responses are preceded by >>.

The heart of ELIZA is a procedure for matching the input sentence against a pattern. The resulting match is applied to another pattern to determine the program reply. The pair of patterns can be considered a stimulus/response pair, where the input is matched against the stimulus and the output generated from the response. A typical stimulus/response pair is

I am ⟨statement⟩   How long have you been ⟨statement⟩?

Using this pair, the response of the program to the input statement "I am unhappy" will be the question "How long have you been unhappy?" The ⟨statement⟩ can be viewed as a slot to be filled.

Program 14.15 is a simple version of ELIZA. It implements the following algorithm:

Read the input.
While the input is not bye,
    choose a stimulus/response pair,
    match the input to the stimulus,
    generate the reply from the response and the above match,
    output the response,
    read the next input.

The stimulus/response pairs are represented as facts of the form `pattern(Stimulus,Response)`, where both `Stimulus` and `Response` are lists of words and slots. Slots in the patterns are represented by integers. The predicate `match(Pattern,Table,Words)` is used for both the second and third steps of the algorithm. It expresses a relation between a pattern `Pattern`, a list of words `Words`, and a table `Table`, where the table records how the slots in the pattern are filled. A central part of the `match` procedure is played by a nondeterministic use of `append` to break up a list of words. The table is represented by an *incomplete data structure*, discussed in more detail in Chapter 15. The missing procedure `lookup/3` is given in Section 15.3. The reply is generated by `reply(Words)`. which is a modified version of Program 12.1 for `writeln` that leaves spaces between words.

The final program presented in this section is Micro SAM or McSAM. It is a simplified version of the SAM (Script Applier Mechanism) program developed in the natural language group at Yale University. The aim of McSAM is to "understand" stories. Given a story, it finds a relevant script and matches the individual events of the story against the patterns in the script. In the process, events in the script not explicitly mentioned in the story are filled in.

eliza ←
Simulates a conversation via side effects.

```
eliza ← read_word_list(Input), eliza(Input), !.
eliza([bye]) ←
    reply(['Goodbye. I hope I have helped you']).
eliza(Input) ←
    pattern(Stimulus,Response),
    match(Stimulus,Dictionary,Input),
    match(Response,Dictionary,Output),
    reply(Output),
    read_word_list(Input1),
    !, eliza(Input1).
```

match(Pattern,Dictionary,Words) ←
Pattern matches the list of words *Words*, and matchings are
recorded in the *Dictionary*.

```
match([N|Pattern],Dictionary,Target) ←
    integer(N), lookup(N,Dictionary,LeftTarget),
    append(LeftTarget,RightTarget,Target),
    match(Pattern,Dictionary,RightTarget).
match([Word|Pattern],Dictionary,[Word|Target]) ←
    atom(Word), match(Pattern,Dictionary,Target).
match([ ],Dictionary,[ ]).

lookup(Key,Dictionary,Value) ← See Program 15.8.
```

pattern(Stimulus,Response) ←
Response is an applicable response pattern to the pattern *Stimulus*.

```
pattern([i,am,1],['How',long,have,you,been,1,?]).
pattern([1,you,2,me],['What',makes,you,think,'I',2,you,?]).
pattern([i,like,1],['Does',anyone,else,in,your,family,like,1,?]).
pattern([i,feel,1],['Do',you,often,feel,that,way,?]).
pattern([1,X,2],['Please',tell,me,more,about,X,.]) ←
    important(X).
pattern([1],['Please',go,on,.]).

important(father).    important(mother).    important(son).
important(sister).    important(brother).   important(daughter).

reply([Head|Tail]) ← write(Head), write(' '), reply(Tail).
reply([ ]) ← nl.

read_word_list(Xs) ← See Program 12.2.
```

Program 14.15   ELIZA

Input: John went to Leones, ate a hamburger, and left.

Output: John went to Leones. He was shown from the door to a seat.
A waiter brought John a hamburger, which John ate by mouth.
The waiter brought John a check, and John left Leones for
another place.

Figure 14.7   A story filled in by McSAM

Both the story and the script are represented in terms of Schank's
theory of conceptual dependency. For example, consider the input story
in Figure 14.7, which is used as an example in our version of McSAM. The
English version

"John went to Leones, ate a hamburger, and left"

is represented in the program as a list of lists:

```
[   [ptrans, john, john, X1, leones],
    [ingest, X2, hamburger, X3],
    [ptrans, Actor, Actor, X4, X5]   ].
```

The first element in each list, `ptrans` and `ingest`, for example, is a term
from conceptual dependency theory. The representation of the story as a
list of lists is chosen as a tribute to the original Lisp version.

Programming McSAM in Prolog is a triviality, as demonstrated by
Program 14.16. The top-level relation is `mcsam(Story,Script)`, which
expands a `Story` into its "understood" equivalent according to a relevant `Script`. The script is found by the predicate `find(Story,Script,`
`Defaults)`. The story is searched for a nonvariable argument that triggers the name of a script. In our example of John visiting Leones, the
atom `leones` triggers the `restaurant` script, indicated by the fact `trig-`
`ger(leones,restaurant)` in Program 14.17.

The matching of the story to the script is done by `match(Script,`
`Story)`, which associates lines in the story with lines in the script. Remaining slots in the script are filled in by `name_defaults(Defaults)`.
The "output" is

```
[ptrans,john,john,place1,leones]
[ptrans,john,john,door,seat]
[mtrans,john,waiter,hamburger]
```

mcsam(*Story,Script*) ←
    Script describes *Story*.

```
mcsam(Story,Script) ←
    find(Story,Script,Defaults),
    match(Script,Story),
    name_defaults(Defaults).

find(Story,Script,Defaults) ←
    filler(Slot,Story),
    trigger(Slot,Name),
    script(Name,Script,Defaults).
```

match(*Script,Story*) ←
    Story is a subsequence of *Script*.

```
match(Script,[ ]).
match([Line|Script],[Line|Story]) ← match(Script,Story).
match([Line|Script],Story) ← match(Script,Story).
```

filler(*Slot,Story*) ←
    Slot is a word in *Story*.

```
filler(Slot,Story) ←
    member([Action|Args],Story),
    member(Slot,Args),
    nonvar(Slot).
```

name_defaults(*Defaults*) ←
    Unifies default pairs in *Defaults*.

```
name_defaults([ ]).
name_defaults([[N,N]|L]) ← name_defaults(L).
name_defaults([[N1,N2]|L]) ← N1 ≠ N2, name_defaults(L).
```

Program 14.16   McSAM

```
[ingest,john,hamburger,[mouth,john]]
[atrans,john,check,john,waiter]
[ptrans,john,john,leones,place2].
```

Its translation to English is given in Figure 14.7.

The work done on the original McSAM was all in the searching and pattern matching. This is accomplished in Prolog by nondeterministic programming and unification.

Testing and data

```
test_mcsam(Name,UnderstoodStory) ←
    story(Name,Story), mcsam(Story,UnderstoodStory).

story(test,[[ptrans, john, john, X1, leones],
    [ingest, X2, hamburger, X3],
    [ptrans, Actor, Actor, X4, X5]  ]).

script(restaurant,
    [  [ptrans, Actor, Actor, EarlierPlace, Restaurant],
       [ptrans, Actor, Actor, Door, Seat],
       [mtrans, Actor, Waiter, Food],
       [ingest, Actor, Food, [mouth, Actor] ],
       [atrans, Actor, Money, Actor, Waiter],
       [ptrans, Actor, Actor, Restaurant, Gone] ],
    [  [Actor, customer], [EarlierPlace, place1],
       [Restaurant, restaurant], [Door, door],
       [Seat, seat], [Food, meal], [Waiter, waiter],
       [Money, check], [Gone, place2]  ]  ).

trigger(leones,restaurant).
trigger(waiter,restaurant).
```

Program 14.17   Testing McSAM

Exercises for Section 14.3

(i)   Extend ANALOGY, Program 14.13, to solve the three problems in Figure 14.8.

(ii)   Extend ELIZA, Program 14.15, by adding new stimulus/response patterns.

(iii) If the seventh statement in Figure 14.6 is changed to be "I like teasing my father," ELIZA responds with "Does any one else in your family like teasing my father." Modify Program 14.15 to "fix" this behavior, changing references such as *I*, *my*, to *you*, *your*, etc.

(iv)   Rewrite McSAM to use structures.

(v)   Reconstruct another AI classic. A good candidate is the general problem solver GPS.

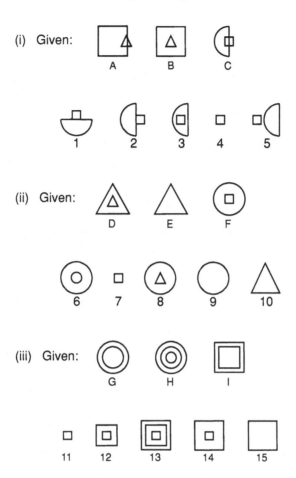

Figure 14.8 Three analogy problems

14.4   Background

Applying Prolog to generate-and-test problems has been very common. Many researchers have discussed the behavior of Prolog in solving the N queens problem and map coloring. A good discussion of how Prolog handles the N queens problem can be found in Elcock (1983). The N queens program given in Exercise 14.1(v), the fastest of which we are aware, is due to Thomas Fruewirth. A classification of generate-and-test programs in Prolog is given in Bansal and Sterling (1989).

Several researchers have used Prolog's behavior on generate-and-test problems as a reason to investigate alternative control of logic programs. Suggestions for improvement include co-routining incorporated in IC-Prolog (Clark and McCabe, 1979) and intelligent backtracking (Bruynooghe and Pereira, 1984). Neither have been widely adopted into Prolog.

Other examples of solving puzzles by instantiating structures are given in a book by Evan Tick (1991) comparing Prolog program performance with concurrent logic programming languages.

The zebra puzzle, Exercise 14.1(iv) did the rounds on the Prolog Digest in the early 1980s. It was used as an unofficial benchmark to test both the speed of Prolog implementations and the ability of Prolog programmers to write clear code. The description of clues given in Program 14.7 was influenced by one of the solutions. The framework of Program 14.6 was tested extensively by Steven Kaminski in a course project at Case Western Reserve University. He took the first 20 puzzles of an available puzzle book and solved them using the framework. Although very much a Prolog novice, he was able to use Prolog fairly easily to find solutions. His experience highlighted some interesting points, namely, how to handle negative information and the undesirability of too many choice points with redundant calls to `select` and `member`.

The definitive discussion of don't-care and don't-know nondeterminism in logic programming appears in Kowalski (1979a).

Program 14.11 for planning is a variant of an example from Kowalski (1979a). The original planning program in Prolog was WARPLAN (Warren, 1976), reproduced in Coelho et al. (1980). Exercise 14.2(ii) was adapted from descriptions of WARPLAN's abilities in Coelho and Cotta (1988).

ANALOGY constituted the Ph.D. thesis of Thomas Evans at MIT in the mid-1960s. A good description of the program appears in *Semantic Information Processing* (Minsky, 1968). Evans's program tackled many aspects of the problem that are made trivial by our choice of representation, for example, identifying that there are triangles, squares, and circles in the diagrams. Our version, Program 14.13, emerged from a discussion group of Leon Sterling with a group of epistemics students at the University of Edinburgh.

ELIZA was originally presented in Weizenbaum (1966). Its performance led people to believe that a limited form of the Turing test had been passed. Weizenbaum, its author, was horrified by people's reactions to the program and to AI more generally, and he wrote an impassioned plea against taking the program too seriously (Weizenbaum, 1976). Our version, Program 14.15, is a slight variant of a teaching program attributed to Alan Bundy, Richard O'Keefe, and Henry Thompson, which was used for AI courses at the University of Edinburgh.

McSAM is a version of the SAM program, which was tailored for teaching AI programming (Schank and Riesbeck, 1981). Our version, Program 14.16, is due to Ernie Davis and Ehud Shapiro. More information about conceptual dependency can be found in Schank and Abelson (1977).

A rational reconstruction of GPS, suggested in Exercise 14.3(v), was shown to us by George Ernst.

15   Incomplete Data Structures

The programs presented so far have been discussed in terms of relations between complete data structures. Powerful programming techniques emerge from extending the discussion to incomplete data structures, as demonstrated in this chapter.

The first section discusses difference-lists, an alternative data structure to lists for representing a sequence of elements. They can be used to simplify and increase the efficiency of list-processing programs. In some respects, difference-lists generalize the concept of accumulators. Data structures built from the difference of incomplete structures other than lists are discussed in the second section. The third section shows how tables and dictionaries, represented as incomplete structures, can be built incrementally during a computation. The final section discusses queues, an application of difference-lists.

15.1   Difference-Lists

Consider the sequence of elements 1,2,3. It can be represented as the difference between pairs of lists. It is the difference between the lists [1,2,3,4,5] and [4,5], the difference between the lists [1,2,3,8] and [8], and the difference between [1,2,3] and [ ]. Each of these cases is an instance of the difference between two incomplete lists [1,2,3|Xs] and Xs.

We denote the difference between two lists as a structure As\Bs, which is called a *difference-list*. As is the *head* of the difference-list and Bs the *tail*. In this example [1,2,3|*Xs*]*Xs* is the most general difference-list representing the sequence 1,2,3, where [1,2,3|*Xs*] is the head of the difference-list and *Xs* the tail.

Logical expressions are unified, not evaluated. Consequently the binary functor used to denote difference-lists can be arbitrary. Of course, the user must be consistent in using the same functor in any one program. Another common choice of functor besides \ is -. The functor for difference-lists can also be omitted entirely, the head and the tail of the difference-list becoming separate arguments in a predicate. While this last choice has advantages from a perspective of efficiency, we use the functor \ throughout for clarity.

Lists and difference-lists are closely related. Both are used to represent sequences of elements. Any list *L* can be trivially represented as a difference-list *L*\[ ]. The empty list is represented by any difference-list whose head and tail are identical, the most general form being *As**As*.

Difference-lists are an established logic programming technique. The use of difference-lists rather than lists can lead to more concise and efficient programs. The improvement occurs because of the combining property of difference-lists. Two incomplete difference-lists can be concatenated to give a third difference-list in constant time. In contrast, lists are concatenated using the standard append program in time linear in the length of the first list.

Consider Figure 15.1. The difference-list *Xs**Zs* is the result of appending the difference-list *Ys**Zs* to the difference-list *Xs**Ys*. This can be expressed as a single fact. Program 15.1 defines a predicate append_dl(As,Bs,Cs), which is true if the difference-list Cs is the result of appending the difference-list Bs to the difference-list As. We use the suffix _dl to denote a variant of a predicate that uses difference-lists.

A necessary and sufficient condition characterizing when two difference-lists As\Bs and Xs\Ys can be concatenated using Program 15.1 is that Bs be unifiable with Xs. In that case, the two difference-lists are *compatible*. If the tail of a difference-list is uninstantiated, it is compatible with any difference-list. Furthermore, in such a case Program 15.1 would concatenate it in constant time. For example, the result of the query append_dl([a,b,c|Xs]\Xs,[1,2]\[ ],Ys)? is (Xs=[1,2],Ys=[a,b,c,1,2]\[ ]).

Difference-lists are the logic programming counterpart of Lisp's *rplacd*, which is also used to concatenate lists in constant time and save consing

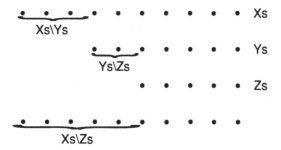

Figure 15.1   Concatenating difference-lists

append_dl(*As,Bs,Cs*) ←
  The difference-list *Cs* is the result of appending *Bs* to *As*,
  where *As* and *Bs* are compatible difference-lists.

```
append_dl(Xs\Ys, Ys\Zs, Xs\Zs).
```

Program 15.1   Concatenating difference-lists

(allocating new list-cells). There is a difference between the two: the former are free of side effects and can be discussed in terms of the abstract computation model, whereas *rplacd* is a destructive operation, which can be described only by reference to the machine representation of S-expressions.

A good example of a program that can be improved by using difference-lists is Program 9.1a for flattening a list. It uses double recursion to flatten separately the head and tail of a list of lists, then concatenates the results. We adapt that program to compute the relation flatten_dl(Xs,Ys), where Ys is a difference-list representing the elements that appear in a list of lists Xs in correct order. The direct translation of Program 9.1a to use difference-lists follows:

```
flatten_dl([X|Xs],Ys\Zs) ←
    flatten_dl(X,As\Bs), flatten_dl(Xs,Cs\Ds),
    append_dl(As\Bs,Cs\Ds,Ys\Zs).
flatten_dl(X,[X|Xs]\Xs) ←
    constant(X), X≠[ ].
flatten_dl([ ],Xs\Xs).
```

flatten(Xs,Ys) ←
  Ys is a flattened list containing the elements in *Xs*.

```
flatten(Xs,Ys) ← flatten_dl(Xs,Ys\[ ]).

flatten_dl([X|Xs],Ys\Zs) ←
    flatten_dl(X,Ys\Ys1), flatten_dl(Xs,Ys1\Zs).
flatten_dl(X,[X|Xs]\Xs) ←
    constant(X), X≠[ ].
flatten_dl([ ],Xs\Xs).
```

Program 15.2 Flattening a list of lists using difference-lists

The doubly recursive clause can be simplified by unfolding the `append_dl` goal with respect to its definition in Program 15.1. Unfolding is discussed in more detail in Chapter 18 on program transformation. The result is

```
flatten_dl([X|Xs],As\Ds) ←
    flatten_dl(X,As\Bs), flatten_dl(Xs,Bs\Ds).
```

The program for *flatten_dl* can be used to implement `flatten` by expressing the connection between the desired flattened list and the difference-list computed by `flatten_dl` as follows:

```
flatten(Xs,Ys) ← flatten_dl(Xs,Ys\[ ]).
```

Collecting the program and renaming variables yields Program 15.2.

Declaratively Program 15.2 is straightforward. The explicit call to append is made unnecessary by flattening the original list of lists into a difference-list rather than a list. The resultant program is more efficient, because the size of its proof tree is linear in the number of elements in the list of lists rather than quadratic.

The operational behavior of programs using difference-lists, such as Program 15.2, is harder to understand. The flattened list seems to be built by magic.

Let us investigate the program in action. Figure 15.2 is a trace of the query `flatten([[a],[b,[c]]],Xs)?` with respect to Program 15.2.

The trace shows that the output, `Xs`, is built top-down (in the terminology of Section 7.5). The tail of the difference-list acts like a pointer to the end of the incomplete structure. The pointer gets set by unification. By using these "pointers" no intermediate structures are built, in contrast to Program 9.1a.

```
flatten([[a],[b,[c]]],Xs)
    flatten_dl([[a],[b,[c]]],Xs\[ ])
        flatten_dl([a],Xs\Xs1)
            flatten_dl(a,Xs\Xs2)                    Xs = [a|Xs2]
                constant(a)
                a ≠ [ ]
            flatten_dl([],Xs2\Xs1)                  Xs2 = Xs1
        flatten_dl([[b,[c]]],Xs1\[ ])
            flatten_dl([b,[c]],Xs1\Xs3)
                flatten_dl(b,Xs1\Xs4)               Xs1 = [b|Xs4]
                    constant(b)
                    b ≠ [ ]
                flatten_dl([[c]],Xs4\Xs3)
                    flatten_dl([c],Xs4\Xs5)
                        flatten_dl(c,Xs4\Xs6)       Xs4 = [c|Xs6]
                            constant(c)
                            c ≠ [ ]
                        flatten_dl([ ],Xs6\Xs5)     Xs6 = Xs5
                    flatten_dl([ ],Xs5\Xs3)         Xs5 = Xs3
                flatten_dl([ ],Xs3\[ ])             Xs3 = [ ]
        Output: Xs = [a,b,c]
```

Figure 15.2   Tracing a computation using difference-lists

The discrepancy between clear declarative understanding and difficult
procedural understanding stems from the power of the logical variable.
We can specify logical relations implicitly and leave their enforcement to
Prolog. Here the concatenation of the difference-lists has been expressed
implicitly, and it is mysterious when it happens in the program.

Building structures with difference-lists is closely related to building
structures with accumulators. Loosely, difference-lists build structures
top-down, while accumulators build structures bottom-up. Exercise 9.1(i)
asked for a doubly recursive version of flatten that avoided the call to
append by using accumulators. A solution is the following program:

```
flatten(Xs,Ys) ← flatten(Xs,[ ],Ys).

flatten([X|Xs],Zs,Ys) ←
    flatten(Xs,Zs,Ys1), flatten(X,Ys1,Ys).
flatten(X,Xs,[X|Xs]) ←
    constant(X), X≠[ ].
flatten([ ],Xs,Xs).
```

reverse(Xs,Ys) ←
   Ys is the reversal of the list *Xs*.

```
reverse(Xs,Ys) ← reverse_dl(Xs,Ys\[ ]).

reverse_dl([X|Xs],Ys\Zs) ←
    reverse_dl(Xs,Ys\[X|Zs]).
reverse_dl([ ],Xs\Xs).
```

Program 15.3   Reverse with difference-lists

The similarity of this program to Program 15.2 is striking. There are only two differences between the programs. The first difference is syntactic. The difference-list is represented as two arguments, but in reverse order, the tail preceding the head. The second difference is the goal order in the recursive clause of `flatten`. The net effect is that the flattened list is built bottom-up from its tail rather than top-down from its head.

We give another example of the similarity between difference-lists and accumulators. Program 15.3 is a translation of naive `reverse` (Program 3.16a) where lists have been replaced by difference-lists, and the append operation has been unfolded away.

When are difference-lists the appropriate data structure for Prolog programs? Programs with explicit calls to append can usually gain in efficiency by using difference-lists rather than lists. A typical example is a doubly recursive program where the final result is obtained by appending the outputs of the two recursive calls. More generally, a program that independently builds different sections of a list to be later combined is a good candidate for using difference-lists.

The logic program for `quicksort`, Program 3.22, is an example of a doubly recursive program where the final result, a sorted list, is obtained from concatenating two sorted sublists. It can be made more efficient by using difference-lists. All the append operations involved in combining partial results can be performed implicitly, as shown in Program 15.4.

The call of `quicksort_dl` by `quicksort` is an initializing call, as for `flatten` in Program 15.2. The recursive clause is the quicksort algorithm interpreted for difference-lists where the final result is pieced together implicitly rather than explicitly. The base clause of `quicksort_dl` states that the result of sorting an empty list is the empty difference-list. Note the use of unification to place the partitioning element X after the smaller

quicksort (*List,SortedList*) ←
  SortedList is an ordered permutation of *List*.

```
quicksort(Xs,Ys) ← quicksort_dl(Xs,Ys\[ ]).

quicksort_dl([X|Xs],Ys\Zs) ←
    partition(Xs,X,Littles,Bigs),
    quicksort_dl(Littles,Ys\[X|Ys1]),
    quicksort_dl(Bigs,Ys1\Zs).
quicksort_dl([ ],Xs\Xs).

partition(Xs,X,Ls,Bs) ← See Program 3.22.
```

Program 15.4 Quicksort using difference-lists

elements Ys and before the bigger elements Ys1 in the call `quicksort_dl(Littles,Ys\[X|Ys1])`.

Program 15.4 is derived from Program 3.22 in exactly the same way as Program 15.2 is derived from Program 9.1a. Lists are replaced by difference-lists and the `append_dl` goal unfolded away. The initial call of `quicksort_dl` by `quicksort` expresses the relation between the desired sorted list and the computed sorted difference-list.

An outstanding example of using difference-lists to advantage is a solution to a simplified version of Dijkstra's Dutch flag problem. The problem reads: "Given a list of elements colored *red, white,* or *blue,* reorder the list so that all the red elements appear first, then all the white elements, followed by the blue elements. This reordering should preserve the original relative order of elements of the same color." For example, the list `[red(1),white(2),blue(3),red(4),white(5)]` should be reordered to `[red(1),red(4),white(2),white(5),blue(3)]`.

Program 15.5 is a simple-minded solution to the problem that collects the elements in three separate lists, then concatenates the lists. The basic relation is `dutch(Xs,Ys)`, where Xs is the original list of colored elements and Ys is the reordered list separated into colors.

The heart of the program is the procedure `distribute`, which constructs three lists, one for each color. The lists are built top-down. The two calls to `append` can be removed by having `distribute` build three distinct difference-lists instead of three lists. Program 15.6 is an appropriately modified version of the program.

The implicit concatenation of the difference-lists is done in the initializing call to `distribute_dls` by `dutch`. The complete list is finally

dutch(Xs,RedsWhitesBlues) ←
   RedsWhitesBlues is a list of elements of *Xs* ordered
   by color: red, then white, then blue.

```
dutch(Xs,RedsWhitesBlues) ←
    distribute(Xs,Reds,Whites,Blues),
    append(Whites,Blues,WhitesBlues),
    append(Reds,WhitesBlues,RedsWhitesBlues).
```

distribute(Xs,Reds,Whites,Blues) ←
   Reds, Whites, and *Blues* are the lists of the red, white,
   and blue elements in *Xs*, respectively.

```
distribute([red(X)|Xs],[red(X)|Reds],Whites,Blues) ←
    distribute(Xs,Reds,Whites,Blues).
distribute([white(X)|Xs],Reds,[white(X)|Whites],Blues) ←
    distribute(Xs,Reds,Whites,Blues).
distribute([blue(X)|Xs],Reds,Whites,[blue(X)|Blues]) ←
    distribute(Xs,Reds,Whites,Blues).
distribute([ ],[ ],[ ],[ ]).

append(Xs,Ys,Zs) ← See Program 3.15.
```

Program 15.5   A solution to the Dutch flag problem

"assembled" from its parts with the satisfaction of the base clause of
`distribute_dls`.

The Dutch flag example demonstrates a program that builds parts of
the solution independently and pieces them together at the end. It is a
more complex use of difference-lists than the earlier examples.

Although it makes the program easier to read, the use of an explicit
constructor such as \ for difference-lists incurs noticeable overhead
in time and space. Using two separate arguments to represent the
difference-list is more efficient. When important, this efficiency can be
gained by straightforward manual or automatic transformation.

Exercises for Section 15.1

(i)   Rewrite Program 15.2 so that the final list of elements is in the
        reverse order to how they appear in the list of lists.

(ii)   Rewrite Programs 3.27 for preorder(Tree,List), inorder(Tree,
        List) and postorder(Tree,List), which collect the elements oc-

dutch(Xs,RedsWhitesBlues) ←
> *RedsWhitesBlues* is a list of elements of *Xs* ordered
> by color: red, then white, then blue.

```
dutch(Xs,RedsWhitesBlues) ←
    distribute_dls(Xs,RedsWhitesBlues\WhitesBlues,
        WhitesBlues\Blues,Blues\[ ]).
```

distribute_dls(Xs,Reds,Whites,Blues) ←
> *Reds*, *Whites*, and *Blues* are the difference-lists of the
> red, white, and blue elements in *Xs*, respectively.

```
distribute_dls([red(X)|Xs],
        [red(X)|Reds]\Reds1,Whites,Blues) ←
    distribute_dls(Xs,Reds\Reds1,Whites,Blues).
distribute_dls([white(X)|Xs],
        Reds,[white(X)|Whites]\Whites1,Blues) ←
    distribute_dls(Xs,Reds,Whites\Whites1,Blues).
distribute_dls([blue(X)|Xs],
        Reds,Whites,[blue(X)|Blues]\Blues1) ←
    distribute_dls(Xs,Reds,Whites,Blues\Blues1).
distribute_dls([ ],Reds\Reds,Whites\Whites,Blues\Blues).
```

Program 15.6   Dutch flag with difference-lists

curring in a binary tree, to use difference-lists and avoid an explicit
call to append.

(iii)   Rewrite Program 12.3 for solving the Towers of Hanoi so that the
list of moves is created as a difference-list rather than a list.

15.2   Difference-Structures

The concept underlying difference-lists is the use of the difference between incomplete data structures to represent partial results of a computation. This can be applied to recursive data types other than lists. This
section looks at a specific example, sum expressions.

Consider the task of normalizing sum expressions. Figure 15.3 contains two sums $(a + b) + (c + d)$ and $(a + (b + (c + d)))$. Standard Prolog
syntax brackets the term $a + b + c$ as $((a + b) + c)$. We describe a procedure converting a sum into a normalized one that is bracketed to the
right. For example, the expression on the left in Figure 15.3 would be

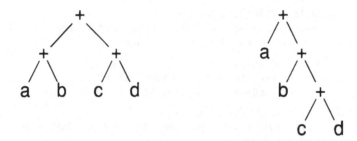

Figure 15.3 Unnormalized and normalized sums

normalize(Sum,NormalizedSum) ←
   NormalizedSum is the result of normalizing the sum expression *Sum*.

```
normalize(Exp,Norm) ← normalize_ds(Exp,Norm++0).

normalize_ds(A+B,Norm++Space) ←
    normalize_ds(A,Norm++NormB), normalize_ds(B,NormB++Space).
normalize_ds(A,(A+Space)++Space) ←
    constant(A).
```

Program 15.7 Normalizing plus expressions

converted to the one on the right. Such a procedure is useful for doing algebraic simplification, facilitating writing programs to test whether two expressions are equivalent.

We introduce a *difference-sum* as a variant of a difference-list. A difference-sum is represented as a structure *E1* ++ *E2*, where *E1* and *E2* are incomplete normalized sums. It is assumed that ++ is defined as a binary infix operator. It is convenient to use 0 to indicate an empty sum.

Program 15.7 is a program for normalizing sums. The relation scheme is `normalize(Exp,Norm)`, where Norm is an expression equivalent to Exp that is bracketed to the right and preserves the order of the constants appearing in Exp.

This program is similar in structure to Program 15.2 for flattening lists using difference-lists. There is an initialization stage, where the difference-structure is set up, typically calling a predicate with the same name but different arity or different argument pattern. The base case passes out the tail of the incomplete structure, and the goals in the body of the recursive clause pass the tail of the first incomplete structure to be the head of the second.

The program builds the normalized sum top-down. By analogy with the programs using difference-lists, the program can be easily modified to build the structure bottom-up, which is Exercise (ii) at the end of this section.

The declarative reading of these programs is straightforward. Operationally the programs can be understood in terms of building a structure incrementally, where the "hole" for further results is referred to explicitly. This is entirely analogous to difference-lists.

Exercises for Section 15.2

(i)   Define the predicate normalized_sum(Expression), which is true if Expression is a normalized sum.

(ii) Rewrite Program 15.7 so that

(a) The normalized sum is built bottom-up;

(b) The order of the elements is reversed.

(iii) Enhance Program 15.7 so that numbers appearing in the addends are added together and returned as the first component of the normalized sum. For example, $(3 + x) + 2 + (y + 4)$ should be normalized to $9 + (x + y)$.

(iv) Write a program to normalize products using difference-products, defined analogously to difference-sums.

15.3 Dictionaries

A different use of incomplete data structures enables the implementation of dictionaries. Consider the task of creating, using, and maintaining a set of values indexed under keys. There are two main operations we would like to perform: looking up a value stored under a certain key, and entering a new key and its associated value. These operations must ensure consistency — for example, the same key should not appear twice

lookup(Key,Dictionary,Value) ←
    Dictionary contains *Value* indexed under *Key.*
    Dictionary is represented as an incomplete
    list of pairs of the form *(Key,Value).*

```
lookup(Key,[(Key,Value)|Dict],Value).
lookup(Key,[(Key1,Value1)|Dict],Value) ←
    Key ≠ Key1, lookup(Key,Dict,Value).
```

Program 15.8 Dictionary lookup from a list of tuples

with two different values. It is possible to perform both operations, looking up values of keys, and entering new keys, with a single simple procedure by exploiting incomplete data structures.

Consider a linear sequence of key-value pairs. Let us see the advantages of using an incomplete data structure for its representation. Program 15.8 defines the relation `lookup(Key,Dictionary,Value)` which is true if the entry under `Key` in the dictionary `Dictionary` has value `Value`. The dictionary is represented as an incomplete list of pairs of the form `(Key,Value)`.

Let us consider an example where the dictionary is used to remember phone extensions keyed under the names of people. Suppose that `Dict` is initially instantiated to `[(arnold,8881),(barry,4513),(cathy,5950) |Xs]`. The query `lookup(arnold,Dict,N)?` has as answer `N=8881` and is used for finding Arnold's phone number. The query `lookup(barry, Dict,4513)?` succeeds, checking that Barry's phone number is 4513.

The entry of new keys and values is demonstrated by the query `lookup(david,Dict,1199)?`. Syntactically this appears to check David's phone number. Its effect is different. The query succeeds, instantiating `Dict` to `[(arnold,8881),(barry,4513),(cathy,5950),(david,1199) |Xs1]`. Thus `lookup` has entered a new value.

What happens if we check Cathy's number with the query `lookup (cathy,Dict,5951)?`, where the number is incorrect? Rather than entering a second entry for Cathy, the query fails because of the test Key ≠ Key1.

The `lookup` procedure given in Program 15.8 completes Program 14.15, the simplified ELIZA. Note that when the program begins, the dictionary is empty, indicated by its being a variable. The dictionary is built up

lookup(*Key,Dictionary,Value*) ←
　　Dictionary contains *Value* indexed under *Key*.
　　Dictionary is represented as an ordered binary tree.

```
lookup(Key,dict(Key,X,Left,Right),Value) ←
   !, X = Value.
lookup(Key,dict(Key1,X,Left,Right),Value) ←
   Key < Key1, lookup(Key,Left,Value).
lookup(Key,dict(Key1,X,Left,Right),Value) ←
   Key > Key1, lookup(Key,Right,Value).
```

Program 15.9　Dictionary lookup in a binary tree

during the matching against the stimulus half of a stimulus-response pair. The constructed dictionary is used to produce the correct response. Note that entries are placed in the dictionary without their values being known: a striking example of the power of logical variables. Once an integer is detected, it is put in the dictionary, and its value is determined later.

Searching linear lists is not very efficient for a large number of key-value pairs. Ordered binary trees allow more efficient retrieval of information than linear lists. The insight that an incomplete structure can be used to allow entry of new keys as well as to look up values carries over to binary trees.

The binary trees of Section 3.4 are modified to be a four-place structure dict(Key,Value,Left,Right), where Left and Right are, respectively, the left and right subdictionaries, and Key and Value are as before. The functor dict is used to suggest a dictionary.

Looking up in the dictionary tree has a very elegant definition, similar in spirit to Program 15.8. It performs recursion on binary trees rather than on lists, and relies on unification to instantiate variables to dictionary structures. Program 15.9 gives the procedure lookup(Key,Dictionary,Value), which as before both looks up the value corresponding to a given key and enters new values.

At each stage, the key is compared with the key of the current node. If it is less, the left branch is recursively checked; if it is greater, the right branch is taken. If the key is non-numeric, the predicates < and > must be generalized. The cut is necessary in Program 15.9, in contrast to

freeze(*A,B*) ←
    Freeze term *A* into *B*.

```
freeze(A,B) ←
    copy_term(A,B), numbervars(B,0,N).
```

melt_new(*A,B*) ←
    Melt the frozen term *A* into *B*.

```
melt_new(A,B) ←
    melt(A,B,Dictionary), !.
melt('$VAR'(N),X,Dictionary) ←
    lookup(N,Dictionary,X).
melt(X,X,Dictionary) ←
    constant(X).
melt(X,Y,Dictionary) ←
    compound(X),
    functor(X,F,N),
    functor(Y,F,N),
    melt(N,X,Y,Dictionary).

melt(N,X,Y,Dictionary) ←
    N > 0,
    arg(N,X,ArgX),
    melt(ArgX,ArgY,Dictionary),
    arg(N,Y,ArgY),
    N1 is N-1,
    melt(N1,X,Y,Dictionary).
melt(0,X,Y,Dictionary).

numbervars(Term,N1,N2) ← See Program 10.8.

lookup(Key,Dictionary,Value) ← See Program 15.9.
```

Program 15.10   Melting a term

Program 15.8, because of the nonlogical nature of comparison operators, which will give errors if keys are not instantiated.

Given a number of pairs of keys and values, the dictionary they determine is not unique. The shape of the dictionary depends on the order in which queries are posed to the dictionary.

The dictionary can be used to melt a term that has been frozen using Program 10.8 for numbervars. The code is given as Program 15.10. Each melted variable is entered into the dictionary, so that the correct shared variables will be assigned.

15.4   Queues

An interesting application of difference-lists is to implement queues. A queue is a first-in, first-out store of information. The head of the difference-list represents the beginning of the queue, the tail represents the end of the queue, and the members of the difference-list are the elements in the queue. A queue is empty if the difference-list is empty, that is, if its head and tail are identical.

Maintaining a queue is different from maintaining a dictionary. We consider the relation queue(S), where a queue processes a stream of commands, represented as a list S. There are two basic operations on a queue—enqueuing an element and dequeuing an element—represented, respectively, by the structures enqueue(X) and dequeue(X), where X is the element concerned.

Program 15.11 implements the operations abstractly. The predicate queue(S) calls queue(S,Q), where Q is initialized to an empty queue. queue/2 is an interpreter for the stream of enqueue and dequeue commands, responding to each command and updating the state of the queue accordingly. Enqueuing an element exploits the incompleteness of the tail of the queue, instantiating it to a new element and a new tail, which is passed as the updated tail of the queue. Clearly, the calls to enqueue and dequeue can be unfolded, resulting in a more concise and efficient, but perhaps less readable, program.

queue(*S*) ←
   S is a sequence of enqueue and dequeue operations,
   represented as a list of terms *enqueue*(*X*) and *dequeue*(*X*).

queue(S) ← queue(S,Q\Q).

queue([enqueue(X)|Xs],Q) ←
   enqueue(X,Q,Q1), queue(Xs,Q1).
queue([dequeue(X)|Xs],Q) ←
   dequeue(X,Q,Q1), queue(Xs,Q1).
queue([ ],Q).

enqueue(X,Qh\[X|Qt],Qh\Qt).
dequeue(X,[X|Qh]\Qt,Qh\Qt).

Program 15.11   A queue process

flatten(Xs,Ys) ←

    Ys is a flattened list containing the elements in *Xs*.

```
flatten(Xs,Ys) ← flatten_q(Xs,Qs\Qs,Ys).

flatten_q([X|Xs],Ps\[Xs|Qs],Ys) ←
    flatten_q(X,Ps\Qs,Ys).
flatten_q(X,[Q|Ps]\Qs,[X|Ys]) ←
    constant(X), X≠[ ], flatten_q(Q,Ps\Qs,Ys).
flatten_q([ ],Q,Ys) ←
    non_empty(Q), dequeue(X,Q,Q1), flatten_q(X,Q1,Ys).
flatten_q([ ],[ ]\[ ],[ ]).

non_empty([ ]\[ ]) ← !, fail.
non_empty(Q).

dequeue(X,[X|Qh]\Qt,Qh\Qt).
```

Program 15.12 Flattening a list using a queue

The program terminates when the stream of commands is exhausted. It can be extended to insist that the queue be empty at the end of the commands by changing the base fact to

```
queue([ ],Q) ← empty(Q).
```

A queue is empty if both its head and tail can be instantiated to the empty list, expressed by the fact `empty([ ]\[ ])`. Logically, the clause `empty(Xs\Xs)` would also be sufficient; however, because of the lack of the occurs check in Prolog, discussed in Chapter 4, it may succeed erroneously on a nonempty queue, creating a cyclic data structure.

We demonstrate the use of queues in Program 15.12 for flattening a list. Although the example is somewhat contrived, it shows how queues can be used. The program does not preserve the order of the elements in the original list.

The basic relation is `flatten_q(Ls,Q,Xs)`, where Ls is the list of lists to be flattened, Q is the queue of lists waiting to be flattened, and Xs is the list of elements in Ls. The initial call of `flatten_q/3` by `flatten/2` initializes an empty queue. The basic operation is enqueuing the tail of the list and recursively flattening the head of the list:

```
flatten_q([X|Xs],Q,Ys)← enqueue(Xs,Q,Q1), flatten_q(X,Q1,Ys).
```

The explicit call to enqueue can be omitted and incorporated via unification as follows:

```
flatten_q([X|Xs],Qh\[Xs|Qt],Ys) ← flatten_q(X,Qh\Qt,Ys).
```

If the element being flattened is a constant, it is added to the output structure being built top-down, and an element is dequeued (by unifying with the head of the difference-list) to be flattened in the recursive call:

```
flatten_q(X,[Q|Qh]\Qt,[X|Ys]) ←
    constant(X), X≠[ ], flatten_q(Q,Qh\Qt,Ys).
```

When the empty list is being flattened, either the top element is dequeued

```
flatten_q([ ],Q,Ys) ←
    non_empty(Q), dequeue(X,Q,Q1), flatten_q(X,Q1,Ys).
```

or the queue is empty, and the computation terminates:

```
flatten_q([ ],[ ]\[ ],[ ]).
```

A previous version of Program 15.12 incorrectly expressed the case when the list was empty, and the top element was dequeued as

```
flatten_q([ ],[Q|Qh]\Qt,Ys) ← flatten_q(Q,Qh\Qt,Ys).
```

This led to a nonterminating computation, since an empty queue Qs\Qs unified with [Q|Qh]\Qt and so the base case was never reached.

Let us reconsider Program 15.11 operationally. Under the expected use of a queue, enqueue(X) messages are sent with X determined and dequeue(X) with X undetermined. As long as more elements are enqueued than dequeued, the queue behaves as expected, with the difference between the head of the queue and the tail of the queue being the elements in the queue. However, if the number of dequeue messages received exceeds that of enqueue messages, an interesting thing happens — the content of the queue becomes *negative*. The head runs ahead of the tail, resulting in a queue containing a negative sequence of undetermined elements, one for each excessive dequeue message.

It is interesting to observe that this behavior is consistent with the associativity of appending of difference-lists. If a queue Qs\[X1,X2,X3|Qs] that contains minus three undetermined elements has the queue [a,b, c,d,e|Xs]\Xs that contains five elements appended to it, then the result will be the queue [d,e|Xs]\Xs with two elements, where the "negative" elements X1,X2,X3 are unified with a,b,c.

15.5 Background

Difference-lists have been in the logic programming folklore since its inception. The first description of them in the literature is given by Clark and Tarnlund (1977).

The automatic transformation of simple programs without difference-lists to programs with difference-lists, for example, reverse and flatten, can be found in Bloch (1984).

Section 15.1 implicitly contains an algorithm for converting from a program with explicit calls to append to an equivalent, more efficient program that uses difference-lists to concatenate the elements and which is much more efficient. Care is needed in application of the algorithm. There are excellent discussions of a correct algorithm and the dangers of using difference-lists without the occurs check in Søndergaard (1990) and Marriott and Søndergaard (1993).

There is an interesting discussion of the Dutch flag problem in O'Keefe (1990).

Automatic removal of a functor denoting difference-lists is described in Gallagher and Bruynooghe (1990).

Maintaining dictionaries and queues can be given a theoretical basis as a perpetual process, as described by Warren (1982) and Lloyd (1987).

Queues are particularly important in concurrent logic programming languages, since their input need not be a list of requests but a stream, which is generated incrementally by the processes requesting the services of the queue.

16   Second-Order Programming

Chapters 14 and 15 demonstrate Prolog programming techniques based directly on logic programming. This chapter, in contrast, shows programming techniques that are missing from the basic logic programming model but can nonetheless be incorporated into Prolog by relying on language features outside of first-order logic. These techniques are called second-order, since they talk about sets and their properties rather than about individuals.

The first section introduces predicates that produce sets as solutions. Computing with predicates that produce sets is particularly powerful when combined with programming techniques presented in earlier chapters. The second section gives some applications. The third section looks at lambda expressions and predicate variables, which allow functions and relations to be treated as "first-class" data objects.

16.1 All-Solutions Predicates

Solving a Prolog query with a program entails finding an instance of the query that is implied by the program. What is involved in finding *all* instances of a query that are implied by a program? Declaratively, such a query lies outside the logic programming model presented in Chapter 1. It is a second-order question, since it asks for the set of elements with a certain property. Operationally, it is also outside the pure Prolog computation model. In pure Prolog, all information about a certain branch of the computation is lost on backtracking. This prevents

```
father(terach,abraham).    father(haran,lot).
father(terach,nachor).     father(haran,milcah).
father(terach,haran).      father(haran,yiscah).
father(abraham,isaac).
male(abraham).    male(haran).     female(yiscah).
male(isaac).      male(nachor).    female(milcah).
male(lot).
```

Program 16.1   Sample data

a simple way of using pure Prolog to find the set of all solutions to a query, or even to find how many solutions there are to a given query.

This section discusses predicates that return all instances of a query. We call such predicates *all-solutions predicates*. Experience has shown that all-solutions predicates are very useful for programming.

A basic all-solutions predicate is findall(Term,Goal,Bag). The predicate is true if and only if Bag unifies with the list of values to which a variable X not occurring in Term or Goal would be bound by successive resatisfaction of call(Goal), X=Term? after systematic replacement of all variables in X by new variables.

Procedurally, findall(Term,Goal,Bag) creates an empty list L, renames Goal to a goal G, and executes G. If G succeeds, a copy of Term is appended to L, and G is reexecuted. For each successful reexecution, a copy of Term is appended to the list. Eventually, when G fails, Bag is unified with L. The success or failure of findall depends on the success or failure of the unification.

We demonstrate the use of all-solutions predicates using part of the biblical database of Program 1.1, repeated here as Program 16.1.

Consider the task of finding all the children of a particular father. It is natural to envisage a predicate children(X,Kids), where Kids is a list of children of X. It is immediate to define using findall, namely,

children(X,Kids) ← findall(Kid,father(X,Kid),Kids).

The query children(terach,Xs)? with respect to Program 16.1 produces the answer Xs = [abraham,nachor,haran].

The query findall(F,father(F,K),Fs)? with respect to Program 16.1 produces the answer F = [terach,haran,terach,haran,terach, haran,abraham]. It would be useful to conceive of this query as asking

for_all(Goal,Condition)
  For all solutions of *Goal*, *Condition* is true.

```
for_all(Goal,Condition) ←
    findall(Condition,Goal,Cases), check(Cases).

check([Case|Cases]) ← Case, check(Cases).
check([ ]).
```

Program 16.2   Applying set predicates

who is a father and to receive as solution [terach,haran,abraham]. This answer can be obtained by removing duplicate solutions.

Another interpretation can be made of the query findall(F,father (F,K),Fs)?. Instead of having a single solution, all fathers, there could be a solution for each child K. Thus one solution would be K=abraham, Fs = [terach]; another would be K=lot, Fs = [haran]; and so on.

Standard Prolog provides two predicates that distinguish between these two interpretations. The predicate bagof(Term,Goal,Bag) is like findall except that alternative solutions are found for the variables in Goal. The predicate setof(Term,Goal,Bag) is a refinement of bagof where the solutions in Bag are sorted corresponding to a standard order of terms and duplicates removed. If we want to emphasize that the solution should be conceived of as a set, we refer to all-solutions predicates as *set predicates*.

Another all-solutions predicate checks whether all solutions to a query satisfy a certain condition. Program 16.2 defines a predicate for_ all(Goal,Condition), which succeeds when Condition is true for all values of Goal. It uses the meta-variable facility.

The query for_all(father(X,C),male(C))? checks which fathers have only male children. It produces two answers: X=terach and X=abra-ham.

A simpler, more efficient, but less general version of for_all can be written directly using a combination of nondeterminism and negation by failure. The definition is

```
for_all(Goal,Condition) ← not (Goal, not Condition).
```

It successfully answers a query such as for_all(father(terach,X), male(X))? but fails to give a solution to the query for_all(father(X, C),male(C))?.

find_all_dl(*X,Goal,Instances*) ←
     Instances is the multiset of
     instances of *X* for which *Goal* is true. The multiplicity
     of an element is the number of different ways *Goal* can be
     proved with it as an instance of *X*.

```
find_all_dl(X,Goal,Xs) ←
    asserta('$instance'('$mark')), Goal,
    asserta('$instance'(X)), fail.
find_all_dl(X,Goal,Xs\Ys) ←
    retract('$instance'(X)), reap(X,Xs\Ys), !.

reap(X,Xs\Ys) ←
    X ≠ '$mark', retract('$instance'(X1)), !,
    reap(X1,Xs\[X|Ys]).
reap('$mark',Xs\Xs).
```

Program 16.3 Implementing an all-solutions predicate using difference-lists, assert, and retract

We conclude this section by showing how to implement a simple variant of findall. The discussion serves a dual purpose. It illustrates the style of implementation for all-solutions predicates and gives a utility that will be used in the next section. The predicate find_all_dl(X,Goal,Instances) is true if Instances is the bag (multiset) of instances of X, represented as a difference-list, where Goal is true.

The definition of find_all_dl is given as Program 16.3. The program can only be understood operationally. There are two stages to the procedure, as specified by the two clauses for find_all_dl. The explicit failure in the first clause guarantees that the second will be executed. The first stage finds all solutions to Goal using a failure-driven loop, asserting the associated X as it proceeds. The second stage retrieves the solutions.

Asserting $mark is essential for nested all-solutions predicates to work correctly, lest one set should "steal" solutions produced by the other all-solutions predicate.

Exercise for Section 16.1

(i)   Define the predicate intersect(Xs,Ys,Zs) using an all-solutions predicate to compute the intersection Zs of two lists Xs and Ys.

What should happen if the two lists do not intersect? Compare the code with the recursive definition of *intersect*.

16.2   Applications of Set Predicates

Set predicates are a significant addition to Prolog. Clean solutions are obtained to many problems by using set predicates, especially when other programming techniques, discussed in previous chapters, are incorporated. This section presents three example programs: traversing a graph breadth-first, using the Lee algorithm for finding routes in VLSI circuits, and producing a keyword in context (KWIC) index.

Section 14.2 presents three programs, 14.8, 14.9, and 14.10, for traversing a graph depth-first. We discuss here the equivalent programs for traversing a graph breadth-first.

The basic relation is connected(X,Y), which is true if X and Y are connected. Program 16.4 defines the relation. Breadth-first search is implemented by keeping a queue of nodes waiting to be expanded. The connected clause accordingly calls connected_bfs(Queue,Y), which is true if Y is in the connected component of the graph represented by the nodes in the Queue.

Each call to connected_bfs removes the current node from the head of the queue, finds the edges connected to it, and adds them to the tail of the queue. The queue is represented as a difference-list, and the all-solutions predicate find_all_dl is used. The program fails when the queue is empty. Because difference-lists are an incomplete data structure, the test that the queue is empty must be made explicitly. Otherwise the program would not terminate.

Consider the edge clauses in Program 16.4, representing the left-hand graph in Figure 14.3. Using them, the query connected(a,X)? gives the values a, b, c, d, e, f, g, j, k, h, i for X on backtracking, which is a breadth-first traversal of the graph.

Like Program 14.8, Program 16.4 correctly traverses a finite tree or a directed acyclic graph (DAG). If there are cycles in the graph, the program will not terminate. Program 16.5 is an improvement over Program 16.4 in which a list of the nodes visited in the graph is kept. Instead of adding all the successor nodes at the end of the queue, each is checked to see if

connected(*X,Y*) ←
  Node *X* is connected to node *Y* in the DAG defined by
  edge/2 facts.

```
connected(X,Y) ← enqueue(X,Q\Q,Q1), connected_bfs(Q1,Y).

connected_bfs(Q,Y) ← empty(Q), !, fail.
connected_bfs(Q,Y) ← dequeue(X,Q,Q1), X=Y.
connected_bfs(Q,Y) ←
    dequeue(X,Q,Q1), enqueue_edges(X,Q1,Q2), connected_bfs(Q2,Y).

enqueue_edges(X,Xs\Ys,Xs\Zs) ← find_all_dl(N,edge(X,N),Ys\Zs), !.

empty([ ]\[ ]).

enqueue/3, dequeue/3 ← See Program 15.11.

find_all_dl(Term,Goal,DList) ← See Program 16.3.
```

Data

```
edge(a,b).    edge(a,c).    edge(a,d).    edge(a,e).    edge(f,i).
edge(c,f).    edge(c,g).    edge(f,h).    edge(e,k).    edge(d,j).
edge(x,y).    edge(y,z).    edge(z,x).    edge(y,u).    edge(z,v).
```

Program 16.4 Testing connectivity breadth-first in a DAG

it has been visited before. This is performed by the predicate `filter` in Program 16.5.

Program 16.5 in fact is more powerful than its depth-first equivalent, Program 14.10. Not only will it correctly traverse any finite graph but it will also correctly traverse infinite graphs in which every vertex has finite degree as well. It is useful to summarize what extensions to pure Prolog have been necessary to increase the performance in searching graphs. Pure Prolog correctly searches finite trees and DAGs. Adding negation allows correct searching of finite graphs with cycles, while set predicates are necessary for infinite graphs. This is shown in Figure 16.1.

Calculating the path between two nodes is a little more awkward than for depth-first search. It is necessary to keep with each node in the queue a list of the nodes linking it to the original node. The technique is demonstrated in Program 20.6.

The next example combines the power of nondeterministic programming with the use of second-order programming. It is a program for calculating a minimal cost route between two points in a circuit using the Lee algorithm.

connected(*X,Y*) ←
>   Node *X* is connected to node *Y* in the graph defined by
>   *edge/2* facts.

```
connected(X,Y) ←
    enqueue(X,Q\Q,Q1), connected_bfs(Q1,Y,[X]).

connected_bfs(Q,Y,Visited) ← empty(Q), !, fail.
connected_bfs(Q,Y,Visited) ← dequeue(X,Q,Q1), X=Y.
connected_bfs(Q,Y,Visited) ←
    dequeue(X,Q,Q1),
    findall(N,edge(X,N),Edges),
    filter(Edges,Visited,Visited1,Q1,Q2),
    connected_bfs(Q2,Y,Visited1).

filter([N|Ns],Visited,Visited1,Q,Q1) ←
    member(N,Visited), !, filter(Ns,Visited,Visited1,Q,Q1).
filter([N|Ns],Visited,Visited1,Q,Q2) ←
    not member(N,Visited), !, enqueue(N,Q,Q1),
    filter(Ns,[N|Visited],Visited1,Q1,Q2).
filter([ ],Visited,Visited,Q,Q).

empty([ ]\[ ]).
```

enqueue/3, dequeue/3 ← See Program 15.11.

Program 16.5   Testing connectivity breadth-first in a graph

(1)   Finite trees and DAGs
       Pure Prolog
(2)   Finite graphs
       Pure Prolog + negation
(3)   Infinite graphs
       Pure Prolog + second order + negation

Figure 16.1   Power of Prolog for various searching tasks

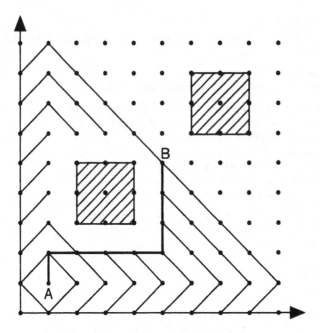

Figure 16.2   The problem of Lee routing for VLSI circuits

The problem is formulated as follows. Given a grid that may have obstacles, find a shortest path between two specified points. Figure 16.2 shows a grid with obstacles. The heavy solid line represents a shortest path between the two points *A* and *B*. The shaded rectangles represent the obstacles.

We first formulate the problem in a suitable form for programming. The VLSI circuit is modeled by a grid of points, conveniently assumed to be the upper quadrant of the Cartesian plane. A route is a path between two points in the grid, along horizontal and vertical lines only, subject to the constraints of remaining in the grid and not passing through any obstacles.

Points in the plane are represented by their Cartesian coordinates and denoted *X-Y*. In Figure 16.2, *A* is 1-1 and *B* is 5-5. This representation is chosen for readability and utilizes the definition of - as an infix binary operator. Paths are calculated by the program as a list of points from B to A, including both endpoints. In Figure 16.2 the route calculated is [5-5,5-4,5-3,5-2,4-2,3-2,2-2,1-2,1-1], and is marked by the heavy solid line.

The top-level relation computed by the program is lee_route(A,B, Obstacles,Path), where Path is a route (of minimal distance) from point A to point B in the circuit. Obstacles are the obstacles in the grid. The program has two stages. First, successive waves of neighboring grid points are generated, starting from the initial point, until the final point is reached. Second, the path is extracted from the accumulated waves. Let us examine the various components of Program 16.6, the overall program for Lee routing.

Waves are defined inductively. The initial wave is the list [A]. Successive waves are sets of points that neighbor a point in the previous wave and that do not already appear in previous waves. They are illustrated by the lighter solid lines in Figure 16.2.

Wave generation is performed by waves(B,WavesSoFar,Obstacles, Waves). The predicate waves/4 is true if Waves is a list of waves to the destination B avoiding the obstacles represented by Obstacles and WavesSoFar is an accumulator containing the waves generated so far in traveling from the source. The predicate terminates when the destination is in the current wave. The recursive clause calls next_wave/4, which finds all the appropriate grid points constituting the next wave using the all-solutions predicate findall.

Obstacles are assumed to be rectangular blocks. They are represented by the term obstacle(L,R), where L is the coordinates of the lower left-hand corner and R the coordinates of the upper right-hand corner. Exercise (i) at the end of this section requires modifying the program to handle other obstacles.

The predicate path(A,B,Waves,Path) finds the path Path back from B to A through the Waves generated in the process. Path is built downward, which means the order of the points is from B to A. This order can be changed by using an accumulator in path.

Program 16.6 produces no output while computing the Lee route. In practice, the user may like to see the computation in progress. This can be easily done by adding appropriate write statements to the procedures next_wave and path.

lee_route(Source,Destination,Obstacles,Path) ←
     Path is a minimal length path from *Source* to
     Destination that does not cross *Obstacles.*

```
lee_route(A,B,Obstacles,Path) ←
    waves(B,[[A],[ ]],Obstacles,Waves),
    path(A,B,Waves,Path).
```

waves(Destination,WavesSoFar,Obstacles,Waves) ←
     Waves is a list of waves including *WavesSoFar*
     (except, perhaps, its last wave) that leads to *Destination*
     without crossing *Obstacles.*

```
waves(B,[Wave|Waves],Obstacles,Waves) ← member(B,Wave), !.
waves(B,[Wave,LastWave|LastWaves],Obstacles,Waves) ←
    next_wave(Wave,LastWave,Obstacles,NextWave),
    waves(B,[NextWave,Wave,LastWave|LastWaves],Obstacles,Waves).
```

next_wave(Wave,LastWave,Obstacles,NextWave) ←
     NextWave is the set of admissible points from *Wave,*
     that is, excluding points from *LastWave,*
     Wave and points under *Obstacles.*

```
next_wave(Wave,LastWave,Obstacles,NextWave) ←
    findall(X,admissible(X,Wave,LastWave,Obstacles),NextWave).

admissible(X,Wave,LastWave,Obstacles) ←
    adjacent(X,Wave,Obstacles),
    not member(X,LastWave),
    not member(X,Wave).

adjacent(X,Wave,Obstacles) ←
    member(X1,Wave),
    neighbor(X1,X),
    not obstructed(X,Obstacles).

neighbor(X1-Y,X2-Y) ← next_to(X1,X2).
neighbor(X-Y1,X-Y2) ← next_to(Y1,Y2).

next_to(X,X1) ← X1 is X+1.
next_to(X,X1) ← X > 0, X1 is X-1.

obstructed(Point,Obstacles) ←
    member(Obstacle,Obstacles), obstructs(Point,Obstacle).

obstructs(X-Y,obstacle(X-Y1,X2-Y2)) ← Y1 ≤ Y, Y ≤ Y2.
obstructs(X-Y,obstacle(X1-Y1,X-Y2)) ← Y1 ≤ Y, Y ≤ Y2.
obstructs(X-Y,obstacle(X1-Y,X2-Y2)) ← X1 ≤ X, X ≤ X2.
obstructs(X-Y,obstacle(X1-Y1,X2-Y)) ← X1 ≤ X, X ≤ X2.
```

Program 16.6 Lee routing

path(Source,Destination,Waves,Path) ←
    Path is a path from *Source* to *Destination* going through *Waves*.

```
path(A,A,Waves,[A]) ← !.
path(A,B,[Wave|Waves],[B|Path]) ←
    member(B1,Wave),
    neighbor(B,B1),
    !, path(A,B1,Waves,Path).
```

Testing and data

```
test_lee(Name,Path) ←
    data(Name,A,B,Obstacles), lee_route(A,B,Obstacles,Path).

data(test,1-1,5-5,[obstacle(2-3,4-5),obstacle(6-6,8-8)]).
```

Program 16.6   (Continued)

Our final example in this section concerns the keyword in context (KWIC) problem. Again, a simple Prolog program, combining nondeterministic and second-order programming, suffices to solve a complex task.

Finding keywords in context involves searching text for all occurrences of a set of keywords, extracting the contexts in which they appear. We consider here the following variant of the general problem: "Given a list of titles, produce a sorted list of all occurrences of a set of keywords in the titles, together with their context."

Sample input to a program is given in Figure 16.3 together with the expected output. The context is described as a rotation of the title with the end of the title indicated by —. In the example, the keywords are *algorithmic, debugging, logic, problem, program, programming, prolog,* and *solving,* all the nontrivial words.

The relation we want to compute is `kwic(Titles,KwicTitles)` where `Titles` is the list of titles whose keywords are to be extracted, and `KwicTitles` is the sorted list of keywords in their contexts. Both the input and output titles are assumed to be given as lists of words. A more general program, as a preliminary step, would convert freer-form input into lists of words and produce prettier output.

The program is presented in stages. The basis is a nondeterministic specification of a rotation of a list of words. It has an elegant definition in terms of append:

Input:	programming in prolog
	logic for problem solving
	logic programming
	algorithmic program debugging
Output:	algorithmic program debugging —,
	debugging — algorithmic program,
	logic for problem solving —,
	logic programming —,
	problem solving — logic for,
	program debugging — algorithmic,
	programming in prolog —,
	programming — logic,
	prolog — programming in,
	solving — logic for problem

Figure 16.3   Input and output for keyword in context (KWIC) problem

```
rotate(Xs,Ys) ← append(As,Bs,Xs), append(Bs,As,Ys).
```

Declaratively, Ys is a rotation of Xs if Xs is composed of As followed by Bs, and Ys is Bs followed by As.

The next stage of development involves identifying single words as potential keywords. This is done by isolating the word in the first call to append. Note that the new rule is an instance of the previous one:

```
rotate(Xs,Ys) ←
    append(As,[Key|Bs],Xs), append([Key|Bs],As,Ys).
```

This definition also improves the previous attempt by removing the duplicate solution when one of the split lists is empty and the other is the entire list.

The next improvement involves examining a potential keyword more closely. Suppose each keyword Word is identified by a fact of the form keyword(Word). The solutions to the rotate procedure can be filtered so that only words identified as keywords are accepted. The appropriate version is

```
rotate_and_filter(Xs,Ys) ← append(As,[Key|Bs],Xs),
    keyword(Key), append([Key|Bs],As,Ys).
```

kwic (*Titles,KWTitles*) ←
  KWTitles is a KWIC index of the list of titles *Titles.*

```
kwic(Titles,KWTitles) ←
    setof(Ys,Xs↑(member(Xs,Titles),
    rotate_and_filter(Xs,Ys)),KWTitles).
```

rotate_and_filter (*Xs,Ys*) ←
  Ys is a rotation of the list *Xs* such that
  the first word of *Ys* is significant and —
  is inserted after the last word of *Xs.*

```
rotate_and_filter(Xs,Ys) ←
    append(As,[Key|Bs],Xs),
    not insignificant(Key),
    append([Key|Bs],['—'|As],Ys).
```

Vocabulary of insignificant words

```
insignificant(a).        insignificant(the).
insignificant(in).       insignificant(for).
```

Testing and data

```
test_kwic(Books,Kwic) ←
    titles(Books,Titles), kwic(Titles,Kwic).

titles(lp,[[logic,for,problem,solving],
    [logic,programming],
    [algorithmic,program,debugging],
    [programming,in,prolog]]).
```

Program 16.7 Producing a keyword in context (KWIC) index

Operationally `rotate_and_filter` considers all keys, filtering out the
unwanted alternatives. The goal order is important here to maximize
program efficiency.

In Program 16.7, the final version, a complementary view to recognizing keywords is taken. Any word `Word` is a keyword unless otherwise
specified by a fact of the form `insignificant(Word)`. Further the procedure is augmented to insert the end-of-title mark —, providing the context information. This is done by adding the extra symbol in the second
append call. Incorporating this discussion yields the clause for `rotate_`
`and_filter` in Program 16.7.

Finally, a set predicate is used to get all the solutions. Quantification
is necessary over all the possible titles. Advantage is derived from the

behavior of setof in sorting the answers. The complete program is given as Program 16.7, and is an elegant example of the expressive power of Prolog. The test predicate is test_kwic/2.

Exercises for Section 16.2

(i)   Modify Program 16.6 to handle other obstacles than rectangles.

(ii)   Adapt Program 16.7 for KWIC so that it extracts keywords from lines of text.

(iii)   Modify rotation of a list so that it uses difference-lists.

(iv)   Write a program to find a minimal spanning tree for a graph.

(v)   Write a program to find the maximum flow in a network design using the Ford-Fulkerson algorithm.

16.3   Other Second-Order Predicates

First-order logic allows quantification over individuals. Second-order logic further allows quantification over predicates. Incorporating this extension into logic programming entails using rules with goals whose predicate names are variables. Predicate names become "first-class" data objects to be manipulated and modified.

A simple example of a second-order relation is the determination of whether all members of a list have a certain property. For simplicity the property is assumed to be described as a unary predicate. Let us define has_property(Xs,P), which is true if each element of Xs has some property P. Extending Prolog syntax to allow variable predicate names enables us to define has_property as in Figure 16.4. Because has_property allows variable properties, it is a second-order predicate. An example of its use is testing whether a list of people Xs is all male with a query has_property(Xs,male)?.

Another second-order predicate is map_list(Xs,P,Ys). Ys is the map of the list Xs under the predicate P. That is, for each element X of Xs there is a corresponding element Y of Ys such that P(X,Y) is true. The

```
has_property([X|Xs],P) ← P(X), has_property(Xs,P).
has_property([ ],P).

map_list([X|Xs],P,[Y|Ys]) ← P(X,Y), map_list(Xs,P,Ys).
map_list([ ],P,[ ]).
```

Figure 16.4 Second-order predicates

order of the elements in Xs is preserved in Ys. We can use map_list to rewrite some of the programs of earlier chapters. For example, Program 7.8 mapping English to French words can be expressed as map_list(Words,dict,Mots). Like has_property, map_list is easily defined using a variable predicate name. The definition is given in Figure 16.4.

Operationally, allowing variable predicate names implies dynamic construction of goals while answering a query. The relation to be computed is not fixed statically when the query is posed but is determined dynamically during the computation.

Some Prologs allow the programmer to use variables for predicate names, and allow the syntax of Figure 16.4. It is unnecessary to complicate the syntax however. The tools already exist for implementing second-order predicates. One basic relation is necessary, which we call apply; it constructs the goal with a variable functor. The predicate apply is defined by a set of clauses, one for each functor name and arity. For example, for functor foo of arity n, the clause is

```
apply(foo,X1, . . . ,Xn) ← foo(X1, . . . ,Xn).
```

The two predicates in Figure 16.4 are transformed into Standard Prolog in Program 16.8. Sample definitions of apply clauses are given for the examples mentioned in the text.

The predicate apply performs structure inspection. The whole collection of apply clauses can be generalized by using the structure inspection primitive, univ. The general predicate apply(P,Xs) applies predicate P to a list of arguments Xs:

```
apply(F,Xs) ← Goal =.. [F|Xs], Goal.
```

We can generalize the function to be applied from a predicate name, i.e., an atom, to a term parameterized by variables. An example is substituting for a value in a list. The relation substitute/4 from Program 9.3

has_property(*Xs,P*) ←
> Each element in the list *Xs* has property *P*.

```
has_property([X|Xs],P) ←
    apply(P,X), has_property(Xs,P).
has_property([ ],P).
```

```
apply(male,X) ← male(X).
```

maplist(*Xs,P,Ys*) ←
> Each element in the list *Xs* stands in relation
> *P* to its corresponding element in the list *Ys*.

```
map_list([X|Xs],P,[Y|Ys]) ←
    apply(P,X,Y), map_list(Xs,P,Ys).
map_list([ ],P,[ ]).
```

```
apply(dict,X,Y) ← dict(X,Y).
```

Program 16.8 Second-order predicates in Prolog

can be viewed as an instance of map_list if parameterization is allowed. Namely, map_list(Xs,substitute(Old,New),Ys) has the same effect in substituting the element New for the element Old in Xs to get Ys — exactly the relation computed by Program 9.3. In order to handle this correctly, the definition of apply must be extended a little:

```
apply(P,Xs) ←
    P =.. L1, append(L1,Xs,L2), Goal =.. L2, Goal.
```

Using apply as part of map_list leads to inefficient programs. For example, using substitute directly rather than through map_list results in far fewer intermediate structures being created, and eases the task of compilation. Hence these second-order predicates are better used in conjunction with a program transformation system that can translate second-order calls to first-order calls at compile-time.

The predicate apply can also be used to implement lambda expressions. A lambda expression is one of the form *lambda*($X_1,\ldots,X_n$).*Expression*. If the set of lambda expressions to be used is known in advance, they can be named. For example, the above expression would be replaced by some unique identifier, foo say, and defined by an apply clause:

```
apply(foo,X1, ... ,Xn) ← Expression.
```

Although possible both theoretically and pragmatically, the use of lambda expressions and second-order constructs such as has_property and map_list is not as widespread in Prolog as in functional programming languages like Lisp. We conjecture that this is a combination of cultural bias and the availability of a host of alternative programming techniques. It is possible that the ongoing work on extending the logic programming model with higher-order constructs and integrating it with functional programming will change the picture.

In the meantime, all-solutions predicates seem to be the main and most useful higher-order construct in Prolog.

Exercise for Section 16.3

(i)   Write a program performing beta reduction for lambda expressions.

16.4 Background

The discussion of findall uses the description contained in the Standard Prolog document (Scowen, 1991). An excellent discussion of the all-solutions predicates bagof and setof in Edinburgh Prolog are given in Warren (1982a). Discussions of "rolling your own" set predicates can be found in both O'Keefe (1990) and Ross (1989).

Set predicates are a powerful extension to Prolog. They can be used (inefficiently) to implement negation as failure and meta-logical type predicates (Kahn, 1984). If a goal G has no solutions, which is determined by a predicate such as findall, then not G is true. The predicate var(X) is implemented by testing whether the goal X=1;X=2 has two solutions. Further discussion of such behavior of set predicates and a survey of different implementations of set predicates can be found in Naish (1985a).

Further description of the Lee algorithm and the general routing problem for VLSI circuits can be found in textbooks on VLSI, for example, Breuer and Carter (1983). A neat graphic version of Program 16.6 has been written by Dave Broderick.

Recent logic programming research has focused somewhat more on higher-order logic programming. Approaches of note are Lambda-Prolog (Miller and Nadathur, 1986) and HiLog (Chen et al., 1989).

KWIC was posed as a benchmark for high-level programming languages by Perlis, and was used to compare several languages. We find the Prolog implementation of it perhaps the most elegant of all.

Our description of lambda expressions is modeled after Warren (1982a). Predicates such as `apply` and `map_list` were part of the utilities package at the University of Edinburgh. They were fashionable for a while but fell out of favor because they were not compiled efficiently, and no source-to-source transformation tools were available.

17   Interpreters

Meta-programs treat other programs as data. They analyze, transform, and interpret other programs. The writing of meta-programs, or meta-programming, is particularly easy in Prolog because of the equivalence of programs and data: both are Prolog terms. We have already presented some examples of meta-programs, namely, the editor of Program 12.5 and the shell process of Program 12.6. This chapter covers interpreters, an important and useful class of meta-programs, and Chapter 18 discusses program transformation.

17.1   Interpreters for Finite State Machines

The sharp distinction between programs and data present in most computer languages is lacking in Prolog. The equivalence of programs and data greatly facilitates the writing of interpreters. We demonstrate the facility in this section by considering the basic computation models of computer science. Interpreters for the various classes of automata are very easily written in Prolog.

It is interesting to observe that the interpreters presented in this section are a good application of nondeterministic programming. The programs that are presented illustrate typical examples of don't-know nondeterminism. The same interpreter can execute both deterministic and nondeterministic automata because of the nondeterminism of Prolog.

Definition

A (nondeterministic) finite automaton, abbreviated NDFA, is a 5-tuple $\langle Q, \Sigma, \delta, I, F \rangle$, where Q is a set of states, Σ is a set of symbols, δ is a

accept(*Xs*) ←
>   The string represented by the list *Xs* is accepted by
>   the NDFA defined by *initial/1, delta/3*, and *final/1*.

```
accept(Xs) ← initial(Q), accept(Xs,Q).

accept([X|Xs],Q) ← delta(Q,X,Q1), accept(Xs,Q1).
accept([ ],Q) ← final(Q).
```

Program 17.1 An interpreter for a nondeterministic finite automaton (NDFA)

mapping from $Q \times \Sigma$ to Q, I is an initial state, and F is a set of final states. If the mapping is a function, then an NDFA is deterministic.

A finite automaton can be specified as a Prolog program by three collections of facts. The predicate `initial(Q)` is true if Q is the initial state. The predicate `final(Q)` is true if Q is a final state. The most interesting is `delta(Q,X,Q1)`, which is true if the NDFA changes from state Q to state Q1 on receipt of symbol X. Note that both the set of states and the set of symbols can be defined implicitly as the constants that appear in the `initial`, `final`, and `delta` predicates.

An NDFA *accepts* a string of symbols from the alphabet Σ^*, if when started in its initial state, and following the transitions specified by δ, the NDFA ends up in one of the final states. An interpreter for an NDFA must determine whether it accepts given strings of symbols. Program 17.1 is an interpreter. The predicate `accept(Xs)` is true if the NDFA defined by the collection of `initial`, `final`, and `delta` facts accepts the string represented as the list of symbols Xs.

Figure 17.1 shows a deterministic automaton that accepts the language $(ab)^*$. There are two states, *q0* and *q1*. If in state *q0* an *a* is received, the automaton moves to state *q1*. The automaton moves back from *q1* to *q0* if a *b* is received. The initial state is *q0*, and *q0* is also the single final state.

To use the interpreter, a specific automaton must be given. Program 17.2 is the realization in Prolog of the automaton in Figure 17.1. The combination of Programs 17.1 and 17.2 correctly accepts strings of alternating *a*'s and *b*'s.

If an arc from *q0* to itself labeled *a* is added to the automaton in Figure 17.1, we get a new automaton that recognizes the language $(a(a^*)b)^*$.

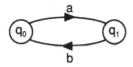

Figure 17.1   A simple automaton

```
initial(q0).

final(q0).

delta(q0,a,q1).
delta(q1,b,q0).
```

Program 17.2   An NDFA that accepts the language $(ab)^*$

This automaton is nondeterministic because on receipt of an *a* in state *q0* it is not determined which path will be followed. Nondeterminism does not affect the interpreter in Program 17.1. All that is needed to produce the new automaton is to add the fact `delta(q0,a,q0)` and the combined program will behave correctly.

Another simple computation model is a pushdown automaton that accepts the class of context-free languages. Pushdown automata extend NDFAs by providing a single stack for memory in addition to the internal state of the automaton. Formally, a (nondeterministic) pushdown automaton, abbreviated NPDA, is a 7-tuple $\langle Q,\Sigma,G,\delta,I,Z,F \rangle$ where Q, Σ, I, F are as before, G is the set of symbols that can be pushed onto the stack, Z is the start symbol on the stack, and δ is changed to take the stack into account.

Specifically, δ is a mapping from $Q \times \Sigma \times G^*$ to $Q \times G^*$. The mapping controls the change of state of the NPDA and the pushing and popping of elements onto and off the stack by the NPDA. In one operation, the NPDA can pop (push) one symbol off (onto) the stack.

Analogously to an NDFA, an NPDA *accepts* a string of symbols from the alphabet Σ^*, if when started in its initial state and with the starting symbol on the stack, and following the transitions specified by δ, the NPDA ends up in one of the final states with the stack empty. An interpreter for an NPDA is given as Program 17.3. The predicate `accept(Xs)` is true if the NDFA defined by the collection of `initial`, `final`, and `delta` facts

accept(*Xs*) ←
    The string represented by the list *Xs* is accepted by
    the NPDA defined by *initial/1*, *delta/5*, and *final/1*.

```
accept(Xs) ← initial(Q), accept(Xs,Q,[ ]).

accept([X|Xs],Q,S) ← delta(Q,X,S,Q1,S1), accept(Xs,Q1,S1).
accept([ ],Q,[ ]) ← final(Q).
```

Program 17.3 An interpreter for a nondeterministic pushdown automaton (NPDA)

```
initial(q0).    final(q1).

delta(q0,X,S,q0,[X|S]).
delta(q0,X,S,q1,[X|S]).
delta(q0,X,S,q1,S).
delta(q1,X,[X|S],q1,S).
```

Program 17.4 An NPDA for palindromes over a finite alphabet

accepts the string represented as the list of symbols Xs. The interpreter is very similar to the interpreter of an NDFA given as Program 17.1. The only change is the explicit manipulation of the stack by the delta predicate.

A particular example of an NPDA is given as Program 17.4. This automaton accepts palindromes over a finite alphabet. A *palindrome* is a nonempty string that reads the same backwards as forwards. Example palindromes are *noon*, *madam*, and *glenelg*. Again, the automaton is specified by initial, final, and delta facts, and the sets of symbols being defined implicitly. The automaton has two states: *q0*, the initial state when symbols are pushed onto the stack, and *q1*, a final state when symbols are popped off the stack and compared with the symbols in the input stream. When to stop pushing and start popping is decided nondeterministically. There are two delta facts that change the state from *q0* to *q1* to allow for palindromes of both odd and even lengths.

Programs 17.1 and 17.2 can be combined into a single program for recognizing the language (*ab*)*. Similarly, Programs 17.3 and 17.4 can be combined into a single program for recognizing palindromes. A program that can achieve this combination is given in Chapter 18.

It is straightforward to build an interpreter for a Turing machine written in a similar style to the interpreters in Programs 17.1 and 17.3. This is posed as Exercise (iii) at the end of this section. Building an interpreter for Turing machines shows that Prolog has the power of all other known computation models.

Exercises for Section 17.1

(i)   Define an NDFA that accepts the language ab^*c.

(ii) Define an NPDA that accepts the language a^nb^n.

(iii) Write an interpreter for a Turing machine.

17.2   Meta-Interpreters

We turn now to a class of especially useful interpreters. A *meta-interpreter* for a language is an interpreter for the language written in the language itself. Being able to write a meta-interpreter easily is a very powerful feature of a programming language. It gives access to the computation process of the language and enables the building of an integrated programming environment. The examples in the rest of this chapter demonstrate the potential of meta-interpreters and the ease with which they can be written. In this section, we also examine issues in writing meta-interpreters.

Throughout the remainder of this chapter, the predicate solve is used for a meta-interpreter. A suitable relation scheme is as follows. The relation solve(Goal) is true if Goal is true with respect to the program being interpreted.

The simplest meta-interpreter that can be written in Prolog exploits the meta-variable facility. It is defined by a single clause:

```
solve(A) ← A.
```

This trivial interpreter is only useful as part of a larger program. For example, a version of the trivial interpreter forms the basis for the interactive shell given as Program 12.6 and the logging facility given as Program 12.7. In general, as we suggest here and see in more detail in

solve(Goal) ←
    Goal is true given the pure Prolog program defined by *clause/2*.

```
solve(true).
solve((A,B)) ← solve(A), solve(B).
solve(A) ← clause(A,B), solve(B).
```

Program 17.5 A meta-interpreter for pure Prolog

Sections 17.3 and 17.4, meta-interpreters are useful and important because of the easily constructed enhancements.

The best known and most widely used meta-interpreter models the
computation model of logic programs as goal reduction. The three
clauses of Program 17.5 interpret pure Prolog programs. This meta-
interpreter, called *vanilla*, together with its enhancements, is the basis of
the rest of this section and Section 17.3.

The interpreter in Program 17.5 can be given a declarative reading. The
solve fact states that the empty goal, represented by the constant true,
is true. The first solve rule states that a conjunction (A,B) is true if A
is true and B is true. The second solve rule states that a goal A is true if
there is a clause A ← B in the interpreted program such that B is true.

We also give a procedural reading of the three clauses in Program
17.5. The solve fact states that the empty goal, represented in Prolog by
the atom true, is solved. The next clause concerns conjunctive goals. It
reads: "To solve a conjunction (A,B), solve A and solve B." The general
case of goal reduction is covered by the final clause. To solve a goal,
choose a clause from the program whose head unifies with the goal, and
recursively solve the body of the clause.

The procedural reading of Prolog clauses is necessary to demonstrate
that the meta-interpreter of Program 17.5 indeed reflects Prolog's choices
of implementing the abstract computation model of logic programming.
The two choices are the selection of the leftmost goal as the goal to
reduce, and sequential search and backtracking for the nondeterministic
choice of the clause to use to reduce the goal. The goal order of the body
of the solve clause handling conjunctions guarantees that the leftmost
goal in the conjunction is solved first. Sequential search and backtracking
comes from Prolog's behavior in satisfying the clause goal.

The hard work of the interpreter is borne by the third clause of Program 17.5. The call to clause performs the unification with the heads

```
solve(member(X,[a,b,c]))
    clause(member(X,[a,b,c]),B)                    {X=a,B=true}
    solve(true)
        true        Output:  X=a
                        ;

    solve(true)
        clause(true,T)      f
    clause(member(X,[a,b,c]),B)                    {B=member(X,[b,c])}
    solve(member(X,[b,c]))
        clause(member(X,[b,c]),B1)                 {X=b,B1=true}
        solve(true)
        true        Output:  X=b
                        ;

        solve(true)
            clause(true,T)      f
        clause(member(X,[b,c]),B1)                 {B1=member(X,[c])}
        solve(member(X,[c]))
            clause(member(X,[c],B2)                {X=c,B2=true}
            solve(true)
            true        Output:  X=c
                            ;

            solve(true)
                clause(true,T)      f
            clause(member(X,[c],B2))               {B2=member(X,[ ])}
            solve(member(X,[ ]))
                clause(member(X,[ ]),B3)      f
                no (more) solutions
```

Figure 17.2   Tracing the meta-interpreter

of the clauses appearing in the program. It is also responsible for giving different solutions on backtracking. Backtracking also occurs in the conjunctive rule reverting from B to A.

Tracing the meta-interpreter of Program 17.5 solving a goal is instructive. The trace of answering the query solve(member(X,[a,b,c])) with respect to Program 3.12 for member is given in Figure 17.2.

The vanilla meta-interpreter inherits Prolog's representation of clauses using the system predicate clause. Alternative representations of clauses are certainly possible, and indeed have been used by alternative Prologs. Lists are one possible representation. The clause $A \leftarrow B_1, B_2, \ldots, B_n$ can be represented by the clause rule(A,[B1,...,Bn]). In

solve(Goal) ←

    Goal is true given the pure Prolog program defined by *clause/2*.

```
solve(Goal) ← solve(Goal,[ ]).

solve([ ],[ ]).
solve([ ],[G|Goals]) ← solve(G,Goals).
solve([A|B],Goals) ← append(B,Goals,Goals1), solve(A,Goals1).
solve(A,Goals) ← rule(A,B), solve(B,Goals).
```

Program 17.6 A meta-interpreter for pure Prolog in continuation style

this representation, the empty list represents the empty goal and list construction represents conjunction. This representation is used in Program 17.6.

    A different representation imposes a different form on the meta-interpreter, as illustrated in Program 17.6. Unlike Program 17.5, this version of the vanilla meta-interpreter makes explicit the remaining goals in the resolvent. Enhancements can be written to exploit the fact that the resolvent is accessible during the computation, for example, allowing a more sophisticated computation rule. The behavior of Program 17.6 can be considered as being in continuation style promoted by languages such as Scheme.

    Differences in meta-interpreters can be characterized in terms of their *granularity*, that is the chunks of the computation that are made accessible to the programmer. The granularity of the trivial one-clause meta-interpreter is too coarse. Consequently there is little scope for applying the meta-interpreter. It is possible, though not as easy, to write a meta-interpreter that models unification and backtracking. The granularity of such a meta-interpreter is very fine. Working at this fine level is usually not worthwhile. The efficiency loss is too great to warrant the extra applications. The meta-interpreter in Program 17.5, at the clause reduction level, has the granularity most suited for the widest range of applications.

    The vanilla meta-interpreter must be extended to handle language features outside pure Prolog. Builtin predicates are not defined by clauses in the program and need different treatment. The easiest way to incorporate builtin predicates is to use the meta-variable facility to call them directly. A table of builtin predicates is necessary. In this chapter, we assume a table of facts of the form builtin(Predicate) for each builtin

```
builtin(A is B).        builtin(A > B).
builtin(read(X)).       builtin(write(X)).
builtin(integer(X)).    builtin(functor(T,F,N)).
builtin(clause(A,B)).   builtin(builtin(X)).
```

Figure 17.3   Fragment of a table of builtin predicates

predicate. Figure 17.3 gives part of that table. A table of builtin predicates is provided in some Prologs by another name but is not present in Standard Prolog.

The clause solve(A) ← builtin(A), A. can be added to the meta-interpreter in Program 17.5 to correctly handle builtin predicates. The resulting program handles four disjoint cases, one per clause, for solving goals: the empty goal, conjunctive goals, builtin goals, and user-defined goals. For compatibility with a number of Prolog systems, the meta-interpreters in the rest of this section contain cuts to indicate that the clauses are mutually exclusive.

The extra solve clause makes the behavior of the builtin predicates invisible to the meta-interpreter. User-defined predicates that one wants to make invisible can be handled similarly with a single clause. Conversely, there are occasions when builtin predicates for negation and second-order programming should be made visible.

The vanilla meta-interpreter needs to be extended to handle cuts correctly. A naive incorporation of cuts treats them as a builtin predicate, effectively adding a clause solve(!) ←!. This clause does not achieve the correct behavior of cut. The cut in the clause commits to the current solve clause rather than pruning the search tree.

To achieve correct behavior of cut in a meta-interpreter, one needs to understand *scope*, that is to which clause the cut commits. The scope of cut, as described in Chapter 11, is the clause in which the cut is a goal in the body. The scope of cut when it is contained within a meta-logical builtin predicate such as conjunction and disjunction is less distinct and varies in different Prologs. If a cut is part of a disjunction, should execution of the cut commit to the current disjunct or to the clause in which the disjunction is embedded? Handling cut correctly in a meta-interpreter is tricky and usually relies on technical details of the scope of cut in a particular implementation of Prolog. Incorporating cuts within

solve_trace(Goal) ←
    Goal is true given the Prolog program defined by *clause/2*.
    The program traces the proof by side effects.

```
solve_trace(Goal) ← solve_trace(Goal,0).

solve_trace(true,Depth) ← !.
solve_trace((A,B),Depth) ←
    !, solve_trace(A,Depth), solve_trace(B,Depth).
solve_trace(A,Depth) ←
    builtin(A), !, A, display(A,Depth), nl.
solve_trace(A,Depth) ←
    clause(A,B), display(A,Depth), nl, Depth1 is Depth + 1,
    solve_trace(B,Depth1).

display(A,Depth) ←
    Spacing is 3*Depth, put_spaces(Spacing), write(A).

put_spaces(N) ←
    between(1,N,I), put_char(' '), fail.
put_spaces(N).

between(1,N,I) ← See Program 8.5.
```

Program 17.7   A tracer for Prolog

meta-interpreters has been widely studied, and references to solutions are given in Section 17.5.

We apply meta-interpreters to develop a simple tracer. Program 17.7 handles success branches of computations and does not display failure nodes in the search tree. It is capable of generating the traces presented in Chapter 6.

The basic predicate is `solve_trace(Goal,Depth)`, where `Goal` is solved at some depth. The starting depth is assumed to be 0. The first `solve_trace/2` clause in Program 17.7 states that the empty goal is solved at any depth. The second clause indicates that each goal in a conjunct is solved at the same depth. The third clause handles builtins. The final `solve_trace/2` clause matches the goal with the head of a program clause, displays the goal, increments the depth, and solves the body of the program clause at the new depth.

The predicate `display(Goal,Depth)` is an interface for printing the traced goal. The second argument, `Depth`, controls the amount of indentation of the first argument, `Goal`. Level of indentation correlates with depth in the proof tree.

solve(Goal,Tree) ←

> *Tree* is a proof tree for *Goal* given the program defined
> by *clause/2*.

```
solve(true,true) ← !.
solve((A,B),(ProofA,ProofB)) ←
    !, solve(A,ProofA), solve(B,ProofB).
solve(A,(A←builtin)) ← builtin(A), !, A.
solve(A,(A←Proof)) ← clause(A,B), solve(B,Proof).
```

Program 17.8   A meta-interpreter for building a proof tree

There is subtlety in the goal order of the clause

```
solve_trace(A,Depth) ←
    clause(A,B), display(A,Depth), nl, Depth1 is Depth + 1,
    solve_trace(B,Depth1).
```

The `display` goal is between calls to `clause` and `solve_trace`, ensuring
that the goal is displayed each time Prolog backtracks to choose another
clause. If the `clause` and `display` goals are swapped, only the initial call
of the goal is displayed.

Using Program 17.7 for the query `solve_trace(append(Xs,Ys,[a,b,
c]))?` with Program 3.15 for append generates a trace like the one pre-
sented in Section 6.1. The output messages and semicolons for alternative solutions are provided by the underlying Prolog. There is only one
difference from the trace in Figure 6.2. The unifications are already performed. Separating out unifications requires explicit representation of
unification and is considerably harder.

A simple application of meta-interpreters constructs a proof tree while
solving a goal. The proof tree is built top-down. A proof tree is essential for the applications of debugging and explanation in the next two
sections.

The basic relation is `solve(Goal,Tree)`, where `Tree` is a proof tree
for the goal `Goal`. Proof trees are represented by the structure `Goal` ←
`Proof`. Program 17.8 implements `solve/2` and is a straightforward enhancement of the vanilla meta-interpreter. We leave as an exercise for
the reader giving a declarative reading of the program.

Here is an example of using Program 17.8 with Program 1.2. The query
`solve(son(lot,haran),Proof)?` has the solution

solve(*Goal,Certainty*) ←
    Certainty is our confidence that *Goal* is true.

```
solve(true,1) ← !.
solve((A,B),C) ←
    !, solve(A,C1), solve(B,C2), minimum(C1,C2,C).
solve(A,1) ← builtin(A), !, A.
solve(A,C) ← clause_cf(A,B,C1), solve(B,C2), C is C1 * C2.

minimum(X,Y,Z) ← See Program 11.3.
```

Program 17.9 A meta-interpreter for reasoning with uncertainty

```
Proof = (son(lot,haran) ←
        ((father(haran,lot)←true),
        (male(lot)←true))).
```

The query `solve(son(X,haran),Proof)?` has the solution `X=lot` and the same value for `Proof`.

Our next enhancement of the vanilla meta-interpreter incorporates a mechanism for uncertainty reasoning. Associated with each clause is a *certainty factor*, which is a positive real number less than or equal to 1. A *logic program with certainties* is a set of ordered pairs ⟨*Clause,Factor*⟩, where *Clause* is a clause and *Factor* is a certainty factor.

The simple meta-interpreter in Program 17.9 implements the uncertainty reasoning mechanism. The program is a straightforward enhancement of the vanilla meta-interpreter. The top-level relation is `solve(Goal,Certainty)`, which is true when `Goal` is satisfied with certainty `Certainty`.

The meta-interpreter computes the combination of certainty factors in a conjunction as the minimum of the certainty factors of the conjuncts. Other combining strategies could be accommodated just as easily. Program 17.9 assumes that clauses with certainty factors are represented using a predicate `clause_cf(A,B,CF)`.

Program 17.9 can be enhanced to prune computations that do not meet a desired certainty threshold. An extra argument constituting the value of the cutoff threshold needs to be added. The enhanced program is given as Program 17.10. The new relation is `solve(Goal,Certainty, Threshold)`.

The threshold is used in the fourth clause in Program 17.10. The certainty of any goal must exceed the current threshold. If the threshold is

solve(Goal,Certainty,Threshold) ←
  Certainty is our confidence, greater than *Threshold*, that *Goal* is true.

```
solve(true,1,T) ← !.
solve((A,B),C,T) ←
    !, solve(A,C1,T), solve(B,C2,T), minimum(C1,C2,C).
solve(A,1,T) ← builtin(A), !, A.
solve(A,C,T) ←
    clause_cf(A,B,C1), C1 > T, T1 is T/C1,
    solve(B,C2,T1), C is C1 * C2.

minimum(X,Y,Z) ← See Program 11.3.
```

Program 17.10   Reasoning with uncertainty with threshold cutoff

exceeded, the computation continues. The new threshold is the quotient of the previous threshold by the certainty of the clause.

Exercises for Section 17.2

(i)   Write a meta-interpreter to count the number of times a procedure is called in a successful computation.

(ii)   Write a meta-interpreter to find the maximum depth reached in a computation.

(iii) Extend Program 17.6 to give a tracer and build a proof tree.

(iv)   Extend Program 17.7 for `solve_trace/2` to print out failed goals.

(v)   Modify Program 17.8 to use a different representation for a proof tree.

17.3   Enhanced Meta-Interpreters for Debugging

Debugging is an essential aspect of programming, even in Prolog. The promise of high-level programming languages is not so much in the prospect for writing bug-free programs but in the power of the computerized tools for supporting the process of program development. For reasons of bootstrapping and elegance, these tools are best implemented in the language itself. Such tools are programs for manipulating, analyzing, and simulating other programs, or in other words, meta-programs.

This section shows meta-programs for supporting the debugging process of pure Prolog programs. The reason for restricting ourselves to the pure part is clear: the difficulties in handling the impure parts of the language.

To debug a program, we must assume that the programmer has some intended behavior of the program in mind, and an intended domain of application on which the program should exhibit this behavior. Given those, debugging consists of finding discrepancies between the program's actual behavior and the behavior the programmer intended. Recall the definitions of an intended meaning and a domain from Section 5.2. An intended meaning M of a pure Prolog program is the set of ground goals on which the program should succeed. The *intended domain D* of a program is a domain on which the program should terminate. We require the intended meaning of a program to be a subset of the intended domain.

We say that A_1 is a *solution* to a goal A if the program returns on a goal A its instance A_1. We say that a solution A is *true* in an intended meaning M if every instance of A is in M. Otherwise it is *false* in M.

A pure Prolog program can exhibit only three types of bugs, given an intended meaning and an intended domain. When invoked on a goal A in the intended domain, the program may do one of three things:

1. Fail to terminate
2. Return some false solution $A\theta$
3. Fail to return some true solution $A\theta$

We describe algorithms for supporting the detection and identification of each of these three types of bugs.

In general, it is not possible to detect if a Prolog program is nonterminating; the question is undecidable. Second best is to assign some a priori bound on the running time or depth of recursion of the program, and abort the computation if the bound is exceeded. It is desirable to save part of the computation to support the analysis of the reasons for nontermination. The enhanced meta-interpreter shown in Program 17.11 achieves this. It is invoked with a call solve(A,D,Overflow), where A is an initial goal, and D an upper bound on the depth of recursion. The call

solve(A,D,Overflow) ←
> *A* has a proof tree of depth less than *D* and
> *Overflow* equals *no_overflow*, or *A* has a
> branch in the computation tree longer than *D*, and
> *Overflow* contains a list of its first *D* elements.

```
solve(true,D,no_overflow) ← !.
solve(A,0,overflow([ ])) ← !.
solve((A,B),D,Overflow) ←
    D > 0, !,
    solve(A,D,OverflowA),
    solve_conjunction(OverflowA,B,D,Overflow).
solve(A,D,no_overflow) ←
    D > 0,
    builtin(A), !, A.
solve(A,D,Overflow) ←
    D > 0,
    clause(A,B),
    D1 is D-1,
    solve(B,D1,OverflowB),
    return_overflow(OverflowB,A,Overflow).

solve_conjunction(overflow(S),B,D,overflow(S)).
solve_conjunction(no_overflow,B,D,Overflow) ←
    solve(B,D,Overflow).

return_overflow(no_overflow,A,no_overflow).
return_overflow(overflow(S),A,overflow([A|S])).
```

Program 17.11   A meta-interpreter detecting a stack overflow

succeeds if a solution is found without exceeding the predefined depth of recursion, with `Overflow` instantiated to `no_overflow`. The call also succeeds if the depth of recursion is exceeded, but in this case `Overflow` contains the stack of goals, i.e., the branch of the computation tree, which exceeded the depth-bound D.

Note that as soon as a stack overflow is detected, the computation returns, without completing the proof. This is achieved by `solve_conjunction` and `return_overflow`.

For example, consider Program 17.12 for insertion sort. When called with the goal `solve(isort([2,2],Xs),6,Overflow)`, the solution returned is

```
isort(Xs,Ys) ←
```
    Ys is an ordered permutation of *Xs*. Nontermination program.
```
isort([X|Xs],Ys) ← isort(Xs,Zs), insert(X,Zs,Ys).
isort([ ],[ ]).

insert(X,[Y|Ys],[X,Y|Ys]) ←
    X < Y.
insert(X,[Y|Ys],[Y|Zs]) ←
    X ≥ Y, insert(Y,[X|Ys],Zs).
insert(X,[ ],[X]).
```

Program 17.12   A nonterminating insertion sort

```
Xs = [2,2,2,2,2,2],
Overflow = overflow([
    isort([2,2],[2,2,2,2,2,2]),
    insert(2,[2],[2,2,2,2,2,2]),
    insert(2,[2],[2,2,2,2,2]),
    insert(2,[2],[2,2,2,2]),
    insert(2,[2],[2,2,2]),
    insert(2,[2],[2,2])]])
```

The overflowed stack can be further analyzed, upon return, to diagnose the reason for nontermination. This can be caused, for example, by a loop, i.e., by a sequence of goals $G_1,G_2,...,G_n$, on the stack, where G_1 and G_n are called with the same input, or by a sequence of goals that calls each goal with increasingly larger inputs. The first situation occurs in the preceding example. It is clearly a bug that should be fixed in the program. The second situation is not necessarily a bug, and knowing whether the program should be fixed or whether a larger machine should be bought in order to execute it requires further program-dependent information.

The second type of bug is returning a false solution. A program can return a false solution only if it has a false clause. A clause C is false with respect to an intended meaning M if it has an instance whose body is true in M and whose head is false in M. Such an instance is called a *counterexample* to C.

Consider, for example, Program 17.13 for insertion sort. On the goal isort([3,2,1],Xs) it returns the solution isort([3,2,1],[3,2,1]) which is clearly false.

isort(Xs,Ys) ←
    Buggy insertion sort.

```
isort([X|Xs],Ys) ← isort(Xs,Zs), insert(X,Zs,Ys).
isort([ ],[ ]).
insert(X,[Y|Ys],[X,Y|Ys]) ←
    X ≥ Y.
insert(X,[Y|Ys],[Y|Zs]) ←
    X > Y, insert(X,Ys,Zs).
insert(X,[ ],[X]).
```

Program 17.13 An incorrect and incomplete insertion sort

The false clause in the program is

```
insert(X,[Y|Ys],[X,Y|Ys]) ← X ≥ Y.
```

and a counterexample to it is

```
insert(2,[1],[2,1]) ← 2 ≥ 1.
```

Given a ground proof tree corresponding to a false solution, one can find a false instance of a clause as follows: Traverse the proof tree in postorder. Check whether each node in the proof tree is true. If a false node is found, the clause whose head is the false node and whose body is the conjunction of its sons is a counterexample to a clause in the program. That clause is false and should be removed or modified.

The correctness of this algorithm follows from a simple inductive proof. The algorithm is embedded in an enhanced meta-interpreter, shown as Program 17.14.

The algorithm and its implementation assume an *oracle* that can answer queries concerning the intended meaning of the program. The oracle is some entity external to the diagnosis algorithm. It can be the programmer, who can respond to queries concerning the intended meaning of the program, or another program that has been shown to have the same meaning as the intended meaning of the program under debugging. The second situation may occur in developing a new version of a program while using the older version as an oracle. It can also occur when developing an efficient program (e.g., quicksort), given an inefficient executable specification of it (i.e., permutation sort), and using the specification as an oracle.

false_solution(A,Clause) ←
    If *A* is a provable false instance, then *Clause* is
    a false clause in the program. Bottom-up algorithm.

```
false_solution(A,Clause) ←
    solve(A,Proof),
    false_clause(Proof,Clause).

solve(Goal,Proof)  ←  See Program 17.8.

false_clause(true,ok).
false_clause((A,B),Clause) ←
    false_clause(A,ClauseA),
    check_conjunction(ClauseA,B,Clause).
false_clause((A←B),Clause) ←
    false_clause(B,ClauseB),
    check_clause(ClauseB,A,B,Clause).

check_conjunction(ok,B,Clause) ←
    false_clause(B,Clause).
check_conjunction((A←B1),B,(A←B1)).

check_clause(ok,A,B,Clause) ←
    query_goal(A,Answer),
    check_answer(Answer,A,B,Clause).
check_clause((A1←B1),A,B,(A1←B1)).

check_answer(true,A,B,ok).
check_answer(false,A,B,(A←B1)) ←
    extract_body(B,B1).

extract_body(true,true).
extract_body((A←B),A).
extract_body(((A←B),Bs),(A,As)) ←
    extract_body(Bs,As).

query_goal(A,true) ←
    builtin(A).
query_goal(Goal,Answer) ←
    not builtin(Goal),
    writeln(['Is the goal ',Goal,' true?']),
    read(Answer).
```

Program 17.14   Bottom-up diagnosis of a false solution

When invoked with the goal `false_solution(isort([3,2,1],X),C)`
the algorithm exhibits the following interactive behavior:

```
false_solution(isort([3,2,1],X),C)?
Is the goal isort([ ],[ ]) true?
true.
Is the goal insert(1,[ ],[1]) true?
true.
Is the goal isort([1],[1]) true?
true.
Is the goal insert(2,[1],[2,1]) true?
false.

X = [3,2,1],
C = insert(2,[1],[2,1]) ← 2 ≥ 1.
```

This returns a counterexample to the false clause.

The proof tree returned by `solve/2` is not guaranteed to be ground, in contrast to the assumption of the algorithm. However, a ground proof tree can be generated by either instantiating variables left in the proof tree to arbitrary constants before activating the algorithm, or by requesting the oracle to instantiate the queried goal when it contains variables. Different instances might imply different answers. Since the goal of this algorithm is to find a counterexample as soon as possible, the oracle should instantiate the goal to a false instance if it can.

One of the main concerns with diagnosis algorithms is improving their query complexity, i.e., reducing the number of queries they require to diagnose the bug. Given that the human programmer may have to answer the queries, this desire is understandable. The query complexity of the preceding diagnosis algorithm is linear in the size of the proof tree. There is a better strategy, whose query complexity is linear in the depth of the proof tree, not its size. In contrast to the previous algorithm, which is bottom-up, the second algorithm traverses the proof tree top-down. At each node it tries to find a false son. The algorithm recurses with any false son found. If there is no false son, then the current node constitutes a counterexample, as the goal at the node is false, and all its sons are true.

The implementation of the algorithm is shown in Program 17.15. Note the use of cut to implement implicit negation in the first clause of `false_goal/2` and the use of `query_goal/2` as a test predicate.

false_solution(A,Clause) ←
    If *A* is a provable false instance, then *Clause*
    is a false clause in the program. Top-down algorithm.

```
false_solution(A,Clause) ←
    solve(A,Proof),
    false_goal(Proof,Clause).

solve(Goal,Proof) ← See Program 17.8.

false_goal((A←B),Clause) ←
    false_conjunction(B,Clause), !.
false_goal((A←B),(A←B1)) ←
    extract_body(B,B1).

false_conjunction(((A←B),Bs),Clause) ←
    query_goal(A,false), !,
    false_goal((A←B),Clause).
false_conjunction((A←B),Clause) ←
    query_goal(A,false), !,
    false_goal((A←B),Clause).
false_conjunction((A,As),Clause) ←
    false_conjunction(As,Clause).

extract_body(Tree,Body) ← See Program 17.14.

query_goal(A,Answer) ← See Program 17.14.
```

Program 17.15   Top-down diagnosis of a false solution

Compare the behavior of the bottom-up algorithm with the following trace of the interactive behavior of Program 17.15:

```
false_solution(isort([3,2,1],X),C)?
Is the goal isort([2,1],[2,1]) true?
```
false.
```
Is the goal isort([1],[1]) true?
```
true.
```
Is the goal insert(2,[1],[2,1]) true?
```
false.
```
X = [3,2,1],
C = insert(2,[1],[2,1]) ← 2 ≥ 1.
```

There is a diagnosis algorithm for false solutions with an even better query complexity, called *divide-and-query*. The algorithm progresses by splitting the proof tree into two approximately equal parts and querying the node at the splitting point. If the node is false, the algorithm is applied recursively to the subtree rooted by this node. If the node is true, its subtree is removed from the tree and replaced by *true*, and a new middle point is computed. The algorithm can be shown to require a number of queries logarithmic in the size of the proof tree. In case of close-to-linear proof trees, this constitutes an exponential improvement over both the top-down and the bottom-up diagnosis algorithms.

The third possible type of bug is a missing solution. Diagnosing a missing solution is more difficult than fixing the previous bugs. We say that a clause *covers* a goal A with respect to an intended meaning M if it has an instance whose head is an instance of A and whose body is in M.

For example, consider the goal insert(2,[1,3],Xs). It is covered by the clause

insert(X,[Y|Ys],[X,Y|Ys]) ← X ≥ Y.

of Program 17.13 with respect to the intended meaning M of the program, since in the following instance of the clause

insert(2,[1,3],[1,2,3]) ← 2 ≥ 1.

the head is an instance of A and the body is in M.

It can be shown that if a program P has a missing solution with respect to an intended meaning M, then there is a goal A in M that is not covered by any clause in P. The proof of this claim is beyond the scope of the book. It is embedded in the diagnosis algorithm that follows.

Diagnosing a missing solution imposes a heavier burden on the oracle. Not only does it have to know whether a goal has a solution but it must also provide a solution, if it exists. Using such an oracle, an uncovered goal can be found as follows.

The algorithm is given a missing solution, i.e., a goal in the intended meaning M of the program P, for which P fails. The algorithm starts with the initial missing solution. For every clause that unifies with it, it checks, using the oracle, if the body of the clause has an instance in M. If there is no such clause, the goal is uncovered, and the algorithm terminates. Otherwise the algorithm finds a goal in the body that fails. At least one of them should fail, or else the program would have solved the body, and hence the goal, in contrast to our assumption. The algorithm is applied recursively to this goal.

missing_solution(A,Goal) ←
    If *A* is a nonprovable true ground goal, then *Goal* is a
    true ground goal that is uncovered by the program.

```
missing_solution((A,B),Goal) ← !,
    (not A, missing_solution(A,Goal) ;
    A, missing_solution(B,Goal)).
missing_solution(A,Goal) ←
    clause(A,B),
    query_clause((A←B)), !,
    missing_solution(B,Goal).
missing_solution(A,A) ←
    not system(A).

query_clause(Clause) ←
    writeln(['Enter a true ground instance of ',Clause,
    'if there is such,  or "no" otherwise']),
    read(Answer),
    !, check_answer(Answer,Clause).

check_answer(no,Clause) ← !, fail.
check_answer(Clause,Clause) ← !.
check_answer(Answer,Clause) ←
    write('Illegal answer'),
    !, query_clause(Clause).
```

Program 17.16   Diagnosing missing solution

An implementation of this algorithm is shown in Program 17.16. The
program attempts to trace the failing path of the computation and to find
a true goal which is uncovered. Following is a session with the program:

```
missing_solution(isort([2,1,3],[1,2,3]),C)?
```

Enter a true ground instance of
(isort([2,1,3],[1,2,3]) ←
    isort([1,3],Xs),insert(2,Xs,[1,2,3]))
if there is such, or "no" otherwise

(isort([2,1,3],[1,2,3]) ←
    isort([1,3],[1,3]),insert(2,[1,3],[1,2,3])).

Enter a true ground instance of
(isort([1,3],[1,3]) ← isort([3],Ys),insert(1,Ys,[1,3]))
if there is such, or 'no' otherwise

```
(isort([1,3],[1,3]) ← isort([3],[3]),insert(1,[3],[1,3])).
```

Enter a true ground instance of
```
(insert(1,[3],[1,3]) ← 1 ≥ 3)
```
if there is such, or 'no' otherwise

no.

```
C = insert(1,[3],[1,3]).
```

The reader can verify that the goal `insert(1,[3],[1,3])` is not covered by Program 17.13.

The three algorithms shown can be incorporated in a high-quality interactive program development environment for Prolog.

17.4   An Explanation Shell for Rule-Based Systems

The final section of this chapter presents an application of interpreters to rule-based systems. An explanation shell is built that is capable of explaining why goals succeed and fail and that allows interaction with the user during a computation. The shell is developed with the methodology of stepwise enhancement introduced in Section 13.3.

The skeleton interpreter in this section is written in the same style as the vanilla meta-interpreter and has the same granularity. It differs in two important respects. First, it interprets a rule language rather than Prolog clauses. Second, the interpreter has two levels to allow explanation of failed goals.

Before describing the interpreter, we give an example of a toy rule-based system written in the rule language. Program 17.17 contains some rules for placing a dish on the correct rack in an oven for baking. Facts have the form `fact(Goal)`. For example, the first fact in Program 17.17 states that `dish1` is of type `bread`.

Rules have the form `rule(Head,Body,Name)`, where `Head` is a goal, `Body` is (possibly) a conjunction of goals, and `Name` is the name of the rule. Individual goals in the body are placed inside a unary postfix functor `is_true`, for reasons to be explained shortly. Conjunctions in the body are denoted by the binary infix operator `&`, which differs from Prolog syntax. Operator declarations for `&` and `is_true` are given in Program 17.17. To paraphrase a sample rule, rule `place1` in Program 17.17 states:

Rule base for a simple expert system for placing dishes in an oven.
The predicates used in the rules are

place_in_oven(Dish,Rack) ←

 Dish should be placed in the oven at level *Rack* for baking.

pastry(Dish) ← *Dish* is a pastry.

main_meal(Dish) ← *Dish* is a main meal.

slow_cooker(Dish) ← *Dish* is a slow cooker.

type(Dish,Type) ← *Dish* is best described as *Type*.

size(Dish,Size) ← The size of *Dish* is *Size*.

The rules have the form `rule(Head,Body,Name)`.

```
:- op(40,xfy,&).
:- op(30,xf,is_true).

rule(place_in_oven(Dish,top),
    pastry(Dish) is_true & size(Dish,small) is_true,place1).
rule(place_in_oven(Dish,middle),
    pastry(Dish) is_true & size(Dish,big) is_true,place2).
rule(place_in_oven(Dish,middle),main_meal(Dish) is_true,place3).
rule(place_in_oven(Dish,bottom),slow_cooker(Dish) is_true,place4).

rule(pastry(Dish),type(Dish,cake) is_true,pastry1).
rule(pastry(Dish),type(Dish,bread) is_true,pastry2).

rule(main_meal(Dish),type(Dish,meat) is_true,main_meal).
rule(slow_cooker(Dish),type(Dish,milk_pudding) is_true,slow_cooker).

fact(type(dish1,bread)).
fact(size(dish1,big)).
```

Program 17.17 Oven placement rule-based system

"A dish should be placed on the top rack of the oven if it is a pastry and
its size is small."

 Why use a separate rule language when the syntax is so close to Prolog?
The first rule, `place1`, could be written as follows.

```
place_in_oven(Dish,top) ← pastry(Dish), size(Dish,small).
```

 There are two main reasons for the rule language. The first is pedagog-
ical. The rule interpreter is neater, avoiding complicated details associated with Prolog's impurities such as the behavior of builtin predicates
when called by `clause`. Avoiding Prolog's impurities also makes it easier
to partially evaluate the interpreter, as described in Chapter 18.

monitor(*Goal*) ←
   Succeeds if a result of yes is returned from solving *Goal*
   at the solve level, or when the end of the computation is reached.

```
monitor(Goal) ← solve(Goal,Result), filter(Result).
monitor(Goal).
```

```
filter(yes).
% filter(no) ← fail.
```

solve(*Goal,Result*) ←
   Given a set of rules of the form *rule*(*A,B,Name*), *Goal* has
   Result yes if it follows from the rules and no if it does not.

```
solve(A,yes) ← fact(A).
solve(A,Result) ← rule(A,B,Name), solve_body(B,Result).
solve(A,no).
```

```
solve_body(A&B,Result) ←
    solve(A,ResultA), solve_and(ResultA,B,Result).
solve_body(A is_true,Result) ← solve(A,Result).
```

```
solve_and(no,A,no).
solve_and(yes,B,Result) ← solve(B,Result).
```

Program 17.18   A skeleton two-level rule interpreter

The second reason is to show by example that the best way to develop a rule-based application in Prolog is to design a rule language on top of Prolog. Although the rule language is largely syntactic sugar, experience has shown that users of a rule-based system are happier working in a customized rule language than in Prolog. Rule languages are straightforward to provide on top of Prolog.

We now start our presentation of the explanation shell. According to the method of stepwise enhancement, the skeleton constituting the basic control flow of the final program is presented first. Program 17.18 contains the skeleton of the rule interpreter. The principal requirement that shaped the skeleton is the desire to handle both successful and failed computations in one interpreter.

The rule interpreter presented in Program 17.18 has two levels. The top level, or *monitor* level, consists of the predicates monitor and filter. The bottom level, or *solve* level, consists of the predicates solve, solve_body, and solve_and. Two levels are needed to correctly handle failed computations.

Let us consider the bottom level first. The three predicates constitute an interpreter at the same level of granularity as the vanilla meta-interpreter. There is one major difference. There is a result variable that says whether a goal succeeds or fails. A goal that succeeds, with the result variable indicating failure, instead of failing gives rise to a different control flow, compensated for by the top level.

The predicate `solve(Goal,Result)` solves a single goal. There are three cases. The result is `yes` if the goal is a fact in the rule base. The result is `no` if no fact or head of a rule matches the goal. If there is a rule that matches the goal, the result will be returned by the predicate `solve_body(Goal,Result)`. The order of the third clause is significant because we only want to report `no` for an individual goal if there is no suitable fact or rule. Effectively, `solve` succeeds for each branch of the search tree, the result being `yes` for successful branches and `no` for failed branches.

`solve_body/2` has two clauses handling conjunctive goals and goals of the form `A is_true`. The functor `is_true` is a wrapper that allows unification to distinguish between the two cases. A Prolog implementation with indexing would produce efficient code. The clause handling conjunctions calls a predicate `solve_and/3`, which uses the result of solving the first conjunct to decide whether to continue. The code for `solve_and` results in behavior similar to the behavior of `solve_conjunction` in Program 17.11.

The monitor level is essentially a generate-and-test program. The solve level generates a branch of the search tree, and the test procedure `filter` accepts successful branches of the search tree, indicated by the result being `yes`. Failed branches, i.e., ones with result `no`, are rejected. Note that the second clause for `filter` could simply be omitted. We leave it in the program, albeit commented out, to make clear the later enhancement step for adding a proof tree.

The first enhancement of the rule interpreter makes it interactive. The interactive interpreter is given as Program 17.19. The user is given the opportunity to supply information at runtime for designated predicates. The designated predicates are given as a table of askable facts. For example, a fact `askable(type(Dish,Type)).` appearing in the table would indicate that the user could ask the type of the dish.

Interaction with the user is achieved by adding a new clause to the solve level:

solve(Goal,Result) ←

> Given a set of rules of the form *rule(A,B,Name)*, *Goal* has
> *Result* yes if it follows from the rules and no if it does not.
> The user is prompted for missing information.

```
solve(A,yes) ← fact(A).
solve(A,Result) ← rule(A,B,Name), solve_body(B,Result).
solve(A,Result) ← askable(A), solve_askable(A,Result).
solve(A,no).

solve_body(A&B,Result) ←
    solve_body(A,ResultA), solve_and(ResultA,B,Result).
solve_body(A is_true,Result) ← solve(A,Result).

solve_and(no,A,no).
solve_and(yes,B,Result) ← solve(B,Result).

solve_askable(A,Result) ←
    not known(A), ask(A,Response), respond(Response,A,Result).
```

The following predicates facilitate interaction with the user.

```
ask(A,Response) ← display_query(A), read(Response).

respond(yes,A,yes) ← assert(known_to_be_true(A)).
respond(no,A,no) ← assert(known_to_be_false(A)).

known(A) ← known_to_be_true(A).
known(A) ← known_to_be_false(A).

display_query(A) ← write(A), write('? ').
```

Program 17.19 An interactive rule interpreter

```
solve(A,Result) ← askable(A), solve_askable(A,Result).
```

An alternative method of making the rule interpreter interactive is to
define a new class of goals in the body. An additional `solve_body` clause
could be added, for example,

```
solve_body(A is_askable,Result) ← solve_askable(A,Result).
```

We prefer adding a `solve` clause and having a table of `askable` facts
to embedding in the rules the information about whether a predicate
is askable. The rules become more uniform. Furthermore, the askable
information is explicit meta-knowledge, which can be manipulated as
needed.

To complete the interactive component of the rule interpreter, code
for `solve_askable` needs to be specified. The essential components are

displaying a query and accepting a response. Experience with users of rule-based systems shows that it is essential not to ask the same question twice. Users get very irritated telling the computer information they feel it should know. Thus answers to queries are recorded using assert. Program 17.19 contains appropriate code. Only the solve level is given. The monitor level would be identical to Program 17.18.

Program 17.19 queries the user. The interaction can be extended to allow the user also to query the program. The user may want to know why a particular question is being asked. A facility for giving a *why explanation* is common in rule-based systems, the answer being the rule containing the queried goal in its body. In order to give this why explanation, we need to extend the rule interpreter to carry the rules that have been used so far.

Program 17.20 is an enhancement of Program 17.18 that carries the list of rules that have been used in solving the query. All the predicates carry the rules as an extra argument. The rule list is initialized to be empty in the first monitor clause. The rule list is updated in the second solve clause when a new rule is invoked.

We now describe how the list of rules can be used to provide a why explanation. A new respond clause needs to be added to Program 17.19. The appropriate behavior is to display the rule, then prompt the user again for the answer to the query.

```
respond(why,A,[Rule|Rules]) ← display_rule(Rule),
    ask(A,Answer), respond(Answer,A,Rules).
```

Repeated responses of why can be handled by giving the rule that invoked the current rule. The correct behavior is achieved by having the recursive respond goal use the rest of the rules. Finally, when there are no more rules to display, an appropriate response must be given. A suitable respond clause is

```
respond(why,A,[ ]) ←
    writeln(['No more explanation possible']), ask(A,Answer),
    respond(Answer,A,[ ]).
```

Now let us consider generating explanations of goals that have succeeded or failed. The explanations will be based on the proof tree for successful goals and the search tree for failed goals. Note that a search

monitor (Goal) ←
>   Succeeds if a result of yes is returned from solving *Goal*
>   at the solve level, or when the end of the computation is reached.

```
monitor(Goal) ← solve(Goal,Result,[ ]), filter(Result).
monitor(Goal).
```

```
filter(yes).
% filter(no) ← fail.
```

solve(Goal,Result,Rules) ←
>   Given a set of rules of the form *rule(A,B,Name)*, *Goal* has
>   *Result* yes if it follows from the rules and no if it does not.
>   *Rules* is the current list of rules that have been used.

```
solve(A,yes,Rules) ← fact(A).
solve(A,Result,Rules) ←
    rule(A,B,Name), RulesB = [Name|Rules],
    solve_body(B,Result,RulesB).
solve(A,no,Rules).
```

```
solve_body(A&B,Result,Rules) ←
    solve_body(A,ResultA,Rules),
    solve_and(ResultA,B,Result,Rules).
solve_body(A is_true,Result,Rules) ← solve(A,Result,Rules).
```

```
solve_and(no,A,no,Rules).
solve_and(yes,B,Result,Rules) ← solve(B,Result,Rules).
```

Program 17.20   A two-level rule interpreter carrying rules

tree is a sequence of branches. Each branch is either a proof tree or a failure branch that is like a proof tree. Program 17.18 can be enhanced to incorporate both cases. The enhanced program is given as Program 17.21. The solve level returns a branch of the search tree, and the monitor level keeps track of the failure branches since the last proof tree. The relation between the predicate solve/3 in Program 17.21 and solve/2 in Program 17.18 is analogous to the relation between Programs 17.8 and 17.5.

Four predicates are added to the monitor level to record and remove branches of the search tree. The fact 'search tree'(Proof) records the current sequence of branches of the search tree since the last success. The predicate set_search_tree, called by the top-level monitor goal, initializes the sequence of branches to the empty list. Similarly,

monitor(Goal,Proof) ←
  Succeeds if a result of yes is returned from solving *Goal* at the
  solve level, in which case *Proof* is a proof tree representing the
  successful computation, or when the end of the computation is reached,
  in which case *Proof* is a list of failure branches since the last success.

```
monitor(Goal,Proof) ←
    set_search_tree, solve(Goal,Result,Proof),
    filter(Result,Proof).
monitor(Goal,Proof) ←
    collect_proof(P), reverse(P,[ ],P1),
    Proof = failed(Goal,P1).

filter(yes,Proof) ← reset_search_tree.
filter(no,Proof) ← store_proof(Proof), fail.
```

solve(Goal,Result,Proof) ←
  Given a set of rules of the form *rule(A,B,Name)*, *Goal* has
  Result yes if it follows from the rules and no if it does not.
  Proof is a proof tree if the result is yes and a failure branch
  of the search tree if the result is no.

```
:- op(40,xfy,because).
:- op(30,xfy,with).

solve(A,yes,Tree) ← fact(A), Tree = fact(A).
solve(A,Result,Tree) ←
    rule(A,B,Name), solve_body(B,Result,Proof),
    Tree = A because B with Proof.
solve(A,no,Tree) ←
    not fact(A), not rule(A,B,Name), Tree = no_match(A).

solve_body(A&B,Result,Proof) ←
    solve_body(A,ResultA,ProofA),
    solve_and(ResultA,B,Result,ProofB),
    Proof = ProofA & ProofB.
solve_body(A is_true,Result,Proof) ← solve(A,Result,Proof).

solve_and(no,A,no,unsearched).
solve_and(yes,B,Result,Tree) ← solve(B,Result,Tree).
```

Program 17.21   A two-level rule interpreter with proof trees

The following predicates use side effects to record and remove branches of the search tree.

```
collect_proof(Proof) ← retract('search tree'(Proof)).
store_proof(Proof) ←
    retract('search tree'(Tree)),
    assert('search tree'([Proof|Tree])).
set_search_tree ← assert('search tree'([ ])).
reset_search_tree ←
    retract('search tree'(Proof)),
    assert('search tree'([ ])).

reverse(Xs,Ys) ← See Program 3.16.
```

Program 17.21   (Continued)

reset_search_tree initializes the search tree but first removes the current set of branches. It is invoked by filter when a successful computation is detected. The predicate store_proof updates the search tree, while collect_proof removes the search tree. The failure branches are reordered in the second clause for monitor/2.

Having generated an explanation, we now consider how to print it. The proof tree is a recursive data structure that must be traversed to be explained. Traversing a recursive data structure is a straightforward exercise. Appropriate code is given in Program 17.22, and a trace of a computation given in Figure 17.4.

The explanation shell is obtained by combining the enhancements of Programs 17.19, 17.20, and 17.21. The final program is given as Program 17.23. Understanding the program is greatly facilitated by viewing it as a sum of the three components.

Exercises for Section 17.4

(i)   Add the ability to explain askable goals to the proof explainer in Program 17.22.

(ii)   Add the ability to execute Prolog builtin predicates to the explanation shell.

(iii) Write a two-level meta-interpreter to find the maximum depth reached in any computation of a goal.

explain(Goal) ←
   Explains how the goal *Goal* was proved.

```
explain(Goal) ← monitor(Goal,Proof), interpret(Proof).

monitor(Goal,Proof) ← See Program 17.21.

interpret(ProofA&ProofB) ←
    interpret(ProofA), interpret(ProofB).
interpret(failed(A,Branches)) ←
    nl, writeln([A,' has failed with the following failure
                                        branches:']),
    interpret(Branches).
interpret([Fail|Fails]) ←
    interpret(Fail), nl, write('NEW BRANCH'), nl,
    interpret(Fails).
interpret([ ]).
interpret(fact(A)) ←
    nl, writeln([A,' is a fact in the database.']).
interpret(A because B with Proof) ←
    nl, writeln([A,' is proved using the rule']),
    display_rule(rule(A,B)), interpret(Proof).
interpret(no_match(A)) ←
    nl, writeln([A,' has no matching fact or rule in the rule base.']).
interpret(unsearched) ←
    nl, writeln(['The rest of the conjunct is unsearched.']).

display_rule(rule(A,B)) ←
    write('IF '), write_conjunction(B), writeln(['THEN ',A ]).

write_conjunction(A&B) ←
    write_conjunction(A), write(' AND '),
    write_conjunction(B).
write_conjunction(A is_true) ← write(A).

writeln(Xs) ← See Program 12.1.
```

Program 17.22   Explaining a proof

`place_in_oven(dish1,middle)` is proved using the rule
IF `pastry(dish1)` AND `size(dish1,big)`
THEN `place_in_oven(dish1,middle)`

`pastry(dish1)` is proved using the rule
IF `type(dish1,bread)`
THEN `pastry(dish1)`

`type(dish1,bread)` is a fact in the database.

`size(dish1,big)` is a fact in the database.
    X = `middle` ;

`place_in_oven(dish1,X)` has failed with the following failure branches:

`place_in_oven(dish1,middle)` is proved using the rule
IF `main_meal(dish1)`
THEN `place_in_oven(dish1,middle)`

`main_meal(dish1)` is proved using the rule
IF `type(dish1,meat)`
THEN `main_meal(dish1)`

`type(dish1,meat)` has no matching fact or rule in the rule base.

NEW BRANCH

`place_in_oven(dish1,low)` is proved using the rule
IF `slow_cooker(dish1)`
THEN `place_in_oven(dish1,low)`

`slow_cooker(dish1)` is proved using the rule
IF `type(dish1,milk_pudding)`
THEN `slow_cooker(dish1)`

`type(dish1,milk_pudding)` has no matching fact or rule in the rule base.

Figure 17.4   Explaining a computation

monitor(*Goal,Proof*) ←
> Succeeds if a result of yes is returned from solving *Goal* at the
> solve level, in which case *Proof* is a proof tree representing the
> successful computation, or when the end of the computation is reached,
> in which case *Proof* is a list of failure branches since the last success.

```
monitor(Goal,Proof) ←
    set_search_tree, solve(Goal,Result,[ ],Proof),
    filter(Result,Proof).
monitor(Goal,Proof) ←
    collect_proof(P), reverse(P,[ ],P1),
    Proof = failed(Goal,P1).
```

```
filter(yes,Proof) ← reset_search_tree.
filter(no,Proof) ← store_proof(Proof), fail.
```

solve(*Goal,Result,Rules,Proof*) ←
> Given a set of rules of the form *rule(A,B,Name)*, *Goal* has
> *Result* yes if it follows from the rules and no if it does not.
> *Rules* is the current list of rules that have been used.
> *Proof* is a proof tree if the result is yes and a failure branch
> of the search tree if the result is no.

```
:- op(40,xfy,because).
:- op(30,xfy,with).
```

```
solve(A,yes,Rules,Tree) ← fact(A), Tree = fact(A).
solve(A,Result,Rules,Tree) ←
    rule(A,B,Name), RulesB = [Name|Rules],
    solve_body(B,Result,RulesB,Proof),
    Tree = A because B with Proof.
solve(A,Result,Rules,Tree) ←
    askable(A), solve_askable(A,Result,Rules), Tree = user(A).
solve(A,no,Rules,Tree) ←
    not fact(A), not rule(A,B,Name), Tree = no_match(A).
```

```
solve_body(A&B,Result,Rules,Proof) ←
    solve_body(A,ResultA,Rules,ProofA),
    solve_and(ResultA,B,Result,Rules,ProofB),
    Proof = ProofA & ProofB.
solve_body(A is_true,Result,Rules,Proof) ←
    solve(A,Result,Rules,Proof).
```

```
solve_and(no,A,no,Rules,unsearched).
solve_and(yes,B,Result,Rules,Tree) ←
    solve(B,Result,Rules,Tree).
```

Program 17.23   An explanation shell

The following predicates use side effects to record and remove branches of the search tree.

```
collect_proof(Proof) ← retract('search tree'(Proof)).
store_proof(Proof) ←
    retract('search tree'(Tree)),
    assert('search tree'([Proof|Tree])).
set_search_tree ← assert('search tree'([ ])).
reset_search_tree ←
    retract('search tree'(Proof)), assert('search tree'([ ])).

reverse(Xs,Ys) ← See Program 3.16.
```

The following predicates facilitate interaction with the user.

```
ask(A,Response) ← display_query(A), read(Response).

respond(yes,A,yes) ← assert(known_to_be_true(A)).
respond(no,A,no) ← assert(known_to_be_false(A)).
respond(why,A,[Rule|Rules]) ←
    display_rule(Rule), ask(A,Answer), respond(Answer,A,Rules).
respond(why,A,[ ]) ←
    writeln(['No more explanation possible']), ask(A,Answer),
    respond(Answer,A,[ ]).

known(A) ← known_to_be_true(A).
known(A) ← known_to_be_false(A).

display_query(A) ← write(A), write('? ').

display_rule(rule(A,B)) ←
    write('IF '), write_conjunction(B), nl, writeln(['THEN ',A]).

write_conjunction(A&B) ←
    write_conjunction(A), write(' AND '), write_conjunction(B).
write_conjunction(A is_true) ← write(A).

writeln(Xs) ← See Program 12.1.
```

Program 17.23   (Continued)

17.5   Background

Our notation for automata follows Hopcroft and Ullman (1979).

There is considerable confusion in the literature about the term meta-interpreter—whether it differs from the term meta-level interpreter, for example. The lack of clarity extends further to the topic of meta-programming. A good discussion of meta-programming can be found in Yalçinalp (1991).

One dimension of the discussion is whether the interpreter is capable of interpreting itself. An interpreter with that capability is also called meta-circular or self-applicable. An important early discussion of meta-circular interpreters can be found in Steele and Sussman (1978). That paper claims that the ability of a language to specify itself is a fundamental criterion for language design.

The vanilla meta-interpreter is rooted in Prolog folklore. A version was in the suite of programs attached to the first Prolog interpreter developed by Colmerauer and colleagues, and was given in the early collection of Prolog programs (Coelho et al., 1980). Subsequently, meta-interpreters, and more generally meta-programs, have been written to affect the control flow of Prolog programs. References are Gallaire and Lasserre (1982), Pereira (1982), and Dincbas and Le Pape (1984). Using enhanced meta-interpreters for handling uncertainties is described by Shapiro (1983c).

There have been several papers on handling cuts in meta-interpreters. A variant of the vanilla meta-interpreter handling cuts correctly is described in Coelho et al. (1980) and attributed to Luis Pereira. One easy method to treat cuts is via ancestor cut, which is only present in a few Prologs like Waterloo Prolog on the IBM and Wisdom Prolog, described in the first edition of this book. There is a good discussion of meta-interpreters in general, and cuts in particular, in O'Keefe (1990).

Shapiro suggested that enhanced meta-interpreters should be the basis of a programming environment. The argument, along with the debugging algorithms of Section 17.3, can be found in Shapiro (1983a). Shapiro's debugging work has been extended by Dershowitz and Lee (1987) and Drabent et al. (1989).

Prolog is a natural language for building rule-based systems. The basic statements are rules, and the Prolog interpreter can be viewed as a backward chaining inference engine. Early advocates of Prolog for expert systems were Clark and McCabe (1982), who discussed how explanation facilities and uncertainty can be added to simple expert systems expressed as Prolog clauses by adding extra arguments to the predicates. Incorporating interaction with the user in Prolog was proposed by Sergot (1983). An explanation facility incorporating Sergot's query_the_user was part of the APES expert system shell, described in Hammond (1984).

Using meta-interpreters as a basis for explanation facilities was proposed by Sterling (1984). Incorporating failure in a meta-interpreter has been discussed by several researchers, including Hammond (1984), Sterling and Lalee (1986), and Bruffaerts and Henin (1989). The first description of an integrated meta-interpreter for both success and failure is in Yalçinalp and Sterling (1989). The rule interpreter given in Section 17.4 is an adaptation of the last paper. The layered approach can be used to explain cuts clearly, as in Sterling and Yalçinalp (1989), and also for uncertainty reasoning, as in Yalçinalp and Sterling (1991) and more completely in Yalçinalp (1991).

18 Program Transformation

As stated in the introduction to Chapter 17, meta-programming, or the writing of programs that treat other programs as data, is particularly easy in Prolog. This chapter gives examples of programs that transform and manipulate Prolog programs. The first section looks at fold/unfold, the operation that underlies most applications of program transformation for Prolog programs. The transformations given in Chapter 15 for using difference-lists to avoid explicit concatenation of lists can be understood as unfold operations, for example. The second section describes a simple system for controlled unfolding and folding, which is especially good for removing layers of interpretation. The final section gives two examples of source-to-source transformation by code walking.

18.1 Unfold/Fold Transformations

Logic programming arose from research on resolution theorem proving. The basic step in the logic programming computation model, goal reduction, corresponds to a single resolution between a query and a program clause. Unfold/fold operations correspond to resolution between two Horn clauses. Loosely, unfolding corresponds to replacing a goal in the body of a clause by its definition, while folding corresponds to recognizing that goal(s) in the body of a clause are an instance of a definition. These two operations, being so similar, are often discussed together.

We demonstrate unfolding and folding with a running example in the first part of this chapter. The example is specializing the interpreter for nondeterministic pushdown automata (Program 17.3) for the particular pushdown automaton for recognizing palindromes (Program 17.4). In general, specializing interpreters is a good application for unfold/fold operations.

Definition

Unfolding a goal B_i in a clause $A \leftarrow B_1,\ldots,B_n$ with respect to a clause $B \leftarrow C_1,\ldots,C_m$ where B and B_i unify with mgu θ, produces a clause $(A \leftarrow B_1,\ldots,B_{i-1},C_1,\ldots,C_m,B_{i+1},\ldots,B_n)\theta$.   ∎

As an example of unfolding, we specialize the clause accept(Xs) ← initial(Q), accept(Xs,Q,[ ]) to a particular initial state by unfolding the initial(Q) goal with respect to a particular initial fact. Specifically, unfolding with respect to the fact initial(push) produces the clause accept(Xs) ← accept(Xs,push,[ ]). (Note that in our running example we use the states push and pop for q0 and q1, respectively, from the NPDA of Program 17.4.)

The effect of the unfolding is to instantiate the initial state for the NPDA to push. In general, the effect of unfolding is to propagate variable bindings to the right, as in this example, and also to the left, to goals in the body of the clause and possibly also to the head.

There may be several clauses whose heads unify with a given goal in the body of a clause. We extend the definition of unfolding accordingly.

Definition

Unfolding a goal B_i in a clause $A \leftarrow B_1,\ldots,B_n$ with respect to a procedure defining B_i is to unfold the goal with respect to each clause in the procedure whose head unifies with B_i.   ∎

Unfolding the delta/5 goal in the clause accept([X|Xs],Q,S) ← delta(Q,X,S,Q1,S1), accept(Xs,Q1,S1) with respect to the following procedure for delta adapted from Program 17.4

```
delta(push,X,S,push,[X|S]).     delta(push,X,S,pop,[X|S]).
delta(push,X,S,pop,S).          delta(pop,X,[X|S],pop,S).
```

produces four clauses, one for each fact.

```
accept([X|Xs],push,S)  ← accept(Xs,push,[X|S]).
accept([X|Xs],push,S)  ← accept(Xs,pop,[X|S]).
accept([X|Xs],push,S)  ← accept(Xs,pop,S).
accept([X|Xs],pop,[X|S]) ← accept(Xs,pop,S).
```

palindrome(Xs) ←
    The string represented by the list *Xs* is a palindrome.

```
palindrome(Xs) ← palindrome(Xs,push,[ ]).

palindrome([X|Xs],push,S) ← palindrome(Xs,push,[X|S]).
palindrome([X|Xs],push,S) ← palindrome(Xs,pop,[X|S]).
palindrome([X|Xs],push,S) ← palindrome(Xs,pop,S).
palindrome([X|Xs],pop,[X|S]) ← palindrome(Xs,pop,S).
palindrome([ ],pop,[ ]).
```

Program 18.1   A program accepting palindromes

This example shows variable bindings being propagated both to the right, and to the head of the clause left of the goal being unfolded.

Folding is the reverse of unfolding. The occurrence of a body of a clause is replaced by its head. It is easiest to show with an example. Folding the goal accept(Xs,push,[ ]) in the clause accept(Xs) ← accept(Xs,push,[ ]) with respect to the clause palindrome(Xs,State, Stack) ← accept(Xs,State,Stack) produces the clause accept(Xs) ← palindrome(Xs,push,[ ]).

Note that if we now unfold the goal palindrome(Xs,push,[ ]) in accept(Xs) ← palindrome(Xs,push,[ ]) with respect to the clause just used for folding, palindrome(Xs,State,Stack) ← accept(Xs,State, Stack), we arrive back at the original clause, accept(Xs) ← accept(Xs, push,[ ]). Ideally, fold/unfold are inverse operations.

Our example of folding used an iterative clause, i.e., one with a single goal in the body. Folding can be performed on a conjunction of goals, but there are technical difficulties arising from the scope of variables. Here we restrict ourselves to iterative clauses. The reader interested in the more general case should study the references given at the end of the chapter.

Specialization of the interpreter of Program 17.3 is completed by unfolding the final(Q) goal in the third clause of Program 17.3, folding all occurrences of accept/3, and folding with respect to the clause palindrome(Xs) ← accept(Xs). Program 18.1 is then obtained.

Propagating bindings leftward in Prolog will not preserve correctness in general. For example, consider unfolding the goal r(X) with respect to the fact r(3) in the clause p(X) ← var(X), r(x). The resulting clause, p(3) ← var(3), clearly always fails, in contrast with the original clause. Unfolding for Prolog can be performed correctly by not propagating bindings leftward, and replacing the unfolded goal by the unifier. For this example, the result would be p(X) ← var(X), X=3. This will not be an issue in the examples we consider.

Exercise for Section 18.1

(i)   Specialize the interpreter of Program 17.1 to the NDFA of Program 17.2, or any other NDFA, by unfold/fold operations.

18.2   Partial Reduction

In this section we develop a simple system for controlled unfold/fold operations according to prescribed user declarations. Systems for controlled unfolding are known in the logic programming literature as partial evaluators. This name reveals the influence of functional programming, where the basic computation model is evaluation. We prefer to refer to the system in terms of the computation model of logic programming, goal reduction. We thus, nonstandardly, say our system is doing partial reduction, and call it a *partial reducer*.

Considerable research on applying partial reduction has shown that partial reduction is especially useful for removing levels of interpretation. The sequence of unfold/fold operations given in Section 18.1 typify what is possible. The general NPDA interpreter was specialized to a specific NPDA, removing interpreter overhead. The resulting program, Program 18.1, only recognizes palindromes but does so far more efficiently than the combination of Programs 17.3 and 17.4.

Let us see how to build a system that can apply the unfold and fold operations that were needed to produce the `palindrome` program. The main idea is to recursively perform unfold/fold until no more "progress" can be achieved. A relation that replaces a goal by its equivalent under these operations is needed. The resulting equivalent goal is known as a *residue*. Let us call our basic relation preduce(Goal,Residue), with intended meaning that Residue is a residue arising from partially reducing Goal by applying unfold and fold operations.

preduce(Goal,Residue) ←
    Partially reduce *Goal* to leave the residue *Residue*.

```
preduce(true,true) ← !.
preduce((A,B),(PA,PB)) ← !, preduce(A,PA), preduce(B,PB).
preduce(A,B) ← should_fold(A,B), !.
preduce(A,Residue) ←
    should_unfold(A), !, clause(A,B), preduce(B,Residue).
preduce(A,A).
```

Program 18.2 A meta-interpreter for determining a residue

Program 18.2 contains code for preduce. There are three possibilities for handling a single goal. It can be folded, unfolded, or left alone. The question immediately arises how to decide between the three possibilities. The easiest for a system is to rely on the user. Program 18.2 assumes that the user gives should_fold(Goal,FoldedGoal) declarations that say which goals should be folded and to what they should be folded, and also should_unfold(Goal) declarations that say which goals should be unfolded. Unification against the program clauses determines to what they should be unfolded. Goals not covered by either declaration are left alone. The remaining clauses in Program 18.2 handle the empty goal, true, and conjunctive goals, which are treated recursively in the obvious way.

Observe that Program 18.2 is essentially a meta-interpreter at the granularity level of vanilla (Program 17.5). The meta-interpreter is enhanced to return the residue. Handling builtins is assigned to the exercises.

The query preduce((initial(Q), accept(Xs,Q,[ ])), Residue)? assuming appropriate should_fold and should_unfold declarations (to be given shortly) has as solution Residue = (true,palindrome(Xs, push,[ ])). It would be preferable to remove the superfluous call to true. This can be done by modifying the clause handling conjunctive goals to be more careful in computing the conjunctive resolvent. A suitable modification is

```
preduce((A,B),Res) ←
    !, preduce(A,PA), preduce(B,PB), combine(PA,PB,Res).
```

The code for combine, removing superfluous empty goals, is given in Program 18.3.

process(Program, RedProgram) ←
    Partially reduce each of the clauses in *Program* to produce
    RedProgram.

```
process(Prog,NewProg) ←
    findall(PC1,(member(Cl,Prog),preduce(Cl,PC1)),NewProg).
```

```
test(Name,Program) ←
    program(Name,Clauses), process(Clauses,Program).
```

preduce(Goal,Residue) ←
    Partially reduce *Goal* to leave the residue *Residue*.

```
preduce((A ← B),(PA ← PB)) ←
    !, preduce(B,PB), preduce(A,PA).
preduce(true,true) ← !.
preduce((A,B),Res) ←
    !, preduce(A,PA), preduce(B,PB), combine(PA,PB,Res).
preduce(A,B) ← should_fold(A,B), !.
preduce(A,Residue) ←
    should_unfold(A), !, clause(A,B), preduce(B,Residue).
preduce(A,A).
```

```
combine(true,B,B) ← !.
combine(A,true,A) ← !.
combine(A,B,(A,B)).
```

Program 18.3   A simple partial reduction system

To extend Program 18.2 into a partial reducer, clauses must be handled as well as goals. We saw a need in the previous section to partially reduce the head and body of a clause. The only question is in which order. Typically, we will want to fold the head and unfold the body. Since unfolding propagates bindings, unfolding first will allow more specific folding. Thus our proposed rule for handling clauses is

```
preduce((A ← B),(PA ← PB)) ←
    !, preduce(B,PB), preduce(A,PA).
```

This goal order is advantageous for the example of the rule interpreter to be presented later in this section.

To partially reduce a program, we need to partially reduce each of its clauses. For each clause, there may be several possibilities because of nondeterminism. For example, the recursive `accept/3` clause led to four rules because of the four possible ways of unfolding the `delta` goal. The

```
program(npda,[(accept(Xs1) ← initial(Q1), accept(Xs1,Q1,[ ]),
     (accept([X2|Xs2],Q2,S2) ← delta(Q2,X2,S2,Q12,S12),
     accept(Xs2,Q12,S12)), (accept([ ],Q3,[ ]) ← true)]).
should_unfold(initial(Q)).
should_unfold(final(Q)).
should_unfold(delta(A,B,C,D,E)).

should_fold(accept(Q,Xs,Q1),palindrome(Q,Xs,Q1)).
should_fold(accept(Xs),palindrome(Xs)).
```

Program 18.4   Specializing an NPDA

cleanest way to get the whole collection of program clauses is to use the all-solutions predicate findall. That gives

```
process(Prog,NewProg) ←
     findall(PCl,(member(Cl,Prog), preduce(Cl,PCl)),NewProg).
```

Putting all the preceding actions together gives a simple system for partial reduction. The code is presented as Program 18.3. The program also contains a testing clause.

We now concentrate on how to specify should_fold and should_unfold declarations. Consider the NPDA example for recognizing palindromes. The initial, final, and delta goals should all be unfolded. A declaration is needed for each. The accept/1 and accept/3 goals should be folded into palindrome goals with the same argument. The declaration for accept/1 is should_fold(accept(Xs),palindrome(Xs)). All the necessary declarations are given in Program 18.4. Program 18.4 also contains the test program as data. Note the need to make all the variables in the program distinct. Applying Program 18.3 to Program 18.4 by posing the query test(npda,P)? produces Program 18.1, with the only difference being an explicit empty body for the last palindrome fact.

We now give a more complicated example of applying partial reduction to remove a level of overhead. We consider a simpler variant of the rule interpreter given in Section 17.4. The variant is at the bottom level of the layered interpreter. The interpreter, whose relation is solve(A,N), counts the number of reductions used in solving the goal A. The code for solve and related predicate solve_body is given in Program 18.5. The rules that we will consider constitute Program 17.17 for determining

Rule interpreter for counting reductions

```
solve(A,1) ← fact(A).
solve(A,N) ← rule(A,B,Name), solve_body(B,NB), N is NB+1.

solve_body(A&B,N) ←
    solve_body(A,NA), solve_body(B,NB), N is NA+NB.
solve_body(A is_true,N) ← solve(A,N).
```

Sample rule base

```
rule(oven(Dish,top),pastry(Dish) is_true
        & size(Dish,small) is_true,place1).
rule(oven(Dish,middle),pastry(Dish) is_true
        & size(Dish,big) is_true,place2).
rule(oven(Dish,middle),main_meal(Dish) is_true,place3).
rule(oven(Dish,bottom),slow_cooker(Dish) is_true,place4).

rule(pastry(Dish),type(Dish,cake) is_true,pastry1).
rule(pastry(Dish),type(Dish,bread) is_true,pastry2).

rule(main_meal(Dish),type(Dish,meat) is_true,main_meal).
rule(slow_cooker(Dish),type(Dish,milk_pudding)
                is_true,slow_cooker).

should_fold(solve(oven(D,P),N),oven(D,P,N)).
should_fold(solve(pastry(D),N),pastry(D,N)).
should_fold(solve(main_meal(D),N),main_meal(D,N)).
should_fold(solve(slow_cooker(D),N),slow_cooker(D,N)).
should_fold(solve(type(D,P),N),type(D,P,N)).
should_fold(solve(size(D,P),N),size(D,P,N)).

should_unfold(solve_body(G,N)).
should_unfold(rule(A,B,Name)).

program(rule_interpreter,[(solve(A1,1) ← fact(A1)),
    (solve(A2,N) ← rule(A2,B,Name), solve_body(B,NB), N is NB+1)]).
```

Program 18.5   Specializing a rule interpreter

where a dish should be placed in the oven. The rules are repeated in Program 18.5 for convenience.

The effect of partial reduction in this case will be to "compile" the rules into Prolog clauses where the arithmetic calculations are done. The resulting Prolog clauses can in turn be compiled, in contrast to the combination of interpreter plus rules. Rule place1 will be transformed to

```
oven(Dish,top,N) ←
    pastry(Dish,N1), size(Dish,small,N2),
    N3 is N1+N2, N is N3+1.
```

The idea is to unfold the calls to rule so that each rule can be handled, and also to unfold the component of the interpreter that handles syntactic structure, specifically solve_body. What gets folded are the individual calls to solve, such as solve(oven(D,P),N), which gets replaced by a predicate oven(D,P,N). The necessary declarations are given in Program 18.5. Program 18.3 applied to Program 18.5 produces the desired effect.

Specifying what goals should be folded and unfolded is in general straightforward in cases similar to what we have shown. Nevertheless, making such declarations is a burden on the programmer. In many cases, the declarations can be derived automatically. Discussing how is beyond the scope of the chapter.

How useful partial reduction is for general Prolog programs is an open issue. As indicated, care must be taken when handling Prolog's impurities not to change the meaning of the program. Further, interaction with Prolog implementations can actually mean that programs that have been partially reduced can perform worse than the original program. It will be interesting to see how much partial reduction will be applied for Prolog compilation.

Exercises for Section 18.2

(i)   Extend Program 18.3 to handle builtins.

(ii) Apply Program 18.3 to the two-level rule interpreter with rules given as Program 17.20.

18.3   Code Walking

The examples of meta-programming given so far in Chapters 17 and 18 are dynamic in the sense that they "execute" Prolog programs by performing reductions. Prolog is also a useful language for writing static meta-programs that perform syntactic transformations of Prolog programs. In this section, we give two nontrivial examples in which programs are explicitly manipulated syntactically.

The first example of explicit program manipulation is program composition. In Section 13.3, stepwise enhancement for systematic construction of Prolog programs was introduced. The third and final step in the method is composition of separate enhancements of a common skeleton. We now present a program to achieve composition that is capable of composing Programs 13.1 and 13.2 to produce Program 13.3.

The running example we use to illustrate the program is a variant of the example in Chapter 13. The skeleton is the same, namely,

```
skel([X|Xs],Ys) ← member(X,Ys), skel(Xs,Ys).
skel([X|Xs],Ys) ← nonmember(X,Ys), skel(Xs,Ys).
skel([ ],Ys).
```

The union program, Program 13.1, is also the same, namely,

```
union([X|Xs],Ys,Us) ← member(X,Ys), union(Xs,Ys,Us).
union([X|Xs],Ys,[X|Us]) ← nonmember(X,Ys), union(Xs,Ys,Us).
union([ ],Ys,Ys).
```

The second program to be composed is different and represents when added goals are present. The relation to be used is common(Xs,Ys,N), which counts the number of common elements N in two lists Xs and Ys. The code is

```
common([X|Xs],Ys,N) ←
    member(X,Ys), common(Xs,Ys,M), N is M+1.
common([X|Xs],Ys,N) ← nonmember(X,Ys), common(Xs,Ys,N).
common([ ],Ys,0).
```

The program for composition makes some key assumptions that can be justified by theory underlying stepwise enhancement. Describing the theory is beyond the scope of this book. The most important assumption is that there is a one-to-one correspondence between the clauses of the two programs being composed, and one-to-one correspondences between the clauses of each of the programs and the common skeleton.

Programs are represented as lists of clauses. The first clause in the first program corresponds to the first clause in the second program and to the first clause in the skeleton. Our assumption implies that the lists of clauses of programs being composed have the same length. The three programs have been written with corresponding clauses in the same order. (That the lists of clauses do have the same length is not checked explicitly.)

In order to perform composition, a composition specification is needed. It states how the arguments of the final program relate to the two extensions. The relation that we will assume is `composition_specification(Program1,Program2,Skeleton,FinalProgram)`. An example of the specification for our running example is `composition_specification(union(Xs,Ys,Us), common(Xs,Ys,N), skel(Xs,Ys), uc(Xs,Ys,Us,N)`. The composition specification is given as part of Program 18.6.

The program for composition is given as Program 18.6. The top-level relation is `compose/4`, which composes the first two programs assumed to be enhancements of the third argument to produce the composite program, which is the fourth argument.

The program proceeds clause by clause in the top loop of Program 18.6, where `compose_clause/4` does the clause composition. The arguments correspond exactly to the arguments for `compose`. To compose two clauses, we have to compose the heads and the bodies. Composition of the heads of clauses happens through unification with the composition specification. The predicate `compose_bodies/4` is used to compose the bodies. Note that the order of arguments has been changed so that we systematically traverse the skeleton. Each goal in the skeleton must be represented in each of the enhancements so that it can be used as a reference to align the goals in each of the enhancements.

The essence of `compose_bodies` is to traverse the body of the skeleton goal by goal and construct the appropriate output goal as we proceed. In order to produce tidy output and avoid superfluous empty goals, a difference-structure is used to build the output body. The first clause for `compose_bodies` covers the case when the body of the skeleton is nonempty. The predicates `first` and `rest`, which access the body of the skeleton, are a good example of data abstraction.

compose(Program1,Program2,Skeleton,FinalProgram) ←
   FinalProgram is the result of composing *Program1* and
   Program2, which are both enhancements of *Skeleton*.

```
compose([Cl1|Cls1],[Cl2|Cls2],[ClSkel|ClsSkel],[Cl |Cls]) ←
    compose_clause(Cl1,Cl2,ClSkel,Cl),
    compose(Cls1,Cls2,ClsSkel,Cls).
compose([ ],[ ],[ ],[ ]).

compose_clause((A1←B1),(A2←B2),(ASkel←BSkel),(A←B)) ←
    composition_specification(A1,A2,ASkel,A),
    compose_bodies(BSkel,B1,B2,B\true).

compose_bodies(SkelBody,Body1,Body2,B\BRest) ←
    first(SkelBody,G), !,
    align(G,Body1,G1,RestBody1,B\B1),
    align(G,Body2,G2,RestBody2,B1\(Goal,B2)),
    compose_goal(G1,G2,Goal),
    rest(SkelBody,Gs),
    compose_bodies(Gs,RestBody1,RestBody2,B2\BRest).
compose_bodies(true,Body1,Body2,B\BRest) ←
    rest_goals(Body1,B\B1), rest_goals(Body2,B1\BRest).

align(Goal,Body,G,RestBody,B\B) ←
    first(Body,G), correspond(G,Goal), !, rest(Body,RestBody).
align(Goal,(G,Body),CorrespondingG,RestBody,(G,B)\B1) ←
    align(Goal,Body,CorrespondingG,RestBody,B\B1).

first((G,Gs),G).
first(G,G) ← G ≠ (A,B), G ≠ true.

rest((G,Gs),Gs).
rest(G,true) ← G ≠ (A,B).

correspond(G,G).
correspond(G,B) ← map(G,B).

compose_goal(G,G,G) ← !.
compose_goal(A1,A2,A) ←
    !, composition_specification(A1,A2,ASkel,A).

rest_goals(true,B\B) ← !.
rest_goals(Body,(G,B)\BRest) ←
    first(Body,G), !, rest(Body,Body1), rest_goals(Body1,B\BRest).
```

Program 18.6 Composing two enhancements of a skeleton

An important assumption made by Program 18.6 concerns finding the goals in the bodies of the program that correspond to the goals in the skeleton. The assumption made, embedded in the predicate `correspond`, is that a mapping will be given from goals in the enhancement to goals in the skeleton. In our running example, the predicates `member` and `non-member` map onto themselves, while both `union` and `common` map onto `skel`. This information, provided by the predicate `map/2`, is needed to correctly align goals from the skeleton with goals of the program being composed. The code for `align` as presented allows for additional goals to be present between goals in the skeleton. The only extra goal in our running example is the arithmetic calculation in `common`, which is after the goals corresponding to the skeleton goals.

The second clause for `compose_bodies` covers the case when the body is empty, either from dealing with a fact or because the skeleton has been traversed. In this case, any additional goals need to be included in the result. This is the function of `rest_goals`.

Program 18.7 contains a testing clause for Program 18.6, along with the specific data for our running example. As with Program 18.4, variables in the programs being composed must be named differently. Automatic generation of composition specifications for more complicated examples is possible.

The second example of explicit manipulation of programs is the conversion of context-free grammar rules to equivalent Prolog clauses. Context-free grammars are defined over a language of symbols, divided into *nonterminal* symbols and *terminal* symbols. A context-free grammar is a set of rules of the form

⟨*head*⟩ → ⟨*body*⟩

where *head* is a nonterminal symbol and *body* is a sequence of one or more items separated by commas. Each item can be a terminal or nonterminal symbol. Associated with each grammar is a starting symbol and a language that is the set of sequences of terminal symbols obtained by repeated (nondeterministic) application of the grammar rules starting from the starting symbol. For compatibility with Chapter 19, nonterminal symbols are denoted as Prolog atoms, terminal symbols are enclosed within lists, and [ ] denotes the empty operation.

The language a(bc)* can be defined by the following context-free grammar consisting of four rules:

```
test_compose(X,Prog) ←
    program1(X,Prog1), program2(X,Prog2),
    skeleton(X,Skeleton), compose(Prog1,Prog2,Skeleton,Prog).
program1(test,[
    (union([X1|Xs1],Ys1,Zs1) ←
        member(X1,Ys1), union(Xs1,Ys1,Zs1)),
    (union([X2|Xs2],Ys2,[X2|Zs2]) ←
        nonmember(X2,Ys2), union(Xs2,Ys2,Zs2)),
    (union([ ],Ys3,Ys3) ← true)]).
program2(test,[
    (common([X1|Xs1],Ys1,N1) ←
        member(X1,Ys1), common(Xs1,Ys1,M1), N1 is M1+1),
    (common([X2|Xs2],Ys2,N2) ←
        nonmember(X2,Ys2), common(Xs2,Ys2,N2)),
    (common([ ],Ys3,0) ← true)]).
skeleton(test,[
    (skel([X1|Xs1],Ys1) ← member(X1,Ys1), skel(Xs1,Ys1)),
    (skel([X2|Xs2],Ys2) ← nonmember(X2,Ys2), skel(Xs2,Ys2)),
    (skel([ ],Ys3) ← true)]).

composition_specification(union(Xs,Ys,Us), common(Xs,Ys,N),
    skel(Xs,Ys),uc(Xs,Ys,Us,N)).

map(union(Xs,Ys,Zs), skel(Xs,Ys)).
map(common(Xs,Ys,N), skel(Xs,Ys)).
```

Program 18.7 Testing program composition

```
s → [a], b.
b → [b], c.
b → [ ].
c → [c], b.
```

Another example of a context-free grammar is given in Figure 18.1. This grammar recognizes the language $a*b*c*$.

A context-free grammar can be immediately written as a Prolog program. Each nonterminal symbol becomes a unary predicate whose argument is the sentence or phrase it identifies. The naive choice for representing each phrase is as a list of terminal symbols. The first grammar rule in Figure 18.1 becomes

```
s(Xs) → a(As), b(Bs),
    c(Cs), append(Bs,Cs,BsCs), append(As,BsCs,Xs).
```

```
s → a, b, c.
a → [a], a.
a → [ ].
b → [b], b.
b → [ ].
c → [c], c.
c → [ ].
```

Figure 18.1   A context-free grammar for the language $a^*b^*c^*$

```
s(As\Xs) ← a(As\Bs), b(Bs\Cs), c(Cs\Xs).

a(Xs\Ys) ← connect([a],Xs\Xs1), a(Xs1\Ys).
a(Xs\Ys) ← connect([ ],Xs\Ys).
b(Xs\Ys) ← connect([b],Xs\Xs1), b(Xs1\Ys).
b(Xs\Ys) ← connect([ ],Xs\Ys).
c(Xs\Ys) ← connect([c],Xs\Xs1), c(Xs1\Ys).
c(Xs\Ys) ← connect([ ],Xs\Ys).

connect([ ],Xs\Xs).
connect([W|Ws],[W|Xs]\Ys) ← connect(Ws,Xs\Ys).
```

Program 18.8   A Prolog program parsing the language $a^*b^*c^*$

Completing the grammar of Figure 18.1 in the style of the previous rule leads to a correct program for parsing, albeit an inefficient one. The calls to append suggest, correctly, that a difference-list might be a more appropriate structure for representing the sequence of terminals in the context of parsing. Program 18.8 is a translation of Figure 18.1 to a Prolog program where difference-lists represent the phrases. The basic relation scheme is s(Xs), which is true if Xs is a sequence of symbols accepted by the grammar.

The predicate connect(Xs,Ws) is true if the list Xs represents the same sequence of elements as Ws. The predicate is used to make explicit the translation of terminal symbols to Prolog programs.

As a parsing program, Program 18.8 is a top-down, left-to-right recursive parser that backtracks when it needs an alternative solution. Although easy to construct, backtracking parsers are in general inefficient. However, the efficiency of the underlying Prolog implementation in general more than compensates.

translate(Grammar,Program) ←
> *Program* is the Prolog equivalent of the context-free
> grammar *Grammar*.

```
translate([Rule|Rules],[Clause|Clauses]) ←
    translate_rule(Rule,Clause),
    translate(Rules,Clauses).
translate([ ],[ ]).
```

translate_rule(GrammarRule,PrologClause) ←
> *PrologClause* is the Prolog equivalent of the grammar
> rule *GrammarRule*.

```
translate_rule((Lhs → Rhs),(Head ← Body)) ←
    translate_head(Lhs,Head,Xs\Ys),
    translate_body(Rhs,Body,Xs\Ys).

translate_head(A,A1,Xs) ←
    translate_goal(A,A1,Xs).

translate_body(A,B),(A1,B1),Xs\Ys) ←
    !, translate_body(A,A1,Xs\Xs1), translate_body(B,B1,Xs1\Ys).
translate_body(A,A1,Xs) ←
    translate_goal(A,A1,Xs).

translate_goal(A,A1,DList) ←
    nonterminal(A), functor(A1,A,1), arg(1,A1,DList).
translate_goal(Terms,connect(Terms,S),S) ←
    terminals(Terms).

nonterminal(A) ← atom(A).

terminals(Xs) ← list(Xs).

list(Xs) ← see Program 3.11.
```

Program 18.9   Translating grammar rules to Prolog clauses

We now present Program 18.9, which translates Figure 18.1 to Program 18.8. As for Program 18.6, the translation proceeds clause by clause. There is a one-to-one correspondence between grammar rules and Prolog clauses. The basic relation is `translate(Rules,Clauses)`. Individual clauses are translated by `translate_rule/2`. To translate a rule, both the head and body must be translated, with the appropriate correspondence of difference-lists, which will be added as additional arguments.

Adding an argument is handled by the predicate `translate_goal`. If the goal to be translated is a nonterminal symbol, a unary predicate with the same functor is created. If the goal is a list of terminal symbols, the appropriate `connect` goal is created. When executed, the `connect` goal connects the two difference-lists. Code for `connect` is in Program 18.8.

Program 18.9 can be extended for automatic translation of definite clause grammar rules. Definite clause grammars are the subject of Chapter 19. Most versions of Edinburgh Prolog provide such a translator.

Exercise for Section 18.3

(i)   Apply Program 18.6 to one of the exercises posed at the end of Section 13.3.

18.4   Background

Often research in logic programming has followed in the steps of related research in functional programming. This is true for unfold/fold and partial evaluation. Burstall and Darlington (1977) wrote the seminal paper on unfold/fold in the functional programming literature. Their work was adapted for logic programming by Tamaki and Sato (1984).

The term *partial evaluation* may have been used first in a paper by Lombardi and Raphael (1964), where a simple partial evaluator for Lisp was described. A seminal paper introducing partial evaluation to computer science is due to Futamura in 1971, who noted the possibility of compiling away levels of interpretation. Komorowski described the first partial evaluator for pure Prolog in his thesis in 1981. He has since preferred the term *partial deduction*. Gallagher in 1983 was the first to advocate using partial evaluation in Prolog for removing interpretation overhead (Gallagher, 1986). Venken (1984) was the first to list some of the problems of extending partial evaluation to full Prolog. The paper that sparked the most interest in partial evaluation in Prolog is due to Takeuchi and Furukawa (1986). They discussed using partial evaluation for removing runtime overhead and showed an order of magnitude speedup. Sterling and Beer (1989) particularize the work for expert systems. Their paper introduces the issue of pushing down meta-arguments, which is subsumed in this chapter by `should_fold` declarations. Specific Prolog partial evaluation systems to read for more details are ProMiX

(Lakhotia and Sterling, 1990) and Mixtus (Sahlin, 1991). An interesting application of partial evaluation is given by Smith (1991), where efficient string-matching programs were developed.

Composition was first discussed in the context of Prolog meta-interpreters in Sterling and Beer (1989) and an informal algorithm was given in Sterling and Lakhotia (1988). A theory is found in Kirschenbaum, Sterling, and Jain (1993).

19   Logic Grammars

A very important application area of Prolog is parsing. In fact, Prolog originated from attempts to use logic to express grammar rules and to formalize the process of parsing. In this chapter, we present the most common logic grammar formalism, definite clause grammars. We show how grammar rules can be considered as a language on top of Prolog, and we apply grammar rules to parse simple English sentences. In Chapter 24, definite clause grammars are used as the parsing component of a simple compiler for a Pascal-like language.

19.1   Definite Clause Grammars

Definite clause grammars arise from adding features of Prolog to context-free grammars. In Section 18.3, we briefly sketched how context-free grammars could be immediately converted to Prolog programs, which parsed the language specified by the context-free grammar. By adding the ability of Prolog to exploit the power of unification and the ability to call builtin predicates, a very powerful parsing formalism is indeed achieved, as we now show.

Consider the context-free grammar for recognizing the language $a^*b^*c^*$, presented in Figure 18.1, with equivalent Prolog program Program 18.8. The Prolog program can be easily enhanced to count the number of symbols that appear in any recognized sequence of a's, b's, and c's. An argument would be added to each predicate constituting the number of symbols found. Arithmetic would be performed to add numbers together. The first clause would become

```
s(As\Xs,N) ←
    a(As\Bs,NA), b(Bs\Cs,NB), c(Cs\Xs,NC), N is NA+NB+NC.
```

The extra argument counting the number of *a*'s, *b*'s, and *c*'s can be added to the grammar rule just as easily, yielding

```
s(N) → a(NA), b(NB), c(NC), N is NA+NB+NC.
```

Adding arguments to nonterminal symbols of context-free grammars, and the ability to call (arbitrary) Prolog predicates, increases their utility and expressive power. Grammars in this new class are called *definite clause grammars*, or *DCGs*. Definite clause grammars are a generalization of context-free grammars that are executable, augmented by the language features of Prolog.

Program 18.9, translating context-free grammars into Prolog programs, can be extended to translate DCGs into Prolog. The extension is posed as Exercise (i) at the end of this section. Throughout this chapter we write DCGs in grammar rule notation, being aware that they can be viewed as Prolog programs. Many Edinburgh Prolog implementations provide support for grammar rules. The operator used for → is -->. Grammar rules are expanded automatically into Prolog clauses with two extra arguments added as the last two arguments of the predicate to represent as a difference-list the sequence of tokens or words recognized by the predicate. Braces are used to delimit goals to be called by Prolog directly, which should not have extra arguments added during translation. Grammar rules are not part of Standard Prolog but will probably be incorporated in the future.

Program 19.1 gives a DCG that recognizes the language $a^*b^*c^*$ and also counts the number of letters in the recognized sequence. The enhancement from Figure 18.1 is immediate. To query Program 19.1, consideration must be taken of the two extra arguments that will be added. For example, a suitable query is s(N,[a,a,b,b,b,c],[ ])?.

Counting the symbols could, of course, be accomplished by traversing the difference-list of words. However, counting is a simple enhancement to understand, which effectively displays the essence of definite clause grammars. Section 19.3 presents a wider variety of enhancements.

Our next example is a striking one of the increase in expressive power possible using extra arguments and unification. Consider recognizing the language $a^N b^N c^N$, which is not possible with a context-free grammar.

```
s(N) → a(NA), b(NB), c(NC), {N is NA+NB+NC}.
a(N) → [a], a(N1), {N is N1+1}.
a(0) → [ ].
b(N) → [b], b(N1), {N is N1+1}.
b(0) → [ ].
c(N) → [c], c(N1), {N is N1+1}.
c(0) → [ ].
```

Program 19.1 Enhancing the language $a^* b^* c^*$

```
s → a(N), b(N), c(N).
a(N) → [a], a(N1), {N is N1+1}.
a(0) → [ ].
b(N) → [b], b(N1), {N is N1+1}.
b(0) → [ ].
c(N) → [c], c(N1), {N is N1+1}.
c(0) → [ ].
```

Program 19.2 Recognizing the language $a^N b^N c^N$

However, there is a straightforward modification to the grammar given
as Program 19.1. All that is necessary is to change the first rule and make
the number of a's, b's, and c's the same. The modified program is given
as Program 19.2.

In Program 19.2, unification has added context sensitivity and increased the expressive power of DCGs over context-free grammars. DCGs
should be regarded as Prolog programs. Indeed, parsing with DCGs is a
perfect illustration of Prolog programming using nondeterministic programming and difference-lists. The top-down, left-to-right computation
model of Prolog yields a top-down, left-to-right parser.

Definite clause grammars can be used to express general programs.
For example, a version of Program 3.15 for append with its last two
arguments swapped can be written as follows.

```
append([ ]) → [ ].
append([X|Xs]) → [X], append(Xs).
```

Using DCGs for tasks other than parsing is an acquired programming
taste.

The grammar for the declarative part of a Pascal program.

```
declarative_part →
    const_declaration, type_declaration,
    var_declaration, procedure_declaration.
```

Constant declarations

```
const_declaration → [ ].
const_declaration →
    [const], const_definition, [;], const_definitions.

const_definitions → [ ].
const_definitions →
    const_definition, [;], const_definitions.

const_definition → identifier, [=], constant.

identifier → [X], {atom(X)}.
constant → [X], {constant(X)}.
```

Type declarations

```
type_declaration → [ ].
type_declaration →
    [type], type_definition, [;], type_definitions.

type_definitions → [ ].
type_definitions → type_definition, [;], type_definitions.

type_definition → identifier, [=], type.

type → ['INTEGER'].
type → ['REAL'].
type → ['BOOLEAN'].
type → ['CHAR'].
```

Variable declarations

```
var_declaration → [ ].
var_declaration →
    [var], var_definition, [;], var_definitions.

var_definitions → [ ].
var_definitions → var_definition, [;], var_definitions.
var_definition → identifiers, [:], type.

identifiers → identifier.
identifiers → identifier, [,], identifiers.
```

Program 19.3   Parsing the declarative part of a Pascal block

Procedure declarations

```
procedure_declaration → [ ].
procedure_declaration → procedure_heading, [;], block.

procedure_heading →
    [procedure], identifier, formal_parameter_part.

formal_parameter_part → [ ].
formal_parameter_part → [(], formal_parameter_section, [)].

formal_parameter_section → formal_parameters.
formal_parameter_section →
    formal_parameters, [;], formal_parameter_section.

formal_parameters → value_parameters.
formal_parameters → variable_parameters.

value_parameters → var_definition.
variable_parameters → [var], var_definition.
```

Program 19.3   (Continued)

We conclude this section with a more substantial example. A DCG is given for parsing the declarative part of a block in a Pascal program. The code does not in fact cover all of Pascal — it is not complete in its definition of types or constants, for example. Extensions to the grammar are posed in the exercises at the end of this section. Parsing the statement part of a Pascal program is illustrated in Chapter 24.

The grammar for the declarative part of a Pascal block is given as Program 19.3. Each grammar rule corresponds closely to the syntax diagram for the corresponding Pascal statement. For example, the syntax diagram for constant declarations is as follows:

```
---> const -----> Constant Definition -------> ; ------->
          |                                     |
          +---------------<--------------------+
```

The second grammar rule for const_declaration in Program 19.3 says exactly the same. A constant declaration is the reserved word const followed by a constant definition, handled by the nonterminal symbol const_definition; followed by a semicolon; followed by the rest of the constant definition, handled by the nonterminal symbol const_definitions. The first rule for const_declaration effectively states that the constant declaration is optional. A constant definition is an identifier followed by =, followed by a constant. The definition for const_definitions is recursive, being either empty or another constant definition; followed by a semicolon; followed by the rest of the constant definition.

The remainder of Program 19.3 is similarly easy to understand. It clearly shows the style of writing grammars in Prolog.

Exercises for Section 19.1

(i)   Extend Program 18.9 so that it translates definite clause grammars to Prolog as well as context-free grammars.

(ii)   Add to Program 19.3 the ability to correctly handle label declarations and function declarations.

(iii)   Enhance Program 19.3 to return the list of variables declared in the declarative part.

(iv)   Write a program to parse the language of your choice in the style of Program 19.3.

19.2   A Grammar Interpreter

Grammar rules are viewed in the previous section as syntactic sugar for Prolog clauses. This view is supported by Prolog systems with automatic grammar rule translation. There is a second way of viewing grammar rules, namely as a rule language.

This section takes the second view and considers grammar rules as an embedded language on top of Prolog. We consider applying the interpreter techniques of Chapter 17 to grammar rules.

Program 19.4 is an interpreter for grammar rules. The basic relation is parse(Symbol,Tokens), which is true if a sequence of grammar rules can be applied to Symbol to reach Tokens. The tokens are represented as a difference-list.

The granularity of the DCG interpreter is at the clause reduction level, the same as for the vanilla meta-interpreter, Program 17.5, and the expert system rule interpreter, Program 17.18. Indeed, the code in Program 19.4 is similar to those interpreters. There are four cases, handled by the

parse(Start,Tokens) ←
　　The sequence of tokens *Tokens* represented as a difference-list
　　can be reached by applying the grammar rules defined by →/2,
　　starting from *Start*.

```
parse(A,Tokens) ←
    nonterminal(A), A → B, parse(B,Tokens).
parse((A,B),Tokens\Xs) ←
    parse(A,Tokens\Tokens1), parse(B,Tokens1\Xs).
parse(A,Tokens) ← terminals(A), connect(A,Tokens).
parse({A},Xs\Xs) ← A.
```

terminals(Xs) ← See Program 18.9.

connect(Xs,Tokens) ← See Program 18.8.

Program 19.4 A definite clause grammar (DCG) interpreter

four clauses for parse in Program 19.4. The first rule handles the basic operation of reducing a nonterminal symbol, and the second rule handles conjunctions of symbols. The third rule handles terminal symbols, and the fourth rule covers the ability to handle Prolog predicates by calling them directly using the meta-variable facility.

Observe that the last argument in parse/2, the DCG interpreter, is a difference-list. This difference-list can be handled implicitly using grammar rule notation. In other words, Program 19.4 could itself be written as a DCG. This task is posed as Exercise 19.2(i).

Recall that the interpreters of Chapter 17 were enhanced. Similarly, the DCG interpreter, Program 19.4, can be enhanced. Program 19.5 gives a simple enhancement that counts the number of tokens used in parsing. As mentioned before, this particular enhancement could be accomplished directly, but it illustrates how an interpreter can be enhanced.

Comparing Programs 19.1 and 19.5 raises an important issue. Is it better to enhance a grammar by modifying the rules, as in Program 19.1, or to add the extra functionality at the level of the interpreter? The second approach is more modular, but suffers from a lack of efficiency.

Exercises for Section 19.2

(i) Write Program 19.4 as a DCG.

parse(Start,Tokens,N) ←
> The sequence of tokens *Tokens*, represented as a difference-list, can be reached by applying the grammar rules defined by →/2, starting from *Start*, and *N* tokens are found.

```
parse(A,Tokens,N) ←
    nonterminal(A), A → B, parse(B,Tokens,N).
parse((A,B),Tokens\Xs,N) ←
    parse(A,Tokens\Tokens1,NA), parse(B,Tokens1\Xs,NB),
    N is NA+NB.
parse(A,Tokens,N) ←
    terminals(A), connect(A,Tokens), length(A,N).
parse({A},Xs\Xs,0) ← A.

terminals(Xs) ← See Program 18.9.

connect(A,Tokens) ← See Program 18.8.

length(Xs,N) ← See Program 8.11.
```

Program 19.5 A DCG interpreter that counts words

(ii)   Use the partial reducer, Program 18.3, to specialize the interpreter of Program 19.4 to a particular grammar. For example, Figure 18.1 should be transformed to Program 19.1.

(iii) Enhance Program 19.4 to build a parse tree.

19.3   Application to Natural Language Understanding

An important application area of logic programming has been understanding natural languages. Indeed, the origins of Prolog lie within this application. In this section, it is shown how Prolog, through definite clause grammars, can be applied to natural language processing.

A simple context-free grammar for a small subset of English is given in Program 19.6. The nonterminal symbols are grammatical categories, parts of speech and phrases, and the terminal symbols are English words that can be thought of as the vocabulary. The first rule in Program 19.6 says that a sentence is a noun phrase followed by a verb phrase. The last rule says that *surprise* is a noun. A sample sentence recognized by the grammar is: "The decorated pieplate contains a surprise."

Grammar Rules

```
sentence → noun_phrase, verb_phrase.

noun_phrase → determiner, noun_phrase2.
noun_phrase → noun_phrase2.

noun_phrase2 → adjective, noun_phrase2.
noun_phrase2 → noun.

verb_phrase → verb.
verb_phrase → verb, noun_phrase.
```

Vocabulary

```
determiner → [the].     adjective → [decorated]
determiner → [a].

noun → [pieplate].      verb → [contains].
noun → [surprise].
```

Program 19.6 A DCG context-free grammar

Using the terminology of stepwise enhancement introduced in Chapter 13, we can view a grammar as a skeleton. We proceed to show how useful grammatical features can be added by enhancement. The next two programs are enhancements of Program 19.6. The enhancements, although simple, typify how DCGs can be used for natural language applications. Both programs exploit the power of the logical variable.

The first enhancement is constructing a parse tree for the sentence as it is being parsed. The program is given as Program 19.7. Arguments representing (subparts of) the parse tree must be added to Program 19.6. The enhancement is similar to adding structured arguments to logic programs, as discussed in Section 2.2. The program builds the parse tree top-down, exploiting the power of the logic variable.

The rules in Program 19.7 can be given a declarative reading. For example, consider the rule

```
sentence(sentence(NP,VP)) → noun_phrase(NP), verb_phrase(VP).
```

This states that the parse tree built in recognizing the sentence is a structure sentence(NP,VP), where NP is the structure built while recognizing the noun phrase and VP is the structure built while recognizing the verb phrase.

```
sentence(sentence(NP,VP)) → noun_phrase(NP), verb_phrase(VP).

noun_phrase(np(D,N)) → determiner(D), noun_phrase2(N).
noun_phrase(np(N)) → noun_phrase2(N).

noun_phrase2(np2(A,N)) → adjective(A), noun_phrase2(N).
noun_phrase2(np2(N)) → noun(N).

verb_phrase(vp(V)) → verb(V).
verb_phrase(vp(V,N)) → verb(V), noun_phrase(N).
```

Vocabulary

```
determiner(det(the)) → [the].
determiner(det(a)) → [a].

noun(noun(pieplate)) → [pieplate].
noun(noun(surprise)) → [surprise].

adjective(adj(decorated)) → [decorated].
verb(verb(contains)) → [contains].
```

Program 19.7   A DCG computing a parse tree

The next enhancement concerns subject/object number agreement. Suppose we wanted our grammar also to parse the sentence "The decorated pieplates contain a surprise." A simplistic way of handling plural forms of nouns and verbs, sufficient for the purposes of this book, is to treat different forms as separate words. We augment the vocabulary by adding the facts

```
noun(noun(pieplates)) → [pieplates].
verb(verb(contain)) → [contain].
```

The new program would parse "The decorated pieplates contain a surprise" but unfortunately would also parse "The decorated pieplates contains a surprise." There is no insistence that noun and verb must both be singular, or both be plural.

Number agreement can be enforced by adding an argument to the parts of speech that must be the same. The argument indicates whether the part of speech is singular or plural. Consider the grammar rule

```
sentence(sentence(NP,VP)) →
    noun_phrase(NP,Num), verb_phrase(VP,Num).
```

The rule insists that both the noun phrase, which is the subject of the sentence, and the verb phrase, which is the object of the sentence, have

```
sentence(sentence(NP,VP)) →
    noun_phrase(NP,Num), verb_phrase(VP,Num).
noun_phrase(np(D,N),Num) →
    determiner(D,Num), noun_phrase2(N,Num).
noun_phrase(np(N),Num) → noun_phrase2(N,Num).
noun_phrase2(np2(A,N),Num) →
    adjective(A), noun_phrase2(N,Num).
noun_phrase2(np2(N),Num) → noun(N,Num).
verb_phrase(vp(V),Num) → verb(V,Num).
verb_phrase(vp(V,N),Num) →
    verb(V,Num), noun_phrase(N,Num1).
```

Vocabulary

```
determiner(det(the),Num) → [the].
determiner(det(a),singular) → [a].

noun(noun(pieplate),singular) → [pieplate].
noun(noun(pieplates),plural) → [pieplates].
noun(noun(surprise),singular) → [surprise].
noun(noun(surprises),plural) → [surprises].

adjective(adj(decorated)) → [decorated].

verb(verb(contains),singular) → [contains].
verb(verb(contain),plural) → [contain].
```

Program 19.8   A DCG with subject/object number agreement

the same number, singular or plural. The agreement is indicated by the sharing of the variable Num. Expressing subject/object number agreement is context-dependent information, which is clearly beyond the scope of context-free grammars.

Program 19.8 is an extension of Program 19.7 that handles number agreement correctly. Noun phrases and verb phrases must have the same number, singular or plural. Similarly, the determiners and nouns in a noun phrase must agree in number. The vocabulary is extended to indicate which words are singular and which plural. Where number is unimportant, for example, with adjectives, it can be ignored, and no extra argument is given. The determiner *the* can be either singular or plural. This is handled by leaving the argument indicating number uninstantiated.

The next example of a DCG uses another Prolog feature, the ability to refer to arbitrary Prolog goals in the body of a rule. Program 19.9 is a grammar for recognizing numbers written in English up to, but not including, 1,000. The value of the number recognized is calculated using the arithmetic facilities of Prolog.

The basic relation is number(N), where N is the numerical value of the number being recognized. According to the grammar specified by the program, a number is zero or a number N of at most three digits, the relation xxx(N). Similarly xx(N) represents a number N of at most two digits, and the predicates rest_xxx and rest_xx denote the rest of a number of three or two digits, respectively, after the leading digit has been removed. The predicates digit, teen, and tens recognize, respectively, single digits, the numbers 10 to 19 inclusive, and the multiples of ten from 20 to 90 inclusive.

A sample rule from the grammar is

```
xxx(N) →
    digit(D), [hundred], rest_xxx(N1), {N is D*100+N1}.
```

This says that a three-digit number N must first be a digit with value D, followed by the word *hundred* followed by the rest of the number, which will have value N1. The value for the whole number N is obtained by multiplying D by 100 and adding N1.

DCGs inherit another feature from logic programming, the ability to be used backward. Program 19.9 can be used to generate the written representation of a given number up to, but not including, 1,000. In technical terms, the grammar generates as well as accepts. The behavior in so doing is classic generate-and-test. All the legal numbers of the grammar are generated one by one and tested to see whether they have the correct value, until the actual number posed is reached. This feature is a curiosity rather than an efficient means of writing numbers.

The generative feature of DCGs is not generally useful. Many grammars have recursive rules. For example, the rule in Program 19.6 defining a noun_phrase2 as an adjective followed by a noun_phrase2 is recursive. Using recursively defined grammars for generation results in a nonterminating computation. In the grammar of Program 19.7, noun phrases with arbitrarily many adjectives are produced before the verb phrase is considered.

```
number(0) → [zero].
number(N) → xxx(N).

xxx(N) →
    digit(D), [hundred], rest_xxx(N1), {N is D*100+N1}.
xxx(N) → xx(N).

rest_xxx(0) → [ ].
rest_xxx(N) → [and], xx(N).

xx(N) → digit(N).
xx(N) → teen(N).
xx(N) → tens(T), rest_xx(N1), {N is T+N1}.

rest_xx(0) → [ ].
rest_xx(N) → digit(N).
```

`digit(1) → [one].`	`teen(10) → [ten].`
`digit(2) → [two].`	`teen(11) → [eleven].`
`digit(3) → [three].`	`teen(12) → [twelve].`
`digit(4) → [four].`	`teen(13) → [thirteen].`
`digit(5) → [five].`	`teen(14) → [fourteen].`
`digit(6) → [six].`	`teen(15) → [fifteen].`
`digit(7) → [seven].`	`teen(16) → [sixteen].`
`digit(8) → [eight].`	`teen(17) → [seventeen].`
`digit(9) → [nine].`	`teen(18) → [eighteen].`
	`teen(19) → [nineteen].`

```
tens(20) → [twenty].
tens(30) → [thirty].
tens(40) → [forty].
tens(50) → [fifty].
tens(60) → [sixty].
tens(70) → [seventy].
tens(80) → [eighty].
tens(90) → [ninety].
```

Program 19.9   A DCG for recognizing numbers

Exercises for Section 19.3

(i)   Write a simple grammar for French that illustrates gender agreement.

(ii)   Extend and modify Program 19.9 for parsing numbers so that it covers all numbers less than 1 million. Don't forget to include things like "thirty-five hundred" and to not include "thirty hundred."

19.4   Background

Prolog was connected to parsing right from its very beginning. As mentioned before, the Prolog language grew out of Colmerauer's interest in parsing, and his experience with developing Q-systems (Colmerauer, 1973). The implementors of Edinburgh Prolog were also keen on natural language processing and wrote one of the more detailed accounts of definite clause grammars (Pereira and Warren, 1980). This paper gives a good discussion of the advantages of DCGs as a parsing formalism in comparison with augmented transition networks (ATNs).

The examples of using DCGs for parsing languages in Section 19.1 were adapted from notes from a tutorial on natural language analysis given by Lynette Hirschman at the Symposium on Logic Programming in San Francisco in 1987. The DCG interpreter of Section 19.2 is adapted from Pereira and Shieber (1987).

Even though the control structure of Prolog matches directly that of recursive-descent, top-down parsers, other parsing algorithms can also be implemented in it quite easily. For example, Matsumoto et al. (1986) describes a bottom-up parser in Prolog.

The grammar in Program 19.3 is taken from Appendix 1 of Findlay and Watt (1985). The grammar in Program 19.6 is taken from Winograd's (1983) book on computational linguistics.

For further reading on logic grammars, refer to Pereira and Shieber (1987) and Abramson and Dahl (1989).

20 Search Techniques

In this chapter, we show programs encapsulating classic AI search techniques. The first section discusses state-transition frameworks for solving problems formulated in terms of a state-space graph. The second discusses the minimax algorithm with alpha-beta pruning for searching game trees.

20.1 Searching State-Space Graphs

State-space graphs are used to represent problems. Nodes of the graph are states of the problem. An edge exists between nodes if there is a transition rule, also called a *move*, transforming one state into the next. Solving the problem means finding a path from a given initial state to a desired solution state by applying a sequence of transition rules.

Program 20.1 is a framework for solving problems by searching their state-space graphs, using depth-first search as described in Section 14.2.

No commitment has been made to the representation of states. The moves are specified by a binary predicate move(State,Move), where Move is a move applicable to State. The predicate update(State,Move, State1) finds the state State1 reached by applying the move Move to state State. It is often easier to combine the move and update procedures. We keep them separate here to make knowledge more explicit and to retain flexibility and modularity, possibly at the expense of performance.

The validity of possible moves is checked by the predicate legal (State), which checks if the problem state State satisfies the constraints of the problem. The program keeps a history of the states visited

solve_dfs(State,History,Moves) ←
   Moves is a sequence of moves to reach a
   desired final state from the current *State*,
   where *History* contains the states visited previously.

```
solve_dfs(State,History,[ ]) ←
    final_state(State).
solve_dfs(State,History,[Move|Moves]) ←
    move(State,Move),
    update(State,Move,State1),
    legal(State1),
    not member(State1,History),
    solve_dfs(State1,[State1|History],Moves).
```

Testing the framework

```
test_dfs(Problem,Moves) ←
    initial_state(Problem,State), solve_dfs(State,[State],Moves).
```

Program 20.1   A depth-first state-transition framework for problem solving

to prevent looping. Checking that looping does not occur is done by see-
ing if the new state appears in the history of states. The sequence of
moves leading from the initial state to the final state is built incrementally in the third argument of `solve_dfs/3`.

To solve a problem using the framework, the programmer must decide
how states are to be represented, and axiomatize the `move`, `update`, and
`legal` procedures. A suitable representation has profound effect on the
success of this framework.

Let us use the framework to solve the wolf, goat, and cabbage problem.
We state the problem informally. A farmer has a wolf, goat, and cabbage
on the left side of a river. The farmer has a boat that can carry at most
one of the three, and he must transport this trio to the right bank. The
problem is that he dare not leave the wolf with the goat (wolves love
to eat goats) or the goat with the cabbage (goats love to eat cabbages).
He takes all his jobs very seriously and does not want to disturb the
ecological balance by losing a passenger.

States are represented by a triple, `wgc(B,L,R)`, where B is the position of the boat (left or right), L is the list of occupants of the
left bank, and R the list of occupants of the right bank. The initial and final states are `wgc(left,[wolf,goat,cabbage],[ ])` and
`wgc(right,[ ],[wolf,goat,cabbage])`, respectively. In fact, it is not
strictly necessary to note the occupants of both the left and right banks.

The occupants of the left bank can be deduced from the occupants of the right bank, and vice versa. But having both makes specifying moves clearer.

It is convenient for checking for loops to keep the lists of occupants sorted. Thus wolf will always be listed before goat, both of whom will be before cabbage if they are on the same bank.

Moves transport an occupant to the opposite bank and can thus be specified by the particular occupant who is the Cargo. The case when nothing is taken is specified by the cargo alone. The nondeterministic behavior of member allows a concise description of all the possible moves in three clauses as shown in Program 20.2: moving something from the left bank, moving something from the right bank, or the farmer's rowing in either direction by himself.

For each of these moves, the updating procedure must be specified, namely, changing the position of the boat (by update_boat/2) and updating the banks (by update_banks). Using the predicate select allows a compact description of the updating process. The insert procedure is necessary to keep the occupant list sorted, facilitating the check if a state has been visited before. It contains all the possible cases of adding an occupant to a bank.

Finally, the test for legality must be specified. The constraints are simple. The wolf and goat cannot be on the same bank without the farmer, nor can the goat and cabbage.

Program 20.2, together with Program 20.1, solves the wolf, goat, and cabbage problem. The clarity of the program speaks for itself.

We use the state-transition framework for solving another classic search problem from recreational mathematics—the water jugs problem. There are two jugs of capacity 8 and 5 liters with no markings, and the problem is to measure out exactly 4 liters from a vat containing 20 liters (or some other large number). The possible operations are filling up a jug from the vat, emptying a jug into the vat, and transferring the contents of one jug to another until either the pouring jug is emptied completely, or the other jug is filled to capacity. The problem is depicted in Figure 20.1.

The problem can be generalized to N jugs of capacity $C_1,...,C_N$. The problem is to measure a volume V, different from all the C_i but less than the largest. There is a solution if V is a multiple of the greatest common divisor of the C_i. Our particular example is solvable because 4 is a multiple of the greatest common divisor of 8 and 5.

States for the wolf, goat and cabbage problem are a structure
wgc(Boat,Left,Right), where *Boat* is the bank on which the boat
currently is, *Left* is the list of occupants on the left bank of
the river, and *Right* is the list of occupants on the right bank.

```
initial_state(wgc,wgc(left,[wolf,goat,cabbage],[ ])).

final_state(wgc(right,[ ],[wolf,goat,cabbage])).

move(wgc(left,L,R),Cargo) ← member(Cargo,L).
move(wgc(right,L,R),Cargo) ← member(Cargo,R).
move(wgc(B,L,R),alone).

update(wgc(B,L,R),Cargo,wgc(B1,L1,R1)) ←
    update_boat(B,B1), update_banks(Cargo,B,L,R,L1,R1).

update_boat(left,right).
update_boat(right,left).

update_banks(alone,B,L,R,L,R).
update_banks(Cargo,left,L,R,L1,R1) ←
    select(Cargo,L,L1), insert(Cargo,R,R1).
update_banks(Cargo,right,L,R,L1,R1) ←
    select(Cargo,R,R1), insert(Cargo,L,L1).

insert(X,[Y|Ys],[X,Y|Ys]) ←
    precedes(X,Y).
insert(X,[Y|Ys],[Y|Zs]) ←
    precedes(Y,X), insert(X,Ys,Zs).
insert(X,[ ],[X]).

precedes(wolf,X).
precedes(X,cabbage).

legal(wgc(left,L,R)) ← not illegal(R).
legal(wgc(right,L,R)) ← not illegal(L).

illegal(Bank) ← member(wolf,Bank), member(goat,Bank).
illegal(Bank) ← member(goat,Bank), member(cabbage,Bank).

select(X,Xs,Ys) ← See Program 3.19.
```

Program 20.2 Solving the wolf, goat, and cabbage problem

Figure 20.1   The water jugs problem

The particular problem we solve is for two jugs of arbitrary capacity, but the approach is immediately generalizable to any number of jugs. The program assumes two facts in the database, `capacity(I,CI)`, for I equals 1 and 2. The natural representation of the state is a structure `jugs(V1,V2)`, where V1 and V2 represent the volumes of liquid currently in the two jugs. The initial state is `jugs(0,0)` and the desired final state either `jugs(0,X)` or `jugs(X,0)`, where X is the desired volume. In fact, the only final state that needs to be specified is that the desired volume be in the larger jug. The volume can be transferred from the smaller volume, if it fits, by emptying the larger jug and pouring the contents of the smaller jug into the larger one.

Data for solving the jugs problem in conjunction with Program 20.1 are given in Program 20.3. There are six moves: filling each jug, emptying each jug, and transferring the contents of one jug to another. A sample fact for filling the first jug is `move(jugs(V1,V2),fill(1))`. The jugs' state is given explicitly to allow the data to coexist with other problem-solving data such as in Program 20.2. The emptying moves are optimized to prevent emptying an already empty jug. The updating procedure associated with the first four moves is simple, while the transferring operation has two cases. If the total volume in the jugs is less than the capacity of the jug being filled, the pouring jug will be emptied and the other jug will have the entire volume. Otherwise the other jug will be filled to capacity and the difference between the total liquid volume and the capacity of the filled jug will be left in the pouring jug. This is achieved by the predicate `adjust/4`. Note that the test for legality is trivial because all reachable states are legal.

Most interesting problems have too large a search space to be searched exhaustively by a program like 20.1. One possibility for improvement is

```
initial_state(jugs,jugs(0,0)).
final_state(jugs(4,V)).
final_state(jugs(V,4).

move(jugs(V1,V2),fill(1)).
move(jugs(V1,V2),fill(2)).
move(jugs(V1,V2),empty(1)) ← V1 > 0.
move(jugs(V1,V2),empty(2)) ← V2 > 0.
move(jugs(V1,V2),transfer(2,1)).
move(jugs(V1,V2),transfer(1,2)).

update(jugs(V1,V2),fill(1),jugs(C1,V2)) ← capacity(1,C1).
update(jugs(V1,V2),fill(2),jugs(V1,C2)) ← capacity(2,C2).
update(jugs(V1,V2),empty(1),jugs(0,V2)).
update(jugs(V1,V2),empty(2),jugs(V1,0)).
update(jugs(V1,V2),transfer(2,1),jugs(W1,W2)) ←
    capacity(1,C1),
    Liquid is V1 + V2,
    Excess is Liquid - C1,
    adjust(Liquid,Excess,W1,W2).
update(jugs(V1,V2),transfer(1,2),jugs(W1,W2)) ←
    capacity(2,C2),
    Liquid is V1 + V2,
    Excess is Liquid - C2,
    adjust(Liquid,Excess,W2,W1).

adjust(Liquid,Excess,Liquid,0) ← Excess ≤ 0.
adjust(Liquid,Excess,V,Excess) ←
    Excess > 0, V is Liquid - Excess.

legal(jugs(V1,V2)).

capacity(1,8).
capacity(2,5).
```

Program 20.3   Solving the water jugs problem

to put more knowledge into the moves allowed. Solutions to the jug problem can be found by filling one of the jugs whenever possible, emptying the other whenever possible, and otherwise transferring the contents of the jug being filled to the jug being emptied. Thus instead of six moves only three need be specified, and the search will be more direct, because only one move will be applicable to any given state. This may not give an optimal solution if the wrong jug to be constantly filled is chosen.

Developing this point further, the three moves can be coalesced into a higher-level move, `fill_and_transfer`. This tactic fills one jug and transfers all its contents to the other jug, emptying the other jug as necessary. The code for transferring from the bigger to the smaller jug is

```
move(jugs(V1,V2),fill_and_transfer(1)).

update(jugs(V1,V2),fill_and_transfer(1),jugs(0,V)) ←
    capacity(1,C1),
    capacity(2,C2),
    C1 > C2,
    V is (C1+V2) mod C2.
```

Using this program, we need only three fill and transfer operations to solve the problem in Figure 20.1.

Adding such domain knowledge means changing the problem description entirely and constitutes programming, although at a different level.

Another possibility for improvement of the search performance, investigated by early research in AI, is heuristic guidance. A general framework, based on a more explicit choice of the next state to search in the state-space graph, is used. The choice depends on numeric scores assigned to positions. The score, computed by an *evaluation function*, is a measure of the goodness of the position. Depth-first search can be considered a special case of searching using an evaluation function whose value is the distance of the current state to the initial state, while breadth-first search uses an evaluation function which is the inverse of that distance.

We show two search techniques that use an evaluation function explicitly: hill climbing and best-first search. In the following, the predicate `value(State,Value)` is an evaluation function. The techniques are described abstractly.

Hill climbing is a generalization of depth-first search where the successor position with the highest score is chosen rather than the leftmost one chosen by Prolog. The problem-solving framework of Program 20.1 is easily adapted. The hill climbing `move` generates all the states that can be reached from the current state in a single move, and then orders them in decreasing order with respect to the values computed by the evaluation function. The predicate `evaluate_and_order(Moves,State,MVs)` determines the relation that `MVs` is an ordered list of move-value tuples corresponding to the list of moves `Moves` from a state `State`. The overall program is given as Program 20.4.

To demonstrate the behavior of the program we use the example tree of Program 14.8 augmented with a value for each move. This is given as Program 20.5. Program 20.4, combined with Program 20.5 and appropriate definitions of `update` and `legal` searches the tree in the order a, d, j. The program is easily tested on the wolf, goat, and cabbage problem using as the evaluation function the number of occupants on the right bank.

Program 20.4 contains a repeated computation. The state reached by `Move` is calculated in order to reach a value for the move and then recalculated by `update`. This recalculation can be avoided by adding an extra argument to `move` and keeping the state along with the move and the value as the moves are ordered. Another possibility if there will be many calculations of the same move is using a memo-function. What is the most efficient method depends on the particular problem. For problems where the `update` procedure is simple, the program as presented will be best.

Hill climbing is a good technique when there is only one hill and the evaluation function is a good indication of progress. Essentially, it takes a local look at the state-space graph, making the decision on where next to search on the basis of the current state alone.

An alternative search method, called *best-first search*, takes a global look at the complete state-space. The best state from all those currently unsearched is chosen.

Program 20.6 for best-first search is a generalization of breadth-first search given in Section 16.2. A frontier is kept as for breadth-first search, which is updated as the search progresses. At each stage, the next best available move is made. We make the code as similar as possible to Program 20.4 for hill climbing to allow comparison.

solve_hill_climb(State,History,Moves) ←
    Moves is the sequence of moves to reach a
    desired final state from the current *State*,
    where *History* is a list of the states visited previously.

```
solve_hill_climb(State,History,[ ]) ←
    final_state(State).
solve_hill_climb(State,History,[Move|Moves]) ←
    hill_climb(State,Move),
    update(State,Move,State1),
    legal(State1),
    not member(State1,History),
    solve_hill_climb(State1,[State1|History],Moves).

hill_climb(State,Move) ←
    findall(M,move(State,M),Moves),
    evaluate_and_order(Moves,State,[ ],MVs),
    member((Move,Value),MVs).
```

evaluate_and_order(Moves,State,SoFar,OrderedMVs) ←
    All the *Moves* from the current *State*
    are evaluated and ordered as *OrderedMVs*.
    SoFar is an accumulator for partial computations.

```
evaluate_and_order([Move|Moves],State,MVs,OrderedMVs) ←
    update(State,Move,State1),
    value(State1,Value),
    insert((Move,Value),MVs,MVs1),
    evaluate_and_order(Moves,State,MVs1,OrderedMVs).
evaluate_and_order([ ],State,MVs,MVs).

insert(MV,[ ],[MV]).
insert((M,V),[(M1,V1)|MVs],[(M,V),(M1,V1)|MVs]) ←
    V ≥ V1.
insert((M,V),[(M1,V1)|MVs],[(M1,V1)|MVs1]) ←
    V < V1, insert((M,V),MVs,MVs1).
```

Testing the framework

```
test_hill_climb(Problem,Moves) ←
    initial_state(Problem,State),
    solve_hill_climb(State,[State],Moves).
```

Program 20.4 Hill climbing framework for problem solving

```
initial_state(tree,a).     value(a,0).      final_state(j).
move(a,b).      value(b,1).     move(c,g).      value(g,6).
move(a,c).      value(c,5).     move(d,j).      value(j,9).
move(a,d).      value(d,7).     move(e,k).      value(k,1).
move(a,e).      value(e,2).     move(f,h).      value(h,3).
move(c,f).      value(f,4).     move(f,i).      value(i,2).
```

Program 20.5   Test data

At each stage of the search, there is a set of moves to consider rather than a single one. The plural predicate names, for example, updates and legals, indicate this. Thus legals(States,States1) filters a set of successor states, checking which ones are allowed by the constraints of the problem. One disadvantage of breadth-first search (and hence best-first search) is that the path to take is not as conveniently calculated. Each state must store explicitly with it the path used to reach it. This is reflected in the code.

Program 20.6 tested on the data of Program 20.5 searches the tree in the same order as for hill climbing.

Program 20.6 makes each step of the process explicit. In practice, it may be more efficient to combine some of the steps. When filtering the generated states, for example, we can test that a state is new and also legal at the same time. This saves generating intermediate data structures. Program 20.7 illustrates the idea by combining all the checks into one procedure, update_frontier.

Exercises for Section 20.1

(i)   Redo the water jugs program based on the two fill-and-transfer operations.

(ii)   Write a program to solve the missionaries and cannibals problem:

Three missionaries and three cannibals are standing on the left bank of a river. There is a small boat to ferry them across with enough room for only one or two people. They wish to cross the river. If ever there are more missionaries than cannibals on a particular bank of the river, the missionaries will convert the cannibals. Find a series of ferryings to transport safely all the missionaries and cannibals across the river without exposing any of the cannibals to conversion.

solve_best (*Frontier,History,Moves*) ←
   Moves is a sequence of moves to reach a desired final state from
   the initial state, where *Frontier* contains the current states under
   consideration, and *History* contains the states visited previously.

```
solve_best([state(State,Path,Value)|Frontier],History,Moves)←
    final_state(State), reverse(Path,Moves).
solve_best([state(State,Path,Value)|Frontier],History,FinalPath)←
    findall(M,move(State,M),Moves),
    updates(Moves,Path,State,States),
    legals(States,States1),
    news(States1,History,States2),
    evaluates(States2,Values),
    inserts(Values,Frontier,Frontier1),
    solve_best(Frontier1,[State|History],FinalPath).
```

updates (*Moves,Path,State,States*) ←
   States is the list of possible states accessible from the
   current *State*, according to the list of possible *Moves*,
   where *Path* is a path from the initial node to *State*.

```
updates([M|Ms],Path,S,[(S1,[M|Path])|Ss]) ←
    update(S,M,S1), updates(Ms,Path,S,Ss).
updates([ ],Path,State,[ ]).
```

legals (*States,States1*) ←
   States1 is the subset of the list of *States* that are legal.

```
legals([(S,P)|States],[(S,P)|States1]) ←
    legal(S), legals(States,States1).
legals([(S,P)|States],States1) ←
    not legal(S), legals(States,States1).
legals([ ],[ ]).
```

news (*States,History,States1*) ←
   States1 is the list of states in *States* but not in *History*.

```
news([(S,P)|States],History,States1) ←
    member(S,History), news(States,History,States1).
news([(S,P)|States],History,[(S,P)|States1]) ←
    not member(S,History), news(States,History,States1).
news([ ],History,[ ]).
```

evaluates (*States,Values*) ←
   Values is the list of tuples of *States* augmented by their value.

```
evaluates([(S,P)|States],[state(S,P,V)|Values]) ←
    value(S,V), evaluates(States,Values).
evaluates([ ],[ ]).
```

Program 20.6   Best-first framework for problem solving

inserts(*States,Frontier,Frontier1*) ←
>   *Frontier1* is the result of inserting *States* into the current *Frontier*.

```
inserts([Value|Values],Frontier,Frontier1) ←
    insert(Value,Frontier,Frontier0),
    inserts(Values,Frontier0,Frontier1).
inserts([ ],Frontier,Frontier).

insert(State,[ ],[State]).
insert(State,[State1|States],[State,State1|States] ←
    lesseq_value(State,State1).
insert(State,[State1|States],[State|States]) ←
    equals(State,State1).
insert(State,[State1|States],[State1|States1]) ←
    greater_value(State,State1), insert(State,States,States1).

equals(state(S,P,V),state(S,P1,V)).

lesseq_value(state(S1,P1,V1),state(S2,P2,V2)) ← S1 ≠ S2, V1 ≤ V2.

greater_value(state(S1,P1,V1),state(S2,P2,V2)) ← V1 > V2.
```

Program 20.6   (Continued)

solve_best (*Frontier,History,Moves*) ←
>   *Moves* is a sequence of moves to reach a desired final state
>   from the initial state. *Frontier* contains the current states
>   under consideration. *History* contains the states visited previously.

```
solve_best([state(State,Path,Value)|Frontier],History,Moves) ←
    final_state(State), reverse(Path,[ ],Moves).
solve_best([state(State,Path,Value)|Frontier],History,FinalPath) ←
    findall(M,move(State,M),Moves),
    update_frontier(Moves,State,Path,History,Frontier,Frontier1),
    solve_best(Frontier1,[State|History],FinalPath).

update_frontier([M|Ms],State,Path,History,F,F1) ←
    update(State,M,State1),
    legal(State1),
    value(State1,Value),
    not member(State1,History),
    insert((State1,[M|Path],Value),F,F0),
    update_frontier(Ms,State,Path,History,F0,F1).
update_frontier([ ],S,P,H,F,F).

insert(State,Frontier,Frontier1) ← See Program 20.6.
```

Program 20.7   Concise best-first framework for problem solving

(iii)   Write a program to solve the five jealous husbands problem (Dudeney, 1917):

> *During a certain flood five married couples found themselves surrounded by water and had to escape from their unpleasant position in a boat that would only hold three persons at a time. Every husband was so jealous that he would not allow his wife to be in the boat or on either bank with another man (or with other men) unless he himself was present. Find a way of getting these five men and their wives across to safety.*

(iv)   Compose a general problem-solving framework built around breadth-first search analogous to Program 20.1, based on programs in Section 16.2.

(v)   Express the 8-queens puzzle within the framework. Find an evaluation function.

20.2   Searching Game Trees

What happens when we play a game? Starting the game means setting up the chess pieces, dealing out the cards, or setting out the matches, for example. Once it is decided who plays first, the players take turns making a move. After each move the game position is updated accordingly.

We develop the vague specification in the previous paragraph into a simple framework for playing games. The top-level statement is

```
play(Game) ←
    initialize(Game,Position,Player),
    display_game(Position,Player),
    play(Position,Player,Result).
```

The predicate `initialize(Game,Position,Player)` determines the initial game position `Position` for `Game`, and `Player`, the player to start.

A game is a sequence of turns, where each turn consists of a player choosing a move, the move being executed, and the next player being determined. The neatest way of expressing this is as a tail recursive procedure, `play`, with three arguments: a game position, a player to move, and the final result. It is convenient to separate the choice of the move by `choose_move/3` from its execution by `move/3`. The remaining

play(Game) ←
    Play game with name *Game*.

```
play(Game) ←
    initialize(Game,Position,Player),
    display_game(Position,Player),
    play(Position,Player,Result).

play(Position,Player,Result) ←
    game_over(Position,Player,Result), !, announce(Result).
play(Position,Player,Result) ←
    choose_move(Position,Player,Move),
    move(Move,Position,Position1),
    display_game(Position1,Player),
    next_player(Player,Player1),
    !, play(Position1,Player1,Result).
```

Program 20.8   Framework for playing games

predicates in the clause for play/3 display the state of the game and determine the next player:

```
play(Position,Player,Result) ←
    choose_move(Position,Player,Move),
    move(Move,Position,Position1),
    display_game(Position1,Player),
    next_player(Player,Player1),
    !,  play(Position1,Player1,Result).
```

Program 20.8 provides a logical framework for game-playing programs. Using it for writing a program for a particular game focuses attention on the important issues for game playing: what data structures should be used to represent the game position, and how strategies for the game should be expressed. We demonstrate the process in Chapter 21 by writing programs to play Nim and Kalah.

The problem-solving frameworks of Section 20.1 are readily adapted to playing games. Given a particular game state, the problem is to find a path of moves to a winning position.

A game tree is similar to a state-space graph. It is the tree obtained by identifying states with nodes and edges with players' moves. We do not, however, identify nodes on the tree, obtained by different sequences of moves, even if they repeat the same state. In a game tree, each layer is called a *ply*.

evaluate_and_choose(Moves,Position,Record,BestMove) ←
    Chooses the *BestMove* from the set of *Moves* from the
    current *Position*. *Record* records the current best move.

```
evaluate_and_choose([Move|Moves],Position,Record,BestMove) ←
    move(Move,Position,Position1),
    value(Position1,Value),
    update(Move,Value,Record,Record1),
    evaluate_and_choose(Moves,Position,Record1,BestMove).
evaluate_and_choose([ ],Position,(Move,Value),Move).

update(Move,Value,(Move1,Value1),(Move1,Value1)) ←
    Value ≤ Value1.
update(Move,Value,(Move1,Value1),(Move,Value)) ←
    Value > Value1.
```

Program 20.9   Choosing the best move

Most game trees are far too large to be searched exhaustively. This section discusses the techniques that have been developed to cope with the large search space for two-person games. In particular, we concentrate on the minimax algorithm augmented by alpha-beta pruning. This strategy is used as the basis of a program we present for playing Kalah in Chapter 21.

We describe the basic approach of searching game trees using evaluation functions. Again, in this section value(Position,Value) denotes an evaluation function computing the Value of Position, the current state of the game. Here is a simple algorithm for choosing the next move:

Find all possible game states that can be reached in one move.
Compute the values of the states using the evaluation function.
Choose the move that leads to the position with the highest score.

This algorithm is encoded as Program 20.9. It assumes a predicate move(Move,Position,Position1) that applies a Move to the current Position to reach Position1. The interface to the game framework of Program 20.8 is provided by the clause

```
choose_move(Position,computer,Move) ←
    findall(M,move(Position,M),Moves),
    evaluate_and_choose(Moves,Position,(nil,-1000),Move).
```

The predicate move(Position,Move) is true if Move is a possible move from the current position.

The basic relation is evaluate_and_choose(Moves,Position,Record, BestMove) which chooses the best move BestMove in the possible Moves from a given Position. For each of the possible moves, the corresponding position is determined, its value is calculated, and the move with the highest value is chosen. Record is a record of the current best move so far. In Program 20.9, it is represented as a tuple (Move,Value). The structure of Record has been partially abstracted in the procedure update/4. How much data abstraction to use is a matter of style and a trade-off among readability, conciseness, and performance.

Looking ahead one move, the approach of Program 20.9, would be sufficient if the evaluation function were perfect, that is, if the score reflected which positions led to a win and which to a loss. Games become interesting when a perfect evaluation function is not known. Choosing a move on the basis of looking ahead one move is generally not a good strategy. It is better to look several moves ahead and to infer from what is found the best move to make.

The *minimax algorithm* is the standard method for determining the value of a position based on searching the game tree several ply ahead.

The algorithm assumes that, when confronted with several choices, the opponent would make the best choice for her, i.e., the worst choice for me. My goal then is to make the move that maximizes for me the value of the position after the opponent has made her best move, i.e., that minimizes the value for her. Hence the name minimax. This reasoning proceeds several ply ahead, depending on the resources that can be allocated to the search. At the last ply the evaluation function is used.

Assuming a reasonable evaluation function, the algorithm will produce better results the more ply are searched. It will produce the best move if the entire tree is searched.

The minimax algorithm is justified by a zero-sum assumption, which says, informally, that what is good for me must be bad for my opponent, and vice versa.

Figure 20.2 depicts a simple game tree of depth 2 ply. The player has two moves in the current position, and the opponent has two replies. The values of the leaf nodes are the values for the player. The opponent wants to minimize the score, so will choose the minimum values, making the positions be worth +1 and −1 at one level higher in the tree. The player wants to maximize the value and will choose the node with value +1.

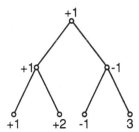

Figure 20.2   A simple game tree

Program 20.10 encodes the minimax algorithm. The basic relation is
`minimax(D,Position,MaxMin,Move,Value)`, which is true if `Move` is the
move with the highest `Value` from `Position` obtained by searching `D` ply
in the game tree. `MaxMin` is a flag that indicates if we are maximizing or
minimizing. It is 1 for maximizing and −1 for minimizing, the particular
values being chosen for ease of manipulation by simple arithmetic operations. A generalization of Program 20.9 is used to choose from the set of
moves. Two extra arguments must be added to `evaluate_and_choose`:
the number of ply `D` and the flag `MaxMin`. The last argument is generalized to return a record including both a move and a value rather than
just a move. The `minimax` procedure does the bookkeeping, changing the
number of moves being looked ahead and also the minimax flag. The initial record is `(nil,-1000)`, where `nil` represents an arbitrary move and
`-1000` is a score intended to be less than any possible score of the evaluation function.

The observation about efficiency that was made about combining the
move generation and update procedures in the context of searching
state-space graphs has an analogue when searching game trees. Whether
it is better to compute the set of positions rather than the set of moves
(with the corresponding change in algorithm) will depend on the particular application.

The minimax algorithm can be improved by keeping track of the results of the search so far, using a technique known as alpha-beta pruning.
The idea is to keep for each node the estimated minimum value found so
far, the alpha value, along with the estimated maximum value, beta. If,
on evaluating a node, beta is exceeded, no more search on that branch is
necessary. In good cases, more than half the positions in the game tree
need not be evaluated.

evaluate_and_choose(Moves,Position,Depth,Flag,Record,BestMove) ←
 Choose the *BestMove* from the set of *Moves* from the current
 Position using the minimax algorithm searching *Depth* ply ahead.
 Flag indicates if we are currently minimizing or maximizing.
 Record records the current best move.

```
evaluate_and_choose([Move|Moves],Position,D,MaxMin,Record,Best) ←
    move(Move,Position,Position1),
    minimax(D,Position1,MaxMin,MoveX,Value),
    update(Move,Value,Record,Record1),
    evaluate_and_choose(Moves,Position,D,MaxMin,Record1,Best).
evaluate_and_choose([ ],Position,D,MaxMin,Record,Record).

minimax(0,Position,MaxMin,Move,Value) ←
    value(Position,V),
    Value is V*MaxMin.
minimax(D,Position,MaxMin,Move,Value) ←
    D > 0,
    findall(M,move(Position,M),Moves),
    D1 is D - 1,
    MinMax is -MaxMin,
    evaluate_and_choose(Moves,Position,D1,MinMax, (nil,-1000),
        (Move,Value)).

update(Move,Value,Record,Record1) ← See Program 20.9.
```

Program 20.10 Choosing the best move with the minimax algorithm

Program 20.11 is a modified version of Program 20.10 that incorporates alpha-beta pruning. The new relation scheme is `alpha_beta`
`(Depth,Position,Alpha,Beta,Move,Value)`, which extends minimax
by replacing the minimax flag with alpha and beta. The same relation
holds with respect to `evaluate_and_choose`.

Unlike the one in Program 20.10, the version of `evaluate_and_choose`
in Program 20.11 does not need to search all possibilities. This is
achieved by introducing a predicate `cutoff`, which either stops searching
the current branch or continues the search, updating the value of alpha
and the current best move as appropriate.

For example, the last node in the game tree in Figure 20.2 does not
need to be searched. Once a move with value −1 is found, which is
less than the value of +1 the player is guaranteed, no other nodes can
contribute to the final score.

The program can be generalized by replacing the base case of `alpha_`
`beta` by a test of whether the position is terminal. This is necessary in
chess programs, for example, for handling incomplete piece exchanges.

evaluate_and_choose(Moves,Position,Depth,Alpha,Beta,Record,BestMove) ←
  Chooses the *BestMove* from the set of *Moves* from the current
  Position using the minimax algorithm with alpha-beta cutoff searching
  Depth ply ahead. *Alpha* and *Beta* are the parameters of the algorithm.
  Record records the current best move.

```
evaluate_and_choose([Move|Moves],Position,D,Alpha,Beta,Move1,
    BestMove) ←
  move(Move,Position,Position1),
  alpha_beta(D,Position1,Alpha,Beta,MoveX,Value),
  Value1 is -Value,
  cutoff(Move,Value1,D,Alpha,Beta,Moves,Position,Move1,BestMove).
evaluate_and_choose([ ],Position,D,Alpha,Beta,Move,(Move,Alpha)).

alpha_beta(0,Position,Alpha,Beta,Move,Value) ←
  value(Position,Value).
alpha_beta(D,Position,Alpha,Beta,Move,Value) ←
  findall(M,move(Position,M),Moves),
  Alpha1 is -Beta,
  Beta1 is -Alpha,
  D1 is D-1,
  evaluate_and_choose(Moves,Position,D1,Alpha1,Beta1,nil,
      i (Move,Value)).

cutoff(Move,Value,D,Alpha,Beta,Moves,Position,Move1,(Move,Value)) ←
  Value ≥ Beta.
cutoff(Move,Value,D,Alpha,Beta,Moves,Position,Move1,BestMove) ←
  Alpha < Value, Value < Beta,
  evaluate_and_choose(Moves,Position,D,Value,Beta,Move,BestMove).
cutoff(Move,Value,D,Alpha,Beta,Moves,Position,Move1,BestMove) ←
  Value ≤ Alpha,
  evaluate_and_choose(Moves,Position,D,Alpha,Beta,Move1,BestMove).
```

Program 20.11 Choosing a move using minimax with alpha-beta pruning

---

20.3 Background

Search techniques for both planning and game playing are discussed in
AI textbooks. For further details of search strategies or the minimax algorithm and its extension to alpha-beta pruning, see, for example, Nilsson
(1971) or Winston (1977).

Walter Wilson originally showed us the alpha-beta algorithm in Prolog.

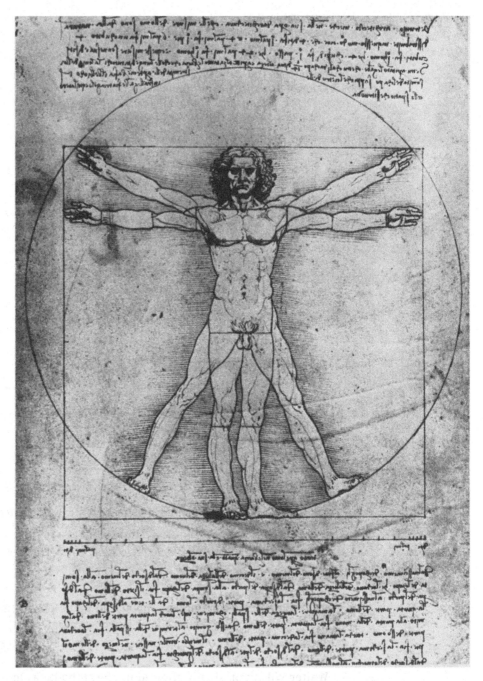

Leonardo Da Vinci, *The Proportions of the Human Figure*, after Vitruvius. Pen and ink. About 1492. Venice Academy.

IV Applications

Prolog has been used for a wide range of applications: expert systems, natural language understanding, symbolic algebra, compiler writing, building embedded languages, and architectural design, to name a few. In this part, we give a flavor of writing application programs in Prolog.

The first chapter looks at programs for playing three games: mastermind, Nim, and Kalah. The next chapter presents an expert system for evaluating requests for credit. The third chapter presents a program for solving symbolic equations, and the final chapter looks at a compiler for a Pascal-like language.

The emphasis in presentation in these chapters is on writing clear programs. Knowledge embedded in the programs is made explicit. Minor efficiency gains are ignored if they obscure the declarative reading of the program.

21   Game-Playing Programs

Learning how to play a game is fun. As well as understanding the rules of the game, we must constantly learn new strategies and tactics until the game is mastered. Writing a program to play games is also fun, and a good vehicle for showing how to use Prolog for writing nontrivial programs.

21.1   Mastermind

Our first program guesses the secret code in the game of mastermind. It is a good example of what can be programmed in Prolog easily with just a little thought.

The version of mastermind we describe is what we played as kids. It is a variant on the commercial version and needs less hardware (only pencil and paper). Player A chooses a sequence of distinct decimal digits as a secret code—usually four digits for beginners and five for advanced players. Player B makes guesses and queries player A for the number of *bulls* (number of digits that appear in identical positions in the guess and in the code) and *cows* (number of digits that appear in both the guess and the code, but in different positions).

There is a very simple algorithm for playing the game: Impose some order on the set of legal guesses; then iterate, making the next guess that is consistent with all the information you have so far until you find the secret code.

Rather than defining the notion of consistency formally, we appeal to the reader's intuition: A guess is consistent with a set of answers to queries if the answers to the queries would have remained the same if the guess were the secret code.

The algorithm performs quite well compared with experienced players: an average of four to six guesses for a code with four digits with an observed maximum of eight guesses. However, it is not an easy strategy for humans to apply, because of the amount of bookkeeping needed. On the other hand, the control structure of Prolog—nondeterministic choice, simulated by backtracking—is ideal for implementing the algorithm.

We describe the program top-down. The entire program is given as Program 21.1. The top-level procedure for playing the game is

```
mastermind(Code) ←
    cleanup, guess(Code), check(Code), announce.
```

The heart of the top level is a generate-and-test loop. The guessing procedure guess(Code), which acts as a generator, uses the procedure selects(Xs,Ys) (Program 7.7) to select nondeterministically a list Xs of elements from a list Ys. According to the rules of the game, Xs is constrained to contain four distinct elements, while Ys is the list of the ten decimal digits:

```
guess(Code) ←
    Code = [X1,X2,X3,X4],
    selects(Code,[1,2,3,4,5,6,7,8,9,0]).
```

The procedure check(Guess) tests the proposed code Guess. It first verifies that Guess is consistent with all (i.e., not inconsistent with any) of the answers to queries already made; then it asks the user for the number of bulls and cows in Guess. The ask(Guess) procedure also controls the generate-and-test loop, succeeding only when the number of bulls is four, indicating the correct code is found:

```
check(Guess) ←
    not inconsistent(Guess), ask(Guess).
```

Ask stores previous answers to queries in the relation query(X,B,C), where X is the guess, B is the number of bulls in it, and C the number of cows. A guess is inconsistent with a previous query if the number of bulls and cows do not match:

```
mastermind(Code) ←
    cleanup, guess(Code), check(Code), announce.
guess(Code) ←
    Code = [X1,X2,X3,X4], selects(Code,[1,2,3,4,5,6,7,8,9,0]).
```

Verify the proposed guess

```
check(Guess) ←
    not inconsistent(Guess), ask(Guess).

inconsistent(Guess) ←
    query(OldGuess,Bulls,Cows),
    not bulls_and_cows_match(OldGuess,Guess,Bulls,Cows).

bulls_and_cows_match(OldGuess,Guess,Bulls,Cows) ←
    exact_matches(OldGuess,Guess,N1),
    Bulls =:= N1,          % Correct number of bulls
    common_members(OldGuess,Guess,N2),
    Cows =:= N2-Bulls.     % Correct number of cows

exact_matches(Xs,Ys,N) ←
    size_of(A,same_place(A,Xs,Ys),N).
common_members(Xs,Ys,N) ←
    size_of(A,(member(A,Xs),member(A,Ys)),N).

same_place(X,[X|Xs],[X|Ys]).
same_place(A,[X|Xs],[Y|Ys]) ← same_place(A,Xs,Ys).
```

Asking a guess

```
ask(Guess) ←
    repeat,
    writeln(['How many bulls and cows in ',Guess,'?']),
    read((Bulls,Cows)),
    sensible(Bulls,Cows), !,
    assert(query(Guess,Bulls,Cows)),
    Bulls =:= 4.

sensible(Bulls,Cows) ←
    integer(Bulls), integer(Cows), Bulls+Cows ≤ 4.
```

Bookkeeping

```
cleanup ← abolish(query,3).

announce ←
    size_of(X,query(X,A,B),N),
    writeln(['Found the answer after ',N,' queries']).

size_of(X,G,N) ← findall(X,G,Xs), length(Xs,N).

length(Xs,N) ← See Program 8.11.

selects(X,Xs) ← See Program 7.7.

abolish(F,N) ← See Exercise 12.5(i).
```

Program 21.1 Playing mastermind

```
inconsistent(Guess) ←
    query(Old,Bulls,Cows),
    not bulls_and_cows_match(Old,Guess,Bulls,Cows).
```

The bulls match between a previous guess OldGuess and a conjectured guess Guess if the number of digits in the same position in the two guesses equals the number of Bulls in OldGuess. It is computed by the predicate exact_matches(OldGuess,Guess,Bulls). The cows match if the number of common digits without respect to order corresponds to the sum of Bulls and Cows; it is computed by the procedure bulls_and_cows_match. It is easy to count the number of matching digits and common digits in two queries, using an all-solutions predicate size_of/3.

The ask(Guess) procedure is a memo-function that records the answer to the query. It performs some limited consistency checks on the input with the procedure sensible/2 and succeeds only if four bulls are indicated. The expected syntax for the user's reply is a tuple (Bulls,Cows).

The remaining (top-level) predicates are for bookkeeping. The first, cleanup, removes unwanted information from previous games. The predicate announce tells how many guesses were needed, which is determined using size_of/3.

A more efficient implementation of the exact_matches and common_members procedures can be obtained by writing iterative versions:

```
exact_matches(Xs,Ys,N) ← exact_matches(Xs,Ys,0,N).

exact_matches([X|Xs],[X|Ys],K,N) ←
    K1 is K+1, exact_matches(Xs,Ys,K1,N).
exact_matches([X|Xs],[Y|Ys],K,N) ←
    X ≠ Y, exact_matches(Xs,Ys,K,N).
exact_matches([ ],[ ],N,N).

common_members(Xs,Ys,N) ← common_members(Xs,Ys,0,N).

common_members([X|Xs],Ys,K,N) ←
    member(X,Ys), K1 is K+1, common_members(Xs,Ys,K1,N).
common_members([X|Xs],Ys,K,N) ←
    common_members(Xs,Ys,K,N).
common_members([ ],Ys,N,N).
```

Using the more efficient versions of exact_matches and common_members saves about 10%–30% of the execution time.

21.2 Nim

We turn our attention now from mastermind to Nim, also a game for two players. There are several piles of matches, and the players take turns removing some of the matches (up to all) in a pile. The winner is the player who takes the last match. Figure 21.1 gives a common starting position, with piles of 1, 3, 5 and 7 matches.

To implement the Nim-playing program, we use the game-playing framework of Program 20.8.

The first decision is the representation of the game position and the moves. A natural choice for positions is a list of integers where elements of the list correspond to piles of matches. A move is a tuple (N,M) for taking M matches from pile N. Writing the procedure move(Move,Position,Position1), where Position is updated to Position1 by Move, is straightforward. The recursive rule counts down match piles until the desired pile is reached. The remaining piles of matches representing the new game position are computed routinely:

```
move((K,M),[N|Ns],[N|Ns1]) ←
    K > 1, K1 is K-1, move((K1,M),Ns,Ns1).
```

There are two possibilities for updating the specified pile of matches, the base case of the procedure. If all the matches are taken, the pile is removed from the list. Otherwise the new number of matches in the pile is computed and checked to be legal:

```
move((1,N),[N|Ns],Ns).
move((1,M),[N|Ns],[N1|Ns]) ← N > M, N1 is N-M.
```

The mechanics of turns for two-person games is specified by two facts.

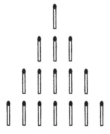

Figure 21.1   A starting position for Nim

The initial piles of matches and who moves first must be decided by the two players. Assuming the computer moves second, the game of Figure 21.1 is specified as

```
initialize(nim,[1,3,5,7],opponent).
```

The game is over when the last match is taken. This corresponds to the game position being the empty list. The person having to move next is the loser, and the output messages of announce are formulated accordingly. The details are in Program 21.2.

It remains to specify how to choose the moves. The opponent's moves are accepted from the keyboard; how much flexibility is allowed in input is the responsibility of the programmer:

```
choose_move(Position,opponent,Move) ←
    writeln(['Please make move']),
    read(Move),
    legal(Move,Position).
```

Choosing a move for the computer requires a strategy. A simple strategy to implement is taking all of the first pile of matches. It is recommended only for use against extremely poor players:

```
choose_move([N|Ns],computer,(1,N)).
```

A winning strategy is known for Nim. It involves dividing game states, or positions, into two classes, safe and unsafe. To determine if a position is safe or unsafe, the binary representation of the number of matches in each pile is computed. The *nim-sum* of these binary numbers is then calculated as follows. Each column is summed independently modulo 2. If the total in each column is zero, the position is *safe*. Otherwise the position is *unsafe*.

Figure 21.2 illustrates the process for the four piles of matches in Figure 21.1. The binary representations of 1, 3, 5, and 7 are 1, 11, 101, and 111 respectively. Calculating the nim-sum: there are four 1's in the units column, two 1's in the 2's column and two 1's in the 4's column; an even number of 1's in each. The nim-sum is zero, making the position [1,3,5,7] safe. On the other hand the position [2,6] is unsafe. The binary representations are 10 and 110. Summing them gives one 1 in the 4's column and two 1's in the 2's column. The single 1 in the 4's column makes the position unsafe.

play(Game) ← See Program 20.8.

Filling in the game-playing framework

initialize(nim,[1,3,5,7],opponent).

display_game(Position,X) ← write(Position), nl.

game_over([ ],Player,Player).

announce(computer) ← write('You won! Congratulations.'), nl.
announce(opponent) ← write('I won.'), nl.

Choosing moves

choose_move(Position,opponent,Move) ←
    writeln(['Please make move']), read(Move), legal(Move,Position).

legal((K,N),Position) ← nth_member(K,Position,M), N ≤ M.

nth_member(1,[X|Xs],X).
nth_member(N,[X|Xs],Y) ← N > 1, N1 is N-1, nth_member(N1,Xs,Y).

choose_move(Position,computer,Move) ←
    evaluate(Position,Safety,Sum),
    decide_move(Safety,Position,Sum,Move).

evaluate(Position,Safety,Sum) ←
    nim_sum(Position,[ ],Sum), safety(Sum,Safety).

safety(Sum,safe) ← zero(Sum), !.
safety(Sum,unsafe) ← not zero(Sum), !.

decide_move(safe,Position,Sum,(1,1)).
    % The computer's ''arbitrary move''
decide_move(unsafe,Position,Sum,Move) ←
    safe_move(Position,Sum,Move).

move(Move,Position,Position1) ←
    Position1 is the result of executing the move
    Move from the current *Position*.

move((K,M),[N|Ns],[N|Ns1]) ←
    K > 1, K1 is K-1, move((K1,M),Ns,Ns1).
move((1,N),[N|Ns],Ns).
move((1,M),[N|Ns],[N1|Ns]) ←
    N > M, N1 is N-M.

next_player(computer,opponent).   next_player(opponent,computer).

Program 21.2 A program for playing a winning game of Nim

nim_sum(Position,SoFar,Sum) ←
    Sum is the nim-sum of the current *Position*,
    and *SoFar* is an accumulated value.

```
nim_sum([N|Ns],Bs,Sum) ←
    binary(N,Ds), nim_add(Ds,Bs,Bs1), nim_sum(Ns,Bs1,Sum).
nim_sum([ ],Sum,Sum).

nim_add(Bs,[ ],Bs).
nim_add([ ],Bs,Bs).
nim_add([B|Bs],[C|Cs],[D|Ds]) ←
    D is (B+C) mod 2, nim_add(Bs,Cs,Ds).

binary(1,[1]).
binary(N,[D|Ds]) ←
    N > 1, D is N mod 2, N1 is N/2, binary(N1,Ds).

decimal(Ds,N) ← decimal(Ds,0,1,N).
decimal([ ],N,T,N).
decimal([D|Ds],A,T,N) ←
    A1 is A+D*T, T1 is T*2, decimal(Ds,A1,T1,N).

zero([ ]).
zero([0|Zs]) ← zero(Zs).
```

safe_move(Position,NimSum,Move) ←
    Move is a move from the current *Position* with
    the value *NimSum* that leaves a safe position.

```
safe_move(Piles,NimSum,Move) ←
    safe_move(Piles,NimSum,1,Move).

safe_move([Pile|Piles],NimSum,K,(K,M)) ←
    binary(Pile,Bs), can_zero(Bs,NimSum,Ds,0), decimal(Ds,M).
safe_move([Pile|Piles],NimSum,K,Move) ←
    K1 is K+1, safe_move(Piles,NimSum,K1,Move).

can_zero([ ],NimSum,[ ],0) ←
    zero(NimSum).
can_zero([B|Bs],[0|NimSum],[C|Ds],C) ←
    can_zero(Bs,NimSum,Ds,C).
can_zero([B|Bs],[1|NimSum],[D|Ds],C) ←
    D is 1-B*C, C1 is 1-B, can_zero(Bs,NimSum,Ds,C1).
```

Program 21.2 (Continued)

```
    1
  1 1
1 0 1
1 1 1
─────
0 0 0
```

Figure 21.2   Computing nim-sums

The winning strategy is to always leave the position safe. Any unsafe position can be converted to a safe position (though not all moves do), while any move from a safe position creates an unsafe one. The best strategy is to make an arbitrary move when confronted with a safe position, hoping the opponent will blunder, and to convert unsafe positions to safe ones.

The current position is evaluated by the predicate `evaluate/3`, which determines the safety of the current position. An algorithm is needed to compute the nim-sum of a position. The nim-sum is checked by the predicate `safety(Sum,Safety)`, which labels the position *safe* or *unsafe* depending on the value of `Sum`.

```
choose_move(Position,computer,Move) ←
    evaluate(Position,Safety,Sum),
    decide_move(Safety,Position,Sum,Move).
```

The move made by the computer computed by `decide_move/4` depends on the safety of the position. If the position is safe, the computer makes the "arbitrary" move of one match from the first pile. If the position is unsafe, an algorithm is needed to compute a move that converts an unsafe position into a safe one. This is done by `safe_move/3`.

In a prior version of the program `evaluate` did not return `Sum`. In the writing of `safe_move` it transpired that the nim-sum was helpful, and it was sensible to pass the already computed value rather than recomputing it.

The nim-sum is computed by `nim_sum(Ns,SoFar,Sum)`. The relation computed is that `Sum` is the nim-sum of the numbers `Ns` added to what has been accumulated in `SoFar`. To perform the additions, the numbers must first be converted to binary, done by `binary/2`:

```
nim_sum([N|Ns],Bs,Sum) ←
    binary(N,Ds), nim_add(Ds,Bs,Bs1), nim_sum(Ns,Bs1,Sum).
```

The binary form of a number is represented here as a list of digits. To overcome the difficulty of adding lists of unequal length, the least significant digits are earliest in the list. Thus 2 (in binary 10) is represented as [0,1], while 6 is represented as [0,1,1]. The two numbers can then be added from least significant digit to most significant digit, as is usual for addition. This is done by `nim_add/3` and is slightly simpler than regular addition, since no carry needs to be propagated. The code for both `binary` and `nim_add` appears in Program 21.2.

The nim-sum `Sum` is used by the predicate `safe_move(Ns,Sum,Move)` to find a winning move `Move` from the position described by `Ns`. The piles of matches are checked in turn by `safe_move/4` to see if there is a number of matches that can be taken from the pile to leave a safe position. The interesting clause is

```
safe_move([Pile|Piles],NimSum,K,(K,M)) ←
    binary(Pile,Bs), can_zero(Bs,NimSum,Ds,0), decimal(Ds,M).
```

The heart of the program is `can_zero(Bs,NimSum,Ds,Carry)`. This relation is true if replacing the binary number `Bs` by the binary number `Ds` would make `NimSum` zero. The number `Ds` is computed digit by digit. Each digit is determined by the corresponding digit of `Bs`, `NimSum`, and a carry digit `Carry` initially set to 0. The number is converted to its decimal equivalent by `decimal/2` in order to get the correct move.

Program 21.2 is a complete program for playing Nim interactively incorporating the winning strategy. As well as being a program for playing the game, it is also an axiomatization of what constitutes a winning strategy.

21.3   Kalah

We now present a program for playing the game of Kalah that uses alpha-beta pruning. Kalah fits well into the paradigm of game trees for two reasons. First, the game has a simple, reasonably reliable evaluation function, and second, its game tree is tractable, which is not true for games such as chess and go. It has been claimed that some Kalah programs are unbeatable by human players. Certainly, the one presented here beats us.

Kalah is played on a board with two rows of six holes facing each other. Each player owns a row of six holes, plus a kalah to the right of the holes.

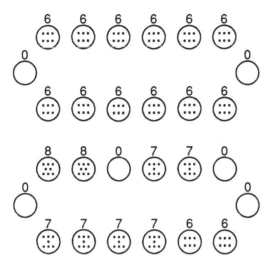

Figure 21.3   Board positions for Kalah

In the initial state there are six stones in each hole and the two kalahs are empty. This is pictured in the top half of Figure 21.3.

A player begins his move by picking up all the stones in one of his holes. Proceeding counterclockwise around the board, he puts one of the picked-up stones in each hole and in his own kalah, skipping the opponent's kalah, until no stones remain to be distributed. There are three possible outcomes. If the last stone lands on the kalah, the player has another move. If the last stone lands on an empty hole owned by the player, and the opponent's hole directly across the board contains at least one stone, the player takes all the stones in the hole plus his last landed stone and puts them all in his kalah. Otherwise the player's turn ends, and his opponent moves.

The bottom kalah board in Figure 21.3 represents the following move from the top board by the owner of the top holes. He took the six stones in the rightmost hole and distributed them, the last one ending in the kalah, allowing another move. The stones in the fourth hole from the right were then distributed.

If all the holes of a player become empty (even if it is not his turn to play), the stones remaining in the holes of the opponent are put in the opponent's kalah and the game ends. The winner of the game is the first player to get more than half the stones in his kalah.

The difficulty for programming the game in Prolog is finding an efficient data structure to represent the board, to facilitate the calculation of moves. We use a four-argument structure board(Holes,Kalah,Opp-Holes,OppKalah), where Holes is a list of the numbers of stones in your six holes, Kalah is the number of stones in your kalah, and OppHoles and OppKalah are, respectively, the lists of the numbers of stones in the opponent's holes and the number of stones in his kalah. Lists were chosen rather than six-place structures to facilitate the writing of recursive programs for distributing the stones in the holes.

A move consists of choosing a hole and distributing the stones therein. A move is specified as a list of integers with values between 1 and 6 inclusive, where the numbers refer to the holes. Hole 1 is farthest from the player's kalah, while hole 6 is closest. A list is necessary rather than a single integer because a move may continue. The move depicted in Figure 21.3 is [1, 4].

The code gives all moves on backtracking. The predicate stones_in_hole(M,Board,N) returns the number of stones N in hole M of the Board if N is greater than 0, failing if there are no stones in the hole. The predicate extend_move(M,Board,N,Ms) returns the continuation of the move Ms. The second clause for move handles the special case when all the player's holes become empty during a move.

Testing whether the move continues is nontrivial, since it may involve all the procedures for making a move. If the last stone is not placed in the kalah, which can be determined by simple arithmetic, the move will end, and there is no need to distribute all the stones. Otherwise the stones are distributed, and the move continues recursively.

The basic predicate for making a move is distribute_stones(Stones, N,Board,Board1), which computes the relation that Board1 is obtained from Board by distributing the number of stones in Stones starting from hole number N. There are two stages to the distribution, putting the stones in the player's holes, distribute_my_holes, and putting the stones in the opponent's holes, distribute_your_holes.

The simpler case is distributing the stones in the opponent's holes. The holes are updated by distribute, and the distribution of stones continues recursively if there is an excess of stones. A check is made to see if the player's board has become empty during the course of the move, and if so, the opponent's stones are added to his kalah.

Distributing the player's stones must take into account two possibilities, distributing from any particular hole, and continuing the distribution for a large number of stones. The `pick_up_and_distribute` predicate is the generalization of `distribute` to handle these cases. The predicate `check_capture` checks if a capture has occurred and updates the holes accordingly; `update_kalah` updates the number of stones in the player's kalah. Some other necessary utilities such as `n_substitute` are also included in the program.

The evaluation function is the difference between the number of stones in the two kalahs:

`value(board(H,K,Y,L),Value)` ← `Value is K-L.`

The central predicates have been described. A running program is now obtained by filling in the details for I/O, for initializing and terminating the game, etc. Simple suggestions can be found in the complete program for the game, given as Program 21.3.

In order to optimize the performance of the program, cuts can be added. Another tip is to rewrite the main loop of the program as a failure-driven loop rather than a tail recursive program. This is sometimes necessary in implementations that do not incorporate tail recursion optimization and a good garbage collector.

21.4 Background

The mastermind program, slightly modified, originally appeared in SIGART (Shapiro, 1983d) in response to a program for playing mastermind in Pascal. The SIGART article provoked several reactions, both of theoretical improvements to algorithms for playing mastermind and practical improvements to the program. Most interesting was an analysis and discussion by Powers (1984) of how a Prolog program could be rewritten to good benefit using the mastermind code as a case study. Eventually, speedup by a factor of 50 was achieved.

A proof of the correctness of the algorithm for playing Nim can be found in any textbook discussing games on graphs, for example, Berge (1962).

Kalah was an early AI target for game-playing programs (Slagle and Dixon, 1969).

Play framework

play(Game) ← See Program 20.8.

Choosing a move by minimax with alpha-beta cutoff

```
choose_move(Position,computer,Move) ←
    lookahead(Depth),
    alpha_beta(Depth,Position,-40,40,Move,Value),
    nl, write(Move), nl.
choose_move(Position,opponent,Move) ←
    nl, writeln(['please make move']), read(Move), legal(Move).

alpha_beta(Depth,Position,Alpha,Beta,Move,Value) ←
    See Program 20.11.

move(Board,[M|Ms]) ←
    member(M,[1,2,3,4,5,6]),
    stones_in_hole(M,Board,N),
    extend_move(N,M,Board,Ms).
move(board([0,0,0,0,0,0],K,Ys,L),[ ]).

stones_in_hole(M,board(Hs,K,Ys,L),Stones) ←
    nth_member(M,Hs,Stones), Stones > 0.

extend_move(Stones,M,Board,[ ]) ←
    Stones =\= (7-M) mod 13, !.
extend_move(Stones,M,Board,Ms) ←
    Stones =:= (7-M) mod 13, !,
    distribute_stones(Stones,M,Board,Board1),
    move(Board1,Ms).
```

Executing a move

```
move([N|Ns],Board,FinalBoard) ←
    stones_in_hole(N,Board,Stones),
    distribute_stones(Stones,N,Board,Board1),
    move(Ns,Board1,FinalBoard).
move([ ],Board1,Board2) ←
    swap(Board1,Board2).
```

distribute_stones(Stones,Hole,Board,Board1) ←
    Board1 is the result of distributing the number of stones
    Stones from *Hole* from the current *Board*.
    It consists of two stages: distributing the stones in the player's
    holes, *distribute_my_holes*, and distributing the stones
    in the opponent's holes, *distribute_your_holes*.

Program 21.3   A complete program for playing Kalah

```
distribute_stones(Stones,Hole,Board,FinalBoard) ←
    distribute_my_holes(Stones,Hole,Board,Board1,Stones1),
    distribute_your_holes(Stones1,Board1,FinalBoard).

distribute_my_holes(Stones,N,board(Hs,K,Ys,L),
        board(Hs1,K1,Ys,L),Stones1) ←
    Stones > 7-N, !,
    pick_up_and_distribute(N,Stones,Hs,Hs1),
    K1 is K+1, Stones1 is Stones+N-7.
distribute_my_holes(Stones,N,board(Hs,K,Ys,L),Board,0) ←
    Stones ≤ 7-N,
    pick_up_and_distribute(N,Stones,Hs,Hs1),
    check_capture(N,Stones,Hs1,Hs2,Ys,Ys1,Pieces),
    update_kalah(Pieces,N,Stones,K,K1),
    check_if_finished(board(Hs2,K1,Ys1,L),Board).

check_capture(N,Stones,Hs,Hs1,Ys,Ys1,Pieces) ←
    FinishingHole is N+Stones,
    nth_member(FinishingHole,Hs,1),
    OppositeHole is 7-FinishingHole,
    nth_member(OppositeHole,Ys,Y),
    Y > 0, !,
    n_substitute(OppositeHole,Ys,0,Ys1),
    n_substitute(FinishingHole,Hs,0,Hs1),
    Pieces is Y+1.
check_capture(N,Stones,Hs,Hs,Ys,Ys,0) ← !.

check_if_finished(board(Hs,K,Ys,L),board(Hs,K,Hs,L1)) ←
    zero(Hs), !, sumlist(Ys,YsSum), L1 is L+YsSum.
check_if_finished(board(Hs,K,Ys,L),board(Ys,K1,Ys,L)) ←
    zero(Ys), !, sumlist(Hs,HsSum), K1 is K+HsSum.
check_if_finished(Board,Board) ← !.

update_kalah(0,Stones,N,K,K) ← Stones < 7-N, !.
update_kalah(0,Stones,N,K,K1) ← Stones =:= 7-N, !, K1 is K+1.
update_kalah(Pieces,Stones,N,K,K1) ← Pieces > 0, !, K1 is K+Pieces.

distribute_your_holes(0,Board,Board) ← !.
distribute_your_holes(Stones,board(Hs,K,Ys,L),board(Hs,K,Ys1,L)) ←
    1 ≤ Stones, Stones ≤ 6,
    non_zero(Hs), !,
    distribute(Stones,Ys,Ys1).
```

Program 21.3   (Continued)

```
distribute_your_holes(Stones,board(Hs,K,Ys,L),Board) ←
    Stones > 6, !,
    distribute(6,Ys,Ys1),
    Stones1 is Stones-6,
    distribute_stones(Stones1,0,board(Hs,K,Ys1,L),Board).
distribute_your_holes(Stones,board(Hs,K,Ys,L),board(Hs,K,Hs,L1)) ←
    zero(Hs), !, sumlist(Ys,YsSum), L1 is Stones+YsSum+L.
```

Lower-level stone distribution

```
pick_up_and_distribute(0,N,Hs,Hs1) ←
    !, distribute(N,Hs,Hs1).
pick_up_and_distribute(1,N,[H|Hs],[0|Hs1]) ←
    !, distribute(N,Hs,Hs1).
pick_up_and_distribute(K,N,[H|Hs],[H|Hs1]) ←
    K > 1, !, K1 is K-1, pick_up_and_distribute(K1,N,Hs,Hs1).

distribute(0,Hs,Hs) ← !.
distribute(N,[H|Hs],[H1|Hs1]) ←
    N > 0, !, N1 is N-1, H1 is H+1, distribute(N1,Hs,Hs1).
distribute(N,[ ],[ ]) ← !.
```

Evaluation function

```
value(board(H,K,Y,L),Value) ← Value is K-L.
```

Testing for the end of the game

```
game_over(board(0,N,0,N),Player,draw) ←
    pieces(K), N =:= 6*K, !.
game_over(board(H,K,Y,L),Player,Player) ←
    pieces(N), K > 6*N, !.
game_over(board(H,K,Y,L),Player,Opponent) ←
    pieces(N), L > 6*N, next_player(Player,Opponent).
announce(opponent) ← writeln(['You won! Congratulations.']).
announce(computer) ← writeln(['I won.']).
announce(draw) ← writeln(['The game is a draw']).
```

Miscellaneous game utilities

```
nth_member(N,[H|Hs],K) ←
    N > 1, !, N1 is N-1, nth_member(N1,Hs,K).
nth_member(1,[H|Hs],H).

n_substitute(1,[X|Xs],Y,[Y|Xs]) ← !.
n_substitute(N,[X|Xs],Y,[X|Xs1]) ←
    N > 1, !, N1 is N-1, n_substitute(N1,Xs,Y,Xs1).
```

Program 21.3 (Continued)

```
next_player(computer,opponent).
next_player(opponent,computer).

legal([N|Ns]) ← 0 < N, N < 7, legal(Ns).
legal([ ]).

swap(board(Hs,K,Ys,L),board(Ys,L,Hs,K)).

display_game(Position,computer) ←
    show(Position).
display_game(Position,opponent) ←
    swap(Position,Position1), show(Position1).

show(board(H,K,Y,L)) ←
    reverse(H,HR), write_stones(HR),
    write_kalahs(K,L), write_stones(Y).

write_stones(H) ←
    nl, tab(5), display_holes(H).

display_holes([H|Hs]) ←
    write_pile(H), display_holes(Hs).
display_holes([ ]) ← nl.

write_pile(N) ← N < 10, write(N), tab(4).
write_pile(N) ← N ≥ 10, write(N), tab(3).

write_kalahs(K,L) ←
    write(K), tab(34), write(L), nl.

zero([0,0,0,0,0,0]).
non_zero(Hs) ← Hs ≠ [0,0,0,0,0,0].
```

Initializing

```
lookahead(2).
initialize(kalah,board([N,N,N,N,N,N],0,[N,N,N,N,N,N],0),opponent) ←
    pieces(N).
pieces(6).
```

Program 21.3   (Continued)

22   A Credit Evaluation Expert System

When the first edition of this book was published, there was a surge of activity in the application of artificial intelligence to industry. Of particular interest were expert systems—programs designed to perform tasks previously allocated to highly paid human experts. One important feature of expert systems is the explicit representation of knowledge.

This entire book is relevant for programming expert systems. The example programs typify code that might be written. For instance, the equation-solving program of Chapter 23 can be, and has been, viewed as an expert system. The knowledge of expert systems is often expressed as rules. Prolog whose basic statements are rules is thus a natural language for implementing expert systems.

22.1   Developing the System

This chapter presents an account of developing a prototype expert system. The example comes from the world of banking: evaluating requests for credit from small business ventures. We give a fictionalized account of the development of a simple expert system for evaluating client requests for credit from a bank. The account is from the point of view of Prolog programmers, or knowledge engineers, commissioned by the bank to write the system. It begins after the most difficult stage of building an expert system, extracting the expert knowledge, has been under way for some time. In accordance with received wisdom, the programmers have been consulting with a single bank expert, Chas E. Manhattan. Chas has told us that three factors are of the utmost importance in considering a request for credit from a client (a small business venture).

The most important factor is the collateral that can be offered by the client in case the venture folds. The various types of collateral are divided into categories. Currency deposits, whether local or foreign, are *first-class* collateral. Stocks are examples of *second-class* collateral, and the collateral provided by mortgages and the like is *illiquid*.

Also very important is the client's financial record. Experience in the bank has shown that the two most important factors are the client's net worth per assets and the current gross profits on sales. The client's short-term debt per annual sales should be considered in evaluating the record, and slightly less significant is last year's sales growth. For knowledge engineers with some understanding of banking, no further explanation of such concepts is necessary. In general, a knowledge engineer must understand the domain sufficiently to be able to communicate with the domain expert.

The remaining factor to be considered is the expected yield to the bank. This is a problem that the bank has been working on for a while. Programs exist to give the yield of a particular client profile. The knowledge engineer can thus assume that the information will be available in the desired form.

Chas uses qualitative terms in speaking about these three factors: "The client had an excellent financial rating, or a good form of collateral. His venture would provide a reasonable yield," and so on. Even concepts that could be determined quantitatively are discussed in qualitative terms. The financial world is too complicated to be expressed only with the numbers and ratios constantly being calculated. In order to make judgments, experts in the financial domain tend to think in qualitative terms with which they are more comfortable. To echo expert reasoning and to be able to interact with Chas further, qualitative reasoning must be modeled.

On talking to Chas, it became clear that a significant amount of the expert knowledge he described could be naturally expressed as a mixture of procedures and rules. On being pressed a little in the second and third interviews, Chas gave rules for determining ratings for collateral and financial records. These involved considerable calculations, and in fact, Chas admitted that to save himself work in the long term, he did a quick initial screening to see if the client was at all suitable.

This information is sufficient to build a prototype. We show how these comments and observations are translated into a system. The top-level basic relation is credit(Client,Answer), where Answer is the reply given to the request by Client for credit. The code has three modules— collateral, financial_rating, and bank_yield—corresponding to the three factors the expert said were important. The initial screening to determine that the client is worth considering in the first place is performed by the predicate ok_profile(Client). The answer Answer is then determined with the predicate evaluate(Profile,Answer), which evaluates the Profile built by the three modules.

Being proud knowledge engineers, we stress the features of the top-level formulation in credit/2. The modularity is apparent. Each of the modules can be developed independently without affecting the rest of the system. Further, there is no commitment to any particular data structure, i.e., data abstraction is used. For this example, a structure profile(C,F,Y) represents the profile of collateral rating C, the financial rating F, and the yield Y of a client. However, nothing central depends on this decision, and it would be easy to change it. Let us consider some of the modular pieces.

Let us look at the essential features of the collateral evaluation module. The relation collateral_rating/2 determines a rating for a particular client's collateral. The first step is to determine an appropriate profile. This is done with the predicate collateral_profile, which classifies the client's collateral as first_class, second_class, or illiquid and gives the percentage each covers of the amount of credit the client requested. The relation uses facts in the database concerning both the bank and the client. In practice, there may be separate databases for the bank and the client. Sample facts shown in Program 22.1 indicate, for example, that local currency deposits are first-class collateral.

The profile is evaluated to give a rating by collateral_evaluation. It uses rules of thumb to give a qualitative rating of the collateral: excellent, good, etc. The first collateral_evaluation rule, for example, reads: "The rating is *excellent* if the coverage of the requested credit amount by first-class collateral is greater than or equal to 100 percent."

Two features of the code bear comment. First, the terminology used in the program is the terminology of Chas. This makes the program (almost) self-documenting to the experts and means they can modify it with

Credit Evaluation

credit(*Client,Answer*) ←
  Answer is the reply to a request by *Client* for credit.

```
credit(Client,Answer) ←
    ok_profile(Client),
    collateral_rating(Client,CollateralRating),
    financial_rating(Client,FinancialRating),
    bank_yield(Client,Yield),
    evaluate(profile(CollateralRating,FinancialRating,Yield),Answer).
```

The collateral rating module

collateral_rating(*Client,Rating*) ←
  Rating is a qualitative description assessing the collateral
  offered by *Client* to cover the request for credit.

```
collateral_rating(Client,Rating) ←
    collateral_profile(Client,FirstClass,SecondClass,Illiquid),
    collateral_evaluation(FirstClass,SecondClass,Illiquid,Rating).

collateral_profile(Client,FirstClass,SecondClass,Illiquid) ←
    requested_credit(Client,Credit),
    collateral_percent(first_class,Client,Credit,FirstClass),
    collateral_percent(second_class,Client,Credit,SecondClass),
    collateral_percent(illiquid,Client,Credit,Illiquid).

collateral_percent(Type,Client,Total,Value) ←
    findall(X,(collateral(Collateral,Type),
        amount(Collateral,Client,X)),Xs),
    sumlist(Xs,Sum),
    Value is Sum*100/Total.
```

Evaluation rules

```
collateral_evaluation(FirstClass,SecondClass,Illiquid,excellent) ←
    FirstClass ≥ 100.
collateral_evaluation(FirstClass,SecondClass,Illiquid,excellent) ←
    FirstClass > 70, FirstClass + SecondClass ≥ 100.
collateral_evaluation(FirstClass,SecondClass,Illiquid,good) ←
    FirstClass + SecondClass > 60,
    FirstClass + SecondClass < 70,
    FirstClass + SecondClass + Illiquid ≥ 100.
```

Bank data - classification of collateral

```
collateral(local_currency_deposits,first_class).
collateral(foreign_currency_deposits,first_class).
collateral(negotiate_instruments,second_class).
collateral(mortgage,illiquid).
```

Program 22.1 A credit evaluation system

Financial rating

financial_rating(Client,Rating) ←
> *Rating* is a qualitative description assessing the financial
> record offered by *Client* to support the request for credit.

```
financial_rating(Client,Rating) ←
    financial_factors(Factors),
    score(Factors,Client,0,Score),
    calibrate(Score,Rating).
```

Financial evaluation rules

```
calibrate(Score,bad) ← Score ≤ -500.
calibrate(Score,medium) ← -500 < Score, Score < 150.
calibrate(Score,good) ← 150 ≤ Score, Score < 1000.
calibrate(Score,excellent) ← Score ≥ 1000.
```

Bank data - weighting factors

```
financial_factors([(net_worth_per_assets,5),
    (last_year_sales_growth,1),
    (gross_profits_on_sales,5),
    (short_term_debt_per_annual_sales,2) ]).

score([(Factor,Weight)|Factors],Client,Acc,Score) ←
    value(Factor,Client,Value),
    Acc1 is Acc + Weight*Value,
    score(Factors,Client,Acc1,Score).
score([ ],Client,Score,Score).
```

Final evaluation

evaluate(Profile,Outcome) ←
> *Outcome* is the reply to the client's *Profile*.

```
evaluate(Profile,Answer) ←
    rule(Conditions,Answer), verify(Conditions,Profile).

verify([condition(Type,Test,Rating)|Conditions],Profile) ←
    scale(Type,Scale),
    select_value(Type,Profile,Fact),
    compare(Test,Scale,Fact,Rating),
    verify(Conditions,Profile).
verify([ ],Profile).

compare('=',Scale,Rating,Rating).
compare('>',Scale,Rating1,Rating2) ←
    precedes(Scale,Rating1,Rating2).
compare('≥',Scale,Rating1,Rating2) ←
    precedes(Scale,Rating1,Rating2) ; Rating1 = Rating2.
```

Program 22.1   (Continued)

```
compare('<',Scale,Rating1,Rating2) ←
    precedes(Scale,Rating2,Rating1).
compare('≤',Scale,Rating1,Rating2) ←
    precedes(Scale,Rating2,Rating1) ; Rating1 = Rating2.
precedes([R1|Rs],R1,R2).
precedes([R|Rs],R1,R2) ← R ≠ R2, precedes(Rs,R1,R2).
select_value(collateral,profile(C,F,Y),C).
select_value(finances,profile(C,F,Y),F).
select_value(yield,profile(C,F,Y),Y).
```

Utilities

```
sumlist(Xs,Sum) ← See Program 8.6b.
```

Bank data and rules

```
rule([condition(collateral,'≥',excellent),
    condition(finances,'≥',good),
    condition(yield,'≥',reasonable)],give_credit).
rule([condition(collateral,'=',good),condition(finances,'=',good),
    condition(yield,'≥',reasonable)],consult_superior).
rule([condition(collateral,'≤',moderate),
    condition(finances,'≤',medium)],
    refuse_credit).

scale(collateral,[excellent,good,moderate]).
scale(finances,[excellent,good,medium,bad]).
scale(yield,[excellent,reasonable,poor]).
```

Program 22.1   (Continued)

little help from the knowledge engineer. Allowing people to think in domain concepts also facilitates debugging and assists in using a domain-independent explanation facility as discussed in Section 17.4. Second, the apparent naivete of the evaluation rules is deceptive. A lot of knowledge and experience are hidden behind these simple numbers. Choosing poor values for these numbers may mean suffering severe losses.

The financial evaluation module evaluates the financial stability of the client. It uses items taken mainly from the balance and profit/loss sheets. The financial rating is also qualitative. A weighted sum of financial factors is calculated by score and used by calibrate to determine the qualitative class.

It should be noted that the modules giving the collateral rating and the financial rating both reflect the point of view and style of a particular expert, Chas Manhattan, rather than a universal truth. Within the bank there is no consensus about the subject. Some people tend to be conservative and some are prepared to take considered risks.

Programming the code for determining the collateral and financial ratings proceeded easily. The knowledge provided by the expert was more or less directly translated into the program. The module for the overall evaluation of the client, however, was more challenging.

The major difficulty was formulating the relevant expert knowledge. Our expert was less forthcoming with general rules for overall evaluation than for rating the financial record, for example. He happily discussed the profiles of particular clients, and the outcome of their credit requests and loans, but was reluctant to generalize. He preferred to react to suggestions rather than volunteer rules.

This forced a close reevaluation of the exact problem we were solving. There were three possible answers the system could give: approve the request for credit, refuse the request, or ask for advice. There were three factors to be considered. Each factor had a qualitative value that was one of a small set of possibilities. For example, the financial rating could be *bad, medium, good,* or *excellent.* Further, the possible values were ranked on an ordinal scale.

Our system clearly faced an instance of a general problem: Find an outcome from some ordinal scale based on the qualitative results of several ordinal scales. Rules to solve the problem were thus to give a conclusion based on the outcome of the factors. We pressed Chas with this formulation, and he rewarded us with several rules. Here is a typical one: "If the client's collateral rating is excellent (or better), her financial rating good (or better), and her yield at least reasonable, then grant the credit request."

An immediate translation of the rule is

```
evaluate(profile(excellent,good,reasonable),give_credit).
```

But this misses many cases covered by the rule, for example, when the client's profile is (excellent,good,excellent). All the cases for a given rule can be listed. It seemed more sensible, however, to build a more general tool to evaluate rules expressed in terms of qualitative values from ordinal scales.

There is potentially a problem with using ordinal scales because of the large number of individual cases that may need to be specified. If each of the N modules have M possible outcomes, there are N^M cases to be considered. In general, it is infeasible to have a separate rule for each possibility. Not only is space a problem for so many rules but the search involved in finding the correct rule may be prohibitive. So instead we defined a small ad hoc set of rules. We hoped the rules defined, which covered many possibilities at once, would be sufficient to cover the clients the bank usually dealt with. We chose the structure rule(Conditions,Conclusion) for our rules, where Conditions is a list of conditions under which the rule applies and Conclusion is the rule's conclusion. A condition has the form condition(Factor,Relation,Rating), insisting that the rating from the factor named by Factor bears the relation named by Relation to the rating given by Rating.

The relation is represented by the standard relational operators: <, =, >, etc. The previously mentioned rule is represented as

```
rule([condition(collateral,'≥',excellent),
    condition(finances,'≥',good),
    condition(yield,'≥',reasonable)],give_credit).
```

Another rule given by Chas reads: "If both the collateral rating and financial rating are good, and the yield is at least reasonable, then consult your superior." This is translated to

```
rule([condition(collateral,'=',good),
    condition(finances,'=',good),
    condition(yield,'≥',reasonable)],consult_superior).
```

Factors can be mentioned twice to indicate they lie in a certain range or might not be mentioned at all. For example, the rule

```
rule([condition(collateral,'≤',moderate),
    condition(finances,'≤',medium)],
    refuse_credit).
```

states that a client should be refused credit if the collateral rating is no better than moderate and the financial rating is at best medium. The yield is not relevant and so is not mentioned.

Client Data

```
bank_yield(client1,excellent).
requested_credit(client1,50000).

amount(local_currency_deposits,client1,30000).
amount(foreign_currency_deposits,client1,20000).
amount(bank_guarantees,client1,3000).

amount(negotiate_instruments,client1,5000).
amount(stocks,client1,9000).

amount(mortgage,client1,12000).
amount(documents,client1,14000).

value(net_worth_per_assets,client1,40).
value(last_year_sales_growth,client1,20).
value(gross_profits_on_sales,client1,45).
value(short_term_debt_per_annual_sales,client1,9).

ok_profile(client1).
```

Program 22.2   Test data for the credit evaluation system

The interpreter for the rules is written nondeterministically. The procedure is: "Find a rule and verify that its conditions apply," as defined by evaluate. The predicate verify(Conditions,Profile) checks that the relation between the corresponding symbols in the rule and the ones that are associated with the Profile of the client is as specified by Conditions. For each Type that can appear, a scale is necessary to give the order of values the scale can take. Examples of scale facts in the bank database are scale(collateral, [excellent,good,moderate]) and scale(finances, [excellent,good,medium,bad]). The predicate select_value returns the appropriate symbol of the factor under the ordinality test that is performed by compare. It is an access predicate, and consequently the only predicate dependent on the choice of data structure for the profile.

At this stage, the prototype program is tested. Some data from real clients are necessary, and the answer the system gives on these individuals is tested against what the corresponding bank official would say. The data for client1 is given in Program 22.2. The reply to the query credit(client1,X) is X = give_credit.

Our prototype expert system is a composite of styles and methods — not just a backward chaining system. Heuristic rules of thumb are used to determine the collateral rating; an algorithm, albeit a simple one, is used to determine the financial rating; and there is a rule language, with an interpreter, for expressing outcomes in terms of values from discrete ordinal scales. The rule interpreter proceeds forward from conditions to conclusion rather than backward as in Prolog. Expert systems must become such composites in order to exploit the different forms of knowledge already extant.

The development of the prototype was not the only activity of the knowledge engineers. Various other features of the expert system were developed in parallel. An explanation facility was built as an extension of Program 17.22. A simulator for rules based on ordinal scales was built to settle the argument among the knowledge engineers as to whether a reasonable collection of rules would be sufficient to cover the range of outcomes in the general case.

Finally, a consistency checker for the rules was built. The following meta-rule is an obvious consistency principle: "If all of client A's factors are better than or equal to client B's, then the outcome of client A must be better than or equal to that of client B."

22.2   Background

More details on the credit evaluation system can be found in Ben-David and Sterling (1986).

23   An Equation Solver

A very natural area for Prolog applications is symbolic manipulation. For example, a Prolog program for symbolic differentiation, a typical symbol manipulation task, is just the rules of differentiation in different syntax, as shown in Program 3.30.

In this chapter, we present a program for solving symbolic equations. It is a simplification of PRESS (PRolog Equation Solving System), developed in the mathematical reasoning group of the Department of Artificial Intelligence at the University of Edinburgh. PRESS performs at the level of a mathematics student in her final year of high school.

The first section gives an overview of equation solving with some example solutions. The remaining four sections cover the four major equation-solving methods implemented in the equation solver.

23.1   An Overview of Equation Solving

The task of equation solving can be described syntactically. Given an equation Lhs = Rhs in an unknown X, transform the equation into an equivalent equation X = Rhs1, where Rhs1 does not contain X. This final equation is the solution. Two equations are equivalent if one is transformed into the other by a finite number of applications of the axioms and rules of algebra.

Successful mathematics students do not solve equations by blindly applying axioms of algebra. Instead they learn, develop, and use various methods and strategies. Our equation solver, modeling this behavior, is accordingly a collection of methods to be applied to an equation to be

(i) $\cos(x) \cdot (1 - 2 \cdot \sin(x)) = 0$

(ii) $x^2 - 3 \cdot x + 2 = 0$

(iii) $2^{2 \cdot x} - 5 \cdot 2^{x+1} + 16 = 0$

Figure 23.1   Test equations

solved. Each method transforms the equation by applying identities of algebra expressed as rewrite rules. The methods can and do take widely different forms. They can be a collection of rules for solving the class of equations to which the method is applicable, or algorithms implementing a decision procedure.

Abstractly, a method has two parts: a condition testing whether the method is applicable, and the application of the method itself.

The type of equations our program can handle are indicated by the three examples in Figure 23.1. They consist of *algebraic functions* of the unknown, that is +, -, *, /, and exponentiation to an integer power, and also trigonometric and exponential functions. The unknown is x in all three equations.

We briefly show how each equation is solved.

The first step in solving equation (i) in Figure 23.1 is factorization. The problem to be solved is reduced to solving $\cos(x) = 0$ and $1 - 2 \cdot \sin(x) = 0$. A solution to either of these equations is a solution to the original equation.

Both the equations $\cos(x) = 0$ and $1 - 2 \cdot \sin(x) = 0$ are solved by making x the subject of the equation. This is possible because x occurs once in each equation.

The solution to $\cos(x) = 0$ is arccos(0). The solution of $1 - 2 \cdot \sin(x) = 0$ takes the following steps:

$$1 - 2 \cdot \sin(x) = 0,$$

$$2 \cdot \sin(x) = 1,$$

$$\sin(x) = 1/2,$$

$$x = \arcsin(1/2).$$

In general, equations with a single occurrence of the unknown can be solved by an algorithmic method called *isolation*. The method repeatedly applies an appropriate inverse function to both sides of the equation until the single occurrence of the unknown is isolated on the left-hand side of the equation. Isolation solves $1 - 2 \cdot \sin(x) = 0$ by producing the preceding sequence of equations.

Equation (ii) in Figure 23.1, $x^2 - 3 \cdot x + 2 = 0$, is a quadratic equation in x. We all learn in high school a formula for solving quadratic equations. The discriminant, $b^2 - 4 \cdot a \cdot c$, is calculated, in this case $(-3)^2 - 4 \cdot 1 \cdot 2$, which equals 1, and two solutions are given: $x = (-(-3) + \sqrt{1})/2$, which equals 2, and $x = (-(-3) - \sqrt{1})/2$, which equals 1.

The key to solving equation (iii) in Figure 23.1 is to realize that the equation is really a quadratic equation in 2^x. The equation $2^{2 \cdot x} - 5 \cdot 2^{x+1} + 16 = 0$ can be rewritten as $(2^x)^2 - 5 \cdot 2 \cdot 2^x + 16 = 0$. This can be solved for 2^x, giving two solutions of the form $2^x = \text{Rhs}$, where Rhs is free of x. Each of these equations are solved for x to give solutions to equation (iii).

PRESS was tested on equations taken from British A-level examinations in mathematics. It seems that examiners liked posing questions such as equation (iii), which involved the student's manipulating logarithmic, exponential, or other transcendental functions into forms where they could be solved as polynomials. A method called *homogenization* evolved to solve equations of these types.

The aim of homogenization is to transform the equation into a polynomial in some term containing the unknown. (We simplify the more general homogenization of PRESS for didactic purposes.) The method consists of four steps, which we illustrate for equation (iii). The equation is first parsed and all maximal nonpolynomial terms containing the unknown are collected with duplicates removed. This set is called the *offenders set*. In the example, it is $\{2^{2x}, 2^{x+1}\}$. The second step is finding a term, known as the *reduced term*. The result of homogenization is a polynomial equation in the reduced term. The reduced term in our example is 2^x. The third step of homogenization is finding rewrite rules that express each of the elements of the offenders set as a polynomial in the reduced term. Finding such a set guarantees that homogenization will succeed. In our example the rewrite rules are $2^{2x} = (2^x)^2$ and $2^{x+1} = 2 \cdot 2^x$. Finally, the rewrite rules are applied to produce the polynomial equation.

We complete this section with a brief overview of the equation solver. The basic predicate is `solve_equation(Equation,X,Solution)`. The relation is true if `Solution` is a solution to `Equation` in the unknown `X`. The complete code appears as Program 23.1.

solve_equation(Equation,Unknown,Solution) ←
    Solution is a solution to the equation *Equation*
    in the unknown *Unknown.*

```
solve_equation(A*B=0,X,Solution) ←
    !,
    factorize(A*B,X,Factors\[ ]),
    remove_duplicates(Factors,Factors1),
    solve_factors(Factors1,X,Solution).

solve_equation(Equation,X,Solution) ←
    single_occurrence(X,Equation),
    !,
    position(X,Equation,[Side|Position]),
    maneuver_sides(Side,Equation,Equation1),
    isolate(Position,Equation1,Solution).

solve_equation(Lhs=Rhs,X,Solution) ←
    polynomial(Lhs,X),
    polynomial(Rhs,X),
    !,
    polynomial_normal_form(Lhs-Rhs,X,PolyForm),
    solve_polynomial_equation(PolyForm,X,Solution).

solve_equation(Equation,X,Solution) ←
    homogenize(Equation,X,Equation1,X1),
    !,
    solve_equation(Equation1,X1,Solution1),
    solve_equation(Solution1,X,Solution).
```

The factorization method

factorize(Expression,Subterm,Factors) ←
    Factors is a difference-list consisting of the factors of
    the multiplicative term *Expression* that contain the *Subterm.*

```
factorize(A*B,X,Factors\Rest) ← !, factorize(A,X,Factors\Factors1),
factorize(B,X,Factors1\Rest).
factorize(C,X,[C|Factors]\Factors) ←
    subterm(X,C),  !.
factorize(C,X,Factors\Factors).
```

solve_factors(Factors,Unknown,Solution) ←
    Solution is a solution of the equation *Factor* = 0 in the
    Unknown for some *Factor* in the list of *Factors.*

```
solve_factors([Factor|Factors],X,Solution) ←
    solve_equation(Factor=0,X,Solution).
solve_factors([Factor|Factors],X,Solution) ←
    solve_factors(Factors,X,Solution).
```

Program 23.1 A program for solving equations

The isolation method

```
maneuver_sides(1,Lhs = Rhs,Lhs = Rhs) ← !.
maneuver_sides(2,Lhs = Rhs,Rhs = Lhs) ← !.

isolate([N|Position],Equation,IsolatedEquation) ←
    isolax(N,Equation,Equation1),
    isolate(Position,Equation1,IsolatedEquation).
isolate([ ],Equation,Equation).
```

Axioms for isolation

```
isolax(1,-Lhs = Rhs,Lhs = -Rhs).                  % Unary minus

isolax(1,Term1+Term2 = Rhs,Term1 = Rhs-Term2).    % Addition
isolax(2,Term1+Term2 = Rhs,Term2 = Rhs-Term1).    % Addition

isolax(1,Term1-Term2 = Rhs,Term1 = Rhs+Term2).    % Subtraction
isolax(2,Term1-Term2 = Rhs,Term2 = Term1-Rhs).    % Subtraction

isolax(1,Term1*Term2 = Rhs,Term1 = Rhs/Term2) ←   % Multiplication
    Term2 ≠ 0.
isolax(2,Term1*Term2 = Rhs,Term2 = Rhs/Term1) ←   % Multiplication
    Term1 ≠ 0.

isolax(1,Term1↑Term2 = Rhs,Term1 = Rhs↑(-Term2)).
    % Exponentiation
isolax(2,Term1↑Term2 = Rhs,Term2 = log(base(Term1),Rhs)).
    % Exponentiation

isolax(1,sin(U) = V,U = arcsin(V)).               % Sine
isolax(1,sin(U) = V,U = π-arcsin(V)).             % Sine
isolax(1,cos(U) = V,U = arccos(V)).               % Cosine
isolax(1,cos(U) = V,U = -arccos(V)).              % Cosine
```

The polynomial method

polynomial(Term,X) ← See Program 11.4.

polynomial_normal_form(Expression,Term,PolyNormalForm) ←
PolyNormalForm is the polynomial normal form of
Expression, which is a polynomial in *Term*.

```
polynomial_normal_form(Polynomial,X,NormalForm) ←
    polynomial_form(Polynomial,X,PolyForm),
    remove_zero_terms(PolyForm,NormalForm), !.

polynomial_form(X,X,[(1,1)]).
polynomial_form(X↑N,X,[(1,N)]).
polynomial_form(Term1+Term2,X,PolyForm) ←
    polynomial_form(Term1,X,PolyForm1),
    polynomial_form(Term2,X,PolyForm2),
    add_polynomials(PolyForm1,PolyForm2,PolyForm).
```

Program 23.1   (Continued)

```
polynomial_form(Term1-Term2,X,PolyForm) ←
    polynomial_form(Term1,X,PolyForm1),
    polynomial_form(Term2,X,PolyForm2),
    subtract_polynomials(PolyForm1,PolyForm2,PolyForm).
polynomial_form(Term1*Term2,X,PolyForm) ←
    polynomial_form(Term1,X,PolyForm1),
    polynomial_form(Term2,X,PolyForm2),
    multiply_polynomials(PolyForm1,PolyForm2,PolyForm).
polynomial_form(Term↑N,X,PolyForm) ← !,
    polynomial_form(Term,X,PolyForm1),
    binomial(PolyForm1,N,PolyForm).
polynomial_form(Term,X,[(Term,0)]) ←
    free_of(X,Term), !.

remove_zero_terms([(0,N)|Poly],Poly1) ←
    !, remove_zero_terms(Poly,Poly1).
remove_zero_terms([(C,N)|Poly],[(C,N)|Poly1]) ←
    C ≠ 0, !, remove_zero_terms(Poly,Poly1).
remove_zero_terms([ ],[ ]).
```

Polynomial manipulation routines

add_polynomials(Poly1,Poly2,Poly) ←
    Poly is the sum of *Poly1* and *Poly2*, where *Poly1*,
    Poly2, and *Poly* are all in polynomial form.

```
add_polynomials([ ],Poly,Poly) ← !.
add_polynomials(Poly,[ ],Poly) ← !.
add_polynomials([(Ai,Ni)|Poly1],[(Aj,Nj)|Poly2],[(Ai,Ni)|Poly]) ←
    Ni > Nj, !, add_polynomials(Poly1,[(Aj,Nj)|Poly2],Poly).
add_polynomials([(Ai,Ni)|Poly1],[(Aj,Nj)|Poly2],[(A,Ni)|Poly]) ←
    Ni =:= Nj, !, A is Ai+Aj, add_polynomials(Poly1,Poly2,Poly).
add_polynomials([(Ai,Ni)|Poly1],[(Aj,Nj)|Poly2],[(Aj,Nj)|Poly]) ←
    Ni < Nj, !, add_polynomials([(Ai,Ni)|Poly1],Poly2,Poly).
```

subtract_polynomials(Poly1,Poly2,Poly) ←
    Poly is the difference of *Poly1* and *Poly2*, where *Poly1*,
    Poly2, and *Poly* are all in polynomial form.

```
subtract_polynomials(Poly1,Poly2,Poly) ←
    multiply_single(Poly2,(-1,0),Poly3),
    add_polynomials(Poly1,Poly3,Poly), !.
```

multiply_single(Poly1,Monomial,Poly) ←
    Poly is the product of *Poly1* and *Monomial*, where *Poly1*
    and *Poly* are in polynomial form, and *Monomial* has the
    form (C,N) denoting the monomial $C*X^N$.

```
multiply_single([(C1,N1)|Poly1],(C,N),[(C2,N2)|Poly]) ←
    C2 is C1*C, N2 is N1+N, multiply_single(Poly1,(C,N),Poly).
multiply_single([ ],Factor,[ ]).
```

Program 23.1 (Continued)

multiply_polynomials (*Poly1,Poly2,Poly*) ←
    Poly is the product of *Poly1* and *Poly2*, where *Poly1*,
    Poly2, and *Poly* are all in polynomial form.

```
multiply_polynomials([(C,N)|Poly1],Poly2,Poly) ←
    multiply_single(Poly2,(C,N),Poly3),
    multiply_polynomials(Poly1,Poly2,Poly4),
    add_polynomials(Poly3,Poly4,Poly).
multiply_polynomials([ ],P,[ ]).

binomial(Poly,1,Poly).
```

Polynomial equation solver

solve_polynomial_equation (*Equation,Unknown,Solution*) ←
    Solution is a solution to the polynomial *Equation* in the unknown
    Unknown.

```
solve_polynomial_equation(PolyEquation,X,X = -B/A) ←
    linear(PolyEquation), !,
    pad(PolyEquation,[(A,1),(B,0)]).
solve_polynomial_equation(PolyEquation,X,Solution) ←
    quadratic(PolyEquation), !,
    pad(PolyEquation,[(A,2),(B,1),(C,0)]),
    discriminant(A,B,C,Discriminant),
    root(X,A,B,C,Discriminant,Solution).

discriminant(A,B,C,D) ← D is B*B - 4*A*C.

root(X,A,B,C,0,X= -B/(2*A)).
root(X,A,B,C,D,X= (-B+sqrt(D))/(2*A)) ← D > 0.
root(X,A,B,C,D,X= (-B-sqrt(D))/(2*A)) ← D > 0.

pad([(C,N)|Poly],[(C,N)|Poly1]) ←
    !, pad(Poly,Poly1).
pad(Poly,[(0,N)|Poly1]) ←
    pad(Poly,Poly1).
pad([ ],[ ]).

linear([(Coeff,1)|Poly]).
quadratic([(Coeff,2)|Poly]).
```

The homogenization method

homogenize (*Equation,X,Equation1,X1*) ←
    The *Equation* in *X* is transformed to the polynomial
    Equation1 in *X1* where *X1* contains *X*.

```
homogenize(Equation,X,Equation1,X1) ←
    offenders(Equation,X,Offenders),
    reduced_term(X,Offenders,Type,X1),
    rewrite(Offenders,Type,X1,Substitutions),
    substitute(Equation,Substitutions,Equation1).
```

Program 23.1   (Continued)

offenders(Equation,Unknown,Offenders) ←
    Offenders is the set of offenders of the *Equation* in the *Unknown*.

```
offenders(Equation,X,Offenders) ←
    parse(Equation,X,Offenders1\[ ]),
    remove_duplicates(Offenders1,Offenders),
    multiple(Offenders).

reduced_term(X,Offenders,Type,X1) ←
    classify(Offenders,X,Type),
    candidate(Type,Offenders,X,X1).
```

Heuristics for exponential equations

```
classify(Offenders,X,exponential) ←
    exponential_offenders(Offenders,X).

exponential_offenders([A↑B|Offs],X) ←
    free_of(X,A), subterm(X,B), exponential_offenders(Offs,X).
exponential_offenders([ ],X).

candidate(exponential,Offenders,X,A↑X) ←
    base(Offenders,A), polynomial_exponents(Offenders,X).

base([A↑B|Offs],A) ← base(Offs,A).
base([ ],A).

polynomial_exponents([A↑B|Offs],X) ←
    polynomial(B,X), polynomial_exponents(Offs,X).
polynomial_exponents([ ],X).
```

Parsing the equation and making substitutions

parse(Expression,Term,Offenders) ←
    Expression is traversed to produce the set of *Offenders* in *Term*,
    that is, the nonalgebraic subterms of *Expression* containing *Term*.

```
parse(A+B,X,L1\L2) ←
    !, parse(A,X,L1\L3), parse(B,X,L3\L2).
parse(A*B,X,L1\L2) ←
    !, parse(A,X,L1\L3), parse(B,X,L3\L2).
parse(A-B,X,L1\L2) ←
    !, parse(A,X,L1\L3), parse(B,X,L3\L2).
parse(A=B,X,L1\L2) ←
    !, parse(A,X,L1\L3), parse(B,X,L3\L2).
parse(A↑B,X,L) ←
    integer(B), !, parse(A,X,L).
parse(A,X,L\L) ←
    free_of(X,A), !.
parse(A,X,[A|L]\L) ←
    subterm(X,A), !.
```

Program 23.1   (Continued)

substitute(Expression,Substitutions,Expression1) ←
> The list of *Substitutions* is applied to *Expression* to produce
> *Expression1.*

```
substitute(A+B,Subs,NewA+NewB) ←
    !, substitute(A,Subs,NewA), substitute(B,Subs,NewB).
substitute(A*B,Subs,NewA*NewB) ←
    !, substitute(A,Subs,NewA), substitute(B,Subs,NewB).
substitute(A-B,Subs,NewA-NewB) ←
    !, substitute(A,Subs,NewA), substitute(B,Subs,NewB).
substitute(A=B,Subs,NewA=NewB) ←
    !, substitute(A,Subs,NewA), substitute(B,Subs,NewB).
substitute(A↑B,Subs,NewA↑B) ←
    integer(B), !, substitute(A,Subs,NewA).
substitute(A,Subs,B) ←
    member(A=B,Subs), !.
substitute(A,Subs,A).
```

Finding homogenization rewrite rules

```
rewrite([Off|Offs],Type,X1,[Off=Term|Rewrites]) ←
    homogenize_axiom(Type,Off,X1,Term),
    rewrite(Offs,Type,X1,Rewrites).
rewrite([ ],Type,X,[ ]).
```

Homogenization axioms

```
homogenize_axiom(exponential,A↑(N*X),A↑X,(A↑X)↑N).
homogenize_axiom(exponential,A↑(-X),A↑X,1/(A↑X)).
homogenize_axiom(exponential,A↑(X+B),A↑X,A↑B*A↑X).
```

Utilities

```
subterm(Sub,Term) ← See Program 9.2.

position(Term,Term,[ ]) ← !.
position(Sub,Term,Path) ←
    compound(Term), functor(Term,F,N), position(N,Sub,Term,Path), !.

position(N,Sub,Term,[N|Path]) ←
    arg(N,Term,Arg), position(Sub,Arg,Path).
position(N,Sub,Term,Path) ←
    N > 1, N1 is N-1, position(N1,Sub,Term,Path).

free_of(Subterm,Term) ← occurrence(Subterm,Term,0).

single_occurrence(Subterm,Term) ← occurrence(Subterm,Term,1).

occurrence(Term,Term,1) ← !.
occurrence(Sub,Term,N) ←
    compound(Term), !, functor(Term,F,M), occurrence(M,Sub,Term,0,N).
occurrence(Sub,Term,0) ← Term ≠ Sub.
```

Program 23.1   (Continued)

```
occurrence(M,Sub,Term,N1,N2) ←
    M > 0, !, arg(M,Term,Arg), occurrence(Sub,Arg,N), N3 is N+N1,
    M1 is M-1, occurrence(M1,Sub,Term,N3,N2).
occurrence(0,Sub,Term,N,N).

remove_duplicates(Xs,Ys) ← no_doubles(Xs,Ys).

no_doubles(Xs,Ys) ← See Program 7.9.

multiple([X1,X2|Xs]).
```

Testing and data

```
test_press(X,Y) ← equation(X,E,U), solve_equation(E,U,Y).

equation(1,cos(x)*(1-2*sin(x))=0,x).

equation(2,x↑2-3*x+2=0,x).

equation(3,2↑(2*x)-5*2↑(x+1)+16=0,x).
```

Program 23.1   (Continued)

Program 23.1 has four clauses for `solve_equation`, one for each of the four methods needed to solve the equations in Figure 23.1. More generally, there is a clause for each equation-solving method. The full PRESS system has several more methods.

Our equation solver ignores several features that might be expected. There is no simplification of expressions, no rational arithmetic, no record of the last equation solved, no help facility, and so forth. PRESS does contain many of these facilities as discussed briefly in Section 23.6.

23.2   Factorization

Factorization is the first method attempted by the equation solver. Note that the test whether factorization is applicable is trivial, being unification with the equation $A * B = 0$. If the test succeeds, the simpler equations are recursively solved. The top-level clause implementing factorization is

```
solve_equation(A*B=0,X,Solution) ←
    factorize(A*B,X,Factors\[ ]),
    remove_duplicates(Factors,Factors1),
    solve_factors(Factors1,X,Solution).
```

The top-level clause in Program 23.1 has a cut as the first goal in the body. This is a green cut: none of the other methods depend on the success or failure of factorization. In general, we omit green cuts from clauses we describe in the text.

23.3 Isolation

A useful concept to locate and manipulate the single occurrence of the unknown is its *position*. The position of a subterm in a term is a list of argument numbers specifying where it appears. Consider the equation $\cos(x) = 0$. The term $\cos(x)$ containing x is the first argument of the equation, and x is the first (and only) argument of $\cos(x)$. The position of x in $\cos(x) = 0$ is therefore [1,1]. This is indicated in the diagram in Figure 23.2. The figure also shows the position of x in $1 - 2 \cdot \sin(x) = 0$ which is [1,2,2,1].

The clause defining the method of isolation is

```
solve_equation(Equation,X,Solution) ←
    single_occurrence(X,Equation),
    position(X,Equation,[Side|Position]),
    maneuver_sides(Side,Equation,Equation1),
    isolate(Position,Equation1,Solution).
```

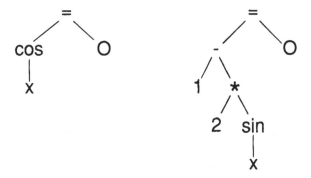

Figure 23.2 Position of subterms in terms

The condition characterizing when isolation is applicable is that there be a single occurrence of the unknown X in the equation, checked by `single_occurrence`. The method calculates the position of X with the predicate `position`. The isolation of X then proceeds in two stages. First, `maneuver_sides` ensures that X appears on the left-hand side of the equation, and second, `isolate` makes it the subject of the formula.

It is useful to define `single_occurrence` in terms of the more general predicate `occurrence(Subterm,Term,N)`, which counts the number of times N that Subterm occurs in the term Term. Both `occurrence` and `position` are typical structure inspection predicates. Both are posed as exercises at the end of Section 9.2. Code for them appears in the utilities section of Program 23.1.

The predicate `maneuver_sides(N,Equation,Equation1)` consists of two facts:

```
maneuver_sides(1,Lhs = Rhs,Lhs = Rhs).
maneuver_sides(2,Lhs = Rhs,Rhs = Lhs).
```

Its effect is to ensure that the unknown appears on the left-hand side of Equation1. The first argument N, the head of the position list, indicates the side of the equation in which the unknown appears. A 1 means the left-hand side, and the equation is left intact. A 2 means the right-hand side, and so the sides of the equation are swapped.

The transformation of the equation is done by `isolate/3`. It repeatedly applies rewrite rules until the position list is exhausted:

```
isolate([N|Position],Equation,IsolatedEquation) ←
    isolax(N,Equation,Equation1),
    isolate(Position,Equation1,IsolatedEquation).
isolate([ ],Equation,Equation).
```

The rewrite rules, or isolation axioms, are specified by the predicate `isolax(N,Equation,Equation1)`. Let us consider an example used in solving $1 - 2 \cdot \sin(x) = 0$. An equivalence transformation on equations is adding the same quantity to both sides of an equation. We show its translation into an `isolax` axiom for manipulating equations of the form $u - v = w$. Note that rules need only simplify the left-hand side of equations, since the unknown is guaranteed to be on that side.

Two rules are necessary to cover the two cases whether the first or second argument of $u - v$ contains the unknown. The term $u - v = w$

can be rewritten to either $u = w + v$ or $v = u - w$. The first argument of `isolax` specifies which argument of the sum contains the unknown. The Prolog equivalent of the two rewrite rules is then

```
isolax(1,Term1-Term2 = Rhs,Term1 = Rhs+Term2).
isolax(2,Term1-Term2 = Rhs,Term2 = Term1-Rhs).
```

Other isolation axioms are more complicated. Consider simplifying a product on the left-hand side of an equation. One of the expected rules would be

```
isolax(1,Term1*Term2 = Rhs,Term1 = Rhs/Term2).
```

If `Term2` equals zero, however, the rewriting is invalid. A test is therefore added that prevents the axioms for multiplication being applied if the term by which it divides is 0. For example,

```
isolax(1,Term1*Term2 = Rhs,Term1 = Rhs/Term2) ← Term2 ≠ 0.
```

Isolation axioms for trigonometric functions illustrate another possibility that must be catered for — multiple solutions. An equation such as $\sin(x) = 1/2$ that is reached in our example has two solutions between 0 and $2 \cdot \pi$. The alternative solutions are handled by having separate `isolax` axioms:

```
isolax(1,sin(U) = V,U = arcsin(V)).
isolax(1,sin(U) = V,U = π - arcsin(V)).
```

In fact, the equation has a more general solution. Integers of the form $2 \cdot n \cdot \pi$ can be added to either solution for arbitrary values of n. The decision whether a particular or general solution is desired depends on context and on semantic information independent of the equation solver.

Further examples of isolation axioms are given in the complete equation solver, Program 23.1.

The code described so far is sufficient to solve the first equation in Figure 23.1, $\cos(x) \cdot (1 - 2 \cdot \sin(x)) = 0$. There are four answers $\arccos(0)$, $-\arccos(0)$, $\arcsin((1 - 0)/2)$, $\pi - \arcsin((1 - 0)/2)$. Each can be simplified, for example, $\arcsin((1 - 0)/2)$ to $\pi/6$, but will not be unless the expression is explicitly evaluated.

The usefulness of an equation solver depends on how well it can perform such simplification, even though simplification is not strictly part of the equation-solving task. Writing an expression simplifier is nontrivial, however. It is undecidable whether two expressions are equivalent in general. Some simple identities of algebra can be easily incorporated, for example, rewriting $0 + u$ to u. Choosing between other preferred forms, e.g., $(1 + x)^3$ and $1 + 3 \cdot x + 3 \cdot x^2 + x^3$, depends on context.

23.4 Polynomial

Polynomial equations are solved by a polynomial equation solver, applying various polynomial methods. Both sides of the equation are checked as to whether they are polynomials in the unknown. If the checks are successful, the equation is converted to a polynomial normal form by `polynomial_normal_form`, and the polynomial equation solver `solve_polynomial_equation` is invoked:

```
solve_equation(Lhs=Rhs,X,Solution) ←
    polynomial(Lhs,X),
    polynomial(Rhs,X),
    polynomial_normal_form(Lhs-Rhs,X,PolyForm),
    solve_polynomial_equation(PolyForm,X,Solution).
```

The polynomial normal form is a list of tuples of the form (A_i, N_i), where A_i is the coefficient of X^{N_i}, which is necessarily nonzero. The tuples are sorted into strictly decreasing order of N_i; for each degree there is at most one tuple. For example, the list $[(1, 2), (-3, 1), (2, 0)]$ is the normal form for $x^2 - 3 \cdot x + 2$. The leading term of the polynomial is the head of the list. The classic algorithms for handling polynomials are applicable to equations in normal form. Reduction to polynomial normal form occurs in two stages:

```
polynomial_normal_form(Polynomial,X,NormalForm) ←
    polynomial_form(Polynomial,X,PolyForm),
    remove_zero_terms(PolyForm,NormalForm).
```

The predicate `polynomial_form(X,Polynomial,PolyForm)` decomposes the polynomial. PolyForm is a sorted list of coefficient-degree tuples, where tuples with zero coefficients may occur.

It is convenient for many of the polynomial methods to assume that all the terms in the polynomial form have nonzero coefficients. Therefore the final step of `polynomial_normal_form` is removing those terms whose coefficients are zero. This is achieved by a simple recursive procedure `remove_zero_terms`.

The code for `polynomial_form` directly echoes the code for `polynomial`. For each clause used in the parsing process, there is a corresponding clause giving the resultant polynomial. For example, the polynomial form of a term x^n is $[(1, n)]$, which is expressed in the clause

```
polynomial_form(X↑N,X,[(1,N)]).
```

The recursive clauses for `polynomial_form` manipulate the polynomials in order to preserve the polynomial form. Consider the clause

```
polynomial_form(Poly1+Poly2,X,PolyForm) ←
    polynomial_form(Poly1,X,PolyForm1),
    polynomial_form(Poly2,X,PolyForm2),
    add_polynomials(PolyForm1,PolyForm2,PolyForm).
```

The procedure `add_polynomials` contains an algorithm for adding polynomials in normal form. The code is a straightforward list of the possibilities that can arise:

```
add_polynomials([ ],Poly,Poly).
add_polynomials(Poly,[ ],Poly).
add_polynomials([(Ai,Ni)|Poly1],[(Aj,Nj)|Poly2],[(Ai,Ni)|Poly]) ←
    Ni > Nj, add_polynomials(Poly1,[(Aj,Nj)|Poly2],Poly).
add_polynomials([(Ai,Ni)|Poly1],[(Aj,Nj)|Poly2],[(A,Ni)|Poly]) ←
    Ni =:= Nj, A is Ai+Aj, add_polynomials(Poly1,Poly2,Poly).
add_polynomials([(Ai,Ni)|Poly1],[(Aj,Nj)|Poly2],[(Aj,Nj)|Poly]) ←
    Ni < Nj, add_polynomials([(Ai,Ni)|Poly1],Poly2,Poly).
```

Similarly, the procedures `subtract_polynomials`, `multiply_polynomials`, and `binomial` are algorithms for subtracting, multiplying, and binomially expanding polynomials in normal form to produce results in normal form. The subsidiary predicate `multiply_single(Poly1,Monomial,Poly2)` multiplies a polynomial by a monomial (C,N) to produce a new polynomial.

Once the polynomial is in normal form, the polynomial equation solver is invoked. The structure of the polynomial solver follows the structure of the overall equation solver. The solver is a collection of methods that are tried in order to see which is applicable and can be used to solve the equation. The predicate `solve_polynomial_equation` is the analogous relation to `solve_equation`.

The second equation in Figure 23.1 is quadratic and can be solved with the standard formula. The equation solver mirrors the human method. The polynomial is identified as being suitable for the quadratic method by checking (with `quadratic`) if the leading term in the polynomial is of second degree. Since zero terms have been removed in putting the polynomial into its normal form, pad puts them back if necessary. The next two steps are familiar: calculating the discriminant, and returning the roots according to the value of the discriminant. Again multiple solutions are indicated by having multiple possibilities:

```
solve_polynomial_equation(Poly,X,Solution) ←
    quadratic(Poly),
    pad(Poly,[(A,2),(B,1),(C,0)]),
    discriminant(A,B,C,Discriminant),
    root(X,A,B,C,Discriminant,Solution).

discriminant(A,B,C,D) ← D is (B*B - 4*A*C).

root(X,A,B,C,0,X= -B/(2*A)).
root(X,A,B,C,D,X= (-B+sqrt(D))/(2*A)) ← D > 0.
root(X,A,B,C,D,X= (-B-sqrt(D))/(2*A)) ← D > 0.
```

Other clauses for `solve_polynomial_equation` constitute separate methods for solving different polynomial equations. Linear equations are solved with a simple formula. In PRESS, cubic equations are handled by guessing a root and then factoring, reducing the equation to a quadratic. Other tricks recognize obvious factors, or that quartic equations missing a cubic and a linear term are really disguised quadratics.

23.5 Homogenization

The top-level clause for homogenization reflects the transformation of the original equation into a new equation in a new unknown, which is recursively solved; its solution is obtained for the original unknown:

```
solve_equation(Equation,X,Solution) ←
    homogenize(Equation,X,Equation1,X1),
    solve_equation(Equation1,X1,Solution1),
    solve_equation(Solution1,X,Solution).
```

The code for `homogenize/4` implements the four stages of homogenization, described in Section 23.1. The offenders set is calculated by `offenders/3`, which checks that there are multiple offenders. If there is only a single offender, homogenization will not be useful:

```
homogenize(Equation,X,Equation1,X1) ←
    offenders(Equation,X,Offenders),
    reduced_term(X,Offenders,Type,X1),
    rewrite(Offenders,Type,X1,Substitutions),
    substitute(Equation,Substitutions,Equation1).
```

The predicate `reduced_term/4` finds a *reduced term*, that is, a candidate for the new unknown. In order to structure the search for the reduced term, the equation is classified into a type. This type is used in the next stage to find rewrite rules expressing each element of the offenders set as an appropriate function of the reduced term. The type of the example equation is *exponential*. PRESS encodes a lot of heuristic knowledge about finding a suitable reduced term. The heuristics depend on the type of the terms appearing in the offenders set. To aid the structuring (and retrieval) of knowledge, finding a reduced term proceeds in two stages — classifying the type of the offenders set, and finding a reduced term of that type:

```
reduced_term(X,Offenders,Type,X1) ←
    classify(Offenders,X,Type),
    candidate(Type,Offenders,X,X1).
```

We look at the set of rules appropriate to our particular equation. The offenders set is of exponential type because all the elements in the offenders set have the form A^B, where A does not contain the unknown but B does. Standard recursive procedures check that this is true.

The heuristic used to select the reduced term in this example is that if all the bases are the same, A, and each exponent is a polynomial in the unknown, X, then a suitable reduced term is A^X:

```
candidate(exponential,Offenders,X,A↑X) ←
    base(Offenders,A), polynomial_exponents(Offenders,X).
```

The straightforward code for base and polynomial_exponents is in the complete program. The heuristics in PRESS are better developed than the ones shown here. For example, the greatest common divisor of all the leading terms of the polynomials is calculated and used to choose the reduced term.

The next step is checking whether each member of the offenders set can be rewritten in terms of the reduced term candidate. This involves finding an appropriate rule. The collection of clauses for homogenize_axiom constitute the possibly applicable rewrite rules. In other words, relevant rules must be specified in advance. The applicable rules in this case are

```
homogenize_axiom(exponential,A↑(N*X),A↑X,(A↑X)↑N).
homogenize_axiom(exponential,A↑(X+B),A↑X,A↑B*A↑X).
```

Substituting the term in the equation echoes the parsing process used by offenders as each part of the equation is checked to see whether it is the appropriate term to rewrite.

Exercises for Chapter 23

(i)   Add isolation axioms to Program 23.1 to handle quotients on the left-hand side of the equation. Solve the equation $x/2 = 5$.

(ii)   Add to the polynomial equation solver the ability to solve disguised linear and disguised quadratic equations. Solve the equations $2 \cdot x^3 - 8 = x^3$, and $x^4 - 5 \cdot x^2 + 6 = 0$.

(iii) The equation $\cos(2 \cdot x) - \sin(x) = 0$ can be solved as a quadratic equation in $\sin(x)$ by applying the rewrite rule $\cos(2 \cdot x) = 1 - 2 \cdot \sin^2(x)$. Add clauses to Program 23.1 to solve this equation. You will need to add rules for identifying terms of type *trigonometric*, heuristics for finding trigonometric reduced terms, and appropriate homogenization axioms.

(iv)   Rewrite the predicate free_of(Term,X) so that it fails as soon as it finds an occurrence of X in Term.

(v) Modify Program 23.1 so that it solves simple simultaneous equations.

23.6 Background

Symbolic manipulation was an early application area for Prolog. Early examples are programs for symbolic integration (Bergman and Kanoui, 1973) and for proving theorems in geometry (Welham, 1976).

The PRESS program, from which Program 23.1 is adapted, owes a debt to many people. The original version was written by Bob Welham. Many of the researchers in the mathematical reasoning group working with Alan Bundy at the University of Edinburgh subsequently tinkered with the code. Published descriptions of the program appear in Bundy and Welham (1981), Sterling et al. (1982), and Silver (1986). The last reference has a detailed discussion of homogenization.

PRESS includes various modules, not discussed in this chapter, that are interesting in their own right: for example, a package for interval arithmetic (Bundy, 1984), an infinite precision rational arithmetic package developed by Richard O'Keefe, and an expression simplifier based on difference-structures as described in Section 15.2, developed by Lawrence Byrd. The successful integration of all these modules is strong evidence for the practicality of Prolog for large programming projects.

The development of PRESS showed up classic points of software engineering. For example, at one stage the program was being tuned prior to publishing some statistics. Profiling was done on the program, which showed that the predicate most commonly called was `free_of`. Rewriting it as suggested in Exercise 23(iv) resulted in a speedup of 35 percent in the performance of PRESS.

Program 23.1 is a considerably cleaned-up version of PRESS. Tidying the code enabled further research. Program 23.1 was easily translated to other logic programming languages, Concurrent Prolog and FCP (Sterling and Codish, 1986). Making the conditions when methods were used more explicit enabled the writing of a program to learn new equation-solving methods from examples (Silver, 1986).

24   A Compiler

Our final application is a compiler. The program is presented top-down. The first section outlines the scope of the compiler and gives its definition. The next three sections describe the three major components: the parser, the code generator, and the assembler.

24.1 Overview of the Compiler

The source language for the compiler is PL, a simplified version of Pascal designed solely for the purposes of this chapter. It contains an assignment statement, an if-then-else statement, a *while* statement, and simple I/O statements. The language is best illustrated with an example. Figure 24.1 contains a program for computing factorials written in PL. A formal definition of the syntax of the language is implicit in the parser in Program 24.1.

The target language is a machine language typical for a one-accumulator computer. Its instructions are given in Figure 24.2. Each instruction has one (explicit) operand, which can be one of four things: an integer constant, the address of a storage location, the address of a program instruction, or a value to be ignored. Most of the instructions also have a second implicit operand, which is either the accumulator or its contents. In addition, there is a pseudoinstruction *block* that reserves a number of storage locations as specified by its integer operand.

The scope of the compiler is clear from its behavior on our example. Figure 24.3 is the translation of the PL program in Figure 24.1 into ma-

```
program factorial;
    begin
        read value;
        count := 1;
        result := 1;
        while count < value do
            begin
                count := count+1;
                result := result*count
            end ;
        write result
    end
```

Figure 24.1   A PL program for computing factorials

```
    Arithmetic
Literals    Memory    Control    I/O, etc.
                      jumpeq     read
addc        add       jumpne     write
subc        sub       jumplt     halt
mulc        mul       jumpgt
divc        div       jumple
loadc       load      jumpge
store                 jump
```

Figure 24.2   Target language instructions

chine language. The compiler produces the columns labeled *Instruction* and *Operand*.

The task of compiling can be broken down into the five stages given in Figure 24.4. The first stage transforms a source text into a list of tokens. The list of tokens is parsed in the second stage, syntax analysis, to give a source structure. The third and fourth stages transform the source structure into relocatable code and assemble the relocatable code into absolute object code, respectively. The final stage outputs the object program.

Our compiler implements the middle three stages. Both the first stage of lexical analysis and the final output stage are relatively uninteresting and are not considered here. The top level of the code handles syntax analysis, code generation, and assembly.

Symbol	Address	Instruction	Operand	Symbol
	1	READ	21	VALUE
	2	LOADC	1	
	3	STORE	19	COUNT
	4	LOADC	20	
	5	STORE	20	RESULT
LABEL1	6	LOAD	19	COUNT
	7	SUB	21	VALUE
	8	JUMPGE	16	LABEL2
	9	LOAD	19	COUNT
	10	ADDC	1	
	11	STORE	19	COUNT
	12	LOAD	20	RESULT
	13	MUL	19	COUNT
	14	STORE	20	RESULT
	15	JUMP	6	LABEL1
LABEL2	16	LOAD	20	RESULT
	17	WRITE	0	
	18	HALT	0	
COUNT	19	BLOCK	3	
RESULT	20			
VALUE	21			

Figure 24.3   Assembly code version of a factorial program

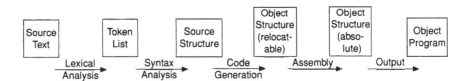

Figure 24.4   The stages of compilation

The basic predicate compile(Tokens,ObjectCode) relates a list of tokens Tokens to the ObjectCode of the program the tokens represent. The compiler compiles correctly any legal PL program but does not handle errors; that is outside the scope of this chapter. The list of tokens is assumed to be input from some previous stage of lexical analysis. The parser performing the syntax analysis, implemented by the predicate parse, produces from the Tokens an internal parse tree Structure.

compile(*Tokens,ObjectCode*) ←
    ObjectCode is the result of compilation of
    a list of *Tokens* representing a PL program.

```
compile(Tokens,ObjectCode) ←
    parse(Tokens,Structure),
    encode(Structure,Dictionary,Code),
    assemble(Code,Dictionary,ObjectCode).
```

The parser

parse(*Tokens,Structure*) ←
    Structure represents the successfully parsed list of *Tokens*.

```
parse(Source,Structure) ←
    pl_program(Structure,Source\[ ]).

pl_program(S) → [program], identifier(X), [';'], statement(S).
statement((S;Ss)) →
    [begin], statement(S), rest_statements(Ss).
statement(assign(X,V)) →
    identifier(X), [':='], expression(V).
statement(if(T,S1,S2)) →
    [if], test(T), [then], statement(S1), [else], statement(S2).
statement(while(T,S)) →
    [while], test(T), [do], statement(S).
statement(read(X)) →
    [read], identifier(X).
statement(write(X)) →
    [write], expression(X).
rest_statements((S;Ss)) → [';'], statement(S), rest_statements(Ss).
rest_statements(void) → [end].

expression(X) → pl_constant(X).
expression(expr(Op,X,Y)) →
    pl_constant(X), arithmetic_op(Op), expression(Y).
arithmetic_op('+') → ['+'].
arithmetic_op('-') → ['-'].
arithmetic_op('*') → ['*'].
arithmetic_op('/') → ['/'].

pl_constant(name(X)) → identifier(X).
pl_constant(number(X)) → pl_integer(X).

identifier(X) → [X], {atom(X)}.
pl_integer(X) → [X], {integer(X)}.

test(compare(Op,X,Y)) →
    expression(X), comparison_op(Op), expression(Y).
```

Program 24.1   A compiler from PL to machine language

```
comparison_op('=') → ['='].
comparison_op('≠') → ['≠'].
comparison_op('>') → ['>'].
comparison_op('<') → ['<'].
comparison_op('≥') → ['≥'].
comparison_op('≤') → ['≤'].
```

The code generator

encode(Structure,Dictionary,RelocatableCode) ←
    RelocatableCode is generated from the parsed *Structure*
    building a *Dictionary* associating variables with addresses.

```
encode((X;Xs),D,(Y;Ys)) ←
    encode(X,D,Y), encode(Xs,D,Ys).
encode(void,D,no_op).
encode(assign(Name,E),D,(Code; instr(store,Address))) ←
    lookup(Name,D,Address), encode_expression(E,D,Code).
encode(if(Test,Then,Else),D,
    (TestCode; ThenCode; instr(jump,L2);
    label(L1); ElseCode; label(L2))) ←
        encode_test(Test,L1,D,TestCode),
        encode(Then,D,ThenCode),
        encode(Else,D,ElseCode).
encode(while(Test,Do),D,
    (label(L1); TestCode; DoCode; instr(jump,L1); label(L2))) ←
        encode_test(Test,L2,D,TestCode), encode(Do,D,DoCode).
encode(read(X),D,instr(read,Address)) ←
    lookup(X,D,Address).
encode(write(E),D,(Code; instr(write,0))) ←
    encode_expression(E,D,Code).
```

encode_expression(Expression,Dictionary,Code) ←
    Code corresponds to an arithmetic *Expression*.

```
encode_expression(number(C),D,instr(loadc,C)).
encode_expression(name(X),D,instr(load,Address)) ←
    lookup(X,D,Address).
encode_expression(expr(Op,E1,E2),D,(Load;Instruction)) ←
    single_instruction(Op,E2,D,Instruction),
    encode_expression(E1,D,Load).

encode_expression(expr(Op,E1,E2),D,Code) ←
    not single_instruction(Op,E2,D,Instruction),
    single_operation(Op,E1,D,E2Code,Code),
    encode_expression(E2,D,E2Code).
```

Program 24.1   (Continued)

```
single_instruction(Op,number(C),D,instr(OpCode,C)) ←
    literal_operation(Op,OpCode).
single_instruction(Op,name(X),D,instr(OpCode,A)) ←
    memory_operation(Op,OpCode), lookup(X,D,A).

single_operation(Op,E,D,Code,(Code;Instruction)) ←
    commutative(Op), single_instruction(Op,E,D,Instruction).
single_operation(Op,E,D,Code,
        (Code;instr(store,Address);Load;instr(OpCode,Address))) ←
    not commutative(Op),
    lookup('$temp',D,Address),
    encode_expression(E,D,Load),
    op_code(E,Op,OpCode).

op_code(number(C),Op,OpCode) ← literal_operation(Op,OpCode).
op_code(name(X),Op,OpCode) ← memory_operation(Op,OpCode).

literal_operation('+',addc).      memory_operation('+',add).
literal_operation('-',subc).      memory_operation('-',sub).
literal_operation('*',mulc).      memory_operation('*',mul).
literal_operation('/',divc).      memory_operation('/',div).

commutative('+').                 commutative('*').
encode_test(compare(Op,E1,E2),Label,D,
        (Code;instr(OpCode,Label))) ←
    comparison_opcode(Op,OpCode),
    encode_expression(expr('-',E1,E2),D,Code).
comparison_opcode('=',jumpne).    comparison_opcode('≠',jumpeq).
comparison_opcode('>',jumple).    comparison_opcode('≥',jumplt).
comparison_opcode('<',jumpge).    comparison_opcode('≤',jumpgt).
lookup(Name,Dictionary,Address) ← See Program 15.9.
```

The assembler

assemble(Code,Dictionary,TidyCode) ←
    TidyCode is the result of assembling *Code* removing
    *no_op*s and *label*s, and filling in the *Dictionary*.

```
assemble(Code,Dictionary,TidyCode) ←
    tidy_and_count(Code,1,N,TidyCode\(instr(halt,0);block(L))),
    N1 is N+1,
    allocate(Dictionary,N1,N2),
    L is N2-N1, !.

tidy_and_count((Code1;Code2),M,N,TCode1\TCode2) ←
    tidy_and_count(Code1,M,M1,TCode1\Rest),
    tidy_and_count(Code2,M1,N,Rest\TCode2).
tidy_and_count(instr(X,Y),N,N1,(instr(X,Y);Code)\Code) ←
    N1 is N+1.
tidy_and_count(label(N),N,N,Code\Code).
tidy_and_count(no_op,N,N,Code\Code).
```

Program 24.1   (Continued)

```
allocate(void,N,N).
allocate(dict(Name,N1,Before,After),N0,N) ←
    allocate(Before,N0,N1),
    N2 is N1+1,
    allocate(After,N2,N).
```

Program 24.1   (Continued)

```
test_compiler(X,Y) ←
    program(X,P), compile(P,Y).
program(test1,[program,test1,';',begin,write,
    x,'+',y,'-',z,'/',2,end]).
program(test2,[program,test2,';',
    begin,if,a,'>',b,then,max,':=',a,else,max,':=',b,end]).
program(factorial,
    [program,factorial,';'
    ,begin
        ,read,value,';'
        ,count,':=',1,';'
        ,result,':=',1,';'
        ,while,count,'<',value,do
            ,begin
                ,count,':=',count,'+',1,';'
                ,result,':=',result,'*',count
            end,';'
        ,write,result
    ,end]).
```

Program 24.2   Test data

The structure is used by the code generator encode to produce relocatable code Code. A dictionary associating variable locations to memory addresses and keeping track of labels is needed to generate the code. This is the second argument of encode. Finally, the relocatable code is assembled into object code by assemble with the aid of the constructed Dictionary.

The testing data and instructions for the program are given as Program 24.2. The program *factorial* is the PL program of Figure 24.1 translated into a list of tokens. The two small programs consist of a single statement each, and test features of the language not covered by the factorial example. The program *test1* tests compilation of a nontrivial arithmetic expression, and *test2* checks the if-then-else statement.

24.2 The Parser

The parser proper is written as a definite clause grammar, as described in Chapter 19. The predicate `parse` as given in Program 24.1 is just an interface to the DCG, whose top-level predicate is `pl_program`. The DCG has a single argument, the structure corresponding to the statements, as described later. A variant of Program 18.9 is assumed to translate the DCG into Prolog clauses. The convention of that program is that the last argument of the predicates defined by the DCG is a difference-list:

```
parse(Source,Structure) ←
    pl_program(Structure,Source\[ ]).
```

The first statement of any PL program must be a program statement. A program statement consists of the word *program* followed by the name of the program. We call words that must appear for rules of the grammar to apply *standard identifiers*, the word *program* being an example. The name of the program is an identifier in the language. What constitutes identifiers, and more generally constants, is discussed in the context of arithmetic expressions. The program name is followed by a semicolon, another standard identifier, and then the program proper begins. The body of a PL program consists of statements or, more precisely, a single statement that may itself consist of several statements. All this is summed up in the top-level grammar rule:

```
pl_program(S) →
    [program], identifier(X), [';'], statement(S).
```

The structure returned as the output of the parsing is the statement constituting the body of the program. For the purpose of code generation, the top-level program statement has no significance and is ignored in the structure built.

The first statement we describe is a *compound statement*. Its syntax is the standard identifier begin followed by the first statement, S, say, in the compound statement, and then the remaining statements Ss. The structure returned for a compound statement is (S;Ss), where ; is used as a two-place infix functor. Note that S, Ss, or both may be compound statements or contain them. The semicolon is chosen as functor to echo its use in PL for denoting sequencing of statements:

```
statement((S;Ss)) →
    [begin], statement(S), rest_statements(Ss).
```

Statements in PL are delimited by semicolons. The rest of the state-ments are accordingly defined as a semicolon followed by a nonempty statement, and recursively the remaining statements:

```
rest_statements((S;Ss)) →
    [';'], statement(S), rest_statements(Ss).
```

The end of a sequence of statements is indicated by the standard iden-tifier end. The atom void is used to mark the end of a statement in the internal structure. The base case of rest_statements is therefore

```
rest_statements(void) → [end].
```

The above definition of statements precludes the possibility of empty statements. Programs and compound statements in PL cannot be empty.

The next statement to discuss is the assignment statement. It has a simple syntactic definition — a left-hand side, followed by the standard identifier is, followed by the right-hand side. The left-hand side is re-stricted to being a PL identifier, and the right-hand side is any arithmetic expression whose definition is to be given:

```
statement(assign(X,E)) →
    identifier(X), [':='], expression(E).
```

The structure returned by the successful recognition of an assignment statement has the form assign(X,E). The (Prolog) variable E represents the structure of the arithmetic expression, and X is the name of the (PL) variable to be assigned the value of the expression. It is implicitly assumed that X will be a PL identifier.

For simplicity of both code and explanation, we restrict ourselves to a subclass of arithmetic expressions. Two rules define the subclass. An expression is either a constant or a constant followed by an arithmetic operator and recursively an arithmetic expression. Examples of expres-sions in the subclass are x, 3, $2 \cdot t$ and $x + y - z/2$, the expression in the first test case in Program 24.2:

```
expression(X) → pl_constant(X).
expression(expr(Op,X,Y)) →
    pl_constant(X), arithmetic_op(Op), expression(Y).
```

This subclass of expressions does not respect the standard precedence of arithmetic operators. The expression $x \cdot 2 + y$ is parsed as $x \cdot (2 + y)$. On the other hand, the expression $x + y - z/2$ is interpreted unambiguously as $x + (y - (z/2))$.

For this example, we restrict ourselves to two types of constants in PL: identifiers and integers. The specification of `pl_constant` duly consists of two rules. Which of the two is found is reflected in the structure returned. For identifiers X, the structure `name(X)` is returned, whereas `number(X)` is returned for the integer X:

```
pl_constant(name(X))    →  identifier(X).
pl_constant(number(X))  →  pl_integer(X).
```

For simplicity we assume that PL integers and PL identifiers are Prolog integers and atoms, respectively. This allows the use of Prolog system predicates to identify the PL identifiers and integers. Recall that the curly braces notation of DCGs is used to specify Prolog goals:

```
identifier(X)  →  [X], {atom(X)}.
pl_integer(X)  →  [X], {integer(X)}.
```

In fact, all grammar rules that use PL identifiers and constants could be modified to call the Prolog predicates directly if greater efficiency is needed.

A list of arithmetic operators is necessary to complete the definition of arithmetic expressions. The form of the statement for addition, represented by +, follows. The grammar rules for subtraction, multiplication, and division are analogous, and appear in the full parser in Program 24.1:

```
arithmetic_op('+')  →  ['+'].
```

The next statement to be discussed is the conditional statement, or if-then-else. The syntax for conditionals is the standard identifier `if` followed by a test (to be defined). After the test, the standard identifier `then` is necessary, followed by a statement constituting the then part, the standard identifier `else` and a statement constituting the else part, in that order. The structure built by the parser is `if(T,S1,S2)`, where T is the test, S1 is the then part, and S2 is the else part:

```
statement(if(T,S1,S2)) →
    [if], test(T), [then], statement(S1),
    [else], statement(S2).
```

Tests are defined to be an expression followed by a comparison operator and another expression. The structure returned has the form compare(Op,X,Y), where Op is the comparison operator, and X and Y are the left-hand and right-hand expressions in the test, respectively:

```
test(compare(Op,X,Y)) →
    expression(X), comparison_op(Op), expression(Y).
```

The definition of comparison operators using the predicate comparison_op is analogous to the use of arithmetic_op to define arithmetic operators. Program 24.1 contains definitions for =, ≠, >, <, ≥, and ≤.

While statements consist of a test and the action to take if the test is true. The structure returned is while(T,S), where T is the test and S is the action. The syntax is defined by the following rule:

```
statement(while(T,S)) →
    [while], test(T), [do], statement(S).
```

I/O is handled in PL with a simple read statement and a simple write statement. The input statement consists of the standard identifier read followed by a PL identifier; it returns the structure read(X), where X is the identifier. Write statements are similar:

```
statement(read(X)) → [read], identifier(X).
statement(write(X)) → [write], expression(X).
```

Collecting the various pieces of the DCG just described gives a parser for the language. Note that ignoring the arguments in the DCG gives a formal BNF grammar for PL.

Let us consider the behavior of the parser on the test data in Program 24.2. The parsed structures produced for the two single statement programs have the form ⟨structure⟩;void, where ⟨structure⟩ represents the parsed statement. The write statement is translated to

```
write(expr(+,name(x),expr(-,name(y),expr(/,name(z),
    number(2)))))),
```

and the if-then-else statement is translated to

```
if(compare(>,name(a),name(b)),assign(max,name(a)),
    assign(max,name(b))).
```

The *factorial* program is parsed into a sequence of five statements followed by void. The output after parsing for all three test programs is

Program test1:

```
write(expr(+,name(x),expr(-,name(y),
    expr(/,name(z),number(2)))));void
```

Program test2:

```
if(compare(>,name(a),name(b)),assign(max,name(a)),
    assign(max,name(b)));void
```

Program test3:

```
read(value);assign(count,number(1));assign(result,number(1));
    while(compare(<,name(count),name(value)),
    (assign(count,expr(+,name(count),number(1)));
    assign(result,expr(*,name(result),name(count)));void));
    write(name(result));void
```

Figure 24.5   Output from parsing

given in Figure 24.5. This is the input for the second stage of compilation, code generation.

24.3   The Code Generator

The basic relation of the code generator is encode(Structure,Dictionary,Code), which generates Code from the Structure produced by the parser. This section echoes the previous one. The generated code is described for each of the structures produced by the parser representing the various PL statements.

Dictionary relates PL variables to memory locations, and labels to instruction addresses. The dictionary is used by the assembler to resolve locations of labels and identifiers. Throughout this section D refers to this dictionary. An incomplete ordered binary tree is used to implement it, as described in Section 15.3. The predicate lookup(Name,D,Value) (Program 15.9) is used for accessing the incomplete binary tree.

The structure corresponding to a compound statement is a sequence of its constituent structures. This is translated into a sequence of blocks of code, recursively defined by encode. The functor ; is used to denote sequencing. The empty statement denoted by void is translated into a null operation, denoted no_op. When the relocatable code is traversed during assembly this "pseudoinstruction" is removed.

The structure produced by the parser for the general PL assignment statement has the form `assign(Name,Expression)`, where `Expression` is the expression to be evaluated and assigned to the PL variable `Name`. The corresponding compiled form calculates the expression followed by a `store` instruction whose argument is the address corresponding to `Name`. The representation of individual instructions in the compiled code is the structure `instr(X,Y)`, where `X` is the instruction and `Y` is the operand. The appropriate translation of the `assign` structure is therefore `(Code; instr(store,Address))`, where `Code` is the compiled form of the expression, which, after execution, leaves the value of the expression in the accumulator. It is generated by the predicate `encode_expression(Expression,D,ExpressionCode)`. Encoding the assignment statement is performed by the clause

```
encode(assign(Name,Expression),D,(Code;instr(store,Address)))
    ← lookup(Name,D,Address), encode_expression(Expression,
        D,Code).
```

This clause is a good example of Prolog code that is easily understood declaratively but hides complicated procedural bookkeeping. Logically, relations have been specified between `Name` and `Address`, and between `Expression` and `Code`. From the programmer's point of view it is irrelevant when the final structure is constructed, and in fact the order of the two goals in the body of this clause can be swapped without changing the behavior of the overall program. Furthermore, the `lookup` goal, in relating `Name` with `Address`, could be making a new entry or retrieving a previous one, where the final instantiation of the address happens in the assembly stage. None of this bookkeeping needs explicit mention by the programmer. It goes on correctly in the background.

There are several cases to be considered for compiling the expression. Constants are loaded directly; the appropriate machine instruction is `loadc C`, where `C` is the constant. Similarly identifiers are compiled into the instruction `load A`, where `A` is the address of the identifier. The two corresponding clauses of `encode_expression` are

```
encode_expression(number(C),D,instr(loadc,C)).
encode_expression(name(X),D,instr(load,Address)) ←
    lookup(X,D,Address).
```

The general expression is the structure expr(Op,E1,E2), where Op is the operator, E1 is a PL constant, and E2 is an expression. The form of the compiled code depends on E2. If it is a PL constant, then the final code consists of two statements: an appropriate load instruction determined recursively by encode_expression and the single instruction corresponding to Op. Again, it does not matter in which order the two instructions are determined. The clause of encode_expression is

```
encode_expression(expr(Op,E1,E2),D,(Load;Instruction)) ←
    single_instruction(Op,E2,D,Instruction),
    encode_expression(E1,D,Load).
```

The nature of the single instruction depends on the operator and whether the PL constant is a number or an identifier. Numbers refer to literal operations, and identifiers refer to memory operations:

```
single_instruction(Op,number(C),D,instr(Opcode,C)) ←
    literal_operation(Op,Opcode).
single_instruction(Op,name(X),D,instr(Opcode,A)) ←
    memory_operation(Op,Opcode), lookup(X,D,A).
```

A separate table of facts is needed for each sort of operation. The respective form of the facts is illustrated for +:

```
literal_operation(+,addc).     memory_operation(+,add).
```

A separate calculation is necessary when the second expression is not a constant and cannot be encoded in a single instruction. The form of the compiled code is determined from the compiled code for calculating E2, and the single operation is determined by Op and E1:

```
encode_expression(expr(Op,E1,E2),D,Code) ←
    not single_instruction(Op,E2,D,Instruction),
    single_operation(Op,E1,D,E2Code,Code),
    encode_expression(E2,D,E2Code).
```

In general, the result of calculating E2 must be stored in some temporary location, called $temp in the following code. The sequence of instructions is then the code for E2, a store instruction, a load instruction for E1, and the appropriate memory operation addressing the stored contents. The predicates shown previously are used to construct the final form of the code:

```
single_operation(Op,E,D,Code,
   (Code;
   instr(store,Address);
   Load;
   instr(OpCode,Address))
) ←
      not commutative(Op),
      lookup('$temp',D,Address),
      encode_expression(E,D,Load),
      op_code(E,Op,OpCode).
```

An optimization is possible if the operation is commutative, e.g., addition or multiplication, which circumvents the need for a temporary variable. In this case, the memory or literal operation can be performed on E1, assuming that the result of computing E2 is in the accumulator:

```
single_operation(Op,E,D,Code,(Code;Instruction)) ←
   commutative(Op), single_instruction(Op,E,D,Instruction).
```

The next statement is the conditional if-then-else parsed into the structure if(Test,Then,Else). To compile the structure, we have to introduce labels to which instructions can jump. For the conditional we need two labels marking the beginning and end of the else part respectively. The labels have the form label(N), where N is the address of the instruction. The value of N is filled in during the assembling stage, when the label statement itself is removed. The schematic of the code is given by the third argument of the following encode clause:

```
encode(if(Test,Then,Else),D,
   (TestCode;
   ThenCode;
   instr(jump,L2);
   label(L1);
   ElseCode;
   label(L2))
)←
      encode_test(Test,L1,D,TestCode),
      encode(Then,D,ThenCode),
      encode(Else,D,ElseCode).
```

In order to compare two arithmetic expressions, we subtract the second from the first and make the jump operation appropriate to the particular comparison operator. For example, if the test is whether two expressions are equal, we circumvent the code if the result of subtracting the two is not equal to zero. Thus `comparison_opcode('=',jumpne)` is a fact. Note that the label that is the second argument of `encode_test` is the address of the code following the test.

```
encode_test(compare(Op,E1,E2),Label,D,
        (Code; instr(OpCode,Label))) ←
    comparison_opcode(Op,OpCode),
    encode_expression(expr('-',E1,E2),D,Code).
```

The next statement to consider is the *while* statement. The statement is parsed into the structure `while(Test,Statements)`. A label is necessary before the test, then the test code is given as for the if-then-else statement, then the body of code corresponding to `Statements` and a jump to reperform the test. A label is necessary after the `jump` instruction for when the test fails.

```
encode(while(Test,Do),D,
    (label(L1);
    TestCode;
    DoCode;
    instr(jump,L1);
    label(L2))
) ←
        encode_test(Test,L2,D,TestCode),
        encode(Do,D,DoCode).
```

The I/O statements are straightforward. The parsed structure for input, `read(X)`, is compiled into a single `read` instruction, and the table is used to get the correct address:

```
encode(read(X),D,instr(read,Address)) ←
    lookup(X,D,Address).
```

The output statement is translated into encoding an expression and then a `write` instruction:

```
encode(write(E),D,(Code; instr(write,0))) ←
    encode_expression(E,D,Code).
```

Program test1:

```
((((instr(load,Z);instr(divc,2));instr(store,Temp);
instr(load,Y);instr(sub,Temp));instr(add,X));
instr(write,0));no_op
```

Program test2:

```
(((instr(load,A);instr(sub,B));instr(jumple,L1));
(instr(load,A);instr(store,Max));instr(jump,L2);label(L1);
(instr(load,B);instr(store,Max));label(L2));no_op
```

Program factorial:

```
instr(read,Value);(instr(loadc,1);instr(store,Count));
    (instr(loadc,1);instr(store,Result));(label(L1);
    ((instr(load,Count);instr(sub,Value));instr(jumpge,L2));
    (((instr(load,Count);instr(addc,1));instr(store,Count));
    ((instr(load,Result);instr(mul,Count));instr(store,Result));
    no_op);instr(jump,L1);label(L2));(instr(load,Result);
    instr(write,0));no_op
```

Figure 24.6   The generated code

Figure 24.6 contains the relocatable code after code generation and before assembly for each of the three examples of Program 24.2. Mnemonic variable names have been used for easy reading.

24.4   The Assembler

The final stage performed by the compiler is assembling the relocatable code into absolute object code. The predicate `assemble(Code,Dictionary,ObjectCode)` takes the `Code` and `Dictionary` generated in the previous stage and produces the object code. There are two stages in the assembly. During the first stage, the instructions in the code are counted, at the same time computing the addresses of any labels created during code generation and removing unnecessary null operations. This tidied code is further augmented by a halt instruction, denoted by `instr(halt,0)`, and a block of *L* memory locations for the *L* PL variables and temporary locations in the code. The space for memory locations is denoted by `block(L)`. In the second stage, addresses are created for the PL and temporary variables used in the program:

```
assemble(Code,Dictionary,TidyCode) ←
    tidy_and_count(Code,1,N,TidyCode\(instr(halt,0);block(L))),
    N1 is N+1,
    allocate(Dictionary,N1,N2),
    L is N2-N1, !.
```

The predicate `tidy_and_count(Code,M,N,TidyCode)` tidies the Code
into TidyCode, where the correct addresses of labels have been filled
in and the null operations have been removed. Procedurally, executing
`tidy_and_count` constitutes a second pass over the code. M is the address of the beginning of the code, and N is 1 more than the address of
the end of the original code. Thus the number of actual instructions in
Code is N+1-M. TidyCode is represented as a difference-structure based
on ; .

The recursive clause of `tidy_and_count` demonstrates both standard
difference-structure technique and updating of numeric values:

```
tidy_and_count((Code1;Code2),M,N,TCode1\TCode2) ←
    tidy_and_count(Code1,M,M1,TCode1\Rest),
    tidy_and_count(Code2,M1,N,Rest\TCode2).
```

Three types of primitives occur in the code: instructions, labels, and
no_ops. Instructions are handled routinely. The address counter is incre-
mented by 1, and the instruction is inserted into a difference-structure:

```
tidy_and_count(instr(X,Y),N,N1,(instr(X,Y);Code)\Code) ←
    N1 is N+1.
```

Both labels and no_ops are removed without updating the current address or adding an instruction to the tidied code:

```
tidy_and_count(label(N),N,N,Code\Code).
tidy_and_count(no_op,N,N,Code\Code).
```

Declaratively, the clauses are identical. Procedurally, the unification of
the label number with the current address causes a major effect in the
program. Every reference to the label address is filled in. This program is
another illustration of the power of the logical variable.

The predicate `allocate(Dictionary,M,N)` has primarily a procedural interpretation. During the code generation as the dictionary is constructed, storage locations are associated with each of the PL variables

Program test1:

```
instr(load,11);instr(divc,2);instr(store,12);instr(load,10);
instr(sub,12);instr(add,9);instr(write,0);instr(halt,0);block(4)
```

Program test2:

```
instr(load,10);instr(sub,11);instr(jumple,7);instr(load,10);
instr(store,12);instr(jump,9);instr(load,11);instr(store,12);
instr(halt,0);block(3)
```

Program factorial:

```
instr(read,21);instr(loadc,1);instr(store,19);instr(loadc,1);
instr(store,20);instr(load,19);instr(sub,21);instr(jumpge,16);
instr(load,19);instr(addc,1);instr(store,19);instr(load,20);
instr(mul,19);instr(store,20);instr(jump,6);instr(load,20);
instr(write,0);instr(halt,0);block(3)
```

Figure 24.7   The compiled object code

in the program, plus any temporary variables needed for computing expressions. The effect of allocate is to assign actual memory locations for the variables and to fill in the references to them in the program.

The variables are found by traversing the Dictionary. M is the address of the memory location for the first variable, and N is 1 more than the address of the last. The order of variables is alphabetic corresponding to their order in the dictionary. The code also completes the dictionary as a data structure.

```
allocate(void,N,N).
allocate(dict(Name,N1,Before,After),N0,N) ←
    allocate(Before,N0,N1),
    N2 is N1+1,
    allocate(After,N2,N).
```

Because the dictionary is an incomplete data structure, the predicate allocate can succeed many times. The variables at the end of the tree match both the fact and the recursive clause. For the compiler, the easiest way to stop multiple solutions is to add a cut to the clause for assemble/3, which commits to the first (and minimal) assignment of memory locations for variables.

The compiled versions of the test programs given in Program 24.2 appear in Figure 24.7.

Exercises for Chapter 24

(i)   Extend the compiler so that it handles repeat loops. The syntax is *repeat ⟨statement⟩ until ⟨test⟩*. Extensions to both the parser and the compiler need to be made. Test the program on the following:

```
program repeat;
    begin
        i := 1;
        repeat
        i begin
        ii write(i);
        ii i := i+1
        i end
        until i = 11
    end.
```

(ii) Extend the definition of arithmetic expressions to allow arbitrary ones. In the encoder, you will have to cater for the possibility of needing several temporary variables.

24.5 Background

The compiler described is based on a delightful paper by Warren (1980).

A Operators

An operator is defined by its name, specifier, and priority. The name is usually an atom. The priority is an integer between 1 and 1200 inclusive. The specifier is a mnemonic that defines two things, class and associativity. There are three classes of operators: prefix, infix, and postfix. Associativity, which determines how to associate terms containing multiple operators, can be one of three possibilities: left-associative, right-associative, and non-associative.

There are seven possible operator types, which are given in Table A.1. A left-associative prefix operator is not possible, nor is a right-associative postfix operator. An operator specifier yfy does not make sense as it would lead to ambiguity. Consequently Standard Prolog does not allow such a specifier.

To explain the associativity, consider a term a :: b :: c. If the infix operator :: was left-associative, the term would be read as (a :: b) :: c. If the operator :: was right-associative, the term would be read as a :: (b :: c). If the operator :: was non-associative, the term would be illegal.

If uncertain about priorities when using operators, terms can always be bracketed. If you prefer not to bracket terms, you must take into account the associativity of the operator(s) involved and the priorities of terms. For example, the following three rules apply.

1. An operand with the same priority as a non-associative operator must be bracketed to avoid a syntax error by the Prolog reader.

2. An operator with the same (or smaller) priority as a right-associative operator that follows that operator need not be bracketed.

3. An operator with smaller priority than a left-associative operator that precedes that operator need not be bracketed.

Table A.1
Types of Operators in Standard Prolog

Specifier	Class	Associativity
fx	prefix	non-associative
fy	prefix	right-associative
xfx	infix	non-associative
xfy	infix	right-associative
yfx	infix	left-associative
xf	postfix	non-associative
yf	postfix	left-associative

Table A.2
Predefined Operators in Standard Prolog

Priority	Specifier	Operator(s)
1200	xfx	(:- -->)
1200	fx	:-
1100	xfy	;
1000	xfy	,
700	xfx	= \=
700	xfx	== \==
700	xfx	=..
700	xfx	is =:= =\= < <= > >=
500	yfx	+ -
400	yfx	* /
200	xfy	& ^
200	fy	-

Standard Prolog specifies some predefined operators. The priorities and specifiers of the operators which have been used in the text are given in Table A.2.

New operators are added with the directive

```
:- op(X,Y,Z).
```

where X is the priority, Y is the operator specifier, and Z is the operator name. These were used in Chapter 17 when defining a new rule language.

The system of operator declarations in Prolog is straightforward and can be used effectively for applications. The reader should be aware, however, that there are some subtle semantic anomalies in how operators are defined and handled. The anomalies, best discovered by trial and error, should not cause problems and can be "programmed around."

References

Abelson, H. and Sussman, G. J., *Structure and Interpretation of Computer Programs*, MIT Press, Cambridge, Massachusetts, 1985.

Abramson, H. and Dahl, V., *Logic Grammars*, Springer-Verlag, New York, 1989.

Abramson, H. and Rogers, M. (eds.), *Meta-Programming in Logic Programming*, MIT Press, Cambridge, Massachusetts, 1989.

Aït-Kaci, H., *The WAM: A (Real) Tutorial*, MIT Press, Cambridge, Massachusetts, 1991.

Apt, K. R., Logic Programming, in *Handbook of Theoretical Computer Science*, J. van Leeuwen (ed.), pp. 493–574, North-Holland, Amsterdam, 1990.

Apt, K. R. and van Emden, M. H., Contributions to the Theory of Logic Programming, *J. ACM* 29, pp. 841–862, 1982.

Bansal, A. and Sterling, L. S., Classifying Generate-and-Test Logic Programs, *International J. of Parallel Processing* 8(4), pp. 401–446, 1989.

Barklund, J., What is a Variable in Prolog? in (Abramson and Rogers, 1989), pp. 383–398.

Ben-David, A. and Sterling, L., A Prototype Expert System for Credit Evaluation, in *Artificial Intelligence in Economics and Management*, L. F. Pau (ed.), pp. 121–128, North-Holland, Amsterdam, 1986.

Berge, C., *The Theory of Graphs and its Applications*, Methuen & Co., London, 1962.

Bergman, M. and Kanoui, H., Application of Mechanical Theorem Proving to Symbolic Calculus, in *Proc. Third International Symposium on Advanced Computing Methods in Theoretical Physics*, CNRS, Marseilles, 1973.

Bloch, C., Source-to-Source Transformations of Logic Programs, Tech. Report CS-84-22, Department of Applied Mathematics, Weizmann Institute of Science, Rehovot, Israel, 1984.

Bowen, D. L., Byrd, L., Pereira, L. M., Pereira, F. C. N., and Warren, D. H. D., Prolog on the DECSystem-10, User's Manual, University of Edinburgh, 1981.

Bowen, K. and Kowalski, R., Amalgamating Language and Meta-Language, in (Clark and Tarnlund, 1982), pp. 153–172.

Boyer, R. S. and Moore, J. S., *A Computational Logic*, Academic Press, ACM Monograph Series, 1979.

Breuer, G. and Carter, H. W., VLSI Routing, in *Hardware and Software Concepts in VLSI*, G. Rabbat (ed.), pp. 368–405, Van Nostrand Reinhold, 1983.

Bruffaerts, A. and Henin, E., Negation as Failure: Proofs, Inference Rules and Meta-interpreters, in (Abramson and Rogers, 1989), pp. 169–190.

Bruynooghe, M., The Memory Management of Prolog Implementations, in (Clark and Tarnlund, 1982), pp. 83–98.

Bruynooghe, M. and Pereira, L. M., Deductive Revision by Intelligent Backtracking, in (Campbell, 1984), pp. 194–215.

Bundy, A., *A Computer Model of Mathematical Reasoning*, Academic Press, New York, 1983.

Bundy, A., A Generalized Interval Package and Its Use for Semantic Checking, *ACM Transactions on Mathematical Software* 10, pp. 392–407, 1984.

Bundy, A. and Welham, R., Using Meta-level Inference for Selective Application of Multiple Rewrite Rules in Algebraic Manipulation, *Artificial Intelligence* 16, pp. 189–212, 1981.

Burstall, R. M. and Darlington, J., A Transformation System for Developing Recursive Programs, *J. ACM* 24, pp. 46–67, 1977.

Byrd, L., Understanding the Control Flow of Prolog Programs, in (Tarnlund, 1980).

Campbell, J. A. (ed.), *Implementations of Prolog*, Ellis Horwood Publication, Wiley, New York, 1984.

Chen, W., Kiefer, M., and Warren, D. S., HiLog: A First-Order Semantics for Higher-Order Logic Programming Constructs, in *Proc. 1989 North American Conference on Logic Programming*, E. Lusk, and R. Overbeek, (eds.), pp. 1090–1114, MIT Press, Cambridge, Massachusetts, 1989.

Chikayama, T., Unique Features of ESP, in *Proc. International Conference on Fifth Generation Computer Systems*, pp. 292-298, ICOT - Institute for New Generation Computer Technology, Tokyo, Japan, 1984.

Ciepielewski, A., Scheduling in OR-parallel Prolog Systems, Frameworks, Survey, and Open Problems, Technical Report 91-02, University of Iowa, 1991.

Clark, K. L., Negation as Failure, in (Gallaire and Minker, 1978), pp. 293-322.

Clark, K. L. and Gregory, S., A Relational Language for Parallel Programming, in *Proc. ACM Symposium on Functional Languages and Computer Architecture*, pp. 171-178, 1981.

Clark, K. L. and Gregory, S., PARLOG: Parallel Programming in Logic, Research Report 84/4, Department of Computing, Imperial College of Science and Technology, England, 1984.

Clark, K. L. and McCabe, F. G., The Control Facilities of IC-Prolog, in *Expert Systems in the Microelectronic Age*, D. Michie (ed.), pp. 153-167, University of Edinburgh Press, 1979.

Clark, K. L. and McCabe, F. G., PROLOG: A Language for Implementing Expert Systems, in *Machine Intelligence* 10, J. Hayes, D. Michie and Y. H. Pao (eds.), pp. 455-470, Ellis Horwood Publication, Wiley, New York, 1982.

Clark, K. L, McCabe, F. G., and Gregory, S., IC-Prolog Language Features, in (Clark and Tarnlund, 1982).

Clark, K. L. and Tarnlund, S.-A., A First Order Theory of Data and Programs, *Information Processing* 77, pp. 939-944, North-Holland, Amsterdam, 1977.

Clark, K. L. and Tarnlund, S.-A. (eds.), *Logic Programming*, Academic Press, London, 1982.

Clocksin, W. F. and Mellish, C. S., *Programming in Prolog*, 2nd Edition, Springer-Verlag, New York, 1984.

Coelho, H. and Cotta, J., *Prolog by Example*, Springer-Verlag, New York, 1988.

Coelho, H., Cotta, J. C., and Pereira, L. M., *How to Solve It in Prolog*, 2nd Edition, Laboratorio Nacional de Engenharia Civil, Lisbon, Portugal, 1980.

Cohen, J., Describing Prolog by Its Interpretation and Compilation, *Comm. ACM* 28, pp. 1311-1324, 1985.

Cohen, J., A View of the Origins and Development of Prolog, *Comm. ACM* 31(1), pp. 26-36, 1988.

Colmerauer, A., Les systemes-*Q* ou un Formalisme pour Analyser et Synthesizer des Phrases sur Ordinateur, Publication Interne No. 43, Dept. d'Informatique, Universite de Montreal, Canada, 1973.

Colmerauer, A., Prolog-II, Manuel de reference et modele theorique, Groupe d'Intelligence Artificielle, Universite d'Aix-Marseille II, France, 1982a.

Colmerauer, A., Prolog And Infinite Trees, in (Clark and Tarnlund, 1982)b, pp. 231-251.

Colmerauer, A., An Introduction to Prolog-III, *Comm. ACM* 33(70), pp. 70–90, 1990.

Colmerauer, A., Kanoui, H., Pasero, R., and Roussel, P., Un Systeme de Communication Homme-machine en Francais, Research Report, Groupe Intelligence Artificielle, Universite Aix-Marseille II, France, 1973.

Colmerauer, A. and Roussel, P., The Birth of Prolog, in *ACM SIGPLAN Notices*, 28(3), pp. 37-52, 1993.

Deo, N., *Graph Theory with Applications to Engineering and Computer Science*, Prentice Hall, Englewood Cliffs, N. J., 1974.

Dershowitz, N. and Lee, Y. J., Deductive Debugging, in *Proc. Third IEEE Symposium on Logic Programming*, San Francisco, pp. 298–306, 1987.

Deville, Y., *Logic Programming—Systematic Program Development*, Addison-Wesley, Reading, Massachusetts, 1990.

Deville, Y., Sterling, L. S. and Deransart, P., Prolog for Software Engineering, Tutorial presented at *Eighth International Conference on Logic Programming*, Paris, France, 1991.

Dincbas, M. and Le Pape, J. P., Metacontrol of Logic Programs in METALOG, in *Proc. International Conference on Fifth Generation Computer Systems*, pp. 361-370, ICOT - Institute for New Generation Computer Technology, Tokyo, Japan, 1984.

Disz, T., Lusk, E., and Overbeek, R., Experiments with OR-Parallel Logic Programs, in *Proc. Fourth International Conference on Logic Programming*, J. L. Lassez (ed.), pp. 576-600, MIT Press, Cambridge, Massachusetts, 1987.

Drabent, W., Nadjm-Tehrani, S., and Maluszynski, J., Algorithmic Debugging with Assertions, in (Abramson and Rogers, 1989), pp. 501-521.

Dudeney, H. E., *Amusements in Mathematics*, Thomas Nelson and Sons, London, 1917.

Dwork, C., Kanellakis, P. C., and Mitchell, J. C., On the Sequential Nature of Unification, *J. Logic Programming* 1, pp. 35-50, 1984.

Eggert, P. R. and Chow, K. P., Logic Programming Graphics with Infinite Terms, Tech. Report University of California, Santa Barbara 83-02, 1983.

Elcock, E. W., The Pragmatics of Prolog: Some Comments, in *Proc. Logic Programming Workshop '83*, pp. 94-106, Algarve, Portugal, 1983.

Even, S., *Graph Algorithms*, Computer Science Press, 1979.

Findlay, W. and Watt, D. A., *PASCAL: An Introduction to Methodical Programming*, 2nd edition, Pitman, 1985.

Futamura, Y., Partial Evaluation of Computation Process—An Approach to a Compiler-Compiler, *Systems, Computers, Controls* 2, pp. 45-50, 1971.

Gallagher, J., Transforming Logic Programs by Specializing Interpreters, in *Proc. Seventh European Conference on Artificial Intelligence*, pp. 109-122, Brighton, England, 1986.

Gallagher, J. and Bruynooghe, M., Some Low-Level Source Transformations for Logic Programs, in *Proc. Second Workshop on Meta-Programming in Logic*, pp. 229-244, Leuven, Belgium, 1990.

Gallaire, H. and Lasserre, C., A Control Metalanguage for Logic Programming, in (Clark and Tarnlund, 1982), pp. 173-185.

Gallaire, H. and Minker, J., *Logic and Databases*, Plenum Publishing Co., New York, 1978.

Gallaire, H., Minker, J., and Nicolas, J. M., Logic and Databases: A Deductive Approach, *Computing Surveys* 16, pp. 153-185, 1984.

Gregory, S., *Parallel Logic Programming in PARLOG*, Addison-Wesley, Reading, Massachusetts, 1987.

Hammond, P., Micro-Prolog for Expert Systems, Chapter 11 in *Micro-Prolog: Programming in Logic*, K. Clark and F. McCabe (eds.), Prentice Hall, Englewood Cliffs, N. J., 1984.

Heintze, N., Michaylov, S., Stuckey, P. and Yap, R., On Meta-Programming in CLP($\mathcal{R}$), in *Proc. 1989 North American Conference on Logic Programming*, E. Lusk, and R. Overbeek, (eds.), pp. 52-66, MIT Press, Cambridge, Massachusetts, 1989.

Hill, P. and Lloyd, J. W., Analysis of Meta-Programs, in (Abramson and Rogers, 1989), pp. 23-51.

Hill, P. and Lloyd, J. W., The Gödel Programming Language, MIT Press, Cambridge, Massachusetts, 1993.

Hill, R., LUSH-Resolution and Its Completeness, DCL Memo 78, Department of Artificial Intelligence, University of Edinburgh, Scotland, 1974.

Hopcroft, J. E. and Ullman, J. D., *Introduction to Automata Theory, Languages, Computation*, Addison-Wesley, Reading, Massachusetts, 1979.

Horowitz, E. and Sahni, S., *Fundamentals of Computer Algorithms*, Computer Science Press, 1978.

Jaffar, J., Lassez, J. L., and Lloyd, J. W., Completeness of the Negation as Failure Rule, in *Proc. of the International Joint Conference on Artificial Intelligence*, pp. 500–506, Karlsruhe, Germany, 1983.

Jaffar, J. and Lassez, J. L., From Unification to Constraints, in *Proc. of Logic Programming '87*, K. Furukawa, H. Tanaka, and T. Fujisaki, (eds.), pp. 1–18, Springer-Verlag LNCS 315, 1987.

Janson, S. and Haridi, S., Programming Paradigms of the Andorra Kernel Language, in *Proc. 1991 International Symposium on Logic Programming*, V. Saraswat, and K. Ueda, (eds.), pp. 167–183, MIT Press, Cambridge, Massachusetts, 1991.

Journal of Logic Programming, Special Issue on Abstract Interpretation, 15, 1993.

Kahn, K. M., A Primitive for the Control of Logic Programs, in *Proc. International IEEE Symposium on Logic Programming*, Atlantic City, pp. 242–251, 1984.

Kirschenbaum, M., Sterling, L., and Jain, A., Relating Logic Programs via Program Maps, *Annals of Mathematics and Artificial Intelligence* 8(3-4), 1993.

Knuth, D., *The Art Of Computer Programming*, Volume 1, Fundamental Algorithms, Addison-Wesley, Reading, Massachusetts, 1968.

Knuth, D., *The Art Of Computer Programming*, Volume 3, Sorting and Searching, Addison-Wesley, Reading, Massachusetts, 1973.

Komorowski, H. J., A Specification of an Abstract Prolog Machine and Its Application to Partial Evaluation, Ph. D. Thesis, available as Report No. 69, Software Systems Research Center, Linköping University, 1981.

Kowalski, R., Predicate Logic as a Programming Language, in *Proc. IFIP Congress*, J. Rosenfeld (ed.), pp. 569–574, North-Holland, Amsterdam, 1974.

Kowalski, R., *Logic For Problem Solving*, North-Holland, Amsterdam, 1979a.

Kowalski, R., Algorithm = Logic + Control, *Comm. ACM* 22, pp. 424–436, 1979b.

Kowalski, R., The Early Years of Logic Programming, *Comm. ACM* 31(1), pp. 38–43, 1988.

Kunen, K., Logic for Logic Programmers, Tutorial Notes T1, *North American Conference on Logic Programming*, Cleveland, October, 1989.

Lakhotia, A., Incorporating 'Programming Techniques' into Prolog programs, in *Proc. 1989 North American Conference on Logic Programming*, E. Lusk, and R. Overbeek, (eds.), pp. 426–440, MIT Press, Cambridge, Massachusetts, 1989.

Lakhotia, A. and Sterling, L. S., ProMiX: A Prolog Partial Evaluation System, in (Sterling, 1990), pp. 137–179.

Lassez, J. L., From LP to LP: Programming with Constraints, Unpublished Technical Report, 1991.

Lassez, J. L., Maher, M., and Marriott, K., Unification Revisited, in *Foundations of Deductive Databases and Logic Programming*, J. Minker, (ed.), pp. 587–625, Morgan Kaufmann, 1988.

Li, D., *A Prolog Database System*, Research Studies Press, Ltd., Wiley, England, 1984.

Lim, P. and Stuckey, P., Meta-Programming as Constraint Programming, in *Proc. NACLP-90*, S. Debray and M. Hermenegildo (eds.), pp. 406–420, MIT Press, Cambridge, Massachusetts, 1990.

Lindholm, T. and O'Keefe, R., Efficient Implementation of a Defensible Semantics for Dynamic Prolog Code, in *Proc. Fourth International Conference on Logic Programming*, J. L. Lassez (ed.), pp. 21–39, MIT Press, Cambridge, Massachusetts, 1987.

Lloyd, J. W., *Foundations Of Logic Programming*, 2nd Edition, Springer-Verlag, New York, 1987.

Lombardi, L. A. and Raphael, B., Lisp as the Language for an Incremental Computer, in *The Programming Language LISP: Operation and Application*, E. C. Berkeley and D. G. Bobrow (eds.), pp. 204–219, MIT Press, Cambridge, Massachusetts, 1964.

Maier, D., *The Theory of Relational Databases*, Computer Science Press, 1983.

Maier, D. and Warren, D. S., *Computing with Logic-Logic Programming with Prolog*, Benjamin-Cummings, 1988.

Marriott, K. and Søndergaard, H., Difference-List Transformation for Prolog, *New Generation Computing* 11(2), pp. 125-157, 1993.

Martelli, A. and Montanari, U., An Efficient Unification Algorithm, *ACM Transactions on Programming Languages and Systems* 4(2), pp. 258-282, 1982.

Matsumoto, Y., Tanaka, H., and Kiyono, M., BUP: A Bottom-Up Parsing System for Natural Languages, in (van Caneghem and Warren, 1986), pp. 262-275.

Mellish, C. S., Some Global Optimizations for a Prolog Compiler, *J. Logic Programming* 2, pp. 43-66, 1985.

Michie, D., "Memo" Functions and Machine Learning, *Nature*, 218, pp. 19-22, 1968.

Miller, D. and Nadathur, G., Higher-Order Logic Programming, in *Proc. Third International Conference on Logic Programming*, E. Y. Shapiro, (ed.), pp. 448-462, Springer-Verlag LNCS 225, 1986.

Minsky, M., *Semantic Information Processing*, MIT Press, Cambridge, Massachusetts, 1968.

Moss, C., Cut and Paste—Defining the Impure Primitives of Prolog, in *Proc. Third International Conference on Logic Programming*, E. Y. Shapiro, (ed.), pp. 686-694, Springer-Verlag LNCS 225, 1986.

Naish, L., All Solutions Predicate in PROLOG, in *Proc. IEEE Symposium on Logic Programming*, Boston, pp. 73-77, IEEE Computer Society Press, 1985a.

Naish, L., Automating Control for Logic Programs, *J. Logic Programming* 2, pp. 167-184, 1985b.

Naish, L., Negation and Control in Prolog, Springer-Verlag LNCS 238, 1986.

Nakashima, H., Tomura S. and Ueda, K., What Is a Variable in Prolog? in *Proc. of the International Conference on Fifth Generation Computer Systems*, pp. 327-332, ICOT - Institute for New Generation Computer Technology, Tokyo, Japan, 1984.

Nilsson, N. J., *Problem Solving Methods in Artificial Intelligence*, McGraw-Hill, New York, 1971.

Nilsson, N. J., *Principles of Artificial Intelligence*, Tioga Publishing Co., Palo Alto, California, 1980.

O'Keefe, R. A., Programming Meta-Logical Operations in Prolog, DAI Working Paper No. 142, University of Edinburgh, Scotland, 1983.

O'Keefe, R. A., On the Treatment of Cuts in Prolog Source-Level Tools, in *Proc. 1985 IEEE Symposium on Logic Programming*, Boston, pp. 68-72, IEEE Computer Society Press, 1985.

O'Keefe, R. A., *The Craft of Prolog*, MIT Press, Cambridge, Massachusetts, 1990.

Paterson, M. S. and Wegman, M. N., Linear Unification, *J. Computer and Systems Sciences* 16, pp. 158-167, 1978.

Pereira, L. M., Logic Control with Logic, in *Proc. First International Logic Programming Conference*, pp. 9-18, Marseilles, France, 1982.

Pereira, F. C. N. and Shieber, S., *Prolog and Natural Language Analysis*, CSLI Lecture Notes No. 10, CSLI, Stanford University, Stanford, 1987.

Pereira, F. C. N. and Warren, D. H. D., Definite Clause Grammars for Language Analysis—A Survey of the Formalism and a Comparison with Augmented Transition Networks, *Artificial Intelligence* 13, pp. 231-278, 1980.

Peter, R., *Recursive Functions*, Academic Press, New York, 1967.

Plaisted, D. A., The Occur-Check Problem in Prolog, *New Generation Computing* 2, pp. 309-322, 1984.

Plümer, L., *Termination Proofs for Logic Programs*, Springer-Verlag, New York, 1990.

Power, A. J. and Sterling, L. S., A Notion of Map between Logic Programs, in *Proc. Seventh International Conference on Logic Programming*, D. H. D. Warren and P. Szeredi (eds.), pp. 390-404, MIT Press, Cambridge, Massachusetts, 1990.

Powers, D., Playing Mastermind More Logically, *SIGART Newsletter* 89, pp. 28-32, 1984.

Quintus Prolog Reference Manual, Quintus Computer Systems Ltd., 1985.

Reiter, R., On Closed World Databases, in (Gallaire and Minker, 1978), pp. 55-76. Also in *Readings in Artificial Intelligence*, Webber and Nilsson (eds.), Tioga Publishing Co., Palo Alto, California, 1981.

Robinson, J. A., A Machine-Oriented Logic Based on the Resolution Principle, *J. ACM* 12, pp. 23-41, January 1965.

Robinson, J. A. and Sibert, E. E., LOGLISP: Motivation, Design and Implementation, in (Clark and Tarnlund, 1982), pp. 299-313.

Ross, P., *Advanced Prolog, Techniques and Examples*, Addison-Wesley, Reading, Massachusetts, 1989.

Sahlin, D., An Automatic Partial Evaluator for Full Prolog, Ph. D. Thesis, available as SICS Dissertation Series 4, Swedish Institute of Computer Science, 1991.

Schank, R. C. and Abelson, R. P., *Scripts, Plans, Goals, and Understanding*, Lawrence Erlbaum, Hillsdale, N. J., 1977.

Schank, R. C. and Riesbeck, C., *Inside Computer Understanding: Five Programs Plus Miniatures*, Lawrence Erlbaum, Hillsdale, N. J., 1981.

Scowen, R., Prolog: Working Draft 5.0, N72, 1991.

Sedgewick, R., *Algorithms*, Addison-Wesley, Reading, Massachusetts, 1983.

Sergot, M., A Query the User Facility for Logic Programming, in *Integrated Interactive Computer Systems*, North-Holland, Amsterdam, 1983.

Shapiro, E., *Algorithmic Program Debugging*, MIT Press, Cambridge, Massachusetts, 1983a.

Shapiro, E., A Subset of Concurrent Prolog and Its Interpreter, Tech. Report TR-003, ICOT—Institute for New Generation Computer Technology, Tokyo, Japan, 1983b.

Shapiro, E., Logic Programs with Uncertainties: A Tool for Implementing Rule-Based Systems, *Proc. Eighth International Joint Conference on Artificial Intelligence*, pp. 529-532, Karlsruhe, Germany, 1983c.

Shapiro, E., Playing Mastermind Logically, *SIGART Newsletter* 85, pp. 28-29, 1983d.

Shapiro, E., Alternation and the Computational Complexity of Logic Programs, *J. Logic Programming* 1, pp. 19-33, 1984.

Shapiro, E., Systems Programming in Concurrent Prolog, in (van Caneghem and Warren, 1986), pp. 50-74.

Shapiro, E. and Takeuchi, A., Object Oriented Programming in Concurrent Prolog, *New Generation Computing* 1, pp. 25-48, 1983.

Shortliffe, E. H., *Computer Based Medical Consultation, MYCIN*, North-Holland, New York, 1976.

Silver, B., *Meta-level Inference*, Elsevier Science, Amsterdam, Netherlands, 1986.

Silverman, W., Hirsch, M., Houri, A. and Shapiro, E., The Logix System User Manual, Weizmann Institute of Science, Rehovot, Israel, 1986.

Slagle, J. and Dixon, J., Experiments with Some Programs That Search Game Trees, *J. ACM* 16, pp. 189–207, 1969.

Smith, D., Partial Evaluation of Pattern Matching in Constraint Logic Programming Languages, *Proc. Symposium on Partial Evaluation and Semantics-Based Program Manipulation, SIGPLAN Notices* 26, pp. 62–71, September 1991.

Søndergaard, H., Semantics-Based Analysis and Transformation of Logic Programs, Ph. D. Thesis, also Tech. Report 89/21, University of Melbourne, 1989.

Steele, G. L., Jr. and Sussman, G. J., The Art of the Interpreter, or the Modularity Complex, Tech. Memorandum AIM-453, MIT AI-Lab, May 1978.

Sterling, L. S., Expert System = Knowledge + Meta-Interpreter, Tech. Report CS84-17, Weizmann Institute of Science, Rehovot, Israel, 1984.

Sterling, L. S. (ed.), *The Practice of Prolog*, MIT Press, Cambridge, Massachusetts, 1990.

Sterling, L. S. and Beer, R. D., Meta-Interpreters for Expert System Construction, *J. Logic Programming* 6(1–2), pp. 163–178, 1989.

Sterling, L. S. and Bundy, A., Meta-Level Inference and Program Verification, in *Proc. of the Sixth Conference on Automated Deduction*, pp. 144–150, Springer-Verlag LNCS 138, 1982.

Sterling, L. S., Bundy, A., Byrd, L., O'Keefe, R., and Silver, B., Solving symbolic equations with PRESS, in *Computer Algebra*, pp. 109–116, Springer-Verlag LNCS 144, 1982.

Sterling, L. S. and Codish, M., PRESSing for Parallelism: A Prolog Program Made Concurrent, *J. Logic Programming* 3, pp. 75–92, 1986.

Sterling, L. S. and Kirschenbaum, M., Applying Techniques to Skeletons, in *Constructing Logic Programs*, J. M. J. Jacquet (ed.), pp.127–140. Wiley, New York, 1993.

Sterling, L. S. and Lalee, M., An Explanation Shell for Expert Systems, *Computational Intelligence* 2, pp. 136–141, 1986.

Sterling, L. S. and Lakhotia, A., Composing Prolog Meta-Interpreters, in *Proc. Fifth International Conference on Logic Programming*, K. Bowen, and R. Kowalski, (eds.), pp. 386–403, MIT Press, Cambridge, Massachusetts, 1988.

Sterling, L. S. and Yalçinalp, L. Ü., Explaining Prolog Computations Using a Layered Meta-Interpreter, in *Proc. IJCAI-89*, pp. 66–71, Morgan Kaufmann, 1989.

Takeuchi, A. and Furukawa, K., Partial Evaluation of Prolog Programs and Its Application to Meta Programming, *Information Processing 86*, H. J. Kugler (ed.), pp. 415–420, Elsevier, New York, 1986.

Tamaki, H. and Sato, T., Unfold/Fold Transformations of Logic Programs, *Proc. Second International Conference on Logic Programming*, pp. 127–138, Uppsala, Sweden, 1984.

Tarnlund, S.-A. (ed.), *Proc. of the Logic Programming Workshop*, Debrecen, Hungary, 1980.

Tick, E., *Parallel Logic Programming*, MIT Press, Cambridge, Massachusetts, 1991.

Ueda, K., Guarded Horn Clauses, ICOT Tech. Report 103, ICOT, Tokyo, Japan, 1985.

Ullman, J. D., *Principles of Database Systems*, 2nd Edition, Computer Science Press, 1982.

Ullman, J. D., *Principles of Database and Knowledge-Base Symbols*, Volume 1, Computer Science Press, 1989.

van Caneghem, M. (ed.), *Prolog-II User's Manual*, 1982.

van Caneghem, M. and Warren, D. H. D. (eds.), *Logic Programming and its Applications*, Ablex Publishing Co., 1986.

van Emden, M., Warren's Doctrine on the Slash, *Logic Programming Newsletter*, December, 1982.

van Emden, M. and Kowalski, R., The Semantics of Predicate Logic as a Programming Language, *Comm. ACM* 23, pp. 733–742, 1976.

Venken, R., A Prolog Meta-Interpreter for Partial Evaluation and its Application to Source-to-Source Transformation and Query Optimization, in *Proc. European Conference on Artificial Intelligence*, pp. 91–100, Pisa, 1984.

Warren, D. H. D., Generating Conditional Plans and Programs, *Proc. AISB Summer Conference*, pp. 344–354, Edinburgh, Scotland, 1976.

Warren, D. H. D., Implementing Prolog—Compiling Logic Programs 1 and 2, DAI Research Reports 39 and 40, University of Edinburgh, Scotland, 1977.

Warren, D. H. D., Logic Programming and Compiler Writing, *Software-Practice and Experience* 10(2), pp. 97-125, 1980.

Warren, D. H. D., Higher-Order Extensions to Prolog: Are They Needed?, *Machine Intelligence* 10, pp. 441–454, Hayes, Michie and Pao (eds.), Ellis Horwood Publications, Wiley, New York, 1982a.

Warren, D. H. D., Perpetual Processes—An Unexploited Prolog Technique, in *Proc. Prolog Programming Environments Workshop*, Sweden, 1982b.

Warren, D. H. D., An Abstract Prolog Instruction Set, Tech. Note 309, SRI International, Menlo Park, California, 1983.

Warren, D. H. D., Optimizing Tail Recursion in Prolog, in (van Caneghem and Warren, 1986), pp. 77–90.

Warren, D. H. D., Pereira, F., and Pereira L. M., User's Guide to DECsystem-10 Prolog, Occasional Paper 15, Department of Artificial Intelligence, University of Edinburgh, Scotland, 1979.

Weizenbaum, J., ELIZA—A Computer Program for the Study of Natural Language Communication between Man and Machine, *CACM* 9, pp. 36–45, 1966.

Weizenbaum, J., *Computer Power and Human Reason*, W. H. Freeman & Co., 1976.

Welham, R., Geometry Problem Solving, Research Report 14, Department of Artificial Intelligence, University of Edinburgh, Scotland, 1976.

Winograd, T., *Language as a Cognitive Process*, Volume I. Syntax, Addison-Wesley, Reading, Massachusetts, 1983.

Winston, P. H., *Artificial Intelligence*, Addison-Wesley, Reading, Massachusetts, 1977.

Yalçinalp, L. Ü., Meta-Programming for Knowledge-Based Systems in Prolog, Ph. D. Thesis, available as Tech. Report TR 91-141, Center for Automation and Intelligent Systems Research, Case Western Reserve University, Cleveland, 1991.

Yalçinalp, L. Ü. and Sterling, L. S., An Integrated Interpreter for Explaining Prolog's Successes and Failures, in (Abramson and Rogers, 1989), pp. 191–203.

Yalçinalp, L. Ü. and Sterling, L. S., Uncertainty Reasoning in Prolog with Layered Meta-Interpreters, in *Proc. Seventh Conference on Artificial Intelligence Applications*, pp. 398–402, IEEE Computer Society Press, February 1991.

Index

Logic Programming

Ehud Shapiro, editor
Koichi Furukawa, Jean-Louis Lassez, Fernando Pereira, and
David H. D. Warren, associate editors

The Art of Prolog: Advanced Programming Techniques, Leon Sterling and
Ehud Shapiro, 1986

Logic Programming: Proceedings of the Fourth International Conference (volumes 1 and 2), edited by Jean-Louis Lassez, 1987

Concurrent Prolog: Collected Papers (volumes 1 and 2), edited by Ehud
Shapiro, 1987

*Logic Programming: Proceedings of the Fifth International Conference and
Symposium* (volumes 1 and 2), edited by Robert A. Kowalski and Kenneth A.
Bowen, 1988

Constraint Satisfaction in Logic Programming, Pascal Van Hentenryck, 1989

Logic-Based Knowledge Representation, edited by Peter Jackson, Han Reichgelt, and Frank van Harmelen, 1989

Logic Programming: Proceedings of the Sixth International Conference, edited
by Giorgio Levi and Maurizio Martelli, 1989

Meta-Programming in Logic Programming, edited by Harvey Abramson and
M. H. Rogers, 1989

Logic Programming: Proceedings of the North American Conference 1989
(volumes 1 and 2), edited by Ewing L. Lusk and Ross A. Overbeek, 1989

Logic Programming: Proceedings of the 1990 North American Conference,
edited by Saumya Debray and Manuel Hermenegildo, 1990

Logic Programming: Proceedings of the Seventh International Conference,
edited by David H. D. Warren and Peter Szeredi, 1990

The Craft of Prolog, Richard A. O'Keefe, 1990

The Practice of Prolog, edited by Leon S. Sterling, 1990

Eco-Logic: Logic-Based Approaches to Ecological Modelling, David Robertson,
Alan Bundy, Robert Muetzelfeldt, Mandy Haggith, and Michael Uschold, 1991

Warren's Abstract Machine: A Tutorial Reconstruction, Hassan Aït-Kaci, 1991

Parallel Logic Programming, Evan Tick, 1991

Logic Programming: Proceedings of the Eighth International Conference, edited by Koichi Furukawa, 1991

Logic Programming: Proceedings of the 1991 International Symposium, edited by Vijay Saraswat and Kazunori Ueda, 1991

Foundations of Disjunctive Logic Programming, Jorge Lobo, Jack Minker, and Arcot Rajasekar, 1992

Types in Logic Programming, edited by Frank Pfenning, 1992

Logic Programming: Proceedings of the Joint International Conference and Symposium on Logic Programming, edited by Krzysztof Apt, 1992

Concurrent Constraint Programming, Vijay A. Saraswat, 1993

Logic Programming Languages: Constraints, Functions, and Objects, edited by K. R. Apt, J. W. de Bakker, and J. J. M. M. Rutten, 1993

Logic Programming: Proceedings of the Tenth International Conference on Logic Programming, edited by David S. Warren, 1993

Constraint Logic Programming: Selected Research, edited by Frédéric Benhamou and Alain Colmerauer, 1993

A Grammatical View of Logic Programming, Pierre Deransart and Jan Maluszyński, 1993

Logic Programming: Proceedings of the 1993 International Symposium, edited by Dale Miller, 1993

The Gödel Programming Language, Patricia Hill and John Lloyd, 1994

The Art of Prolog: Advanced Programming Techniques, second edition, Leon Sterling and Ehud Shapiro, 1994

Printed in the United States
by Baker & Taylor Publisher Services